The Fujifilm X-T3

**Rico Pfirstinger** studied communications and has been working as a journalist, publicist, and photographer since the mid-'80s. He has written numerous books on a diverse range of topics, from computing technology to digital desktop publishing to sled dog racing. He worked as the department head of special assignments for Hubert Burda Media in Munich, Germany, and he also served as chief editor for a winter sports website.

After eight years as a freelance film critic in Los Angeles, Rico now lives in Germany and devotes his time to digital photography and compact camera systems.

Rico writes the popular X-Pert Corner blog and leads workshops called Fuji X Secrets where he offers insights, tips, and tricks on using the Fujifilm X-series cameras.

Rico Pfirstinger

# The Fujifilm X-T3

150 X-Pert Tips to Get the Most
Out of Your Camera

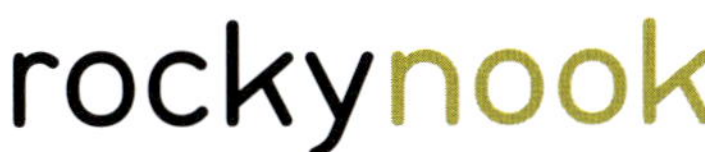

The Fujifilm X-T3
150 X-Pert Tips to Get the Most Out of Your Camera
Rico Pfirstinger

Project editor: Maggie Yates
Project manager: Lisa Brazieal
Marketing manager: Mercedes Murray
Copyeditor: Joan Dixon
Layout and type: Petra Strauch
Cover design: Wolfson Design
Video consultant: Wolfgang Url
Indexer: Maggie Yates

ISBN: 978-1-68198-488-9
1st Edition (1st printing, December 2019)
© 2020 Rico Pfirstinger
All images © Rico Pfirstinger unless otherwise noted

Rocky Nook, Inc.
1010 B Street, Suite 350
San Rafael, CA 94901
U.S.A.

www.rockynook.com

Distributed in the UK and Europe by Publishers Group UK
Distributed in the U.S. and all other territories by Ingram Publisher Services

Library of Congress Control Number: 2018958101

# Table of Contents

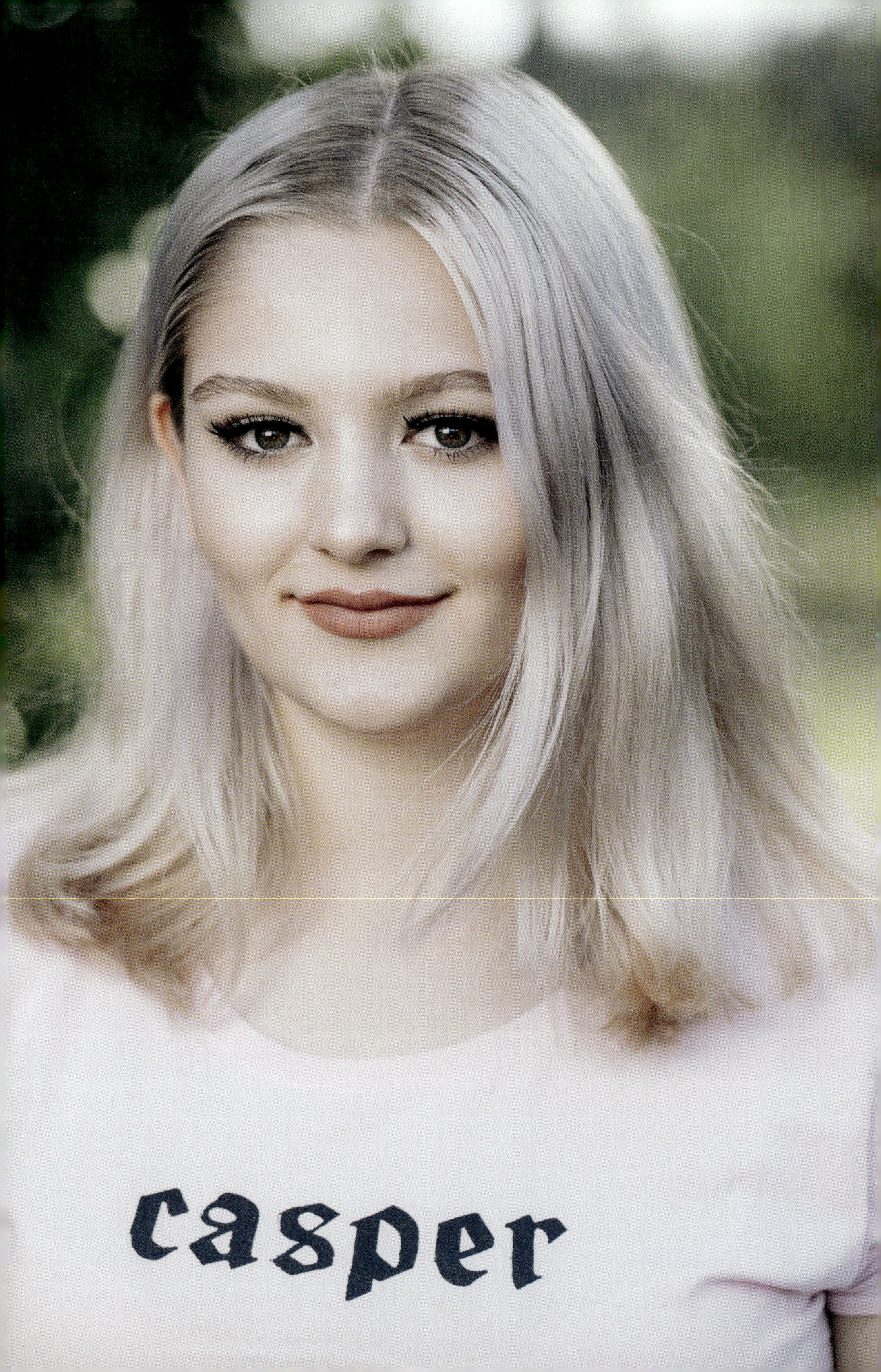

casper

# 1. YOUR X-T3 SYSTEM

To start off, here's a brief overview of the buttons and controls on your Fujifilm X-T3:

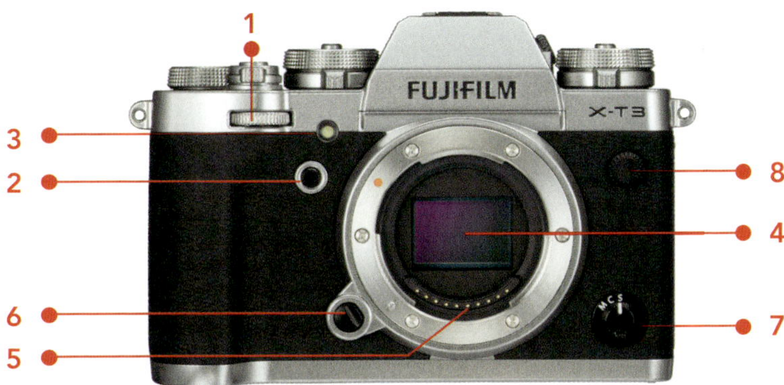

Fig. 1: **X-T3 front view:** front command dial with integrated button (1), Fn button (2), AF assist lamp/self-timer indicator lamp (3), X-Trans sensor (4), electronic lens contacts (5), lens release button (6), focus selector (7), flash sync connector (8)

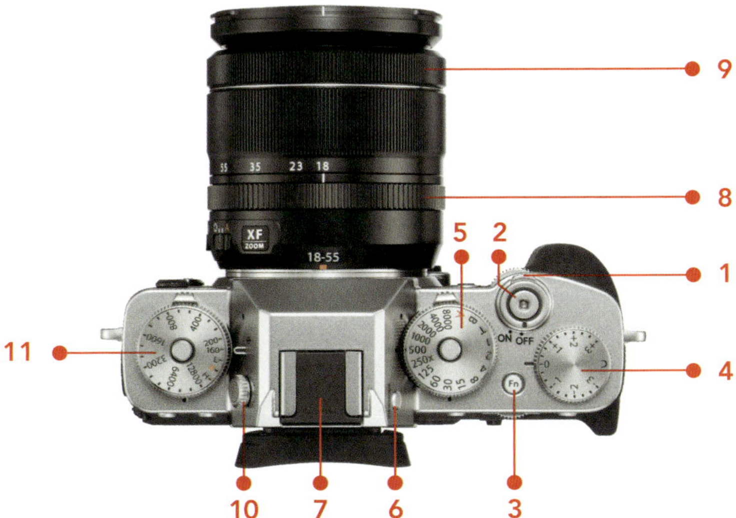

Fig. 2: **X-T3 top view (with XF18–55mmF2.8–4 R LM OIS lens):** on/off switch (1), shutter release button (2), Fn button (3), exposure compensation dial (4), shutter speed dial with stacked metering mode selection dial (5), view mode button (6), hot shoe (7), aperture ring (8), focus ring (9), diopter adjustment dial (10), ISO dial with stacked DRIVE mode dial (11)

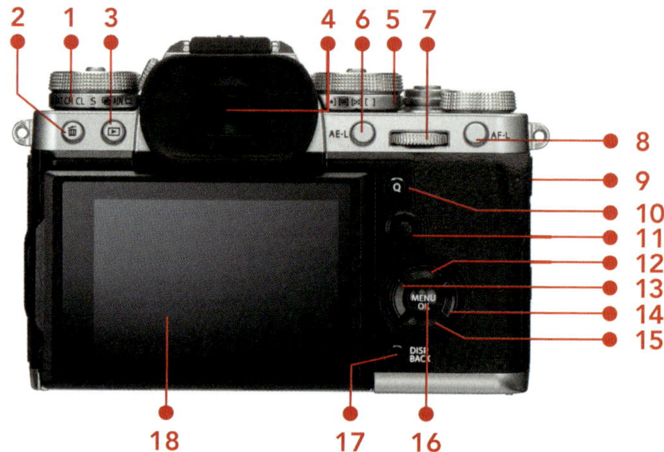

Fig. 3: **X-T3 rear view:** DRIVE mode dial (1), delete ("trash") button (2), playback button (3), viewfinder (4), metering mode selection dial (5), AE-L button/Fn button (6), rear command dial with integrated Fn button (7), AF-L button/Fn button (8), status indicator lamp (9), Q button for Quick menu (10), focus stick with integrated button (11), upper selector/Fn button (12), left selector/Fn button (13), right selector/ Fn button (14), lower selector/Fn button (15), MENU/OK button (16), DISP/BACK button (17), LCD monitor (18)

## 1.1 THE BASICS (1): THINGS YOU SHOULD KNOW ABOUT YOUR CAMERA

| RTFM! Read the Fuji Manual! | TIP 1 |

In case you have misplaced your user manual, or if you want the most recent edition, you can obtain downloadable PDF versions [1] in all supported languages from Fujifilm. You will also find updates and supplementary material that cover new features and changes based on firmware updates.

Please do yourself a big favor and thoroughly study the manual to get acquainted with the functions of your camera, and don't forget that your lenses come with user manuals, as well. This book doesn't replace the camera manual; it serves as an *enhancement* to the manual and offers valuable tips and background information about how to use the various features and functions to get the most out of your equipment.

| Spare batteries and third-party knock-offs | TIP 2 |

The X-T3 is a small, portable camera, which means the rechargeable battery is also small. Depending on how you use your camera, a fully charged battery can last for 250 to 400 shots.

I recommend setting the camera to Boost mode (SET UP > POWER MANAGEMENT > PERFORMANCE > BOOST) for maximum autofocus speed and the best overall performance.

Please note:

■ The X-T3 features an accurate battery indicator with five bars and a percentage display. However, the display's accuracy depends on using original equipment manufacturer (OEM) NP-W126S batteries.

■ In shooting mode, the percentage display is available only in the INFO display. To activate the INFO display, (repeatedly) press the DISP/BACK button until the INFO display appears. In playback mode, the percentage indicator is also available in the INFO display, which can be accessed with the DISP/BACK button *or* by pressing the upper selector key to cycle through two extended image information pages.

■ When the battery indicator shows one remaining red bar, it's almost time to replace/recharge the battery.

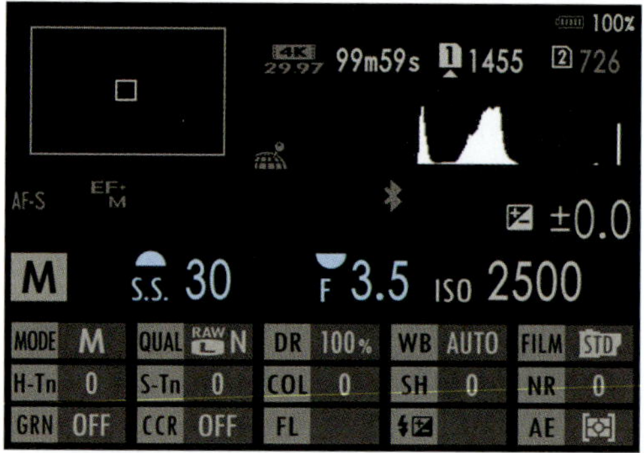

Fig. 4: The **INFO display** features an accurate battery life indicator with a percentage display. You can access the INFO display with the DISP/BACK button.

Your X-T3 uses NP-W126S rechargeable batteries. This type of battery is also used in Fujifilm's X-Pro1, X-Pro2, X-Pro3, X-E1, X-E2, X-E2S, X-E3, X-T1, X-T2, X-H1, X-T10, X-T20, X-T30, X-T100, X-M1, X-A1, X-A2, X-A3, X-A5, X-A7, X-A10, X-A20, and X100F cameras and can be interchanged between these models.

You can also use older NP-W126 batteries from Fujifilm, but this isn't recommended. The main difference between the regular and the S-type batteries is their ability to manage heat and maintain maximum power over an extended time period. For high-performance applications such as long 4K video recordings in a hot environment or shooting in Boost mode, the newer NP-W126S battery is clearly preferred. If you are using an older NP-W126 battery, the X-T3 will issue a warning when you switch it on.

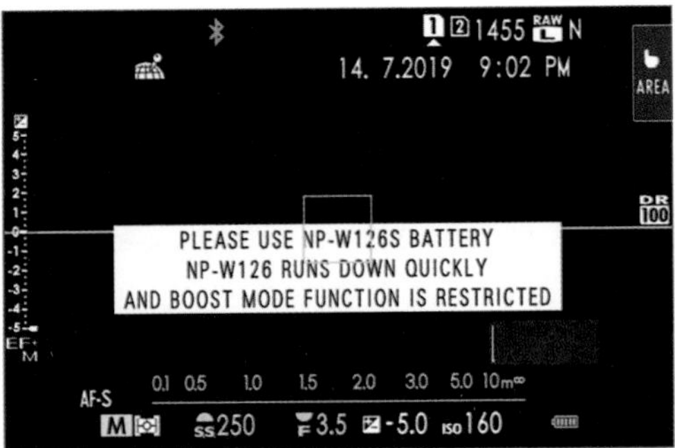


Fig. 5: Using older NP-W126 batteries prompts your X-T3 to issue this **friendly warning** when you switch it on. In addition, the battery symbol is now displayed in yellow instead of white. This warning also appears with many third-party knock-offs, and if it doesn't, it simply means that the third-party battery is "faking it." Your camera may still work, but it may not work as well as it could. In demanding situations, there is also a higher risk of system hang-ups and freezes.

You can obtain NP-W126S batteries from Fujifilm, or you can use compatible products from a variety of third-party vendors. Sadly, none of the aftermarket batteries offer the same quality and capacity as the more expensive Fujifilm batteries. Most third-party batteries will prompt a warning when the X-T3 is switched-on, and most of them use "tricks" to camouflage them as original NP-W126S batteries in order to suppress the switch-on warning.

You may also experience inaccurate battery life displays with third-party offerings, and the camera may unexpectedly switch off due to a depleted battery even though the indicator showed there was still power left. To avoid such trouble, I recommend using original NP-W126S batteries from Fujifilm.

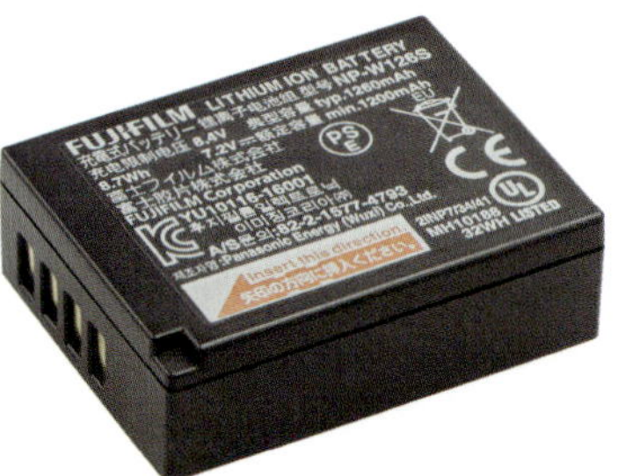

Fig. 6:
Fujifilm's original **NP-W126S** battery is without doubt the best choice. It's also more expensive than third-party knock-offs.

If you store your camera for several days (or longer) without a charged battery, the X-T3's built-in emergency power source may run out of juice, and all camera and user settings will reset to factory conditions.

| TIP 3 | Battery chargers and travel adapters |
| --- | --- |

Along with spare batteries, the aftermarket also offers chargers that work with regular power outlets, USB ports, or a car's cigarette lighter jack. This way, you can charge your batteries not only at home or in your hotel room, but also on your computer's USB port or when you are traveling in a car or plane.

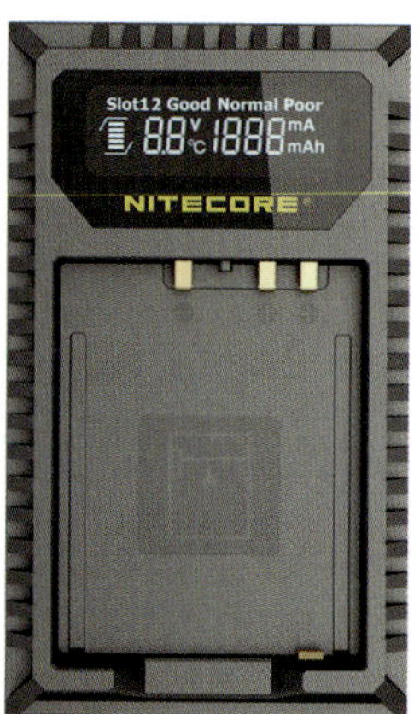


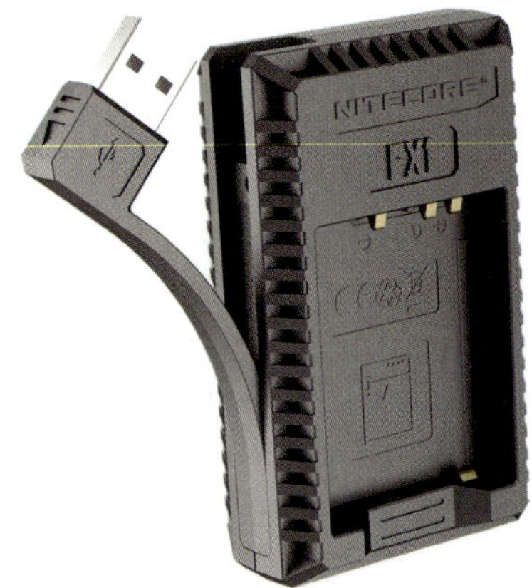


Fig. 7:  My personal travel charger is the **Nitecore FX1** [2] with dual slots and a status display (left). This charger connects to any USB-A port (right) and can smart-charge original Fujifilm NP-W126 and NP-W126S batteries with temperature monitoring.

While traveling, don't forget that different countries use different formats for power outlets, so you may want to carry a suitable travel adapter.

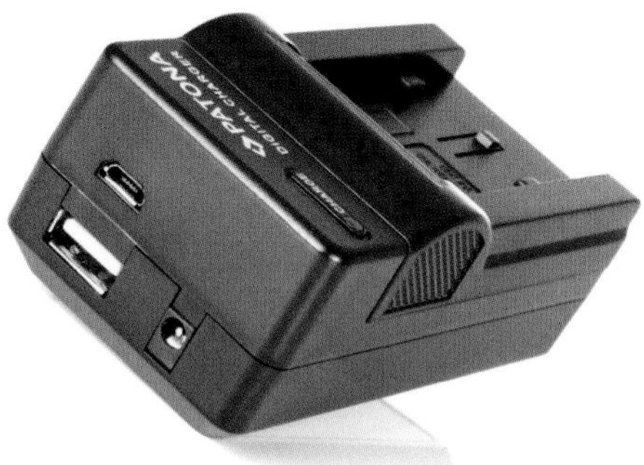

Fig. 8: Some **third-party chargers** can get their power from more than one source, such as power outlets, USB ports, and car cigarette lighter jacks.

As an alternative to external battery chargers, the battery can also be charged inside the camera via the camera's built-in USB port. Use an USB-A to USB-C or an USB-C to USB-C cable to connect the camera to pretty much any power source with an USB port, such as your laptop, phone charger, power bank, or a USB power supply. The X-T3 supports USB-C with Power Delivery so you can speed-up charging by using a USB-C power supply with at least 30W and a USB-C to USB-C cable that supports Power Delivery.

USB chargers and mobile power banks not only charge your X-T3, they can also power your camera while it is switched on and in use. You can find more information on compatible X cameras and batteries in a support document on Fujifilm's website [3].

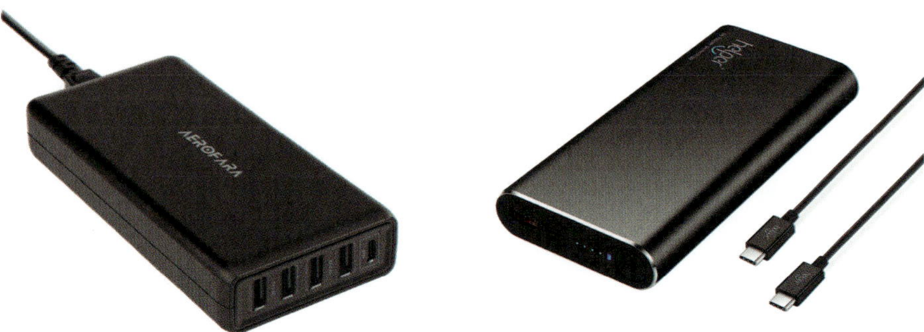

Fig. 9: **USB chargers** (left) and **power banks** (right) are useful accessories for road warriors and users who want to power their camera externally for long exposures, video, time-lapse photography, and interval shooting.

<table><tr><td>TIP 4</td><td>Where to find the latest firmware</td></tr></table>

Fujifilm keeps improving the firmware of your cameras and lenses.

■ To check which firmware version is installed in your camera and lens, switch the camera on while pressing and holding the DISP/BACK button.

■ You can and should download the latest firmware versions for your cameras and lenses online from Fujifilm [4]. While you are there, you can also download current versions of Fuji's application software, such as RAW File Converter EX, Fujifilm X RAW Studio, and Fujifilm X Acquire.

■ A step-by-step video guide illustrating the firmware upgrade process is available online [5]. At this Fujifilm support website, macOS [6] and Windows [7] users can also find detailed firmware download instructions for their operating systems.

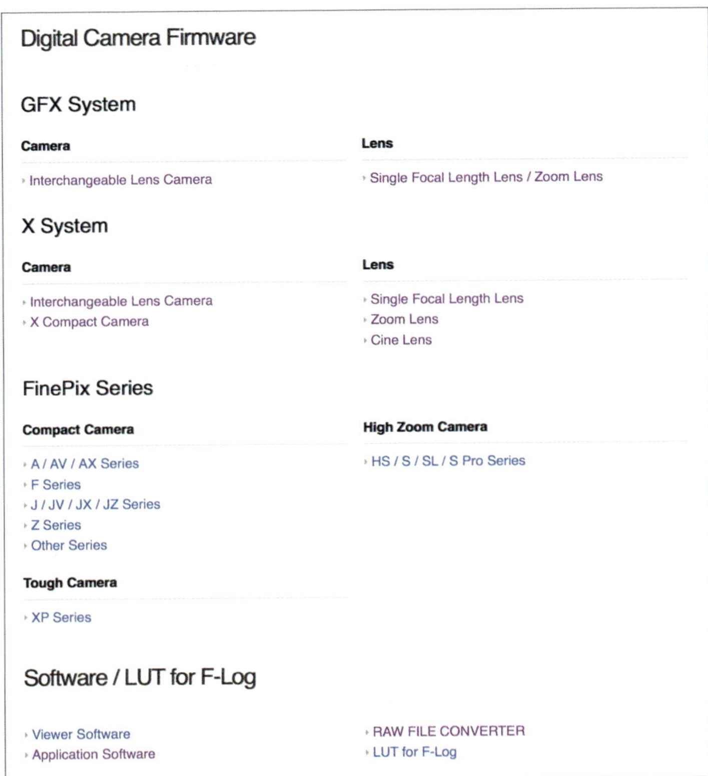

Fig. 10: Fujifilm's **Download Software & Firmware** webpage is your hub to obtain firmware updates for your X-T3 and lenses as well as current versions of supplementary software such as X RAW Studio and RAW File Converter EX.

| Updating your firmware | TIP 5 |
| --- | --- |

- Always use card slot number 1 for firmware updates.

- If you can't find a new firmware version on Fuji's firmware update page, there's a chance your web browser is still caching an older version of this page. In this case, either delete your browser cache or force your browser to reload the webpage from the server.

- Make sure your computer doesn't change the name of the new firmware files you download due to naming conflicts caused by previous firmware versions that are still residing in your download folder. The correct file name of the camera firmware for your X-T3 is always FWUP0019.DAT.

- Make sure your battery is fully charged when updating your firmware.

- Always copy new firmware files for your camera or lenses into the top directory of your SD memory card, and always use cards that have been freshly formatted in your camera. After you have copied the firmware to the card, make sure to properly unmount the card from your computer before removing it.

- If you want to update the firmware for a specific lens, make sure that lens is attached to the camera when you initiate the update process.

- To start the update process for your camera or a lens, switch on the camera while pressing and holding the DISP/BACK button and follow the instructions on the screen.

- Never switch the camera off during the update process. The camera will tell you when the update is complete. Only then can you safely switch it off.

If the firmware in your camera or lens needs to be updated due to compatibility issues, the camera may alert you of this problem when you switch it on. If that's the case, download the new firmware from the website links provided in tip 4 and update your camera and/or lens.

| Wireless firmware updates using Bluetooth and Wi-Fi | TIP 6 |
| --- | --- |

Since your camera supports Bluetooth, you can perform wireless firmware updates using your smartphone or tablet and Fujifilm's free Camera Remote app, which is available for iOS and Android. You can find a useful manual explaining the app's various functions online [8]. Wireless updates are available for only the camera body's firmware, not for lenses or accessories.

When your X-T3 is paired with your wireless device, the Camera Remote App will announce the availability of new camera firmware and offer to download it to your smartphone or tablet. From there, the firmware file is transferred to the camera via the camera's Wi-Fi hotspot.

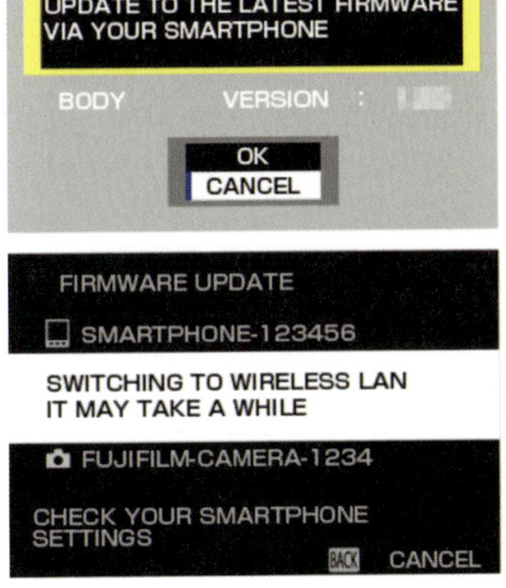


Fig. 11: **Wireless firmware update:** After the Camera Remote app on your smartphone or tablet has finished downloading new camera firmware, its Wi-Fi network must be switched to the camera's own hotspot to transfer the firmware file to the camera.

Using Camera Remote is a good option for users who want to install new firmware without accessing a personal computer. You can find step-by-step instructions for wireless firmware updates online [9].

<table>
<tr><td>TIP 7</td><td>Which memory cards to use</td></tr>
</table>

Turbo-charge your camera and its built-in buffer memory by using the fastest and most reliable UHS-I and UHS-II memory cards as follows:

- Since your X-T3 offers two fast UHS-II slots with transmission speeds of up to 300 MB/s, I highly recommend **Sony SF-G** or **Sony SF-G Tough** cards with write speeds up to 299 MB/s. These cards are also known to be particularly reliable and hang-up resistant when used with high-performance cameras like the X-T3.

- If the speed and performance of your X-T3 doesn't concern you, you can also use cards with the slower UHS-I standard and transfer rates of 95 MB/s or less. In this category, I recommend **SanDisk Extreme Pro 95 MB/s** cards, which are now also marketed as cards with "170 MB/s". However, this doesn't affect the write speed.

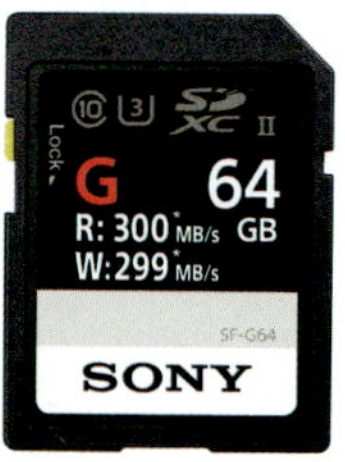

Fig. 12:
For maximum UHS-II performance and compatibility, I recommend superfast **Sony SF-G** cards.

Look out for fakes! Sadly, there's a fair share of fake SD cards on the market. High-end brands and models are particularly affected, so make sure to buy your fast UHS-I and UHS-II cards from reputable sources. Fake cards aren't just slower and less reliable than the originals, they also tend to lie about their actual capacity. A fake 64 GB card could, in reality, contain a cheap 8 GB chip with a manipulated controller that simulates 64 GB to the camera, resulting in severe data loss.

<table><tr><td>Working with dual card slots</td><td>TIP 8</td></tr></table>

Your X-T3 offers two SD card slots numbered 1 and 2. This means you can use two SD cards at the same time.

Please note:

- The primary SD card slot of your X-T3 is always slot 1. If you are only working with a single SD card, always put it in this slot.
- Firmware upgrades are only supported in slot 1.
- Both slots support UHS-II, making them suitable for very fast memory cards like the Sony SF-G series.

Using two memory cards at the same time gives you three options to configure how image data is transferred to your SD cards. To do so, select SET UP > SAVE DATA SET-UP > CARD SLOT SETTING (STILL IMAGE) and pick one of the following options:

- **SEQUENTIAL:** In this default mode, the camera saves all image data (RAW and JPEG) to a manually selected card slot. To change the slot, choose SET UP > SAVE DATA SET-UP > SELECT SLOT (SEQUENTIAL).

- **BACKUP:** In this mode, the X-T3 is sending all image data (RAW and JPEG) to both slots at the same time, creating a backup copy that can be useful when one of the cards gets lost or suffers data loss. In this mode, the overall data transfer rate is limited by the slower of the two cards that are in use. This can become a performance issue in situations that require many images being taken with high burst rates while shooting FINE+RAW, so make sure the cards in both slots are equally fast.

- **RAW/JPEG:** This setting splits the image data up by saving RAW files to slot 1 and JPEGs to slot 2, so this setting is useful only when you are shooting FINE+RAW or NORMAL+RAW. If you shoot RAW-only or JPEG-only, RAW/JPEG mode becomes BACKUP mode, saving your RAW or JPEG data to both cards at the same time.

I always recommend shooting FINE+RAW or NORMAL+RAW. If you follow this advice, then selecting RAW/JPEG mode (and using the fastest UHS-II cards available in slots 1 and 2, respectively) will give you the best camera performance in terms of continuous burst rates.

However, RAW/JPEG data save mode also has its quirks:

- Splitting up RAW and JPEG image data to slots 1 and 2 only works in regular shooting mode (i.e., when you take a new picture), not when you are using the camera's built-in RAW converter to create a JPEG from a RAW file on card 1. JPEGs generated from RAWs on card 1 are also saved on card 1 (the RAW card) instead of card 2 (the JPEG card).

- In playback mode, the X-T3 will display smaller-sized JPEG images that are embedded in the RAW files on card 1 instead of showing the full-resolution JPEGs on card 2. To access the full-resolution JPEGs (e.g., in order to zoom in and check critical focus), you have to manually switch slots in playback mode by pressing and holding the play-back button until the camera confirms the switch. Sadly, the camera will revert back to the other card as soon as you take another picture, so you'll have to go through the motions of switching slots in playback mode each time you take a shot.

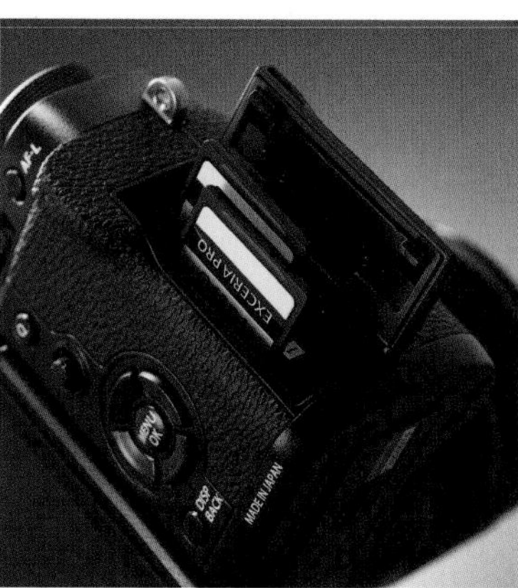

Fig. 13:
Your X-T3 can work with **two SD memory cards at the same time**. For maximum performance, you should use fast UHS-II cards.

<table>
<tr><td>Resetting the frame counter and assigning a new image starting number</td><td>TIP 9</td></tr>
</table>

Make sure you only use a single SD card in slot 1 and then follow these steps to reset the image counter to zero:

■ First select SET UP > SAVE DATA SET-UP > FRAME NO. > RENEW, then format the SD card with SET UP > USER SET-TING > FORMAT > SLOT 1 and take a picture. The frame counter will start from zero.

■ To avoid another automatic image counter reset when you are reformatting an SD card, select SET UP > SAVE DATA SET-UP > FRAME NO. > CONTINUOUS.

If you like, you can assign pretty much *any* number as the camera's frame-counter starting number. The method is similar to the above but involves an extra step in your computer. Again, only use a single SD card in slot 1:

■ Select SET UP > SAVE DATA SET-UP > FRAME NO. > RE-NEW, and then format the SD card with SET UP > USER SETTING > FORMAT > SLOT 1. The frame counter will start from zero.

■ Take one image, then remove the SD card from your camera and insert it in your computer. Locate your image (for example DSCF0001.JPG or DSCF0001.RAF) in the DCIM folder and change the frame-number portion of the file name (0001) to the number you'd like to use as your new starting point. For example, you can change the file name to DSCF2000.JPG.

■ Properly unmount and remove the SD card from your computer and put the card back into your camera. Now take another picture. The camera will use the modified frame number as a starting point. In our example, the next image's name would be DSCF2001.

- To avoid another automatic frame-counter reset when you are reformatting an SD card, select SET UP > SAVE DATA SET-UP > FRAME NO. > CONTINUOUS.

<table><tr><td>TIP 10</td><td>Use Boost mode!</td></tr></table>

In its default setting, the X-T3 operates with limited performance in order to conserve power. To enjoy the camera's full capabilities, it's necessary to select SET UP > POWER MANAGEMENT > PERFORMANCE > BOOST or assign Boost mode to one of the camera's Fn buttons.

If you have the Vertical Battery Grip (VG-XT3) attached to your X-T3, Boost mode is set with the switch on the back of the grip. Since the X-T3 consumes more power in Boost mode, it's even more important: to always have replacement batteries at hand.

Boost mode offers better autofocus performance and a higher frame rate in the electronic real-time live view. It also reduces the shooting interval, the shutter time lag, and the live view blackout time between burst shots.

*Important: When Boost mode is off, the camera will enter an energy saving mode after approximately 10 seconds of user inactivity. This results in a dramatic reduction of the live view's frame rate. As soon as a button is pushed or a dial is turned, the live view goes back to normal.*

<table><tr><td>TIP 11</td><td>Keeping the camera sensor clean</td></tr></table>

Sooner or later, all cameras with interchangeable lenses get dust or dirt on the sensor. This manifests as spots on your image, especially in photos taken at small apertures. You can prevent this from happening by taking measures to avoid sensor dust as much as possible. You can clean dust by using your camera's built-in cleaning mechanism:

- Select SET UP > USER SETTING > SENSOR CLEANING > OK to activate the built-in cleaning mechanism that helps loosen dust particles. By default, this mechanism will be employed when you switch *off* the camera. I recommend setting the camera to also automatically activate this mechanism when the X-T3 is switched *on:* to do this, select SET UP > USER SETTING > SENSOR CLEANING > WHEN SWITCHED ON > ON.

In addition, it's sensible to adhere to a regimen that avoids exposing the camera to dust and dirt:

- Never leave the camera without a lens mounted or without its protective body cap in place.

- Don't change lenses in dusty environments.

- When changing lenses, always hold the camera with the open lens mount pointed downward—never upward.

- When you attach a new lens, make sure the rear glass of the lens is clean and free of dust particles. Otherwise, dust from the lens could travel to the sensor.

- Never touch the sensor!

Fig. 14: **Dust spots** on the sensor made visible. This sensor badly needs cleaning.

<table><tr><td style="background:olive; color:white;">TIP 12</td><td>Do-it-yourself sensor cleaning</td></tr></table>

When the built-in sensor-cleaning function doesn't do a proper job, you have three basic options for cleaning the sensor by yourself:

- Touchless cleaning
- Dry cleaning
- Wet cleaning

**Touchless cleaning** involves using a blower, like the *Giottos Rocket Air Blower,* to rid the sensor of dust particles. An important feature of such devices is a filter in the intake valve that prevents contaminated (dusty) air from being blown against the sensor.

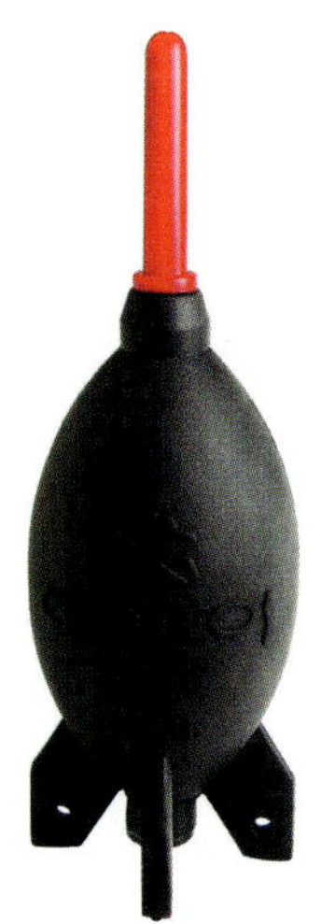

Fig. 15:
Touchless sensor cleaning: **Giottos Rocket Air Blower**

*Important: Don't use compressed air from aerosol cans that contain propellants. Particles could hit the sensor like tiny projectiles and damage the protective surface!*

A popular means to **dry clean** the sensor is to use the *Pentax Sensor Cleaning Kit.* The sticky head of this funny-looking cleaning device picks up dust and dirt from the sensor surface and transfers it to sticky paper sheets that are included with the product.

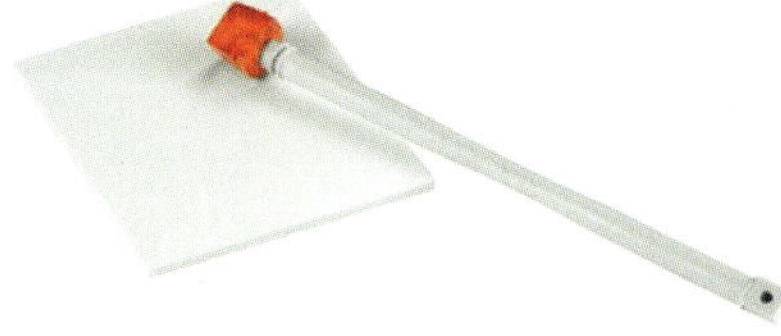

Fig. 16:
Dry cleaning:
**Pentax Sensor Cleaning Kit**

Tough sensor dirt (like water or oil stains) requires **wet cleaning** with a *sensor swab*. Suitable but expensive products are offered by companies likes Photographic Solutions and Visible Dust. They consist of wipers that are wetted with special cleaning fluids (such as Eclipse). Wipe one side of the swab from left to right over the full width of the sensor, and then from right to left with the other side of the swab. Your X-mount camera requires swabs that match APS-C-sized sensors. At Photographic Solutions, this translates into product size number 2.

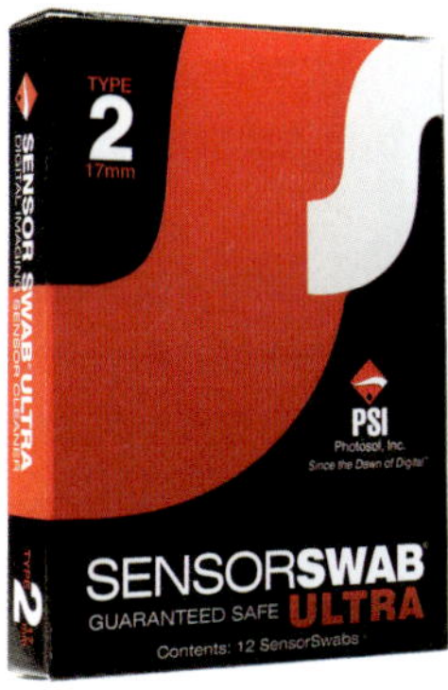

Fig. 17:
Wet cleaning: **sensor swabs** from Photographic Solutions.

Inexpensive and effective alternatives to products from Visible Dust or Photographic Solutions are APS-C-sized swabs from the brand VSGO.

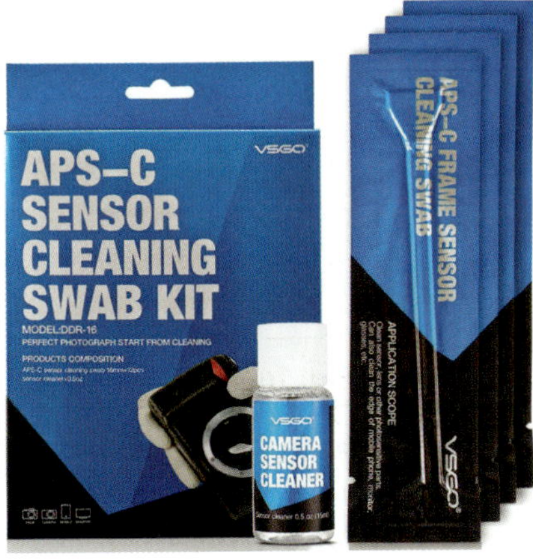

Fig. 18:
My personal sensor cleaning choice for X-mount cameras: **VSGO** swabs and cleaning fluid.

*Important: There's a small chance that sensor spots are caused by dust particles enclosed **behind** the protective surface of the sensor. If some spots simply won't go away, the camera needs to be serviced by Fujifilm.*

<table><tr><td>**TIP 13**</td><td>Pixel Mapping</td></tr></table>

Your X-T3 includes an automatic pixel-mapping feature. To use it, select SHOOTING MENU > IMAGE QUALITY SETTING > PIXEL MAPPING. Pixel mapping detects defective pixels on your sensor and maps them out, meaning they are interpolated with the information of surrounding pixels. Since the number of hot pixels increases with sensor temperature, pixel mapping is only available when the camera hasn't already heated up.

Please note that a few defective pixels are perfectly normal in every digital camera. As the sensor ages (even when the camera is not in use), the number of dead pixels increases. In addition to the manufacturing process, defective pixels are also caused by cosmic radiation. For example, frequently taking your camera on long-haul flights will increase the risk.

Knowing all this, it's a good idea to regularly use the pixel-mapping function in order to keep the defective pixel map inside your camera up-to-date. It takes just a few seconds.

## 1.2 THE BASICS (2): THINGS YOU SHOULD KNOW ABOUT YOUR LENSES

Your camera is compatible with the following native X-mount lenses:

- Fujinon XF lenses (prime and zoom lenses)

- Fujinon XC lenses (compact and affordable lenses)

- Zeiss Touit X-mount lenses (primes)

Confused about which lens category does what? Here's the low-down as of summer 2019:

- Fujinon zoom lenses (except for the XF16–55mmF2.8 and the XF8–16mmF2.8) feature an optical image stabilizer (OIS).

- Zeiss Touit lenses and Fujinon XF lenses (with the exception of the XF27mmF2.8 pancake lens) feature an aperture ring.

- Fujinon XC lenses don't feature an aperture ring. With these lenses, the aperture is set using the camera's command dial.

- Zeiss Touit lenses and Fujinon XF and XC lenses (with the exception of the XF56mm APD prime lens) support fast phase detection autofocus (PDAF). However, lacking adequate firmware updates, the autofocus performance of the Touits cannot keep up with Fujifilm's own lenses.

- Fujinon XF lenses offer LMO (lens modulation optimizer) support. The LMO mitigates undesirable optical effects such as diffraction, which occurs when a lens is stopped-down to a small aperture.

- Zeiss Touit lenses and Fujinon XC lenses do *not* support the LMO.

In addition to native X-mount lenses, you can also attach a host of current and older lenses from other manufacturers to the X-T3 via a suitable mechanical adapter. Remember that adapted lenses will always operate either wide open or at the set working aperture. Autofocus, program AE, and shutter priority AE will not be available, either, unless you use a so-called "smart" adapter.

 **Samyang lenses aren't native!**

Manual focus lenses from Samyang, Rokinon, Walimex, and similar brands are not native X-mount lenses. They simply come with a compatible mechanical mount, so you don't have to buy an additional mechanical adapter. These lenses behave like other adapted third-party lenses: they don't communicate with the camera (there's no data transmission because there aren't any electronic contacts), there's no autofocus, the live view [10] operates with the currently set working aperture, and you can only use AE modes **A** and **M**.

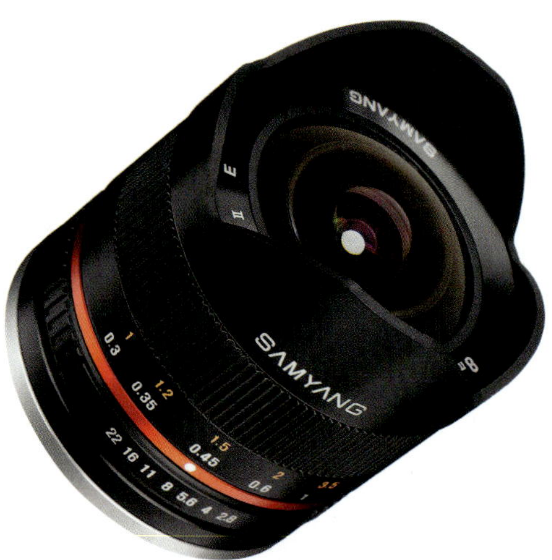

Fig. 19: The affordable **Samyang 8mmF2.8 Fisheye II** manual focus lens for Fujifilm X-mount is a popular choice to take images with extreme angles of view.

 **Zeiss Touit lenses**

Even though Touit lenses with native X-mount compatibility offer great image quality and work like Fujinon XF lenses, Zeiss tends to be hesitant to support new camera features with lens firmware updates. It took Zeiss about half a year longer than Fuji to offer PDAF support, and to date there is still no LMO support. There's also no indication that Zeiss wants to continue with the Touit line of lenses.

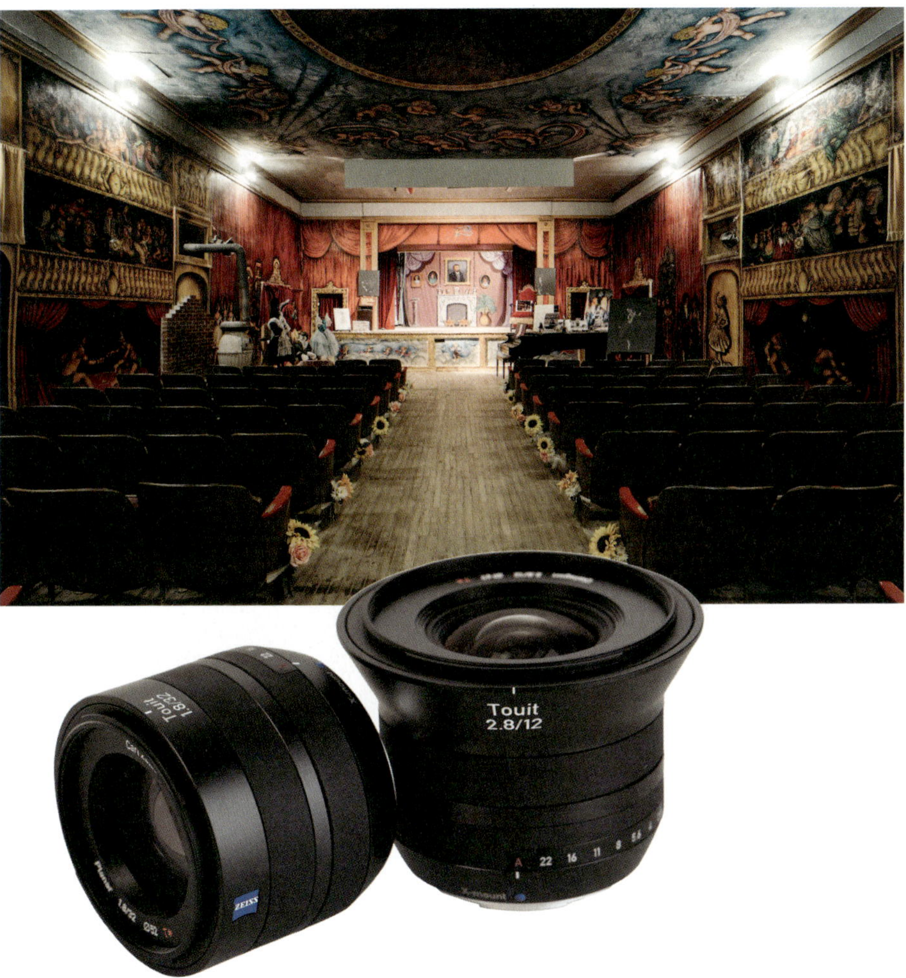

Fig. 20: **Zeiss Touit** 1.8/32mm and 2.8/12mm are autofocus lenses with native X-mount compatibility. The wide field of view of the Touit 2.8/12mm lens makes it ideal for landscape or interior shots.

 | Viltrox autofocus lenses

China-based manufacturer Viltrox is offering a growing selection of affordable AF prime lenses for different mounts, including the Fujifilm X-mount. Please note that Viltrox X-mount lenses aren't licensed or supported by Fujifilm, so their firmware and autofocus function is based on reverse engineering. This can lead to performance and compatibility issues, so please proceed at your own risk.

 | Decoding XF18–135mmF3.5–5.6 R LM OIS WR

This tip is of the "what you always wanted to know but never dared to ask" variety:

- **XF:** "X" means X-mount or X series; "F" means Fine, designating Fuji's premium line of lenses. There's also the smaller, more affordable XC line ("C" stands for Compact or Casual). And let's not forget GF lenses for GFX medium format cameras (G-mount).

- **18–135mm:** This is the focal length range of the zoom lens. To translate the numbers to their full-frame equivalents, you must multiply them by the APS-C crop factor [11] of 1.5. Hence, the field of view (FOV) of an 18–135mm zoom on your X-mount camera is identical to the FOV of a 27–202mm zoom lens on a full-frame (35mm format) camera.

- **F3.5–5.6:** This range describes the maximum aperture opening at the low and high ends of the focal length range. In this case, the lens offers a maximum aperture of f/3.5 at 18 mm and f/5.6 at 135 mm.

- **R:** This stands for Ring and indicates that the lens features an aperture ring. This is a standard feature of all Fujinon XF lenses except the XF27mmF2.8 pancake lens. XC zooms don't offer an aperture ring, either. With ringless lenses, the aperture setting is always controlled with the command dial when you are using exposure modes **A** or **M**.

- **LM:** This stands for Linear Motor, which ensures quick and silent autofocus operation.

- **OIS:** This is the Optical Image Stabilizer [12]. This feature allows you to perform handheld shots at a shutter speed of up to five stops slower than you would usually need in order to eliminate camera shake. For example, in situations that would normally require a shutter speed of 1/160 s to ensure a clear image, you could shoot with 1/8 s and still get usable results. It's important to remember that motion blur often plays a role at slower shutter speeds since many subjects tend to move. Obviously, the OIS cannot reduce motion blur [13]—only blurring that occurs due to camera shake (i.e., the shaky hands of the photographer).

- **WR** denotes weather resistant lenses.

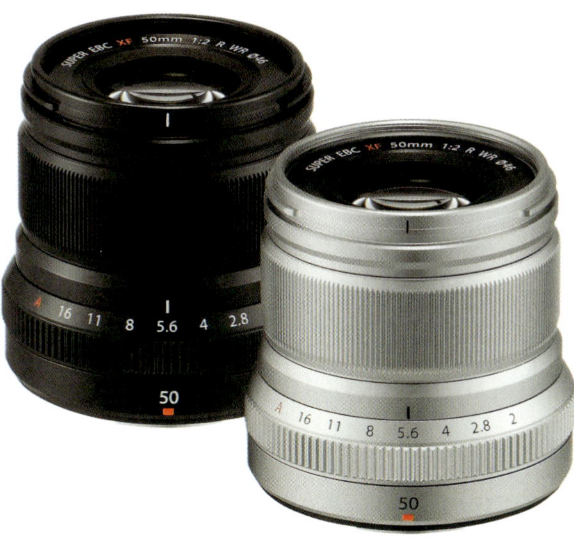

Fig. 21: Along with the XF35mmF2 R WR, XF23mmF2 R WR, and XF16mmF2.8 R WR, the affordable **XF50mmF2 R WR** is one of Fujifilm's popular compact prime lenses for the X series. These lenses are weather resistant and their lean design doesn't obscure the optical viewfinder of the X-Pro1, X-Pro2 and X-Pro3. These lenses come in black and silver.

<table><tr><td>**TIP 18**</td><td>Using the optical image stabilizer (OIS)</td></tr></table>

Most XF and XC zoom lenses, and a few selected prime lenses feature built-in optical image stabilization (OIS). Switch on the OIS to prevent camera shake and blurry images in situations that require you to take handheld shots at slower-than-usual shutter speeds. Most XF lenses offer a dedicated OIS on/off switch on the lens barrel. The OIS in XC lenses and the XF16–80mmF4 is controlled through the camera menu.

For handheld shots, an old rule of thumb recommends using shutter speeds that are at least as fast as the reciprocal of the full–frame equivalent focal length that is currently in use. For example, with a 50 mm lens and an APS-C crop factor of 1.5, the minimum safe shutter speed for handheld camera use would be *[1/(50 × 1.5)] s = 1/75 s*. In other words, when you are shooting handheld with a 50 mm lens and don't want blurry images, you should use shutter speeds at least as fast as 1/75 s. Or you can use the OIS to add a few more stops.

Of course, rules of thumb don't apply to everybody. Some users have quite steady hands, and some are rather shaky. The settings and equipment that work for me may not work for you. However, the OIS will always give you a few extra stops of shutter-speed headroom.

In SHOOTING MENU > SHOOTING SETTING > IS MODE, you can choose between two basic OIS modes:

- **OIS mode 1** (CONTINUOUS) is the default setting. It's always stabilizing the image, even when you are just looking through the viewfinder before you press the shutter button.

- **OIS mode 2** (SHOOTING ONLY) engages only when you fully press the shutter button to take an image (or half-press it in AF-C mode).

Please note that the OIS can also *introduce* camera shake, especially at fast shutter speeds. This adverse effect is more likely to occur in OIS mode 1 than in mode 2. However, OIS mode 1 is more effective when used at very slow shutter speeds, such as 1/15 s, 1/8 s, or even 1/4 s.

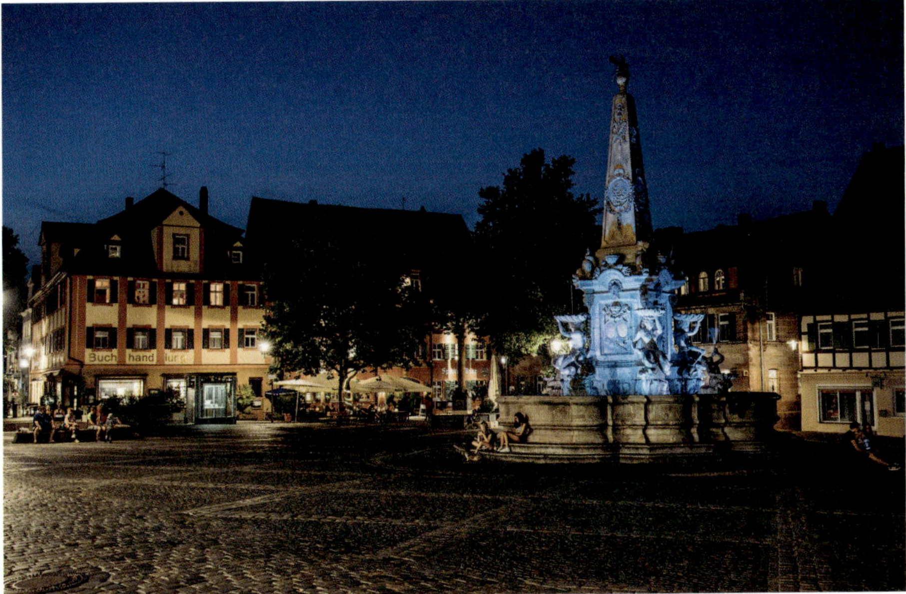

Fig. 22: The **optical image stabilizer** of the XF16–80mmF4 R OIS WR in action: Thanks to a slow shutter speed of 1/2 s, I could still use ISO 160 for this handheld night shot. The OIS was able to successfully compensate for camera shake caused by my hands.

These are my recommendations for using the OIS:

- Only use (switch on) OIS when necessary. When you are using fast shutter speeds that don't require image stabilization, you can safely turn the OIS off to eliminate it as a potential interference. That said, I found the OIS useful even at shutter speed of 1/2000 s and 1/4000 s when I was shooting with an XF18–55mm lens from a small helicopter with extreme high-frequency vibration.

- I often prefer to use the OIS in mode 2 ("shooting only"). However, mode 1 is more useful at very slow shutter speeds and when you are using telephoto lenses, because in mode 1, the OIS will also stabilize the live view image, making it easier to compose and focus a shot.

- Consider turning off the OIS when you are working from a stable tripod or with shutter speeds that are slower than a second. Of course, this decision very much depends on the sturdiness of the tripod, prevailing wind conditions, and vibrations caused by traffic. Shooting in bustling cities, one encounters many situations where leaving OIS on is a good idea even with the sturdiest of tripods. The XF16–80mmF4 R OIS WR features built-in "tripod recognition" and will disable its 6-stop OIS automatically when appropriate.

- Depending on the lens, you might also want to switch OIS off for panning shots [14] in case you find it difficult to smoothly track your subject with the OIS turned on. Again, the XF16–80mmF4 promises to detect your panning motion and adapt accordingly.

By the way, OIS and IBIS both emit a soft humming sound, even when the function is turned off. Don't worry about the noise—it's perfectly normal.

| TIP 19 | How the XF23mmF1.4 R, XF16mmF1.4 R WR, and XF14mmF2.8 R differ |
| --- | --- |

Unlike standard X-mount lenses, the wide-angle primes XF14mmF2.8 R, XF16mmF1.4 R WR, and XF23mmF1.4 R feature a more traditional manual focus ring with a clutch mechanism.

- Pull the focus ring toward the camera to set the lens to manual focus.

- Push the focus ring away from the camera to set the lens to autofocus.

- Alternatively, you can use the camera's own focus mode selector to set it to manual focus mode. In this case, the lens remains in autofocus mode, and you can only use Instant AF (usually assigned to the AF-L button) to change the focus. This also means you cannot manually adjust focus on the lens after focusing with Instant AF.

- You cannot use Instant AF (AF-L button) to focus when the focus ring of the lens is set to manual focus. In this case, you can only use the manual focus ring to change or adjust focus.

- The analog depth-of-field (DOF) [15] markers on the lens barrel are less conservative (and in my opinion less useful) than the camera's pixel-based scale. This is because the pixel-based scale is using a much smaller circle of confusion [16] to display DOF ranges for pixel-sharp results at 100% magnification, whereas the engraved scale on the lens uses a value that's based on looking at typically sized prints from a typical distance with typical eyesight. Some photographers regard the engraved scale (which equals your camera's electronic film format-based scale) as more practical. Personally, I prefer the pixel-based scale. In any case, the actual difference between the two scales is about 3.66 aperture stops.

- It's not possible to reverse the focusing direction of the manual focus ring with the 14 mm, 16 mm, or 23 mm lenses.

- If you set your camera to AF+MF mode (SHOOTING MENU > AF/MF SETTING > AF+MF > ON), you can use this feature only when the lens clutch is set to MF and the camera is set to AF-S. In this configuration, you can autofocus by half-pressing the shutter button, and then manually adjust the focus with the focus ring (while keeping the shutter button half-pressed).

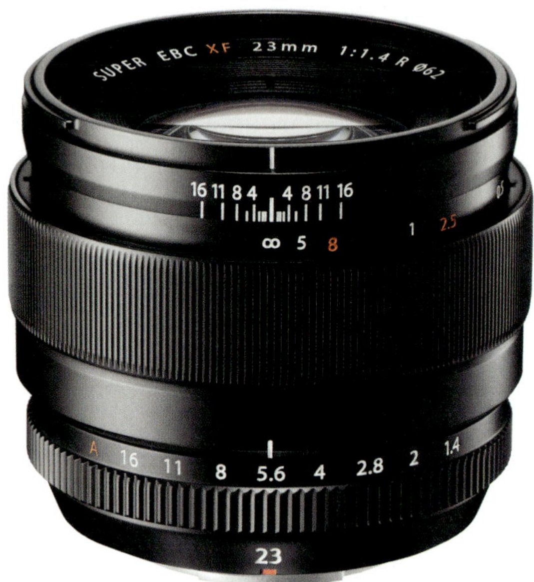



Fig. 23: **Fujinon XF23mmF1.4 R** with engraved distance and DOF markers. It's a nice retro touch, but you lose some state-of-the-art digital functionality.

| TIP 20 | Using the Lens Modulation Optimizer (LMO) |

The X-T3 supports the Lens Modulation Optimizer or LMO. This feature premiered in the X100S and X20 fixed-lens cameras (where it can't be switched off). It counteracts common optical phenomena (like diffraction [17] and corner softness) when the camera converts the RAW data into JPEG images. To make it work, the firmware of the attached lens sends its LMO correction data to the camera as hidden metadata with every image.

- Neither Fujinon XC lenses nor Zeiss Touit lenses support the LMO.

- LMO data is proprietary and not available to external RAW converters.

If your lens supports the LMO (all Fujinon XF lenses do), you should enable the function by selecting SHOOTING MENU > IMAGE QUALITY SETTING > LENS MODULATION OPTIMIZER > ON. You can also use the built-in RAW converter of your camera (PLAYBACK MENU > RAW CONVERSION) to enable or disable the LMO for a specific JPEG result. With this method, it's easy to create and compare versions of a shot with and without LMO enhancements.

The LMO takes care of the following optical effects:

- **Diffraction softness:** This effect increasingly occurs when the lens is stopped down beyond a certain point. APS-C cameras with 26 MP typically exhibit diffraction at apertures of 9 and smaller. While stopping down increases the overall depth of field (DOF), it also reduces the maximum resolution of the lens/camera combination. The LMO counteracts this effect and reconstructs some of the lost detail.

- **Corner softness:** Even the best lenses aren't as sharp in the corners as they are in the center. The LMO can digitally compensate for that loss of quality.

LMO corrections are currently supported only in-camera with the built-in RAW converter. External converters such as Adobe Lightroom, Adobe Camera Raw, Capture One Pro, Silkypix, Iridient Developer, or Photo Ninja can't process LMO data. This means LMO corrections are visible only in JPEGs that have been generated by the camera.

That said, Capture One Pro now offers specific Fujifilm lens profiles that not only replace Fujifilm's built-in digital lens corrections but can also reduce diffraction blur and enhance corner sharpness.

<table><tr><td>**TIP 21**</td><td>Things you should know about digital lens corrections</td></tr></table>

Most modern lenses achieve their optimal image quality through a combination of optical and digital corrections. Corrections are mostly applied to the three following phenomena:

- **Vignetting:** This effect results in a loss of brightness from center to corner. Vignetting [18] is more pronounced at large (open) apertures.

- **Distortion:** There are pincushion- and barrel-type distortions [19], both of which make straight lines seem curved. Several premium primes like the XF14mm, XF23mm (F1.4 and F2), XF35mmF1.4, XF56mm, and XF90mm are fully optically corrected for distortion. Others (such as the Zeiss Touit range, compact pancake lenses, the XF35mmF2 and XF16mmF2.8, or zoom lenses) require a combination of optical and digital distortion correction.

- **Chromatic aberration:** Chromatic aberration [20] results in color fringing. This effect can be corrected (or mitigated) with apochromatic lenses, or digitally corrected during RAW conversion.

Some camera makers rely on dedicated correction profiles that must be provided by each RAW converter maker. Fujifilm isn't one of these companies. Instead, all current Fujifilm cameras store digital corrections as metadata in the RAW file. RAW converters can access this lens-specific metadata and use it to apply appropriate corrections. This way, the built-in RAW converter and external RAW conversion software, such as Adobe Lightroom, Silkypix, Iridient Developer, and Capture One, can use the metadata in the RAW file to correct or mitigate vignetting, distortion, and chromatic aberration.

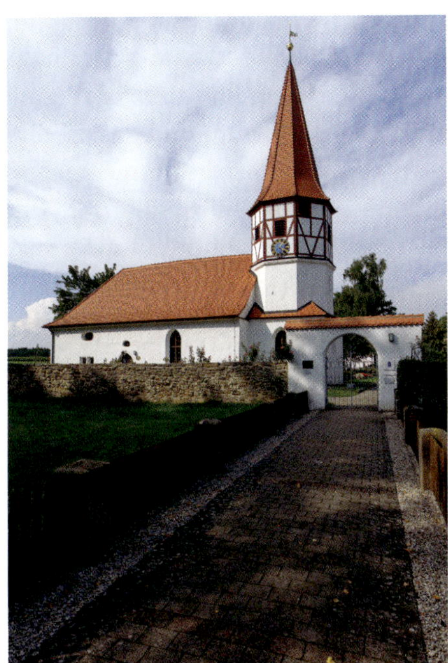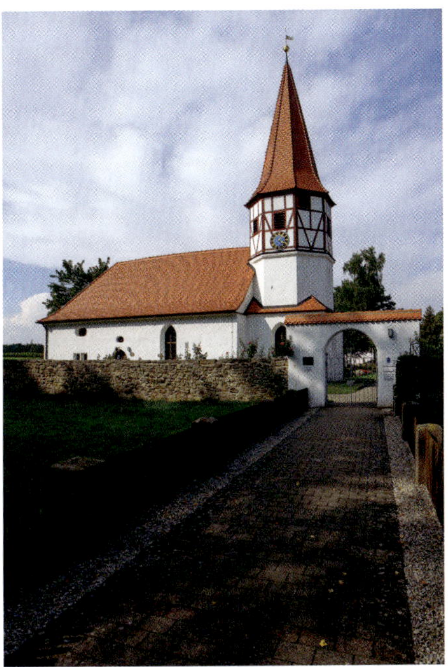

**Fig. 24:** This XF16–80mmF4 R OIS WR example shows the same image with (left) and without (right) digital lens corrections for distortion, vignetting and chromatic aberration. It was shot at f/8 with a focal length of 16 mm.

A major benefit of this method is that many RAW converters automatically support new lenses since Fujifilm delivers the correction data via the RAW metadata. However, there's also a drawback. Some RAW converters (such as Lightroom, Adobe Camera Raw, and Silkypix) don't give you the option to switch off metadata-based digital lens corrections, even if you're convinced they aren't necessary. Since digital distortion correction always results in some loss of image sharpness and detail due to the required stretching and interpolation of pixels, this can be a headache for some users. Obviously, not all subjects or images require the same amount of digital correction (it can also be a simple matter of taste), so full user control over the application of digital lens corrections is a very nice feature.

Luckily, software like Iridient Developer and Capture One offer control over how much digital metadata distortion (or vignetting) correction should be applied. Other programs (like Photo Ninja and AccuRaw) simply ignore lens-correction metadata. With such programs, all corrections must be applied either manually or by using a dedicated profile.

Capture One Pro even supports both options: it can apply RAW metadata-based lens corrections, and it offers a set of dedicated lens correction profiles for a quickly rising number of X-mount lenses. It's up to you to choose the digital lens correction option that suits you.

| TIP 22 | Using teleconverters |
|---|---|

A teleconverter is installed between the camera body and a compatible XF lens, where it extends the effective focal length of the lens by a factor of either 1.4 or 2. This leads to losing either one or two aperture stops of brightness, and it puts a (small) toll on image resolution. Hence, teleconverters should be used in concert with premium lenses that offer a resolution reserve robust enough to make the toll on image quality negligible.

As of the writing of this book, the following teleconverters are available from Fujifilm:

- The **XF1.4x TC WR** and **XF2x TC WR** for X-mount are mechanically compatible with the XF50–140mmF2.8 R LM OIS WR, the XF100–400mmF4.5–5.6 R LM OIS WR, and the XF80mmF2.8 R LM OIS WR Macro. It is *not* recommended to use them with the XF200mmF2 R LM OIS WR.

- The **XF1.4x TC F2 WR** is compatible and included with the XF200mmF2 R LM OIS WR high-end telephoto prime. After applying lens firmware updates that were released in late December of 2018, it can also be used with the

XF50–140mmF2.8 R LM OIS WR, XF100–400mmF4.5–5.6 R LM OIS WR, and XF80mmF2.8 R LM OIS WR Macro lenses.

Unlike screw-on conversion lenses for the X70 and X100 series cameras, XF teleconverters have an impact on the speed (maximum brightness) of the resulting lens combination. To give you an example, the XF2x TC WR effectively turns the ultra-sharp XF80mmF2.8 R LM OIS WR Macro lens into an XF160mmF5.6 R LM OIS WR Macro. Setting the aperture of this combo to f/2.8 actually means setting an effective aperture of f/5.6. Using a 2x teleconverter, the light loss comprises two stops, whereas 1.4x converters take away one stop of light.

Luckily, these issues are recognized and handled by the camera and lens firmware (as long as you have kept them up to date). The firmware will automatically adjust the on-screen displays and the EXIF [21] data to reflect the *effective* aperture values. It will also change the lens-correction metadata (factoring in updated values for distortion, vignetting, and chromatic aberration) and include the presence of the teleconverter in the EXIF lens description.

Depending on the quality of your individual lens copy, using the XF100–400mmF4.5–5.6 R LM OIS WR in concert with an XF2x TC WR tends to stretch things thin in regard to performance and image quality, particularly at the long end of the lens. At an effective focal length of 800 mm (the full-frame equivalent of 1200 mm) the wide-open aperture of this combo is f/11, which can make it hard for your camera's autofocus to gather enough light to operate quickly and precisely. There also will be some loss of resolution—not only because of the optics involved, but also due to atmospheric effects when you are capturing distant subjects.

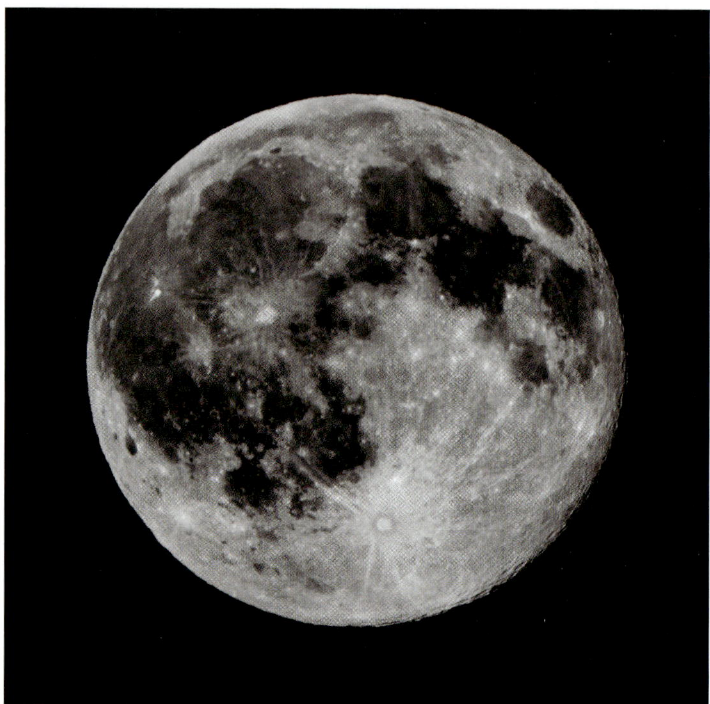

Fig. 25: XF100–400mmF4.5–5.6 R LM OIS WR and XF2x TC WR: Shooting the moon with and effective focal length of 800 mm (or 1200 mm in full-frame terms) on a warm summer night resulted in some unwelcome atmospheric effects. That's why astronomic telescopes are usually placed on mountaintops or in space. This example is based on a square 5 MP crop.

| TIP 23 | Use the included lens hood! |
|--------|------------------------------|

With the exception of the XF27mmF2.8 pancake lens, all Fujifilm XF and most XC lenses come with a fitted lens hood, which should be used whenever possible. In addition to its optical benefits, the hood protects the lens and the front glass element from damage.

Lens hoods can pose problems too. They make the lens bigger than it actually is, and they can shade the camera flash or the autofocus assist light. They also use up extra space in your bag, although most hoods can be reverse-mounted on the lens for transport purposes.

When you shoot with a small shoe-mounted flash, or when you depend on using the AF assist lamp, it's best to remove the lens hood.

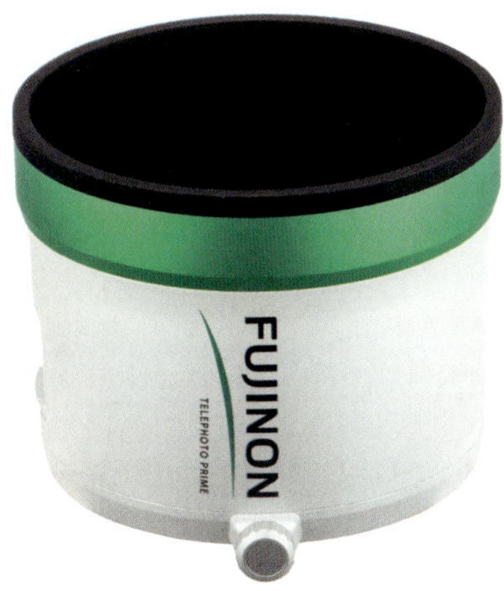

Fig. 26:  Lens hoods like this large attachment for the **XF200mmF2 R LM OIS WR** offer optical benefits and robust lens protection.

*Important: Don't use screw-on lens hoods with lenses that feature a retractable inner tube, such as the XF27mmF2.8, XF60mmF2.4 R Macro, or the XF35mmF1.4 R. The inner tube of these lenses doesn't respond well to shocks and pressure. By using a screw-on hood, you'd directly transfer pressure or shocks from the lens hood to the delicate inner lens tube. It's a recipe for disaster.*

| Lens protection filters—yes or no? | TIP 24 |
| --- | --- |

Digital cameras like the X-T3 don't require the UV or sky-light filters that were popular in the days of analog film photography. This means that a permanently affixed filter has no optical purpose, and only serves as protective glass. This additional glass can have a negative effect on image quality, especially at night or when you shoot against a bright light source. Filters increase the risks of ghosting, unwanted reflections, and a loss of contrast.

I recommend using protective glass only in situations that require this additional protective layer. In most situations, the lens hood should provide sufficient protection. If you still decide to use a filter, make sure to choose a high-quality product. Fujifilm offers suitable protective filters that feature the same Super EBC coating used on their XF and XC lenses. Be prepared to pay a premium, though.

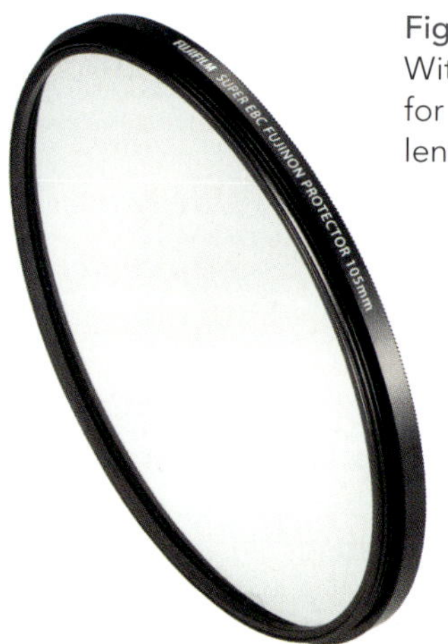

Fig. 27:
With a diameter of 105 mm, the **PRF-105** for the XF200mmF2 is (so far) the largest lens protection filter for the X series.

| TIP 25 | 39 mm filters can be tricky! |
| --- | --- |

The XF60mmF2.4 R and XF27mmF2.8 lenses require filters with a 39 mm thread. These filters are designed to allow the inner lens barrel to freely retract into the outer barrel while the filter is attached. If this isn't possible (for example, because a thin step-up ring is directly attached to the lens or because the filter's overall diameter is too large), the lens can be damaged when the filter or step-up ring collides with the outer barrel of the lens.

A typical indicator for this and other mechanical lens problems is a message alerting you that the camera needs to be switched off and on again. A possible solution is putting a spacer (a fitting 39 mm filter, for example) between the lens and the step-up ring. You should remove the glass from the spacer. You can refit a cheap, old, or unused 39 mm filter to do the job as long as it doesn't interfere with the outer lens barrel when the inner barrel is retracting.

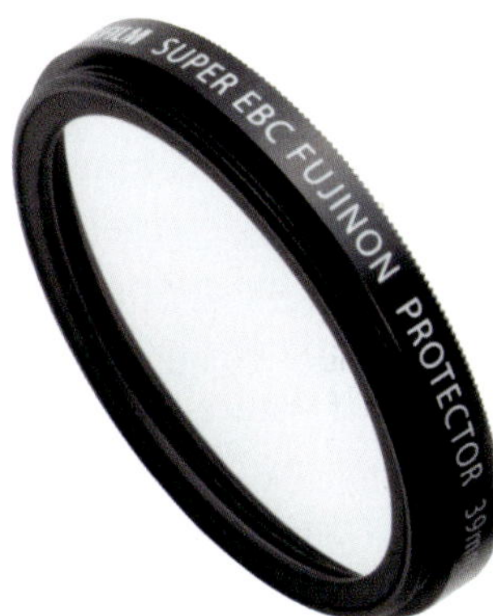


Fig. 28:
A **39mm protection filter** by Fujifilm. A filter like this can also be used as a spacer between the lens (XF60mm or XF27mm) and a step-up ring.

Don't forget that screw-in lens hoods are an absolute no-go for a lens with retractable inner barrels like the XF27mmF2.8.

| Switch off the camera when changing lenses! | TIP 26 |
| --- | --- |

The user manual of your camera tells you to switch off the camera before changing lenses. Then again, who cares, right? In the heat of the moment, many of us forget (or simply don't have the time) to follow this advice, and so far, nothing terrible has happened.

However, instead of getting into a bad habit, we should consider why Fujifilm is telling us to change lenses only when the camera is turned off:

■ Several lenses (like the XF60mmF2.4 R Macro or the XF27mmF2.8) have moving inner barrels. During focusing, the inner barrel can protrude beyond the protective edge of the outer barrel. The secure storage and transport state for these lenses is always with a fully retracted inner barrel, and this secure state is automatically entered when you turn off the camera *before* you remove the lens.

- The same applies to lenses like the XC15–45mmF3.5–5.6 OIS PZ power zoom. Switch off the camera while the lens is still attached and the power zoom will safely retract to its compact transport and storage position. If you remove the lens before turning off the camera, your lens may end up in a less compact and more vulnerable state.

- When the camera/lens is powering off, a lock mechanism holds the linear motor driven inner-focusing element of the XF200mmF2 R LM OIS WR in place. This suppresses clacking noises (caused by the loose lens group) when you carry the lens around off-camera. If you remove the lens while the camera is still powered on, this locking mechanism will not be activated. By the way, clacking sounds are perfectly normal for other lenses with inner-focusing mechanisms, such as the XF90mmF2 R LM or XF50–140mmF2.8 R LM OIS WR, so don't worry, nothing is broken. Off-camera, there's simply no camera-powered magnetic field to hold the rear element in place, so it will loosely move in the barrel when you shake the lens.

# 1.3 THE BASICS (3): USEFUL ACCESSORIES

There is a rich selection of accessories for your X-T3. Whether or not you believe such add-ons are useful, I'll cover a few select items that can, in my opinion and experience, improve the functionality of your camera.

<table><tr><td>**Optional handgrips**</td><td>TIP 27</td></tr></table>

An optional handgrip can improve the ergonomics of the X-T3 when you are using large, heavy lenses or if you have large hands.

The **MHG-XT3 Metal Handgrip** provides full access to the battery compartment and is compatible with Arca-Swiss-type tripod heads, so you don't need a dedicated quick release plate: the handgrip *is* the quick release plate.

Fig. 29: The optional **MHG-XT3** handgrip provides direct access to the battery compartment and can be mounted on an Arca-Swiss-type tripod head.

The **Vertical Battery Grip** is another useful option to enhance both the ergonomics and the performance of your X-T3. The grip can hold two batteries to boost the maximum number of shots per charge to more than 1,000.

For improved vertical shooting, the grip mirrors the camera body's shutter release button, Q button, focus stick, both command dials, the AE-L and AF-L buttons, and one Fn button. The tripod-mounting socket is in line with the camera's optical axis, and the grip is resistant to dust and water. It offers its own battery-charging functionality and, with the included power supply, it is capable of fully charging two batteries in two hours.

The Vertical Battery Grip also features a dedicated Boost mode switch that improves the AF speed and the EVF refresh rate, as well as the shooting interval, the shutter release time lag, and the blackout time.

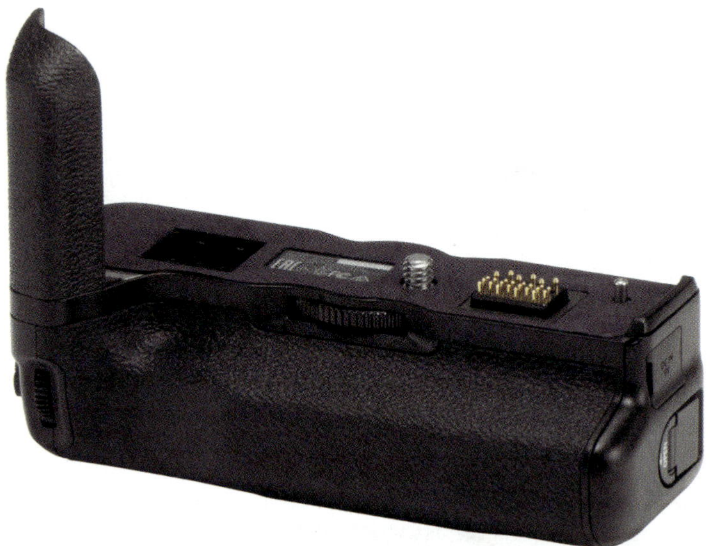

Fig. 30:  The **Vertical Battery Grip** is a useful companion for the X-T3. Personally, I rarely take it off. It enhances the camera's usability when large and heavy lenses are mounted, and offers improved ergonomics for vertical shooting. With a total of three batteries in the camera body and the grip, users can spend a day of intense shooting without changing or charging batteries. The Vertical Battery Grip can also be used to quickly charge two batteries on or off-camera.

**TIP 28** | Remote shutter release options

From time to time you may encounter situations that require you to remotely release the shutter without vibration. A quick-and-dirty method is to use the camera's self-timer with a delay of either two or ten seconds, although a better way is to use a remote shutter release.

Your X-T3 offers three remote shutter release options:

- A **mechanical thread** in the shutter release button allows you to connect a traditional cable release.

- You can connect electronic remote shutter releases to the camera's **RR-100 remote release port** (a 2.5 mm input on the right side of the body).

- You can trigger the shutter via **Bluetooth** using Fujifilm's free Camera Remote app [22].

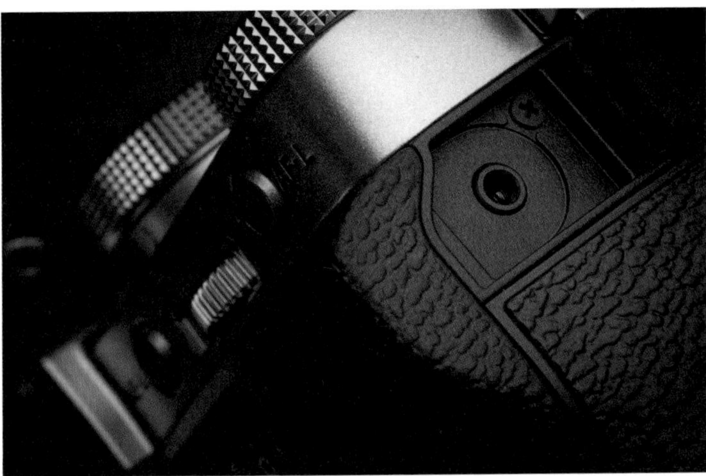

Fig. 31: The electronic **RR-100 remote release port** is located at the upper-right side of the body.

Electronic shutter releases are available in tethered and wireless versions. Wireless options always consist of a transmitter and a receiver. The transmitter sends a trigger signal that is picked up by the receiver, which triggers the camera with an electronic cable that's connected to the RR-100 remote release port.

Fujifilm offers a simple RR-100-compatible remote shutter release cable, but there are more sophisticated (both tethered and wireless) solutions available from third parties, such as programmable intervalometers.

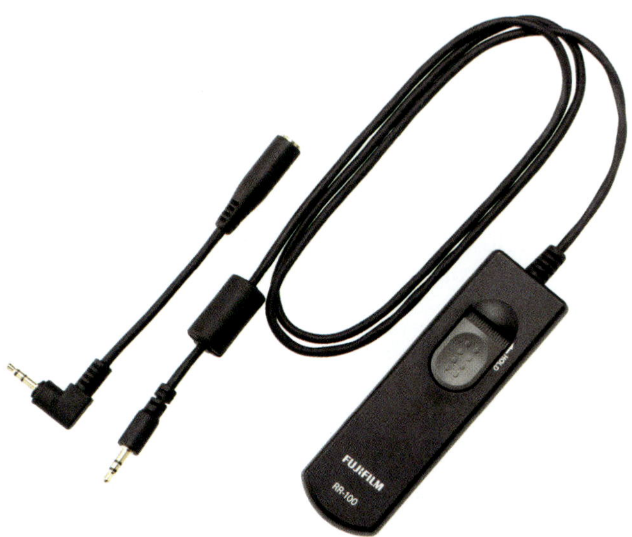

Fig. 32: Fujifilm's **RR-100** is a simple and reliable remote release for your X-T3.

The RR-100 remote release port of the X-T3 is compatible with a widely used Canon remote shutter release standard. Among others, it is compatible to the following camera models: Canon EOS Digital Rebel, Canon EOS 1000D, Canon EOS 100D, Canon EOS 1100D, Canon EOS 300D, Canon EOS 350D, Canon EOS 400D, Canon EOS 450D, Canon EOS 500D, Canon EOS 550D, Canon EOS 600D, Canon EOS 60D, Canon EOS 60Da, Canon EOS 650D, Canon EOS 700D, Canon EOS Kiss Digital, Canon EOS Kiss F, Canon EOS Kiss Digital N, Canon EOS Kiss X2, Canon EOS Kiss X3, Canon EOS Kiss X4, Canon EOS Kiss X5, Canon EOS Kiss X50, Canon EOS Kiss X6i, Canon PowerShot G1 X, Canon PowerShot G10, Canon PowerShot G11, Canon PowerShot G12, Canon PowerShot G15, Canon PowerShot SX50 HS, Canon EOS Rebel SL1, Canon EOS Rebel T1i, Canon EOS Rebel 70 T2i, Canon EOS Rebel T3, Canon EOS Rebel T3i, Canon EOS Rebel T4i, Canon EOS Rebel XS, Canon EOS Rebel XSi, Canon EOS Rebel XT, Canon EOS Rebel XTi, Canon EOS Rebel T5i, Contax 645, Contax N, Contax N Digital, Contax N1, Contax NX, Hasselblad

H1, Hasselblad H3D, Hasselblad H4D-200MS, Hasselblad H4D-31, Hasselblad H4D-40, Hasselblad H4D-50, Hasselblad H4D-50MS, Hasselblad H4D-60, Pentax 645D, Pentax *ist D, Pentax *ist DL, Pentax *ist DL2, Pentax *ist DS, Pentax *ist DS2, Pentax K-30, Pentax K-5, Pentax K-7, Pentax K-m, Pentax K10 Grand Prix, Pentax K100D, Pentax K100D Super, Pentax K10D, Pentax K110D, Pentax K200D, Pentax K20D, Pentax MZ-6, Pentax MZ-L, Pentax ZX-L, Samsung GX-1L, Samsung GX-1S, Samsung GX-20, Samsung NX10, Samsung NX100, Samsung NX11, Samsung NX5, Sigma SD1, Sigma SD1 Merrill, and Sigma SD15.

This list isn't complete, but it's a pretty good start. Remote shutter releases that are compatible with any of these listed cameras should also work with your X-T3.

Personally, I'm a big fan of Canon's simple yet effective **RS-60E3** electronic remote shutter release. It's small and affordable, and it shines with a nice attention to detail.

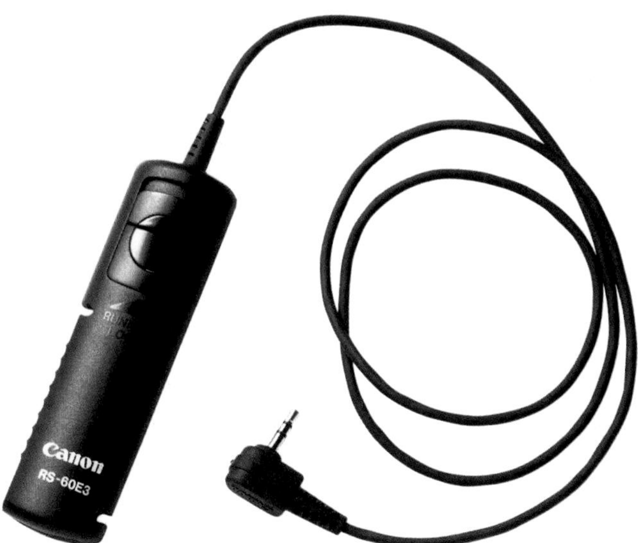


Fig. 33: The **Canon RS-60E3** is my favorite electronic cable release for Fujifilm X cameras—thanks to its attention to detail. Two notches make it easy to neatly spool the cable around the release after shooting. There is also a built-in socket for the 2.5 mm plug that prevents the cable from unspooling in the bag.

Since your X-T3 offers Bluetooth, you can use this semi-permanent wireless connection to your smartphone or tablet to release the shutter [23] with the Camera Remote app [24]. Alternatively, you can remotely control your X-T3 via a Wi-Fi connection. Step-by-step instructions are available online [25].

# 2. USING THE FUJIFILM X-T3

## 2.1 READY, SET, GO!

New users often ask about how to achieve the perfect settings for their camera. Short answer: there are no perfect settings. If they existed, Fuji could have saved us the trouble of navigating the menu options and simply implemented those ideal settings as the factory default. That said, allow me to suggest some basic settings that are meant to provide good overall performance along with as much flexibility as possible.

■ Many settings (such as film simulation modes, color saturation, contrast, sharpness, noise reduction, film grain effect, etc.) belong in the "JPEG settings" category. They don't affect the RAW files but only affect the out-of-camera JPEGs that are generated during RAW conversion. These settings aren't global or camera-specific—they are *image-specific*, and each image should be adjusted individually.

■ In addition to the recommended standard settings, there are many shortcuts and key combinations that can make selecting the optimal camera settings for any situation much easier.

| Recommended default settings for your X-T3 | TIP 29 |
|---|---|

There is no perfect set of basic camera settings that could suit all users in all situations. However, the following settings will allow you to use the X-T3 in a flexible manner with good overall performance:

- Select **FINE+RAW** or **NORMAL+RAW** under SHOOTING MENU > IMAGE QUALITY SETTING > IMAGE QUALITY. This will get you high-resolution out-of-camera JPEGs (digital prints) *and* flexible RAW files (digital negatives). Using the RAW files, you can create a variety of diverse JPEGs with different looks and settings using the camera's built-in RAW converter (PLAYBACK MENU > RAW CONVERSION). Specifically, you can adjust JPEG parameters such as white balance, film simulation, contrast, brightness, noise reduction, and color saturation. This enables you to create different versions of a shot from a single RAW file; for example, you can make color and black-and-white versions of the same image, including different contrast settings. You don't have to worry about finding the perfect JPEG settings prior to taking a shot because you can always change and optimize those settings afterward in the camera's internal RAW converter.

- Make sure to use **electronic front curtain + mechanical shutter** as your default shutter setting by selecting SHOOTING MENU > SHOOTING SETTING > SHUTTER TYPE > EF+M. Use of the electronic shutter (ES or MS+ES) can create all kinds of issues and should be limited to the rare cases where the ES is beneficial, such as shooting with a wide-open aperture (and without an ND filter) in bright daylight, situations that require you to shoot in complete silence (with the alternative of not shooting at all), or situations that require high blackout-free burst rates up to 30 fps.

- As a typical standard setting, most photographers use **single shot drive** (select S on the DRIVE dial) and **single shot autofocus** (AF-S; select S with the focus selector on the front of the camera).

- The most flexible AF mode setting is **ALL** (SHOOTING MENU > AF/MF SETTING > AF MODE > ALL), so please use this mode as your default setting. This way, you can seamlessly cycle between Single-Point, Zone, and Wide/ Tracking AF modes simply by changing the AF frame size (press the focus stick and change the AF frame size with the rear command dial).

■ Set your X-T3 to **Boost mode** for maximum performance by selecting SET UP > POWER MANAGEMENT > PERFOR- MANCE > BOOST. This option is *not* enabled by default, so you have to manually select it. Only Boost mode unleashes the full potential of the camera, offering the fastest available live view readout and best autofocus performance. This mode also uses up more energy, so make sure to always carry one or two fully charged re- placement batteries.

■ Set **Focus Priority** via SHOOTING MENU > AF/MF SET- TING > RELEASE/FOCUS PRIORITY > FOCUS for both AF-S and AF-C. Focus Priority makes sure that the camera records a picture only when the autofocus thinks that it has locked onto a target. In RELEASE mode, the camera will take the shot even if the autofocus couldn't lock on a target. Please note that if you are using AF+MF mode, AF-S will always operate with release priority. That's why my recommended default setting for AF/MF SETTING > AF+MF is OFF.

■ If you want to quickly take a series of single shots, I recommend selecting SET UP > SCREEN SET-UP > IMAGE DISP. > OFF to not interrupt your flow. However, I *nor- mally* set **Image Display** to the shortest available time span of 0.5 SEC. Why? I like to see a quick preview of the final image that represents the camera's exposure and dynamic range (DR) settings. To cancel an ongoing image preview and continue shooting, simply half-press the shutter button.

■ Use the VIEW MODE button to activate the **eye sensor,** which will allow the camera to automatically switch between the viewfinder (EVF) and the LCD depending on which view is in use. There's also an alternative mode called EVF ONLY + EYE SENSOR, which is an energy-saving mode. This mode can make it more difficult to operate the camera, because the LCD won't be available for changing menus while in shooting mode.

- For **exposure metering,** I recommend using MULTI metering as your default mode. Intelligent matrix metering usually delivers results that don't require a massive amount of exposure correction. You can select the metering mode with the metering dial, which is located just below the shutter speed dial.

- Set **white balance** to Auto via SHOOTING MENU > IMAGE QUALITY SETTING > WHITE BALANCE > AUTO to let the camera determine and set the correct white balance for a scene. Since you are shooting FINE+RAW or NORMAL+RAW, you can always adjust the white balance later, either with the camera's built-in RAW converter or with external RAW conversion software such as Lightroom. That said, AUTO will deliver very good results in most scenarios.

- Set **Dynamic Range** by selecting SHOOTING MENU > (IMAGE QUALITY SETTING >) DYNAMIC RANGE > DR100% as your default setting. If you require more **highlight dynamic range** (DR) for a specific subject in order to avoid blown highlights, you can manually set DR200% (for *one* extra stop of dynamic range in the highlights) or DR400% (for *two* extra stops of dynamic range in the highlights). Setting DYNAMIC RANGE to AUTO is *not* recommended. Extending the dynamic range can bring back texture to otherwise blown out areas of your shot (such as in white clouds on a sunny day).

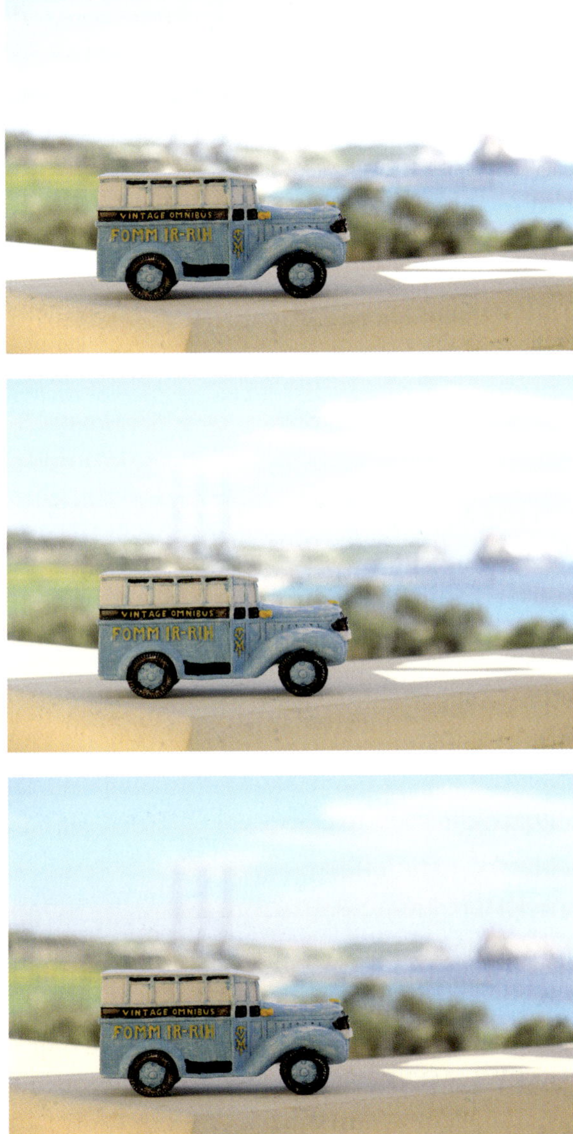

**Fig. 34:** All Fujifilm X cameras feature a powerful and often misunderstood **DR function** that can increase highlight dynamic range by up to two full stops (EV). The default setting is DR100% (top). Seeing blown out highlights that you do not like? Increase dynamic range to DR200% (center) or DR400% (bottom) to get an extra one or two stops worth of highlight detail.

- To use **adapted lenses** with your X-T3, you need either Fujifilm's Leica M adapter or a suitable third-party adapter. In order to make mechanical third-party adapters work, you have to select SET UP > BUTTON/DIAL SETTING > SHOOT WITHOUT LENS > ON. This is necessary because adapted lenses (and third-party lens adapters) do not feature electronic X-mount contacts, so the lens will not register as being connected to the camera. When you are working with a mechanically adapted lens, you should also enter its focal length in SHOOTING MENU > SHOOTING SETTING > MOUNT ADAPTOR SETTING. This ensures that the EXIF [26] data will reflect the proper focal length.

- Do you sometimes shoot with very slow shutter speeds lasting several seconds? In this case, I recommend setting SHOOTING MENU > IMAGE QUALITY SETTING > LONG EXPOSURE NR > ON to improve the quality of your results. In this **Long Exposure** mode, the camera performs a so-called dark-frame subtraction [27] to reduce noise and eliminate hot pixels. With this process, the total exposure time is at least doubled because the camera is taking the shot twice: once normally and once with a closed shutter curtain. The second shot is then subtracted from the first to improve the overall result.

- I recommend *not* using the AUTO setting for the **brightness control for the EVF** because it tends to show an overly bright live view image in bright sunlight and a very subdued image when it's dark. Instead, I select SET UP > SCREEN SET-UP > EVF BRIGHTNESS > MANUAL > 0.

- For the purpose of this book, we assume that SHUTTER AF and SHUTTER AE (in the SET UP > BUTTON DIAL SETTING menu) are both set to ON, which is also the factory default setting. This ensures that autofocus and exposure (including the working aperture) are locked when you half-press the shutter button in AF-S mode, so the camera is primed for the least possible shutter lag once you fully press the shutter button. In AF-C mode, SHUTTER AF ON means the AF keeps tracking a subject while the shutter button is half-pressed or pressed, and SHUTTER AE ON makes sure the exposure is locked as long as you half-press or press the shutter button.

■ I select SET UP > BUTTON DIAL SETTING > COMMAND DIAL SETTING > *front command dial* 1 > S.S. and COMMAND DIAL SETTING > *rear command dial* > F to ensure that the X-T3 stays in line with other X-series cameras that use the front command dial to adjust the shutter speed, and the rear command dial to adjust the aperture (when a lens without an aperture ring is used). All related recommendations in this book are based on this setting. In the same menu, my settings for *front command dial* 2 and *front command dial* 3 are ISO and EXPOSURE COMPENSATION, respectively. This means you can cycle between shutter speed, ISO, and exposure compensation settings by pressing the front command dial. Of course, you are free to set-up your X-T3 differently, as long as you remember which dial is supposed to perform a specific function that I mention in this book.

<table><tr><td>Avoiding the camera menus: practical shortcuts for your X-T3</td><td>TIP 30</td></tr></table>

Navigating nested camera menus can be cumbersome. That's why the X-T3 offers the Quick menu (Q button) and user-configurable Fn keys that can provide direct access to important and frequently used camera functions and settings.

The X-T3 also offers seven custom user settings (C1 through C7) that can hold sets of frequently used camera settings. You can select one of these sets (or profiles) via the Quick menu or an appropriately configured Fn button. C1 through C7 aren't camera *modes;* they are memory locations. Each one conveniently stores a preconfigured profile.

Use these as shortcuts to immediately change your current camera settings to another predefined set of options.

Finally, the X-T3 offers the MY MENU settings, where you can arrange frequently used menu items on two configurable menu pages for quick and easy access.

Speaking of shortcuts—there are plenty, and most of them are available at your fingertips:

- Pull up the Quick menu, then press and hold the Q button again for a few seconds to directly open the configuration menu for your custom user settings (C1 to C7).

- Press and hold the Q button while the Quick menu is *not* opened to directly access the Quick menu configuration page. In this mode, you can customize the Quick menu to meet your personal requirements. You can assign one of more than two-dozen settings to any of the 16 available Quick menu elements. If you don't need 16 shortcuts, you can even select NONE to reduce the size of the Quick menu and make it easier to navigate.

- To see where the Fn and Touch-Fn buttons are located and what's assigned to each of them, simply press and hold the DISP/BACK button. In this menu, you can also reassign all Fn and Touch-Fn buttons.

- To confirm a new menu selection in shooting mode, you can either press the MENU/OK button or half-press the shutter button.

- Half-press the shutter button to switch from playback mode to shooting mode.

- Half-press the shutter button during an ongoing image preview (SET UP > SCREEN SET-UP > IMAGE DISP.) to immediately cancel the preview.

- Half-press the shutter button for a few seconds to wake-up the camera from sleep mode.

- In AF-S shooting mode (with Single Point AF) or MF mode, press the rear command dial to zoom into the currently active focus frame. When zoomed-in, you can select various magnification levels by turning the rear command dial. You can also use the focus stick to change the magnified portion of the live view by jumping to another focus frame. Please note that this magnifier tool is the default configuration for the rear command dial Fn button. If you assign a different function to the R-DIAL Fn button, this useful zoom shortcut won't be available.

- Press and hold the rear command dial in MF mode to cycle between the available manual focus assist modes, such as standard, focus peaking, and digital split image. The X-T3 also offers the new digital microprism mode.

- Press and hold the focus stick in shooting mode to access the focus stick options. You can choose to deactivate the focus stick completely, activate the stick by pressing it, or keep it activated continually. For this book, we choose the last option (ON) to ensure the focus stick is always directly available.

- While in shooting mode, press the focus stick to access the FOCUS AREA screen. Here, you can use the focus stick to move the active focus frame or zone, and you can change their size by turning one of the command dials. In this selection screen, you can press the focus stick again to center the focus frame or zone.

- In the FOCUS AREA screen (which pops up when you press the focus stick), you can also use the four selector (arrow) keys to move the selected AF frame or zone. Press the DISP/BACK button to reset the position of the AF frame or AF zone to the center. You can change the size of the selected AF frame or zone by turning one of the command dials. To reset the size of the AF frame or zone to default, press one of the command dials.

- In shooting mode, you can move the focus stick directly in eight directions to change the position of the active focus frame or zone. However, their size can't be changed before pressing the focus stick.

- In playback mode (while viewing an image), use the front command dial to browse through the images that are on file.

- During playback, you can turn the rear command dial to zoom in and out of an image. By pressing the DISP/BACK button, you can directly return to the standard-size view. Press the rear command dial to zoom in to a 100% view of a shot. When you are zoomed in, pressing the dial again returns the camera to its regular view, displaying the full image.

- While displaying a RAW image in playback mode, you can press the Q button to directly access the built-in RAW converter. This function allows you to create new JPEG versions of your image using different settings.

- In playback mode, press the upper selector button to view the first of two information pages that show additional shooting parameters and the position of the focus point. This function is not available in the FAVORITES display mode.

- In playback mode, you can use the focus stick as an alternative to the selector buttons and the MENU/OK button.

- Press and hold the playback button in playback mode to directly switch between the two memory card slots (if you are using two cards at the same time).

- For direct access to the SD card formatting menu, press and hold the DELETE ("trash") button for about three seconds. Then keep the DELETE button pressed while you press the rear command dial.

<table><tr><td>Suggested Fn button assignment</td><td>TIP 31</td></tr></table>

Thoughtful assignment of your X-T3's Fn and Touch-Fn buttons will save you many cumbersome trips to the camera menu. You can display and change the assignment of all available Fn buttons in one convenient menu: while in shooting mode, press and hold the DISP/BACK button until the configuration page called FUNCTION (Fn) SETTING appears.

Here are my suggested Fn and Touch-Fn button assignments:

- **Fn1: HISTOGRAM.** Your X-T3 features an RGB live histogram with live overexposure warnings, also known as "blinkies." The only way to access this essential feature is via an Fn or a Touch-Fn button, so please make sure it is assigned to one. Personally, I am using Fn1.

- **Fn2: ELECTRONIC LEVEL.** In addition to the regular single-axis indicator, the X-T3 offers a dual-axis electronic level display. The dual-axis indicator helps you correctly align the camera to avoid non-parallel vertical lines, especially in city and architecture shots. Like the RGB histogram, this feature is accessible only via an Fn or a Touch-Fn button.

- **Fn3: AF-C CUSTOM SETTINGS.** AF-C Custom Settings allow fine-tuning the X-T3 for action photography and everything that involves moving subjects. In situations like this, time is of the essence, which is why I want quick, direct access to this menu.

- **Fn4: SPORTS FINDER MODE.** This feature reduces the image area to a crop of a bit more than 16 MP. This can come in handy for sports and action scenes with fast-moving and suddenly appearing subjects. Alternatively, I assign

**ISO** to this Fn button for quick access to the AUTO-ISO settings.

- **Fn5: DYNAMIC RANGE.** Fujifilm cameras offer a very powerful and high-quality DR function to extend the highlight dynamic range of an image, so it's a very good idea to keep this function right at your fingertips.

- **Fn6: FACE SELECT.** With firmware 3.00 and higher, FACE SELECT (which automatically enables face detection) allows you to select a specific face in scenes with more than one detected face. You can select a different face by moving the focus stick in the desired direction.

- **Touch-Fn1: DRIVE.** Accessing the DRIVE options menu via Fn or Touch-Fn is beneficial because, unlike the regular menu, it is context sensitive and only displays DRIVE options that apply to the DRIVE mode that has been currently selected with the DRIVE dial. For example, in DRIVE mode CH, flicking T-Fn4 will only show you options that apply to High Speed Burst mode.

- **Touch-Fn2: PERFORMANCE.** This touch button quickly toggles the camera between Normal and Boost mode. In concert with the Vertical Battery Grip (which has its own dedicated Normal/Boost switch), Touch-Fn2 is free for other tasks, for example the FLASH FUNCTION SETTING page, AUTO-ISO settings or TTL-LOCK.

- **Touch-Fn3: WHITE BALANCE.** T-Fn3 is one of my "wild card" buttons where I can assign any function that I want to be accessible for a particular task at hand. My current default setting is WHITE BALANCE.

- **Touch-Fn4: FACE DETECTION ON/OFF.** Face Detection is another function that should be at your disposal when it's required (and only then), so assigning it to an Fn button makes perfect sense.

- **AF-L & AE-L: AF-ON and PREVIEW EXP. IN MANUAL MODE.** The dedicated AF-L and AE-L buttons can also serve as Fn keys, so you can repurpose them as needed. That said, I don't tend to *radically* change their assignment. Instead, I turn the AF-L button into the AF-ON (i.e., back-button focusing) function. And since I shoot more than 95% of my images in manual exposure mode (where AE-Lock is meaningless), I assign the PREVIEW EXP./WB IN MANUAL MODE toggle to the AE-L button.

- **R-DIAL: FOCUS CHECK.** Pressing the rear command dial also serves as an Fn button. The factory default setting is FOCUS CHECK, which allows you to zoom into the live view image on the electronic viewfinder or LCD monitor. Since this is an important and convenient function, I do not recommend changing this default assignment. Please note that all related tips in this book assume that FOCUS CHECK is assigned to the rear command dial button.

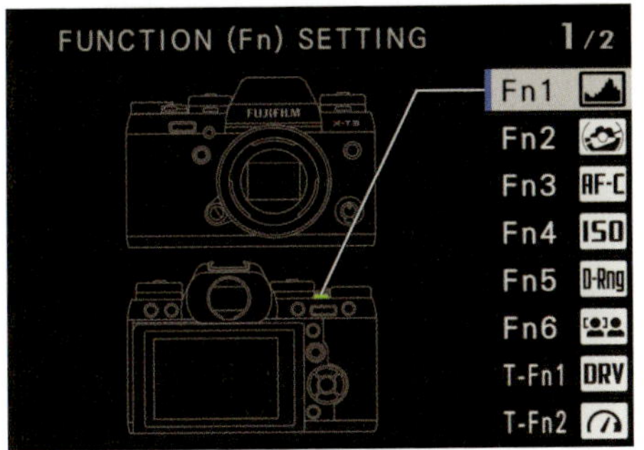


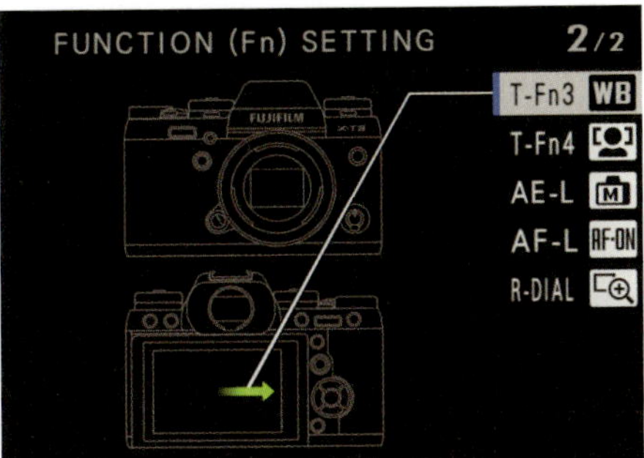


Fig. 35: This is the **Fn button assignment of my X-T3**. To edit the Fn buttons of your camera, press and hold the DISP/BACK button until the configuration page appears.

| Recommended My Menu and Quick menu configuration | TIP 32 |
| --- | --- |

To keep the shooting process effortless and free of interruptions, it's vital to assign frequently used functions to Fn buttons that are easily accessible. However, the number of available buttons is often limited. Luckily, we also have My Menu and the Quick menu (Q button) to quickly access frequently used functions and menus that don't fit into the Fn button lineup.

- To configure **My Menu,** select SET UP > USER SETTING > MY MENU SETTING, where you can add new items, rank existing items (i.e., change their positions in My Menu), or remove items from the menu.

- To configure the **Quick menu,** press and hold the Q button until the Quick menu configuration page appears, where you can change each of the 16 items and assign them either a new function or no function at all (NONE).

The following figures illustrate the My Menu and Quick menu settings in my X-T3. Neither is set in stone.

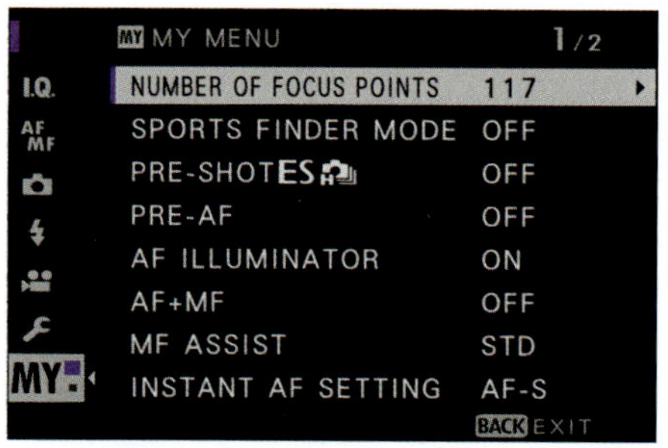

Fig. 36: **My Menu** in my X-T3 and other current X-series cameras consists of two menu pages with a total of 16 possible entries. I use the first page to quickly change and review the autofocus configuration.

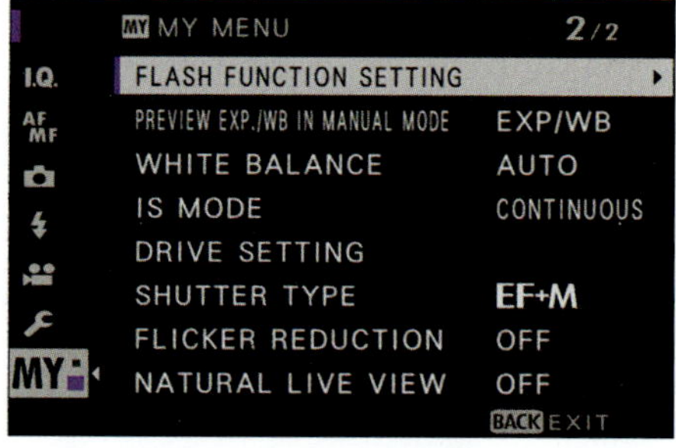

Fig. 37: The second **My Menu** page is reserved for exposure settings and general parameters such as OIS mode, shutter type, flash configuration, or DRIVE mode options.

The OIS mode menu is only available when a lens with OIS has been attached. In a similar fashion, manual exposure mode M must be enabled to access the PREVIEW EXP./WB IN MANUAL MODE setting.

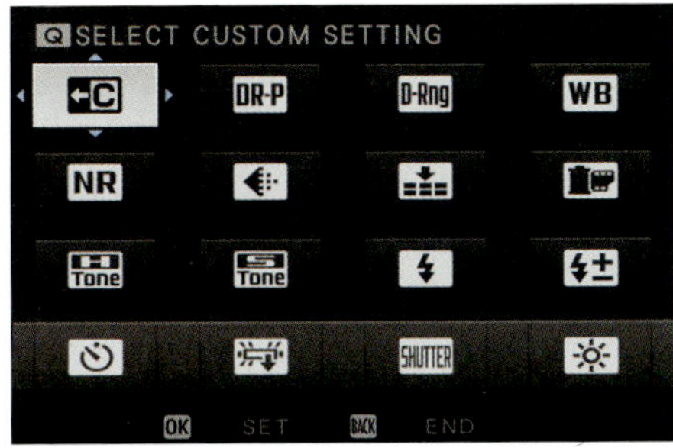



Fig. 38: The **Quick menu** page of my X-T3 isn't very different from the factory default setting. I always make sure I can access the flash mode and the flash exposure compensation directly from this menu, and I like to have direct access to the shutter-type setting and flicker reduction. Since I don't need quick access to the COLOR and SHARP-NESS items, I replaced them with the flash configuration items.

<table>
<tr><td>Always shoot FINE+RAW or NORMAL+RAW!</td><td>TIP 33</td></tr>
</table>

Should you shoot RAW [28] or JPEG [29]? The best option is to use both formats by setting SHOOTING MENU > IM-AGE QUALITY SETTING > IMAGE QUALITY > FINE+RAW (or NORMAL+RAW). It doesn't matter if you consider yourself a diehard RAW shooter or a JPEG shooter.

This is how **RAW shooters** benefit from shooting FINE+RAW or NORMAL+RAW:

- During external RAW processing, the camera-made JPEG can be used as a (sometimes hard-to-beat) reference image.

- Checking critical focus is only possible at 100% magnifi-cation, which only a full-size JPEG can provide. The JPEG that's embedded in the RAW file for preview purposes is too small. Make sure you select one of the available L (Large) options under SHOOTING MENU > IMAGE QUALITY SETTING > IMAGE SIZE.

- The IMAGE SIZE menu isn't available in RAW-only mode. Different image formats, such as 1:1 or 16:9, are only available in JPEG-only mode or FINE+RAW (or NORMAL+RAW) mode. Autofocus and exposure metering adapt to the currently selected format (aspect ratio) and deliver more accurate readings when you are shooting with odd formats like 1:1. No worries, though: the RAW image is always recorded in the sensor's native format (3:2 or 4:3, depending on your camera model), so you don't lose any image information.

This is how **JPEG shooters** benefit from shooting FINE+RAW or NORMAL+RAW:

- Nobody is capable of always setting the *perfect* shooting parameters (exposure, white balance, and dynamic range, as well as JPEG parameters such as film simulation, color, sharpness, noise reduction, shadow and highlight contrast, grain effect, etc.) in advance. FINE+RAW solves this problem by allowing you to change and adjust those settings *after* the fact, either with the built-in RAW converter or with external RAW conversion software. This means you can worry about those JPEG settings later and concentrate on more important factors of your shot, such as focusing, framing, and timing.

- Even if you chose the perfect settings in advance, it's possible that you'd like to have more than one version of a shot, such as a color version and a black-and-white version, or versions with different color film simulations. Again, FINE+RAW (or NORMAL+RAW) does the trick because you can use the built-in RAW converter to create (and compare) different JPEG versions of a shot.

- Progress is continually being made in the digital domain. Things that appear impossible today may be a reality in just a few years. It's perfectly feasible that future RAW converters will be able to extract much better image quality from your RAW files than is possible with today's cameras and RAW processors. It pays to be prepared by archiving the RAW files of your valuable shots. Storage space is cheap; some of your images may be priceless.

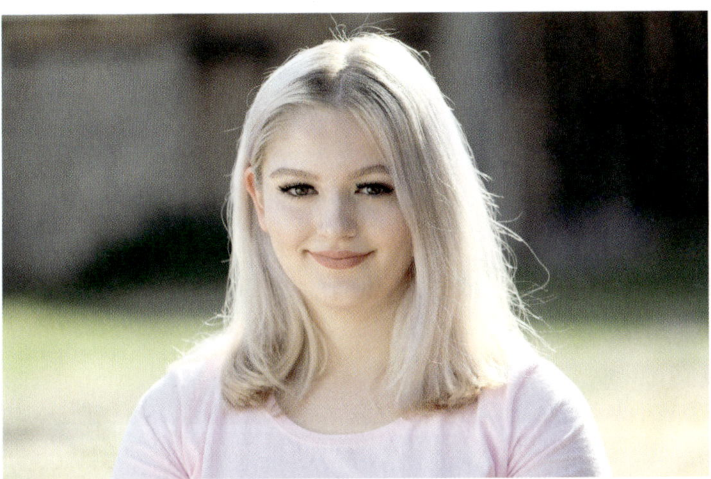

Fig. 39: The X-T3 features a **built-in RAW converter** that allows you to quickly create different JPEG versions of a shot. It only takes a few seconds to modify exposure, contrast settings, and noise reduction of a color image (above), or to create a black-and-white version (below). All you need is the shot's RAW file.

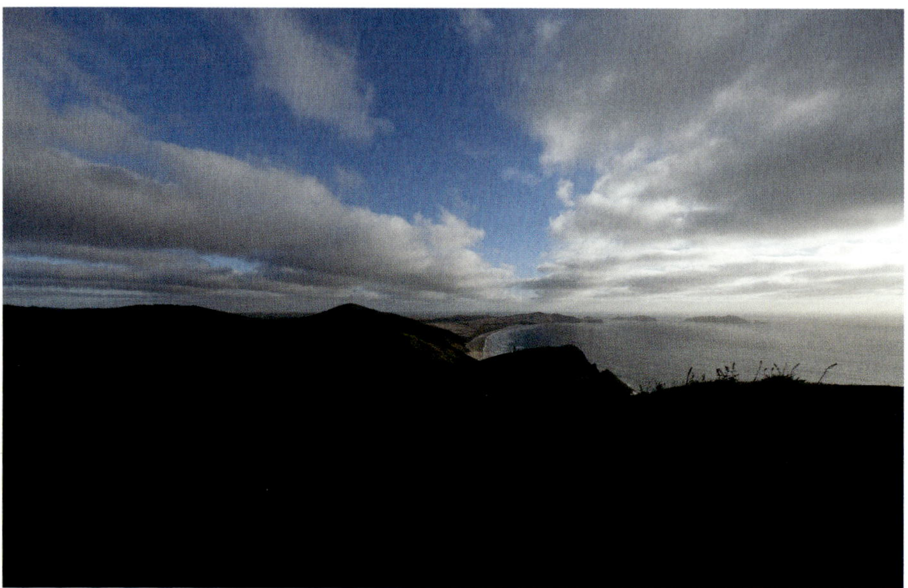

**Fig. 40:**  X series cameras feature competent JPEG engines with terrific film simulations, but that doesn't mean **JPEG-only shooting** is the best way to go. This JPEG was processed with the Pro Neg. Hi film simulation, and while this result may be exactly what you're looking for, it clearly illustrates the limited dynamic range of straight-out-of-camera JPEGs, which often render high-contrast scenes with blown out highlights or blocked shadows (or both). There is no meaningful way to restore what has been lost in processing the JPEG. Instead, you must process the RAW file of this shot.

- Your skills may improve as well! Several months or a few years from now, you may be more adept at using post-processing software than you are today. Wouldn't it be sad if you couldn't revisit great shots of the past and process them in a better way? Don't forget, only RAW files contain the full potential of an image. JPEGs are a processed and compressed subset with limited latitude for post-processing. RAW files feature much better tonality and dynamic range. By the way, using the built-in RAW converter of your X-T3 isn't more complex or complicated than using the camera's JPEG settings in the shooting menu (which should be familiar to you as a JPEG shooter).

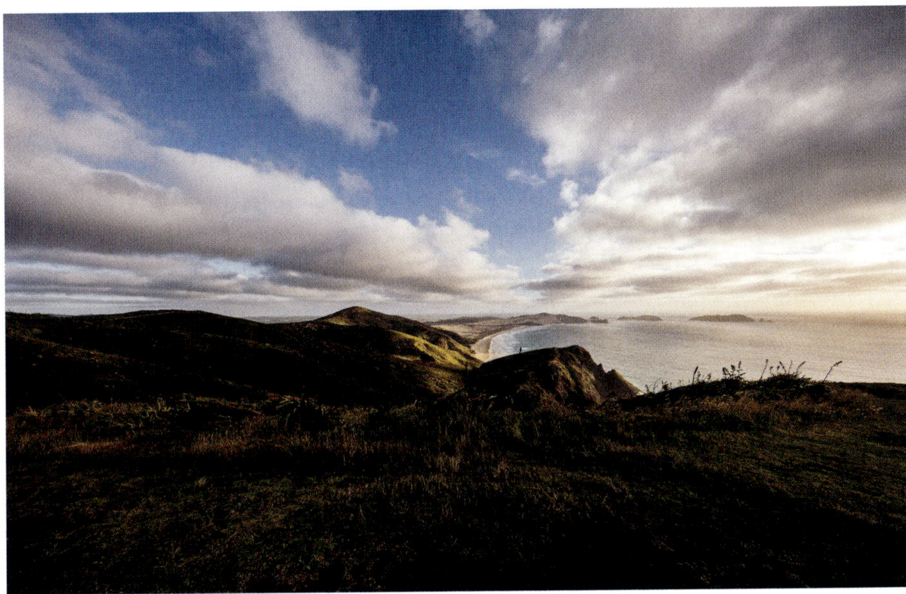

Fig. 41: This is a **Lightroom-processed version** of the RAW file of the previous shot, showcasing the superior dynamic range of the camera's original sensor data. Despite its small size and affordable price, your Fujifilm APS-C camera offers a dynamic range that rivals or even surpasses that of several current full-frame cameras from Canon and Leica, but you need the RAW file to unlock that potential.

As you can see, FINE+RAW is the best and most flexible choice. The one detrimental aspect of using FINE+RAW (or NORMAL+RAW) is that it results in larger amounts of data being recorded. This doesn't matter much in practical terms, since your camera can quickly transfer large amounts of data to the memory card. Just make sure to use a fast card.

Let me use this opportunity to address a widespread misconception: RAW files aren't images that you can directly look at. RAWs contain image *data* that still must be *interpreted* or *processed* into an actual image—either in-camera or with external software. Every digital image (including the live view on the monitor, JPEGs from the camera, or TIFF files from Lightroom) is the result of such a translation.

A JPEG shooter who doesn't keep RAW files must settle for only one of the many possible interpretations of RAW data into an image, and it's unlikely this single JPEG from the camera is the best of all possible versions of the image. Basically, discarding the RAW file turns your X camera into an instant camera: you only get one (most likely not the best) image per shot.

| TIP 34 | Compressed or uncompressed RAW files? |

The X-T3 offers you a choice of uncompressed and compressed RAW files (SHOOTING MENU > IMAGE QUALITY SETTING > RAW RECORDING). Compression cuts the size of RAW files roughly in half, so you can store more of them on a memory card or your computer. The compression also helps speed up camera processes: it takes longer to fill the fast camera buffer, and since the files are smaller, they take less time to transfer to the memory card.

It's important to note that Fujifilm's RAW compression is lossless, so there's no difference in image quality between uncompressed and compressed RAWs. However, not all external RAW converters may be able to process compressed RAWs, because the compression format is proprietary. RAW converter manufacturers can obtain a free SDK from Fujifilm in order to support the compressed RAW file format.

Windows users should always install the latest version of RAW FILE CONVERTER EX, even if you never intend to use it. This software is available as a free download [30]. It installs a codec that allows Windows to display thumbnail images of lossless compressed Fuji RAW files anywhere on your PC.

| TIP 35 | Picking a suitable image format |

The full resolution of the X-T3 (about 26 megapixels) is available only in its native image format (3:2). However, using a different image format (such as 1:1 or 16:9) can still be reasonable. For example, some people prefer to view their images on a 16:9 HD television, while others are fans of the classic (square) medium format look.

No matter what format (aspect ratio) and resolution you choose in SHOOTING MENU > IMAGE QUALITY SETTING > IMAGE SIZE, it will only affect the JPEGs coming from your camera. RAW files are always recorded in full resolution in the native 3:2 sensor format. This means that as long as you kept your RAW files, you can generate new full-size 3:2-format JPEGs with the built-in RAW converter or an external RAW processor.

If you want to compose shots in the 1:1 or 16:9 formats, you should select the desired format in the shooting menu. Here's why:

- The live view in the viewfinder or on the LCD will automatically adjust to the new format, making it easier to compose an image.

- The camera's autofocus frames will adapt to the selected image format.

- The camera's exposure metering and live histogram are based on what's displayed in the live view. Changing the live view to 16:9 or 1:1 will enhance metering accuracy for the respective format.

| The magical half-press | TIP 36 |
|---|---|

A basic rule for successfully using mirrorless cameras is minimizing the delay between pressing the shutter button and the camera taking the image. It's about not missing the decisive moment due to shutter lag.

It's up to you to anticipate these decisive moments. By half-pressing the shutter button, you are preparing the camera: exposure and autofocus (unless you are using AF-C) will be set and locked, and the lens aperture will move to its working position. The camera is now ready to record an image with minimal shutter lag—all that's left to do is to fully press the already half-pressed shutter button at the right instant.

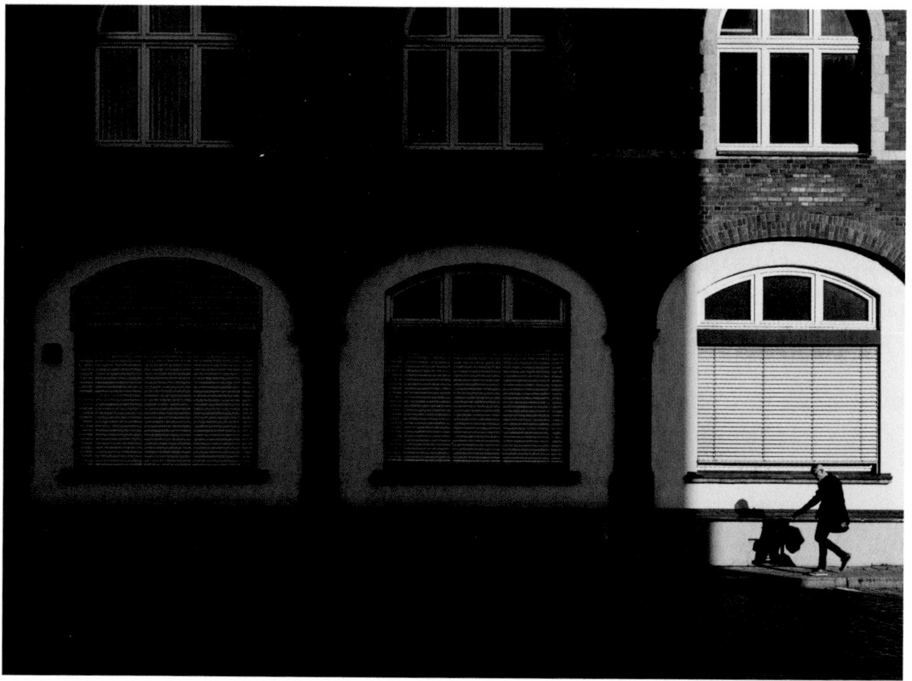

Fig. 42: To make sure your camera is ready when you are, it's useful to prime the camera by **half-pressing the shutter button**.

Don't forget that priming the camera by half-pressing the shutter button only works if SHUTTER AE and SHUTTER AF are set to ON in the SET UP > BUTTON DIAL SETTING menu for AF-S and AF-C.

## 2.2 MONITOR AND VIEWFINDER

The X-T3 features a large, high-resolution electronic view-finder (EVF) along with an LCD touchscreen. Both can be used for image composition and playback.

| Make use of the eye sensor! | TIP 37 |

Use the VIEW MODE button to activate the built-in eye sensor. The camera will now automatically switch to which-ever view (the electronic viewfinder or the LCD screen) is in use when you are taking and reviewing images or making changes to the camera menu.

When you are working with a tripod or holding the LCD display very close to your body, the eye sensor can get con-fused. In such cases, use the VIEW MODE button to set the camera to LCD ONLY.

| Instant image review | TIP 38 |

To instantly review an image right after you have taken it, you can select SET UP > SCREEN SET-UP > IMAGE DISP. and then set a display period of 0.5 SEC, 1.5 SEC, or CONTINUOUS. The image will be displayed in the currently active view (LCD or EVF).

You can cancel an ongoing image review and continue shooting by half-pressing the shutter button. With the CONTINUOUS option, you can also zoom into the image by pressing the rear command dial.

In situations that require you to take a series of shots in quick succession, it may be advisable to switch image review off. To do so, select SET UP > SCREEN SET-UP > IMAGE DISP. > OFF. Even without image review, you can still immediately check your latest shot by pressing the playback button.

Please don't forget that the maximum magnification (to check critical focus) is only available when the camera is set to record RAW *and* JPEG files in size L.

By repeatedly pressing the VIEW MODE button, you can enable a different instant review mode named EYE SENSOR + LCD IMAGE DISPLAY. In this view mode, if you take a shot with the EVF and then immediately remove the camera from your eye, you can review the image you just took on the rear LCD display for the time period selected in the SET UP > SCREEN SET-UP > IMAGE DISP. menu. This mode was implemented at the request of former DLSR users who just couldn't help themselves with their so-called "chimping" habit: taking a shot with the viewfinder and immediately reviewing it on the rear LCD display. Of course, with mirrorless EVF cameras, you can simply review your last shot in the electronic viewfinder. The EVF displays the image larger, with higher resolution, without interference from surrounding light, and you save the time and effort of removing the camera from your eye after each shot. That said, the "chimping mode" might still be useful for those who don't want to review every shot but want to see a few specific images.

| TIP 39 | The DISP/BACK button can be tricky! |
|---|---|

The DISP/BACK button serves two different purposes:

- As a BACK button, it returns the camera to a higher menu or selection level without saving any changes you may have made in the menu sub-level.

- As a DISPLAY button, it changes the display mode of the currently active view (LCD monitor or viewfinder).

It's important to remember that changing the display mode only affects the currently active view. For example, in order to change the display mode of the EVF, the EVF must be in use when you press the DISP/BACK button. This means that when you are using the eye sensor, you must actually look through the EVF while you are pressing the DISP/BACK button. If you don't, you will only change the display mode of the LCD monitor.

When the camera is in shooting mode, the viewfinder and the LCD monitor can each use a different display mode at the same time.

In playback mode, the EVF and LCD are synched to the same display mode. In this case it doesn't matter which view (EVF or LCD) is active when you change the display mode with the DISP/BACK button.

If you select a display with information overlays in shooting mode, you can choose which elements and indicators will appear in the viewfinder or on the LCD monitor. Select SET UP > SCREEN SET-UP > DISP. CUSTOM SETTING, and then check the items in the list that you want displayed in the EVF and on the LCD. Personally, I check all available boxes except for LIVE VIEW HIGHLIGHT ALERT.

| WYSIWYG—What You See Is What You Get! | TIP 40 |
| --- | --- |

The EVF and LCD screens of mirrorless cameras normally operate in WYSIWYG mode [31]: What You See Is What You Get. This means that the viewfinder and monitor are always trying to display a live view [32] image that closely resembles how the resulting JPEG will look. The live view simulates exposure, colors, contrast, and white balance. When you half-press the shutter button, the camera will set the selected working aperture, so the live view will also display a preview of the depth of field.

The live view's exposure simulation is quite helpful because it allows you to recognize exposure problems *before* you take the picture. Please note the live histogram is always based on the contents of the current live view image.

The live view's WYSIWYG simulation is available in all four of the camera's exposure modes: program AE **P**, aperture priority **A**, shutter priority **S**, and manual exposure mode **M**.

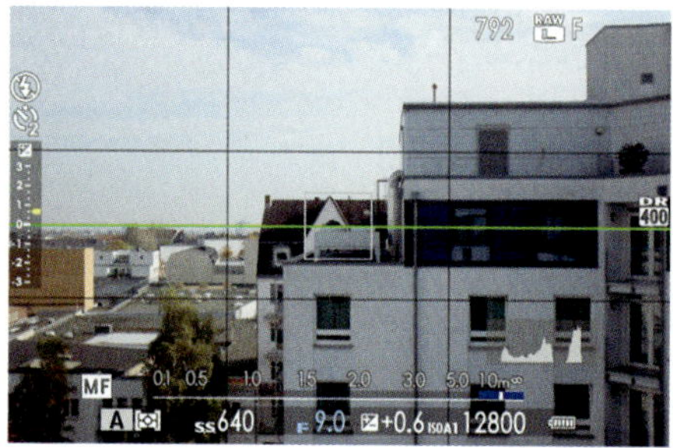 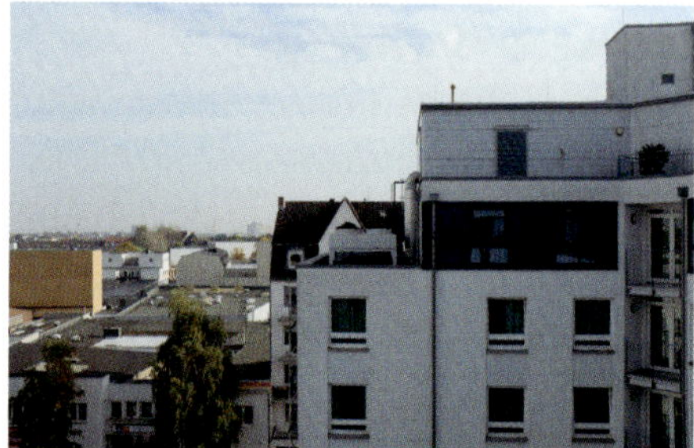

Fig. 43:  **WYSIWYG:** This example illustrates how closely the live view (left) represents the JPEG actually taken from the camera (right). The live view doesn't just simulate exposure, white balance, film simulation, and other JPEG settings, it also previews fixed dynamic range settings like DR400%.

In manual exposure mode **M**, the X-T3 allows you to switch off the exposure simulation by selecting SET UP > SCREEN SET-UP > PREVIEW EXP./WB IN MANUAL MODE > OFF. This way, the camera will always display a bright live view image in manual mode, regardless of the actually selected exposure parameters (shutter speed, aperture, and ISO). This can be useful in a studio setting with flash photography. For example, you may want to eliminate the surrounding-light component by stopping down the aperture and fully illuminating your subject with strobes.

Please note that in this mode, both the live view and the live histogram aren't representing the actual exposure of your image, so don't forget to switch the exposure simulation back on if you want to work with a proper exposure simulation and live histogram in manual mode **M**.

The live view's exposure simulation may be restricted in situations with very low light and slow shutter speeds of several seconds—the live view and the live histogram may appear darker than the actual result. In such scenarios, you should first take a test shot and review it in playback mode. The information display (which you can select with the DISP/BACK button) will show you a playback histogram of the recorded JPEG image. This includes a preview with "blinkies," which indicate blown (overexposed) highlights.

<table><tr><td>**Using the Natural Live View**</td><td>TIP 41</td></tr></table>

The so-called Natural Live View disables the WYSIWYG simulation of JPEG settings such as Film Simulation, Highlight Tone, Shadow Tone, or Color. Instead, it will display a rather flat live view image with increased dynamic range in the highlights and shadows, and with colors that are supposed to resemble what our eyes would see through an optical viewfinder. It will also set the live view to Auto white balance, so there will be no simulation of any white balance custom settings or presets. However, all current JPEG and white balance settings will still be applied to the *actual image* that is recorded.

To set the camera to Natural Live View mode, select SET UP > SCREEN SET-UP > NATURAL LIVE VIEW > ON. This setting enables generic-looking previews for color, black-and-white, and sepia shots that do *not* reflect the look of the actual JPEG results.

*Important: The Natural Live View of the X-T3 extends highlight dynamic range by two stops, rendering the live view and live histogram highly inaccurate when shooting with DR100%, DR200%, or DR-AUTO dynamic range settings as well as DR-P WEAK or DR-P AUTO. Do **not** engage the Natural Live View if you want to use the live view and/or the live histogram to judge and set the exposure!*

<table><tr><td>**Using the LCD touchscreen**</td><td>TIP 42</td></tr></table>

The X-T3 features a touchscreen that can perform several functions in shooting mode and playback mode. To use the touchscreen, make sure to select SET UP > BUTTON/ DIAL SETTING > TOUCH SCREEN SETTING > *Camera* TOUCH SCREEN SETTING > ON.

In *shooting mode,* you can use the touchscreen to pick a focus frame or zone; to autofocus with the selected focus frame or zone; or to autofocus and shoot with the selected focus frame or zone.

- **AREA:** Select a focus frame or zone by tapping once on the LCD touchscreen.

- **AF:** Tap on the LCD touchscreen to pick a focus frame or zone and trigger the autofocus. In MF mode, this option will focus the camera using Instant AF.

- **SHOT:** Tap on the touchscreen to select a focus area or zone, trigger the autofocus through this frame or zone, and take a picture without further delay. In MF mode, this option will immediately take a shot without (re-) focusing.

- **OFF:** Temporarily disable shooting with the touchscreen. This prevents you from accidentally triggering any of the three other touchscreen functions.

Apart from focusing and triggering the camera, the touchscreen offers several additional functionalities:

- In *playback mode,* you can use the touchscreen like a smartphone to browse through images. You can also zoom in and out of an image by double-tapping, or by pinching the image with two fingers. To use the touchscreen in playback mode, make sure to select SET UP > BUTTON/DIAL SETTING > TOUCH SCREEN SETTING > *Playback* TOUCH SCREEN SETTING > ON.

- You can still use the touchscreen when you are shooting with the electronic viewfinder (EVF). In this usage scenario, the touchscreen works like a trackpad that allows you to blindly move the active focus frame. To define the active touchscreen area for EVF operation, select SET UP > BUTTON/DIAL SETTING > TOUCH SCREEN SETTING > EVF TOUCH SCREEN AREA SETTINGS. You will be given a choice of seven active areas and OFF.

- You can also double-tap the touchscreen in shooting and playback mode to zoom-into the picture. This function has the same effect as pressing the rear command dial in its default FOCUS CHECK configuration. To make sure this feature is available to you in shooting mode, select SET UP > BUTTON/DIAL SETTING > TOUCH SCREEN SETTING > *Camera* DOUBLE TAP SETTING > ON. Double-tap also works when you are looking through the EVF as long as you have defined an active touchscreen area for EVF operation.

- Last but not least, the touchscreen gives you access to four virtual Fn buttons, so-called Touch-Fn or T-Fn buttons. You can "press" one of these virtual buttons by flicking your finger left, right, up or down on the screen. You can assign new T-Fn functions by pressing and holding the DISP/BACK button until the FUNCTION (Fn) SETTING screen appears. Please note that T-Fn buttons are available only if SET UP > BUTTON/DIAL SETTING > TOUCH SCREEN SETTING > TOUCH FUNCTION is set to ON.

## 2.3 EXPOSING RIGHT

It's not the job of the camera to find and set the correct exposure; it's the job of the photographer. That said, the X-T3 features the usual set of AE (auto exposure) modes: aperture priority **A**, shutter priority **S**, and program AE **P**.

- **Aperture priority A** will automatically set a suitable shutter speed to match a preset aperture based on your exposure.

- **Shutter priority S** will automatically set a suitable aperture to match a preset shutter speed based on your exposure.

- **Program AE** P will automatically set a suitable aperture and shutter speed combination based on your exposure.

- **Auto-ISO** can contribute a suitable ISO setting (within predefined limits). In digital cameras, ISO is the level of signal amplification applied to an image that has been recorded by the camera's sensor. ISO impacts the brightness of the final image.

- Auto exposure (AE) modes are typically set with the aperture ring on the lens and the shutter speed dial on the camera body: Pre-selecting an aperture and setting the shutter speed dial to "A" activates *aperture priority* mode. Selecting "A" on the aperture ring or lens in concert with a specific shutter speed activates *shutter priority* mode. Finally, selecting "A" on both the lens and the shutter speed dial selects *program AE*.

It is important to understand that these auto exposure (AE) modes (including Auto-ISO) are not responsible for correctly exposing images: exposure is always the responsibility of the photographer. AE modes automatically fill variables (such as the shutter speed in aperture priority A) in a way that matches the exposure you've set manually. Auto exposure will only deliver good results if the photographer is exposing correctly.

EXPOSING CORRECTLY—HOW DOES THIS WORK?
Don't panic! Unlike conventional DSLR cameras, mirrorless cameras make things easy. Up to four different metering modes (multi, spot, center-weighted, and average), the WYSIWYG live view, and the live (RGB) histogram help you determine the correct exposure for any given scene. If you shoot in one of the three AE modes, the most important tool is the exposure compensation dial, which allows you to correct the metered exposure up to ±3 EV in convenient steps of 1/3 EV. EV means Exposure Value, and 1 EV is equivalent to one full aperture stop. The correct exposure isn't what

the camera is metering, it's what *you* make of the metering by adjusting the exposure compensation dial or manual exposure settings.

<table><tr><td>Choosing the right metering method</td><td>TIP 43</td></tr></table>

There are up to four different metering methods available to measure the amount of light that goes through the lens and hits the image sensor:

- **Average** metering calculates an unweighted average of the total light that hits the entire sensor area.

- **Spot** metering considers only two percent of the sensor area. The metering area covers a standard-sized focus frame in the center of the image. Alternatively, you can link spot metering to the size and position of the active focus frame (in SINGLE POINT AF and MF mode).

- **Center-weighted** metering is a cross between average and spot metering. While it encompasses the entire image area, it puts special emphasis on the image center.

- **Multi** or **matrix** metering calculates a weighted average of the total light that hits the sensor. The weighting is a result of 256 metering areas (the matrix) that the camera evaluates and compares to typical scenarios, which is why multi metering is considered "smarter" than the other methods. For example, multi metering is designed to recognize when you are shooting against the sun.

Average, spot, and center-weighted metering return exposure recommendations based on middle gray. In other words, when you take a picture of a black wall and then a picture of a white wall with auto exposure (AE), the results will both look middle gray. This means:

- If you want the black wall to look black in the resulting image, you must manually adjust the exposure downward.

- If you want the white wall to look bright white in the resulting image, you must manually adjust the exposure upward.

**Fig. 44:** This illustration shows a black sheet of paper and a white sheet of paper. Both were photographed with the camera's spot metering without any exposure correction. As you can see, the camera delivered a **middle-gray exposure** in both cases. To get an image that reflects the actual brightness of the subject, the metered exposure must be adjusted.

Fujifilm recommends a correction of +1 EV when you are shooting in snowfields, or −2/3 EV when you are shooting subjects in spotlight. Instead of following these rules, I recommend a more precise and methodical course of action using the live view and the live histogram. To minimize corrective adjustments, it's best to select a metering method that fits the subject and the job at hand:

- **Multi** metering is a general-purpose method. Since it is supposed to be "smarter" than the other methods, there's a good chance you won't have to apply (m)any corrective adjustments to the proposed exposure.

- **Average** and, to a lesser degree, **center-weighted** metering are rather neutral metering methods that will likely stay more consistent despite small changes in composition (or framing) than multi metering and spot metering. I recommend average metering if you want to take a series of shots of the same subject under similar conditions. In such cases, average metering will help you keep the exposure consistent.

■ **Spot** metering bases its measurements on one spot of the overall image. This means you must work very precisely to make sure you are metering the appropriate part (spot) of the scene. The resulting exposure recommendation will expose this spot with middle-gray brightness. For example, if you spot meter a backlit face against the sun, the metered exposure will display the face with middle-gray brightness (or zone 5 in the famous Ansel Adams zone system [33]). If that's too dark for your taste, you can use the exposure compensation dial to lift the exposure by +1/3 EV or +2/3 EV. On the other hand, if the person has dark skin, you may want to reduce the exposure with a correction in the opposite direction. It's up to you to choose the zone (brightness) of the spot-metered part of the image.

Spot metering is the most powerful and challenging metering method. It's useful when the light is very difficult—too difficult for multi and average metering. Typical examples are isolated bright objects in front of a dark background (and vice versa), such as a musician or an actor on a stage, or strongly backlit subjects. Whenever your exposure must be spot on, spot metering is your friend.

With that said, it's obvious that spot metering requires you to meter very precisely. Even small changes in the camera's direction can lead to dramatic changes in the metered result. Therefore, it can be useful to combine spot metering with the camera's AE-L function. AE-L will lock your exposure to prevent it from changing when you alter your composition, or when your subject starts to move away from your metering spot.

The best way to use spot metering is in manual mode **M**. In this mode, metering doesn't affect the exposure because you are manually setting all the exposure parameters (shutter speed, aperture, and ISO). Spot metering in manual mode helps you determine the brightness level of any part of your image for any set exposure. The exposure scale in the viewfinder or LCD tells you exactly how much brighter or darker than middle gray (zone 5) the spot metered object would appear in your shot (either ±3 EV or ±5 EV, depending on your exposure compensation dial mode setting).

Don't forget to *disable* Auto-ISO in manual mode **M**. If you don't, the camera will still operate in some kind of AE mode (I call it "misomatic"); in this mode, the ISO setting will be the exposure variable that's automatically adjusted.

| TIP 44 | Linking spot metering to focus frames |
|---|---|

Traditionally, spot metering covers the center of the image with an area that's about as large as a standard-sized focus frame. However, by selecting SHOOTING MENU > AF/MF SETTING > INTERLOCK SPOT AE & FOCUS AREA > ON, you can link the spot metering area to the position and size(!) of the active focus frame in Single Point AF and MF mode.

This is a very useful feature if you are using one of the camera's many off-center AF frames, since it's likely that your focus area covers the same part of your subject that is also relevant for exposure metering (such as the brightly lit face of a musician or stage actor who is standing in front of a dark background).

Fig. 45: **Spot metering and manual exposure mode:** Metering different parts of an image is easy with spot metering. Simply set an exposure (aperture, shutter speed, and ISO), and then point the small spot-metering area at different parts of the scene. The exposure scale at the left or bottom of your live view tells you the brightness of any metered spot, with 0 representing middle gray (zone 5 in the Ansel Adams zone system). To make things easier and most effective, interlock spot metering with the size and position of the currently active focus frame and select the smallest available focus frame size in AF-S or MF mode.

In this example, I spot-metered the darkest part of the model horse at −4 EV (top), its brightest part at +2 EV (center), and the brightest overall part of the scene at +2.66 EV (bottom). This means that the dynamic range of this scene comprises less than 7 EV (2.66 + 4 = 6.66), a range that fits neatly into a regular DR100% JPEG image.

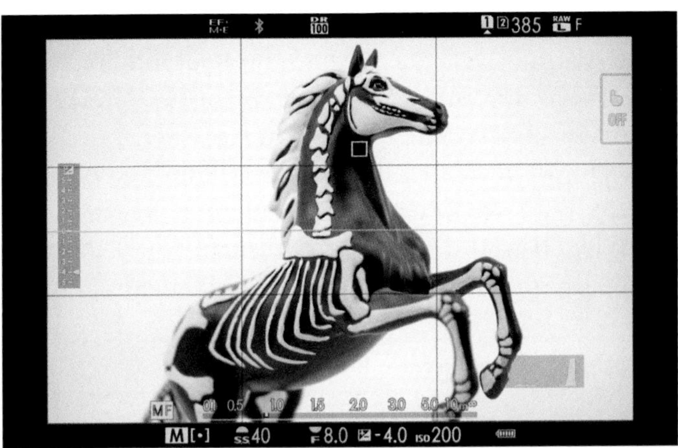

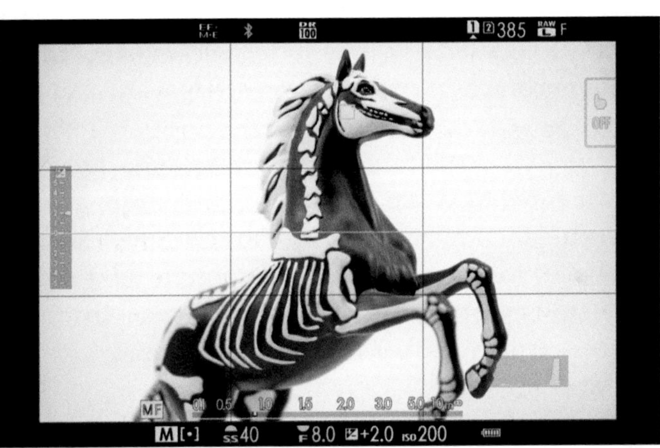

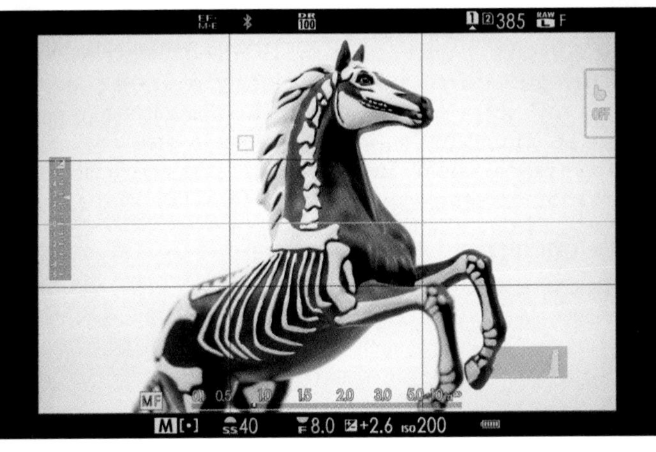

If you want to decouple spot metering from the AF area and limit it to the very center of the frame, make sure to select SHOOTING MENU > AF/MF SETTING > INTERLOCK SPOT AE & FOCUS AREA > OFF.

Please remember that the camera will not interlock spot metering with the focus area if you set it to either Zone AF or Wide/Tracking AF. Interlocking only works in concert with Single Point AF or manual focus (MF) mode.

| TIP 45 | Using the live view and live histogram |

Unlike optical viewfinders in DSLRs, the electronic live view of modern mirrorless cameras like your X-T3 provides an accurate simulation of the resulting JPEG image. The live preview encompasses color, contrast, exposure, and effect settings.

In standard display mode, this WYSIWYG preview is complemented by a live histogram [34]. I strongly recommend using the live histogram because it provides a useful overview of the brightness distribution in your scene. It also helps you identify areas of over- and underexposure in advance, so you can take corrective measures:

- If bars are piling up like a bell curve at the right end of the histogram, but are cut off mid-peak, parts of your shot will be overexposed with blown highlights. If this affects important parts of your image, you should correct the exposure downward. Alternately, you can expand the shot's dynamic range by selecting DR200% or DR400% in the respective menu.

- If the histogram leans to the left, leaving plenty of unused space on the right, the shot might end up underexposed. In this case, you can adjust the exposure upward.

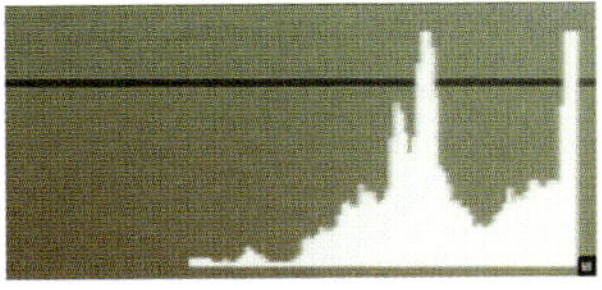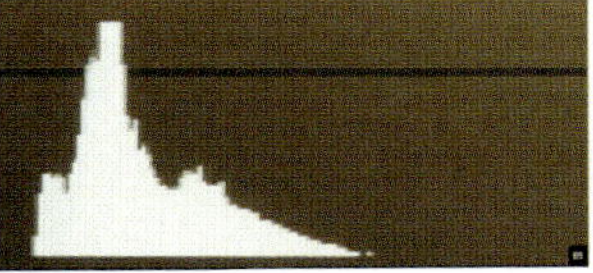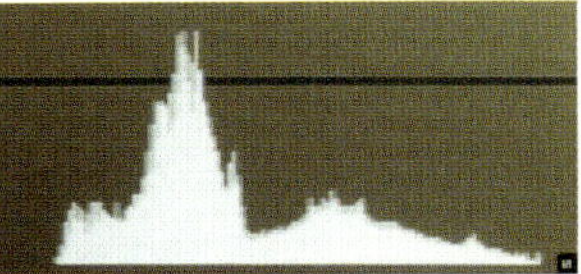

Fig. 46: Three **live histograms** that show overexposure, underexposure, and a balanced exposure of the same scene.

The histogram provides a technical representation of the live view simulation. When the Natural Live View is turned off, both the live view and the live histogram will reflect the current JPEG settings of the camera (white balance, film simulation, color, and highlight and shadow contrast). For example, the VELVIA film simulation delivers more contrast and more saturated colors than ETERNA, and this is reflected in the live view and the live histogram.

It's important to note that the live view and live histogram also represent (simulate) the effect of manual DR200% or DR400% dynamic range settings. However, if you set the camera to DR-AUTO, the live view and live histogram will always display a DR100% preview.

When you half-press the shutter button, the camera's live view will also try to give you an accurate representation of the resulting image's dynamic range. That said, there is no live histogram when you half-press the shutter button, so you'll have to fully rely on the visual impression provided by the live view image.

The X-T3 also offers an **RGB histogram** [35], which is available only by assigning it to an Fn or Touch-Fn button. The RGB histogram is once again based on the current live view image, so it represents the resulting JPEG image. In fact, the color histogram displays four different histograms at once: overall luminance distribution (a larger version of the standard histogram) and separate histograms for the three color channels: red, green, and blue. That way, you can immediately recognize clipping of individual color channels in your JPEG. For example, shooting a red rose, the red channel is the first to clip and, thus, lose texture.

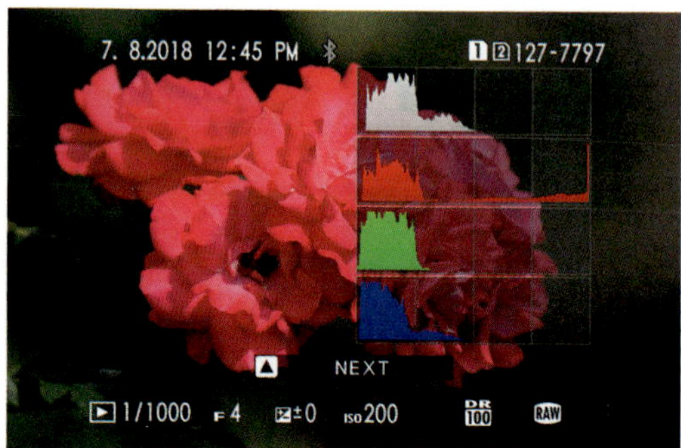

Fig. 47: The **RGB histogram** of this image of a rose illustrates how the red channel is already clipping (indicated by the peaking line at the right edge of the red channel histogram), while green, blue, and overall luminance are barely touching the right half of the histogram. Please note that as long as the Natural Live View is turned off, the histogram always reflects the current JPEG settings (film simulation, contrast settings, color saturation setting, etc.).

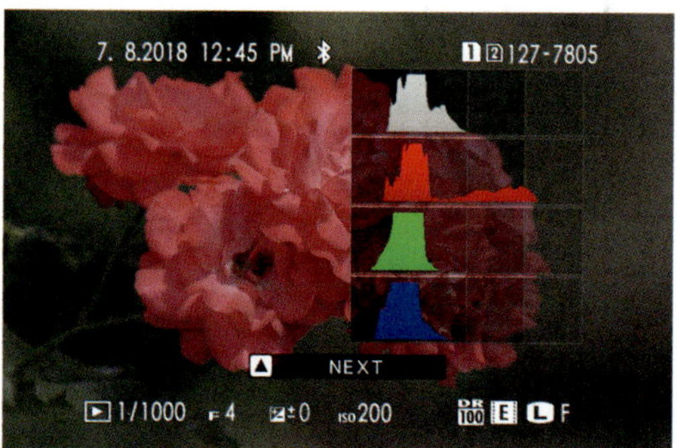

Fig. 48:  This is the same RAW image, but this time processed with **flat JPEG settings:** Eterna film simulation, Shadow Tone −2, Highlight Tone −2, and Color −4. These settings reflect the flattest possible color profile you can achieve in your X-T3, and there's now plenty of additional headroom in the shadows and highlights. Thanks to the much higher dynamic range of the flat JPEG, there's also no clipping of the red channel in the histogram. This flat JPEG reflects the dynamic range of the actual RAW file much better than the camera's default JPEG settings, and many RAW shooters use these or similar flat JPEG settings in concert with the RGB histogram because it makes it easier to determine the optimal exposure right at the sensor's saturation limit.

The RGB histogram also includes "blinkies," which are live overexposure or clipping warnings. If bright parts of your scene start to blink in RGB histogram mode, the blinking areas will be blown out in the resulting JPEG (i.e., losing texture and detail). The blinkies make it easy to set an exposure where important highlights are protected (i.e., not blinking in the RGB histogram view).

| Auto exposure (AE) with modes **P**, **A**, and **S** | TIP 46 |
| --- | --- |

The three auto exposure modes of your X-T3 are **P** (program AE), **A** (aperture priority), and **S** (shutter priority).

A brief reminder:

- **Program AE P** will automatically set a suitable aperture and shutter-speed combination.

- **Aperture priority A** will automatically set a suitable shutter speed to match a preset aperture.

- **Shutter priority S** will automatically set a suitable aperture to match a preset shutter speed.

To take a picture in one of these modes, you can follow these steps:

- Meter the exposure with one of the metering modes: multi, center-weighted, average, or spot.

- After metering, adjust the exposure to taste using the exposure compensation dial. Use the live view and the histogram to determine the best setting. Remember: it's not the camera that's setting the exposure; it's you. Don't blindly follow what the camera is proposing. Instead, always keep an eye on the live view and the live histogram.

- When you half-press the shutter button, your exposure will be locked as long as you keep the button half-pressed. As long as the shutter button remains half-pressed, you can adjust the framing or composition of your shot without changing the exposure.

■ Instead of half-pressing the shutter button, you can also use the AE-L button to meter a scene and lock the exposure. You can configure the AE-L button to either lock the exposure as long as you press the AE-L button (SET UP > BUTTON/DIAL SETTING > AE/AF LOCK MODE > AE&AF ON WHEN PRESSING), or use the button as a toggle to lock and unlock the exposure (SET UP > BUTTON/DIAL SETTING > AE/AF LOCK MODE > AE&AF ON/OFF SWITCH). Personally, I highly recommend the latter option. When the exposure is locked with AE-L, you can still further adjust it with the exposure compensation dial.

■ To take the shot, fully press the shutter button.

Metering and exposure are two different things. After metering a scene, the photographer sets the actual exposure with the exposure compensation dial:

■ **Metering** is performed using either multi, center-weighted, average, or spot metering.

■ Use the **exposure compensation dial** to adjust the metering result. Use the information from the live view and live histogram to adjust your settings. Of course, there are instances where the initial metering is already spot-on, so you won't have to apply any further correction.

■ **Expose** the image using one of three AE modes: aperture priority, shutter priority, or program AE.

*Note: If you set the exposure compensation dial to its C position, exposure compensation will be performed by one of the command dials with an extended range of ±5 EV instead of ±3 EV. To configure a specific command dial to serve as your exposure compensation dial, go to the SET UP > BUTTON/ DIAL SETTING > COMMAND DIAL SETTING screen.*

In manual exposure mode, you manually specify all three exposure parameters: aperture, shutter speed, and ISO amplification. For this to work, Auto-ISO must be turned off. Otherwise, ISO would become an exposure variable that the camera would automatically fill.

For the live view and live histogram to correctly display the set exposure in manual mode, make sure that SET UP > SCREEN SET-UP > PREVIEW EXP./WB IN MANUAL MODE > PREVIEW EXP./WB is set. I recommend setting the metering to spot metering.

Here's how you can expose in manual mode:

- Select and set an aperture and shutter speed that suits your subject and image idea. Aperture controls the depth of field [36]; shutter speed controls the amount of motion blur [37] and camera shake in your exposure.

- Next, select an ISO value that will yield the desired brightness in your shot. You can (and should) use the live view and live histogram to find a suitable setting. As usual, try not to blow out important highlights. The live histogram is your friend.

- You can check specific parts of your scene by spot metering them. The exposure scale in the live view screen tells you how much above or below middle gray (zone 5) the spot-metered selection will be exposed. This tool helps you ensure that important parts of your image (such as skin tones or snow) will be exposed exactly like you want them to be.

- Finally, you may want to readjust or fine-tune aperture, shutter speed, and ISO according to your metering. Once everything is set, you can take the shot(s).

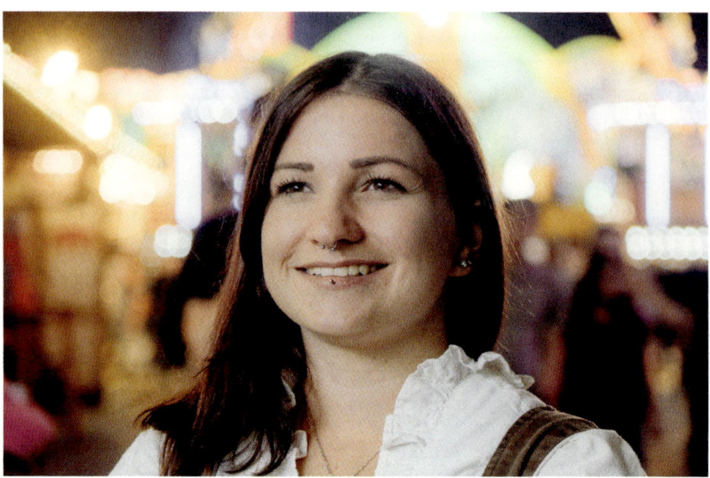

Fig. 49: I shoot in **manual exposure mode** most of the time. And maybe you should too. Not only can the camera make fewer mistakes when you are in charge, but manual mode also gives you full control over aperture (depth of field), shutter speed (motion blur, camera shake), and ISO (noise level, effective dynamic range). Manual mode also ensures that multiple shots of a scene will have the same consistent exposure, because the exposure doesn't change unless *you* change it. It also forces you to think about your actual exposure parameters: Why are you using a particular setting for aperture, shutter speed, and ISO? Thanks to the WYSIWYG nature of mirrorless cameras, manual exposure mode can help you avoid unpleasant surprises: You *set* the exposure, you *see* the exposure in the live view, and you *get* the exposure you set and saw in your JPEG.

**TIP 48**    Using aperture priority A

In aperture priority AE [38], you manually set the aperture [39] and the camera automatically selects a suitable shutter speed based on your chosen exposure (as set with the exposure compensation dial). Which aperture should you select? Let's look at some basics:

- As the aperture gets smaller (i.e., the aperture number gets higher), your depth of field (DOF) [40] increases. DOF is the zone in front of and behind the focus plane that appears in perfect focus when you look at the finished image. In standard display mode, the viewfinder and LCD offer a focus and DOF scale that displays the focus distance as well as the calculated depth-of-field zone that surrounds it.

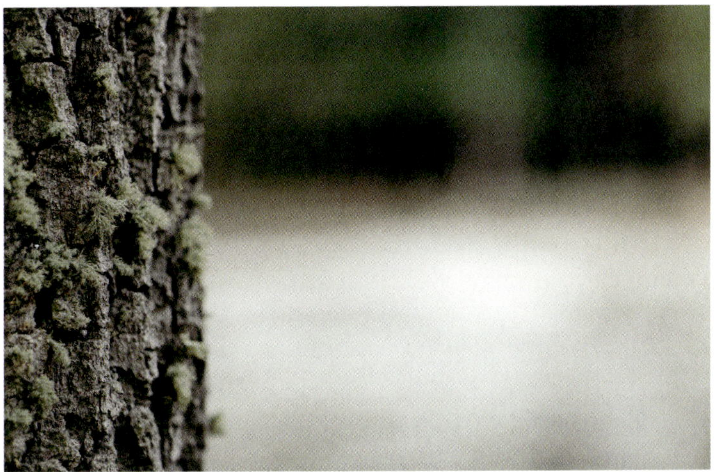

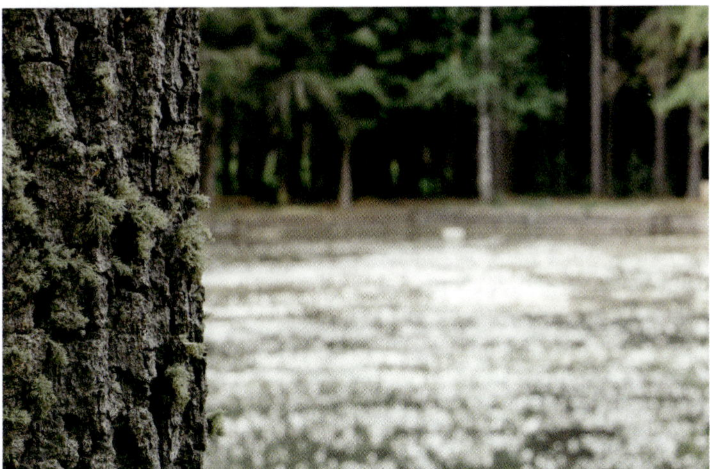

**Fig. 50:** This example shows the same scene shot twice with the XF90mmF2 R LM WR lens. The image at top was shot wide open at f/2; the image at bottom was stopped down to the maximum of f/16. While stopping down clearly increases the depth of field, the look of the remaining out-of-focus area (also known as *bokeh*) is still smooth and silky, which is a trademark of the XF90mmF2 lens. Within the Fujifilm X-mount universe, I consider this the "perfect lens" because it doesn't show relevant weaknesses in any field of use.

- Fast lenses like the XF56mmF1.2 R or the XF35mmF1.4 R often exhibit a tight DOF of less than an inch when used wide open, so in a portrait shot, only one of the subject's eyes may be perfectly in focus. If that's the case, you can stop down the lens or change the position of your subject so that both eyes are the same distance from the camera.

- Stopping down a lens beyond f/9 leads to increased diffraction blur [41] across the image area. While increasing the depth of field enlarges the in-focus zone, maximum detail within that zone is reduced. In other words, when you shoot with f/22 using a wide-angle lens, there's a good chance your scene will be in focus from front to infinity. However, its overall crispness will be significantly lower than it would be at f/8. The Lens Modulation Optimizer (LMO) in your camera can compensate for diffraction blur to a degree, but its effect only extends to JPEGs created in-camera by the built-in RAW converter. External RAW converters can't support the LMO.

- When you shoot wide open or with a high ISO setting, it's possible that the suitable shutter speed is faster than the camera's maximum mechanical shutter speed of 1/8000 s. If that's the case, the shutter speed will be displayed in red (overexposure warning). You can use shutter speeds beyond the mechanical threshold by activating the electronic shutter.

| TIP 49 | Using shutter priority S |
| --- | --- |

Shutter priority AE [42] works like aperture priority, except you are manually setting a shutter speed [43], and the camera automatically selects a fitting aperture value based on your exposure. Shutter priority is available only when you're using native X-mount lenses with electronic contacts. Adapted lenses (at least those with mechanical adapters) can only be used with aperture priority or in manual mode.

Setting the right shutter speed depends on two factors:

- Motion blur [44]: The faster your subject is moving, the faster your shutter speed must be to avoid shots with motion blur. This doesn't mean motion blur is always bad; it can be used as a conscious choice to add dynamic punch to your image. For instance, panning [45] the camera blurs the background behind a sharp main subject. Motion blur can be a benefit of long exposures—exposure times [46] of several seconds or minutes can smooth water surfaces, blur cloudy skies, or add star trails.

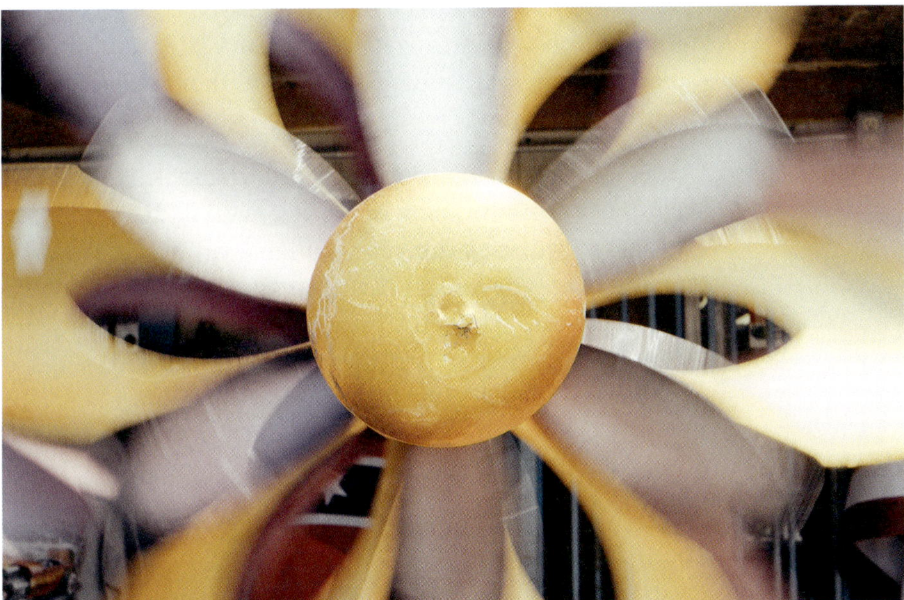

Fig. 51: In this handheld shot of a spinning wind wheel, **motion blur** was a conscious choice. Shot with the versatile XF27mmF2.8 pancake lens at f/13, the selected shutter speed of 1/30 s at base ISO was slow enough to illustrate the motion of the propellers around the stationary (and thus sharply focused) node. At the same time, it was fast enough to avoid camera shake which would have blurred the non-moving parts, as well.

- Blur due to camera shake [47]: If you don't hold the camera steady when you take a shot, the resulting image can be blurred. The optical image stabilizer [48] (OIS) can help, or you can put the camera on a tripod or a solid surface and use the self-timer or a remote shutter release to take the shot. A rule of thumb suggests using at least the reciprocal of the "full-frame" equivalent focal length as your shutter speed. For example, if you are using a 200 mm lens on your APS-C camera (and the OIS has been switched off), your minimum shutter speed should be 1/300 s, since you must multiply the focal length with the APS-C crop factor [49] of 1.5. Of course, rules of thumb don't apply to everyone in every situation. It really depends on your technique and whether you're blessed with steady hands.

If you set a very slow shutter speed or choose a high ISO setting in shutter priority mode, it's possible that even the smallest aperture opening of your lens will still be too large to avoid overexposure. In this case, the aperture value will be displayed in red.

Since your camera features a dedicated shutter speed dial, you can use it to quickly change the shutter speed in full-stop increments. You can also use the command dial to fine-tune your selection in 1/3 EV intermediate steps.

*Hint: Setting the shutter speed dial to **T** (Time) allows you to select the **full** range of available shutter speeds (in 1/3 EV steps) by turning a command dial. You can assign shutter speed control to one of the command dials in SET UP > BUTTON/DIAL SETTING > COMMAND DIAL SETTING. Personally, I always assign shutter speed to the front command dial.*

Using program AE P and program shift     **TIP 50**

In program AE, the X-T3 will automatically pick a combination of aperture *and* shutter speed settings that correspond to your set exposure. This mode can be useful for inexperienced photographers or in situations when you don't have the time to manually adjust the aperture or shutter speed.

In program AE, the slowest possible shutter speed is limited to a maximum duration is 4 seconds. When this (in concert with an already wide-open aperture) is not sufficiently slow enough to achieve the set exposure, the camera will display a red underexposure warning.

Even in program AE, you can influence shutter speed and aperture to a degree by using program shift [50]. Program shift allows you to select more suitable combinations of aperture and shutter speed compared to the one originally proposed by the camera's program AE. You can cycle through various combinations of apertures and shutter speeds that all result in the same exposure. When the camera is in program AE mode, you can activate program shift by turning the command dial that is otherwise responsible for adjusting the shutter speed.

Let's say you are shooting a portrait with the XF16–55mmF2.8 R LM WR zoom lens. It's a bright day, so program AE offers a shutter speed of 1/500 s with an aperture of f/5.6. However, you prefer to shoot the portrait wide open at f/2.8 to achieve a blurrier background. In this situation, you have two choices: you can either switch to aperture priority mode by manually setting an aperture of f/2.8, or you can use program shift by turning the command dial until the aperture display shows f/2.8. Opening the aperture two stops, from f/5.6 to f/2.8, won't change the original exposure because program shift will automatically adjust the shutter speed two stops from 1/500 s to 1/2000 s.

***Important:*** *Program shift is **not** available if Dynamic Range is set to AUTO or if a TTL flash unit is in use.*

<table><tr><td>**TIP 51**</td><td>Playing it safe with auto exposure bracketing</td></tr></table>

As you know by now, the automatic exposure (AE) modes **P**, **A**, and **S** are merely responsible for automatically filling exposure variables. The exposure itself is the responsibility of the photographer. You can use metering (multi, center-weighted, average, or spot), the live view, and the live histogram to determine the correct exposure.

Nobody is perfect! If you want to play it safe, auto exposure bracketing [51] can be a helpful feature. In this mode, the camera takes a series of at least two shots in quick succession, each with a different exposure (known as exposure bracketing). With this method, there will often be one shot with normal exposure, one underexposed shot, and one overexposed shot.

Exposure bracketing is especially useful with subjects that don't move. After you've taken the shot, you can decide which of the differently exposed versions you want to keep.

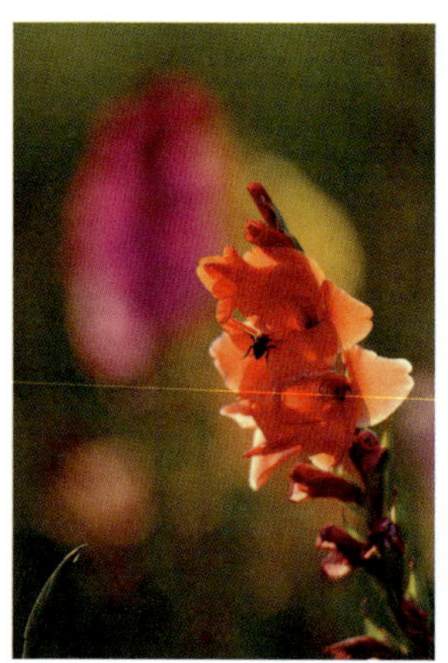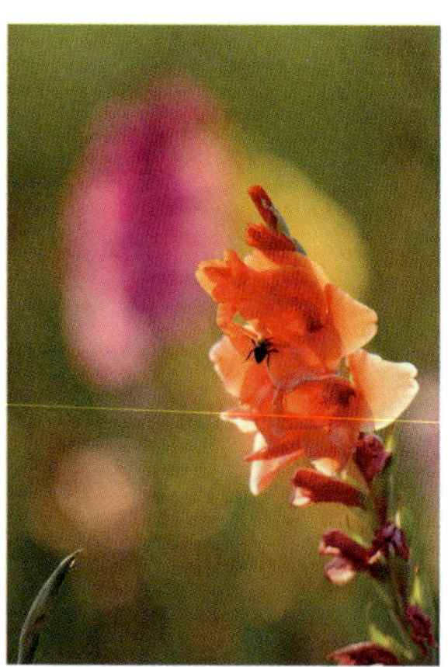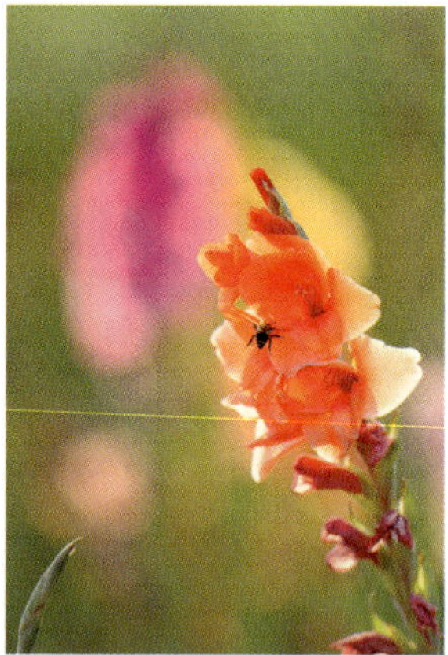

Fig. 52: **Auto exposure bracketing** automatically takes two or more images with varying exposure. Contrary to its name, AE bracketing even works in manual exposure mode, so you can manually set an exposure (aperture, shutter speed, ISO) you think is right, and AE bracketing will give you additional options with different shutter speeds that are brighter and/or darker than your original exposure. In this example, the image in the middle shows the originally set exposure. The image to the left was bracketed 2/3 EV darker, and the one on the right was bracketed 2/3 EV brighter.

You can activate AE BKT by selecting BKT on the DRIVE dial. You have to make sure that AE bracketing is selected in the shooting menu (SHOOTING SETTING > DRIVE SETTING > BKT SETTING > BKT SELECT > AE BKT). You can also configure AE bracketing parameters such as the exposure difference between images (SHOOTING MENU > SHOOTING SETTING > DRIVE SETTING > BKT SETTING > AE BKT > FRAMES/STEP SETTING).

| Long exposures | TIP 52 |
| --- | --- |

Long exposures can lead to impressive results. With fireworks, night shots, interesting water surfaces, stars, and clouds; exposure times of several seconds, or even minutes, capture the course of time in a single photograph. Of course, this only works if you put the camera on a tripod or a solid, non-vibrating surface.

You have two basic options:

- Set the shutter-speed dial to **T** (Time) and then use the corresponding command dial to set the shutter speed. To avoid camera shake, use a remote shutter release or the self-timer to take the shot.

- Set the shutter speed dial to **B** (Bulb), then press and hold the shutter button for as long as you want the camera to expose. Obviously, it makes sense to use a remote shutter release that can be locked for the duration of the shot.

For good-quality results, make sure to set SHOOTING MENU > IMAGE QUALITY SETTING > LONG EXPOSURE NR > ON. By doing so, the camera will perform a dark-frame subtraction [52] depending on what ISO and exposure time you used. Dark-frame subtraction doubles the duration of the effective exposure, so be patient.

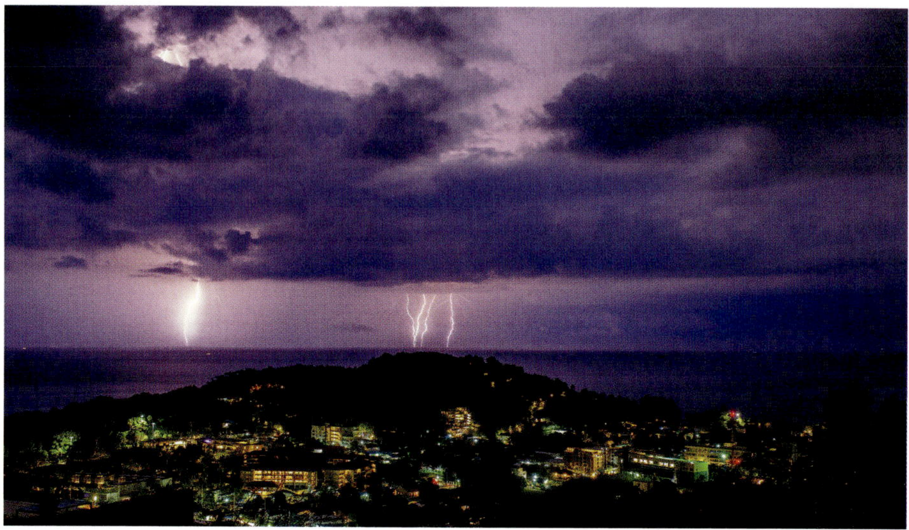

Fig. 53:  A **long exposure** of 30 seconds taken in T mode. Make sure to use a tripod for these kinds of shots.

| TIP 53 | Long exposures in bright daylight |

To achieve long exposure times under normal daylight conditions, you can't just stop down the lens. Even at f/22, your shutter speed would still be too fast. Besides, diffraction blur will kick in beyond f/9, so stopping down beyond this point is only recommended when it cannot be avoided.

To realize long shutter speeds in good light, it's best to use a so-called ND filter [53], or neutral density filter. This is a fancy name for a gray filter you can put in front of the lens to block a portion of the light from reaching the sensor.

For example, a filter with an ND 3.0 specification will extend your exposure time by a factor of about 1000 (or 10 f-stops). This means that by using this filter, a scene that would normally require a shutter speed of 1/50 s at f/8 can be shot at the same aperture with an exposure time of 20 seconds.

However, there's a catch. Since X series cameras are equipped with a rather weak infrared (IR) cut filter in front of their sensors, long exposures (typically one minute or longer) in bright daylight should be performed with a regular neutral density (ND) filter *and* a dedicated IR cut filter in front of the lens. This will help to avoid false colors. A few ND filters already include an IR cut filter.

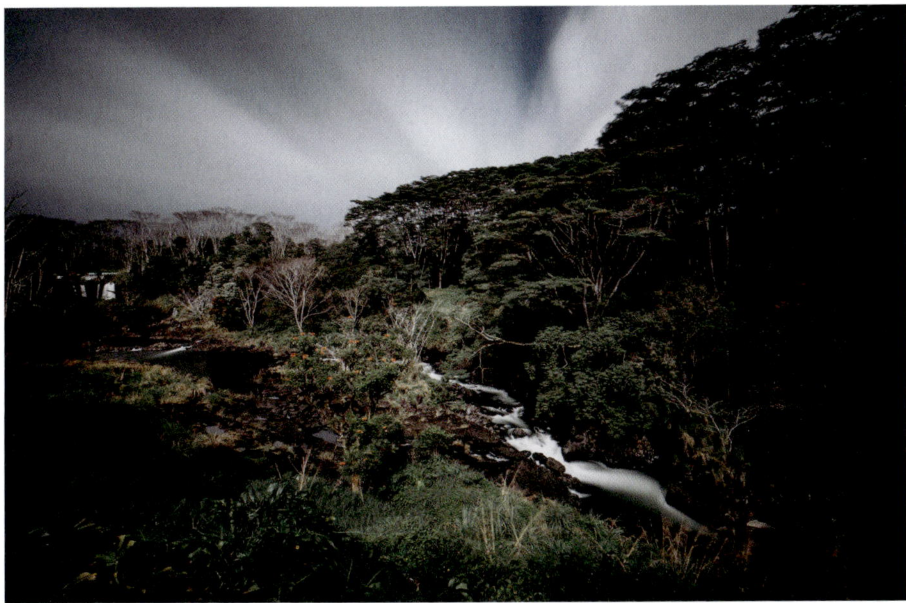

Fig. 54: This **long daylight exposure** lasted almost 4 minutes and was made possible by using a strong ND filter.

| ISO settings—what's the deal? | TIP 54 |
| --- | --- |

The meaning of ISO in the digital realm is often misunderstood. Unlike film, higher ISO settings *don't* increase the sensor's sensitivity. The sensor in your X-T3 is calibrated to a native ISO 160 (based on the popular SOS standard) [54], and this remains the same no matter what ISO you set.

To be clear, there's no difference between taking a shot with f/5.6 and 1/60 s at either ISO L (80) or at ISO H (51200). In both cases, the sensor is exposed to the exact same amount of light (or photons) due to the fixed f/5.6 and 1/60 s setting. The amount of light that hits the sensor (the actual exposure) is solely determined by aperture and shutter speed.

So, what exactly is ISO doing? ISO determines the amount of *signal amplification* that's applied to the image. ISO 160, the sensor's native setting, is the camera's basic calibration. At ISO 320, the signal (or sensor data) is amplified by one aperture stop (1 EV) to brighten the image and increase its exposure. At ISO 640, the amplification amounts to two stops (2 EV), and so on. At ISO 12800, the additional amplification of the light recorded by the sensor amounts to more than six stops. It's not surprising that image quality decreases when ISO amplification increases because noise and artifacts are amplified along with the actual image data.

The amplification we are talking about means brightening the image by increasing its exposure. This concept of amplification isn't limited to the camera itself by setting the ISO—it's also part of the entire workflow from in-camera exposure via RAW file (digital negative) to the final JPEG or TIFF file (digital print). If you are familiar with RAW converters such as Lightroom, you know there's an exposure slider. Moving this slider to the left or right changes the exposure (and hence the ISO brightness) of an image after the fact.

If you take a shot with an ISO 640 setting, you're telling the camera's Auto-exposure (AE) to expose the image two stops darker than it would at its base ISO of 160, then to amplify (brighten) that image two stops to compensate for the underexposure.

Regarding image quality and ISO, there's a basic rule: lower ISO settings lead to higher-quality results—hence the general recommendation to keep the ISO settings as low as possible. However, we obviously can't shoot with base ISO all the time, especially in low-light situations.

There are two basic methods to amplify a digital image:

- **Analog/digital hybrid amplification** *prior* **to writing the RAW file:** This method applies a mix of analog and digital signal processing to amplify or push the image to the brightness level that corresponds to the ISO setting. The digitized result of this process is then saved as a RAW file.

- **Digital amplification (push)** *after* **writing the RAW file:** This method changes the brightness of an image during RAW processing, *after* the RAW file has been written. The metadata (i.e., instructions) in the RAW file tell the RAW converter what to do. You can also use the camera's built-in RAW converter to adjust the effective brightness (and hence, ISO) of an image after it has been recorded, or by moving your external RAW converter's exposure slider.

Digital amplification during RAW processing is beneficial because it's reversible. If the digital amplification (exposure) was too strong (leading to blown highlights), you can always reduce it. If it was too weak, you can push it up. ISO (i.e., exposure amplification) is a volatile aspect of the photographic process because it can be applied anytime: in-camera, prior to writing the RAW file, or later during RAW processing.

The sensor in your X-T3 is a so-called ISO-less sensor. This means there's no significant quality difference between conventional signal amplification prior to writing a RAW file and digital amplification later during RAW conversion. This is great, because it allows you to digitally increase the ISO (i.e., brightness/exposure) of your shots during RAW processing, either in-camera or with external software such as Lightroom. Pushing the exposure up later in your RAW converter won't look much different from choosing a higher ISO setting when you take the shot.

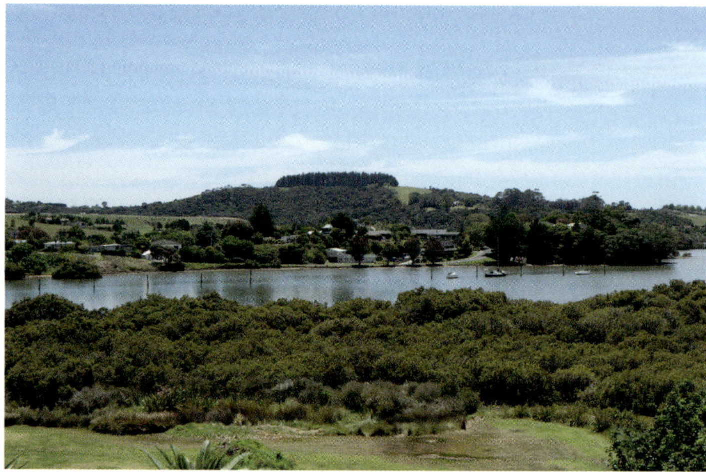

Fig. 55: **ISO-less sensor (1):** This shot was taken at ISO 1250, with classic analog/digital in-camera amplification. The ISO 1250 result was then burned into the RAW file and the RAW converted to a JPEG.

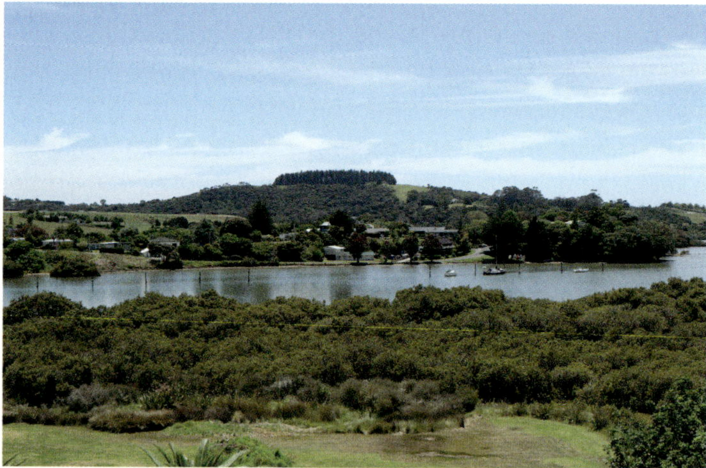

Fig. 56: **ISO-less sensor (2):** This shot was also *effectively* taken at ISO 1250. However, it was shot with an ISO 160 base setting, using the same aperture and shutter speed as the previous image, effectively underexposing it three stops (3 EV). The amplification from ISO 160 to ISO 1250 took place digitally during RAW conversion, simply by moving the exposure slider 3 EV to the right, thus compensating for the underexposure. You won't be able to see any quality difference between the two shots in this book, so I invite you to look at full-size samples that are uploaded to Flickr [55].

Fig. 57: **ISO-less sensor (3):** This is the same as the previous shot as it was actually recorded as an ISO 160 RAW file—before the push of 3 EV that effectively turned it into an image with ISO 1250 brightness.

While the sensors of previous X series APS-C cameras, from the classic X100 up to the X-H1, are calibrated to base ISO 200, the X-T3, X-T30, and additional models with an X-Trans CMOS 4 sensor use a base ISO setting of 160. This means they can accept an additional 1/3 EV of light without blowing critical highlights, which also increases their dynamic range by 1/3 EV.

| What you should know about extended ISO | TIP 55 |
| --- | --- |

You have probably noticed that in addition to the standard ISO settings (ISO 160 to ISO 12800), your X-T3 offers three additional settings: L (80), H (25600), and H (51200).

- **H means High:** In these modes, image data is digitally amplified further. This enormous amplification leads to a visible decrease in image quality. While ISO 25600 is still quite usable (especially for black-and-white JPEGs using the ACROS film simulation), ISO 51200 is only for emergencies.

- **L means LOW:** In ISO L (80) mode, an ISO 160 RAW is over-exposed by one stop. During RAW conversion, the JPEG is pulled down one stop and saved, resulting in an ISO 80 JPEG file. A digital pull is the direct opposite of a digital push operation: Digital pull decreases the exposure of the resulting image. The ISO L (80) RAW and JPEG files contain one stop *less* dynamic range than normal ISO 160 files. This means bright areas like clouds in the sky can easily appear blown out. On the other hand, ISO L (80) can add contrast and punch to scenes with dull lighting and little contrast.

While shooting in extended ISO L diminishes highlight dynamic range, this fact is *not* reflected in the live view and live histogram. This means the live view and live histogram become pretty much useless for determining the correct exposure to the highlights when you are using ISO L. Only when you half-press and hold the shutter button to lock the exposure will the live view adapt, but at that stage there is no histogram available.

Practically, this means it's not recommended that you use extended ISO in one of the auto exposure (AE) modes: **P**, **A**, and **S**. Instead, you should first set the correct exposure to the highlights in manual mode **M** at ISO 160 using the live view and live histogram, and then change the ISO setting to ISO L (80) without further adjustments to shutter speed and aperture. This will keep your highlights intact and will add contrast to the image by lowering the midtones and shadows to the new ISO L (80) settings.

The X-T3 also offers extended ISO L (125) and ISO L (100) settings, which are derived from ISO 250 and ISO 200 by first overexposing the shot one stop and then pulling it back down one stop during RAW conversion to match the brightness of the selected ISO L setting of 125 or 100. Doing so deducts one stop of dynamic range. I strongly advise against using these two additional extended ISO L settings.

**Important:** *Extended ISO settings are not available when the electronic shutter (ES) is selected.*

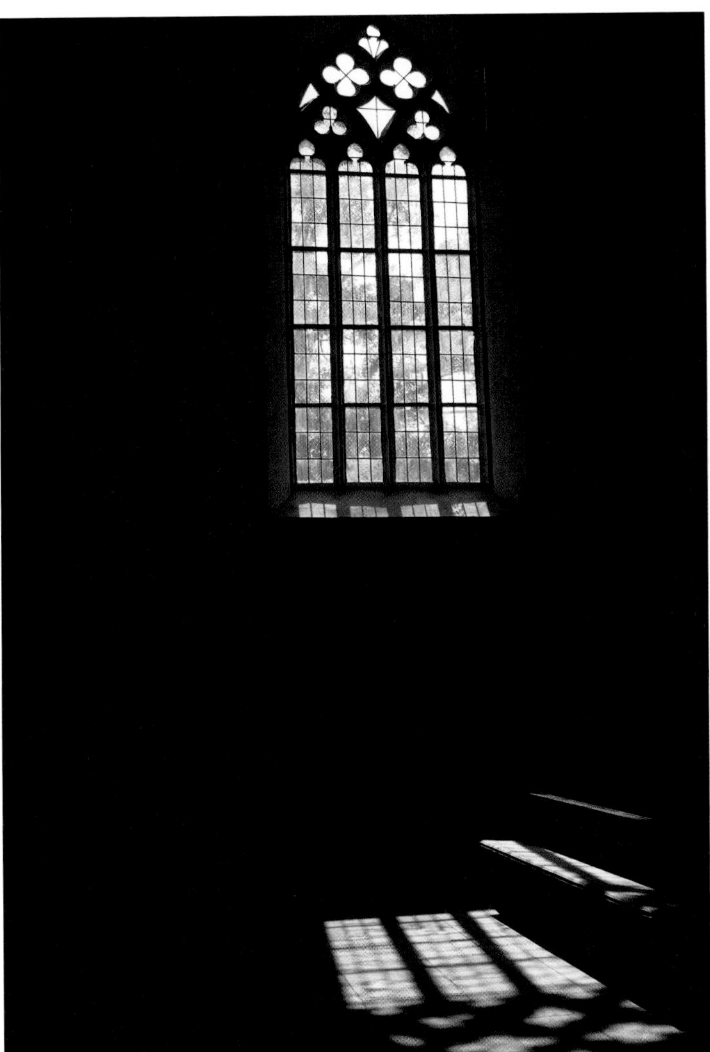

Fig. 58: **Extended ISO L** can add punch thanks to its decreased dynamic range. To pull it off, set your camera to manual exposure mode, select base ISO 160, and expose the scene to the highlights using the live view and live histogram. Exposing to the highlights means that the brightest, important parts of the scene are exposed as bright as possible, but without clipping (i.e., losing highlight detail). After the exposure to the highlights is manually set, change the ISO setting from 160 to L (80) without changing aperture or shutter speed. This will increase the contrast of the image by darkening the shadows and midtones one stop, while bright highlights remain where they were.

<table><tr><td>**TIP 56**</td><td>Auto-ISO and minimum shutter speed</td></tr></table>

You can automate the task of selecting the best (or lowest) ISO setting possible for any given shooting situation. Auto-ISO is an option with up to three configurable presets (AUTO1, AUTO2, and AUTO3) that can be configured in the ISO menu of your camera (SHOOTING MENU > SHOOTING SETTING > ISO AUTO SETTING):

- DEFAULT SENSITIVITY: This is the lower ISO limit. The camera will always try to use this ISO setting as long as the other parameters permit it.

- MAX. SENSITIVITY: This is the upper ISO limit. The camera's Auto-ISO will never go beyond this level.

- MIN. SHUTTER SPEED: Auto-ISO will automatically increase the ISO setting (up to the MAX. SENSITIVITY threshold) when the minimum shutter speed cannot be realized. There's also an AUTO setting here: If you set MIN. SHUTTER SPEED to AUTO, the camera will adjust the minimum shutter speed depending on the current focal length, using the formula *Minimum Shutter Speed = [1 ÷ (Focal Length × 1.5)] s.*

Obviously, MIN. SHUTTER SPEED is only relevant in auto exposure (AE) modes **A** and **P**, because the shutter speed is already set manually in modes **M** and **S**. Auto-ISO minimum shutter speed makes sure that within the lower and upper ISO limits, the camera will always use a shutter speed that is at least as fast as the set minimum shutter speed.

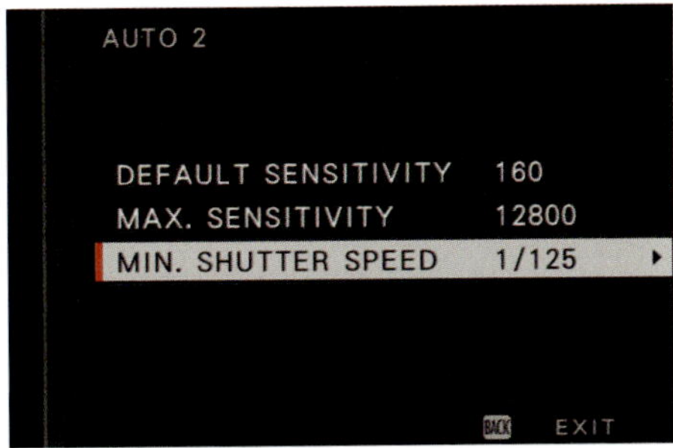

Fig. 59: **Auto-ISO** works with an ISO range between DEFAULT SENSITIVITY (the bottom) and MAX. SENSITIVITY (the ceiling). It will always try to keep ISO as close to the bottom as possible, but only as long as the resulting shutter speed isn't slower than the set MIN. SHUTTER SPEED.

Here's an example: Let's say you are shooting in mode **A** (aperture priority) in bright light conditions using f/5.6. Auto-ISO is set to ISO 160 as the lower limit and ISO 12800 as the upper limit. You have set 1/125 s as your minimum shutter speed, because you want to avoid motion blur while taking pictures of people walking in the street.

As long as the scene is brightly lit, there is no problem. The camera will use ISO 160 with shutter speeds at least as fast as 1/125 s. However, as the sun sets and it becomes impossible to successfully use 1/125 s at f/5.6 and ISO 160, Auto-ISO will increase the ISO to ensure the shutter speed doesn't drop below 1/125 s. This automatic adjustment continues as the light conditions deteriorate until Auto-ISO reaches the upper ISO limit (in our case, ISO 12800). What now? Since the camera can't increase the ISO any further, it will start to reduce the shutter speed to values slower than 1/125 s to still ensure a correct exposure.

In mode **S** (shutter priority), the photographer sets the shutter speed. In this mode, Auto-ISO will increase the ISO setting only when the aperture is already wide open and can't be opened further. This can be a problem with fast lenses like the XF56mmF1.2, XF35mmF1.4, or XF23mmF1.4. When shot wide open, the depth of field of these lenses is quite limited (to say the least). This is why Auto-ISO is better used in modes P or A, at least in concert with fast lenses.

<table><tr><td>TIP 57</td><td>Auto-ISO in manual mode M: the "misomatic" mode</td></tr></table>

Manual mode in concert with Auto-**ISO** turns into another auto**MATIC** exposure mode: the so-called "**misomatic**" mode. In this mode, you select the aperture and shutter speed, and the camera automatically selects a suitable ISO setting that matches the exposure that has been determined by the currently active metering mode.

To be useful in a misomatic setup, Auto-ISO should be able to use the full ISO bandwidth, so you should configure it with the camera's base ISO 160 as the lower limit and the highest available upper limit (ISO 12800).

Misomatic gives you full manual control over aperture (depth of field) and shutter speed (motion blur and camera shake). You can tailor shutter speed and aperture to the requirements of the task at hand; there will be no surprises. At the same time, you still enjoy the comfort of automatic exposure (AE).

Misomatic also allows you to adjust the camera-metered exposure with the exposure compensation dial. For this to be effective, it's even more important to set the Auto-ISO DEFAULT SENSITIVITY as low as possible and the MAX. SENSITIVITY as high as possible.

If you don't want to spend time with exposure compensation while you are in misomatic mode, you can use Fuji's DR function as a workaround by selecting DR200% in concert with the misomatic. This setting is your insurance against accidental overexposure by the camera's AE, because it gives you at least one stop of extra latitude for after-the-fact overexposure corrections with the internal or an external RAW converter. To correct a poor auto-exposure after the fact, you can use the PUSH or PULL commands of the camera's internal RAW converter or move the exposure slider of your external RAW processing software.

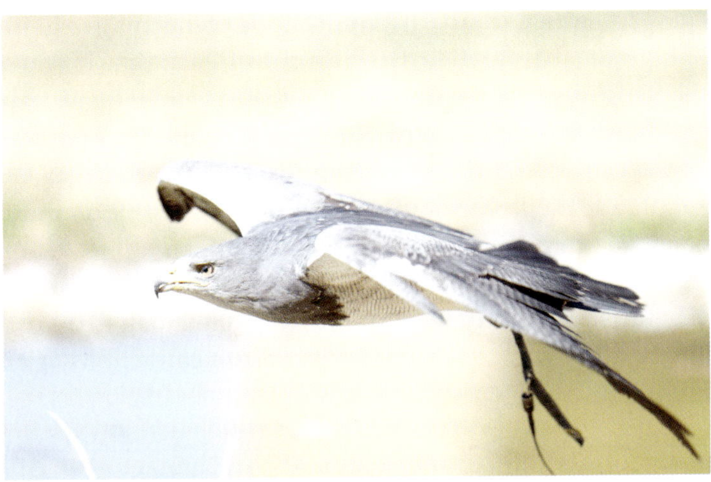

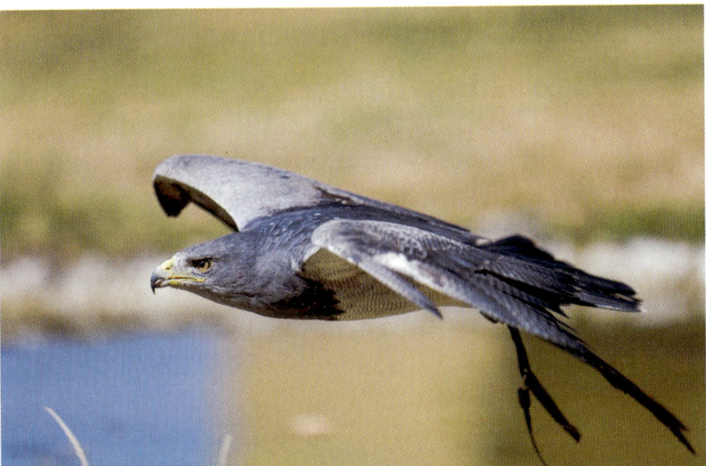

Fig. 60: **Misomatic** mode combines manual exposure with Auto-ISO. It can be helpful in situations with quickly and suddenly changing light conditions, such as with concerts and other stage events, sporting events, action shots, and street photography. Basically, it's about situations that don't leave you enough time to manually adjust the exposure, and where catching the decisive moment is your priority. In misomatic mode, you can set the desired depth-of-field (aperture) and motion blur (shutter speed), while the camera auto-exposes the images by applying the right amount of ISO amplification. To protect against accidental overexposure (top image), you can buy "insurance" by setting the camera to DR200% in misomatic mode. This way, overexposures can be corrected during RAW conversion (bottom image).

Don't forget: ISO is just an amplification of the image signal. Using misomatic mode, the amount of light that reaches the sensor is solely determined by your manual aperture and shutter speed settings. It always stays the same, regardless of the automatic ISO setting chosen by the camera. In misomatic mode, the only exposure variable is the amount of signal amplification (i.e., ISO); and with an ISO-less sensor, this variable can also be adjusted later during RAW conversion. In this context, choosing DR200% ensures there's ample leeway for after-the-fact exposure corrections of at least ±1 EV.

| **TIP 58** | Extending the dynamic range |
|---|---|

If the dynamic range of a subject is larger than the dynamic range of the camera's sensor or image processing, one of the following phenomena occurs:

- The highlights of the image are blown out or appear too bright (overexposed).

- Midtones appear too dark (underexposed) and shadows lose detail in the dark areas.

In both cases, the shot's exposure is out of balance. Sadly, it's very difficult (if not impossible) to restore detail in blown highlights. It's much easier to lift underexposed midtones and blocked shadows. This procedure is called *tone mapping,* and it's the only way to access the full potential of a digital camera's full dynamic range. Certain tonal values of the original exposure are reassigned and changed, either by employing a tone curve or by using a more complex procedure known as adaptive tone mapping.

To record the full tonal range of a high-contrast scene, it's best to expose the image in a way that preserves the color and texture of the important bright parts of the scene. Of course, doing so can lead to an image with underexposed midtones and blocked shadows that needs further processing to look natural, realistic, and pleasing. You can correct these issues with most external RAW converters.

While every RAW converter is different, most programs offer functions to selectively manipulate the exposure of a shot after the fact. For example, you can change the overall exposure with the exposure slider, and you can restore blown highlights with a highlight recovery slider. Most converters also offer sliders that only target shadow tones.

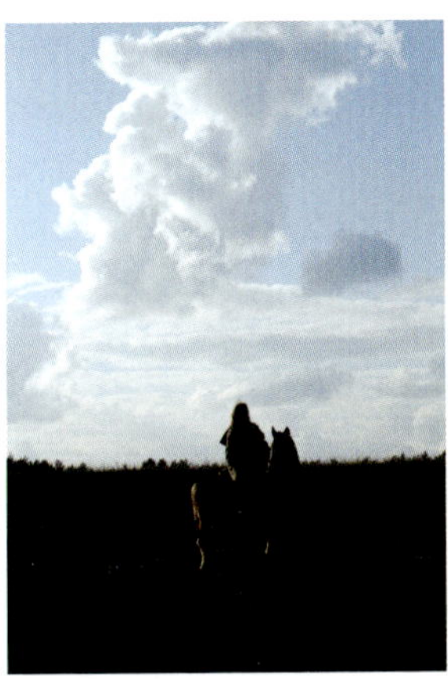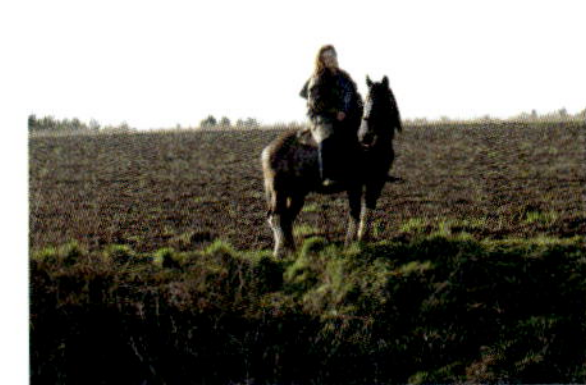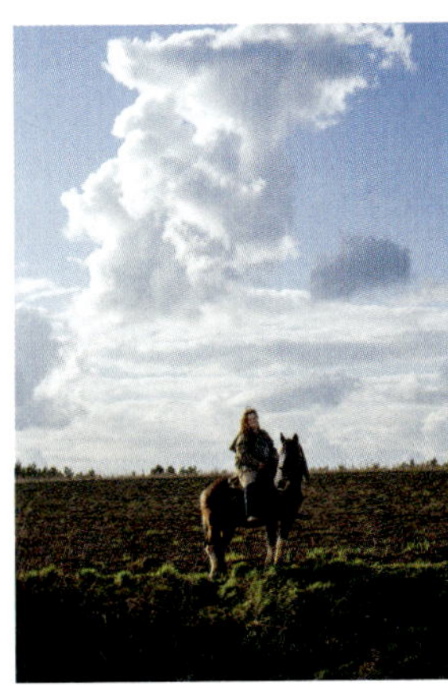

Fig. 61: In many instances, the **dynamic range** of a JPEG is smaller than the dynamic range of the scene, so no matter how you expose it in your camera, some parts of the resulting image will end up either too dark or too bright (or both). Here's a practical example:

The image on the left was exposed to the highlights, showing color and texture in the blue sky and white clouds. However, the darker foreground is clearly underexposed, resulting in blocked shadows. Horse and rider are almost reduced to a silhouette.

The image in the middle depicts the same scene, but this time it was exposed about two stops (EV) brighter, removing blocked shadows and adding detail to the main subject. However, the cloudy blue sky is now overexposed and has all but disappeared.

This is a Catch-22, because no matter how you expose this scene, the JPEG from the camera will always display essential parts either too dark or too bright. Quite obviously, different parts of this scene require different exposures. To pull this off, we use the RAW file of the image on the left, which was exposed to preserve the clouds and the sky. By applying tone mapping in a state-of-the-art RAW converter, we selectively push (brighten) shadows and midtones without further brightening the highlights of the clouds and sky. We can even add additional contrast to the clouds and darken the sky a bit. The example on the right shows the result out of Adobe Lightroom Classic, where certain pixels received different levels of (after-the-fact) amplification.

The built-in DR function of your X-T3 can help you automate the tone mapping procedure. It works in two stages:

■ The RAW file is exposed one (DR200%) or two (DR400%) stops darker than indicated in order to preserve bright highlights of a scene.

■ During the RAW conversion in the camera, the under-exposed shadows and midtones are digitally amplified by one (DR200%) or two (DR400%) stops to restore their natural brightness, while the (already correctly exposed) highlights are mostly left alone in order to preserve them.

The resulting JPEG from the camera has undergone a selective exposure correction. The DR function restores the shadows and midtones of a shot that was initially exposed one or two stops darker to preserve the highlights of the scene. Looking at the resulting JPEGs, this leads to an effective gain in dynamic range (DR): one additional stop of highlight DR at DR200%, and two stops of additional highlight DR at DR400%.

In DR-Auto mode, the camera will automatically select a suitable DR setting. Please note that in this mode, the X-T3 will only choose either DR100% (no highlight DR expansion) or DR200% (one stop of highlight DR expansion). DR400% (two stops of highlight DR expansion) is available only when it is manually selected.

You can change the DR settings of your camera in the Quick menu or by selecting SHOOTING MENU > IMAGE QUALITY SETTING > DYNAMIC RANGE and then either AUTO, DR100%, DR200%, or DR400%.

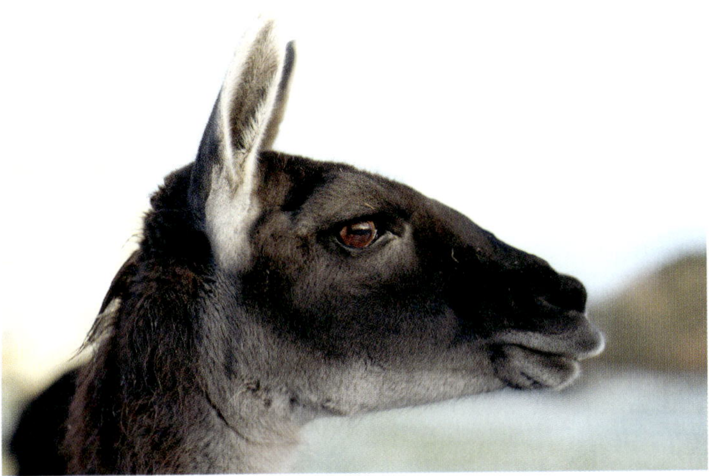

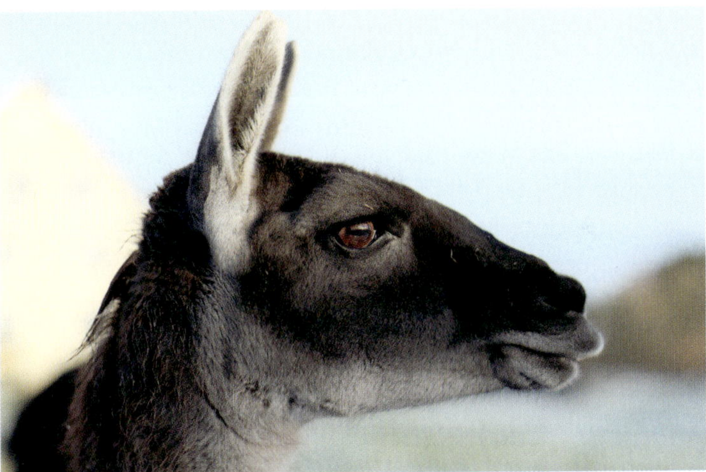

**Fig. 62:** These examples show the same shot with **DR100%** (above) and **DR400%** (below). At DR100%, the dark llama (our main subject) is correctly exposed in the foreground, but the much brighter colors in the sunny background are almost completely blown out because they were outside of the camera's dynamic range. In the DR400% version of the shot, the exposure (brightness) of the llama didn't change, however, the bright background is now perfectly colored and textured. To pull this off, the camera exposed the RAW file of the scene two stops (EV) darker than indicated, and then boosted shadows and midtones two stops brighter during RAW conversion. The result is a DR400% JPEG with 2 EV of extended dynamic range.

<table><tr><td>TIP 59</td><td>Extending the dynamic range for RAW shooters.</td></tr></table>

RAW shooters typically set the camera to DR100% and perform the tone mapping of their shots later during RAW processing. DR100% provides a realistic live view and live histogram (WYSIWYG).

The normal strategy of a RAW shooter is to expose toward the essential highlights of a high-contrast scene, making sure that there's sufficient color texture in the bright parts of the shot. This can result in an image with dark midtones and blocked shadows. However, while blown highlights are difficult, or even impossible, to restore, blocked shadows can be lifted (pushed) later. Balanced results from scenes with a very high dynamic range can be achieved in almost any good external RAW conversion software.

Here's what to do:

- Use the live view and live histogram to adjust the exposure in a way that ensures the important highlights of your scene are not blown out. This will preserve the highlights, but it may also lead to darkened midtones and blocked shadows, which you must deal with later during the RAW conversion of your shot.

- After taking the shot, enhance darkened shadows and midtones by selectively lifting the exposure in your RAW conversion software. For example, you could first lift the overall exposure and then restore the highlights with a highlight-recovery slider, or you could lift only the shadow tones with a shadow-tone slider. You can also combine both methods: Many RAW converters are quite flexible and offer several sliders to selectively change the exposure. Lightroom and Adobe Camera RAW (ACR), for example, feature five different controls (exposure, whites, blacks, shadows, and highlights) to perform this task. Whenever you change an exposure slider, you are effectively changing the ISO of any part of the image that is affected by that slider. However, in the digital domain of the RAW conversion stage, nothing is lost, and everything is fully reversible. *Selectively* changing the exposure of an image is known as tone mapping.

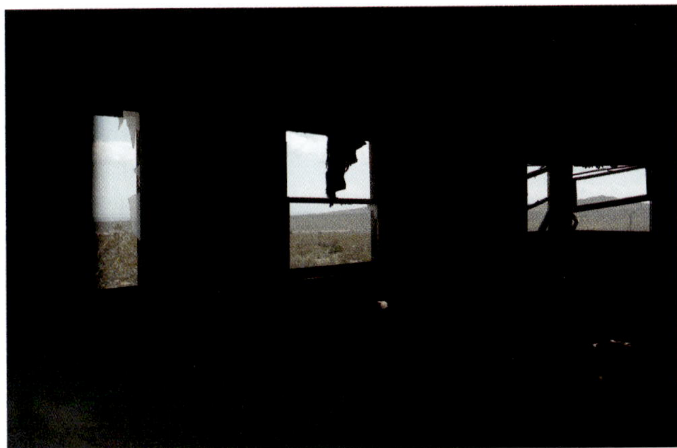

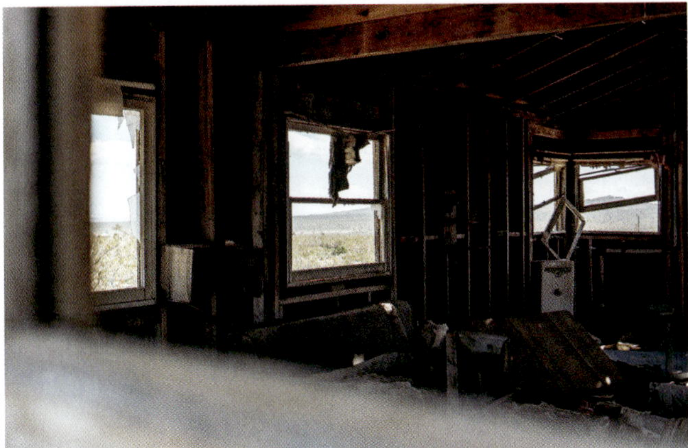

Fig. 63: The example above shows an image that has been **exposed to the highlights**. The exterior is perfectly exposed, but this means the interior is literally left in the dark. If that's what you want, great! If not, you must apply some tone mapping to the RAW file.

The example below shows the same image after tone mapping in Lightroom. The dark shadow regions have been lifted, revealing plenty of detail, where the previous image only displayed a dark patch. This method is also known as applying adaptive ISO, because different parts of the image received a different degree of exposure-push amplification. While the shadows were pushed up (ISO increase), the highlights mostly remained as they were.

| TIP 60 | JPEG settings for RAW shooters |

The previous tip explained the procedure to capture, compress, and later decompress scenes with high dynamic range. Since our exposure relies on the live view and the live histogram, it's useful to find camera settings that force the live histogram and live view to display as much dynamic range as possible. After all, we are shooting RAW and aren't really interested in the JPEGs from the camera, so we want the live view and live histogram to closely represent the data that will be recorded in the RAW files. This goal can be achieved by choosing JPEG parameters in the IMAGE QUALITY SETTING menu that display as much dynamic range as possible:

- Set FILM SIMULATION to ETERNA. This setting results in JPEGs with less contrast than the other film simulation modes.

- Set HIGHLIGHT TONE to −2. This setting reduces the highlight contrast of the JPEG in the live view and in the live histogram.

- Set SHADOW TONE to −2. This setting reduces the shadow contrast of the JPEG in the live view and the live histogram.

- If you are shooting scenes with bright and saturated tones of red, blue, or green, you can also dial back the COLOR setting.

The JPEG settings listed above give you a live view and live histogram with maximum dynamic range. JPEGs that are generated with these settings may look flat, but we usually don't intend to keep them anyway. We are only interested in the RAW file, which isn't affected by JPEG settings. However, the live view and live histogram *are* affected, and a flat live view image with a correspondingly flat live histogram is exactly what we want. It helps us to better fine-tune our exposure to preserve important highlights.

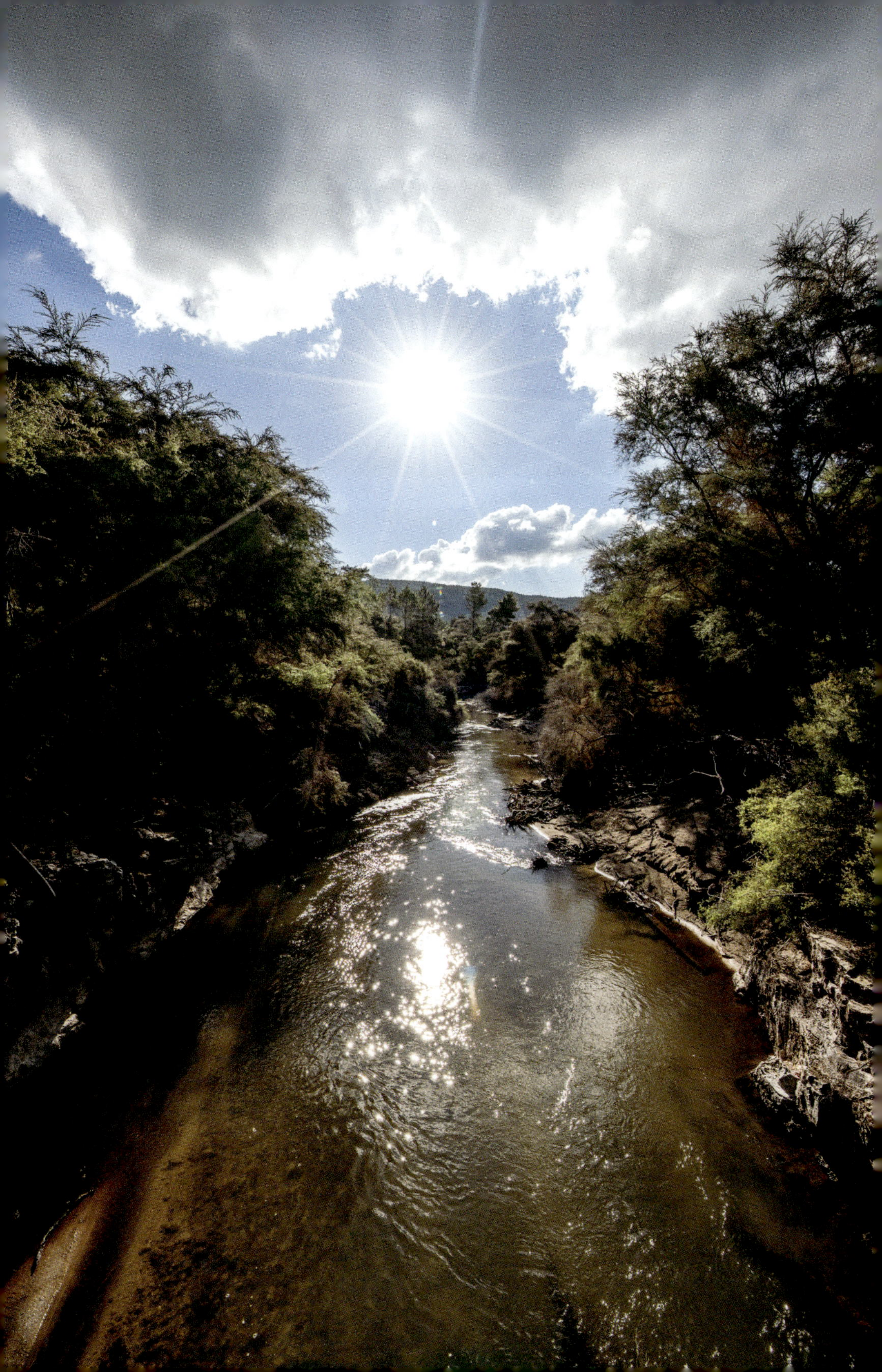

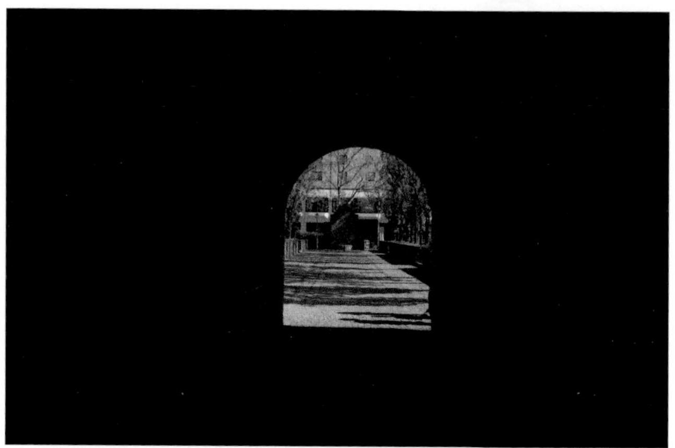

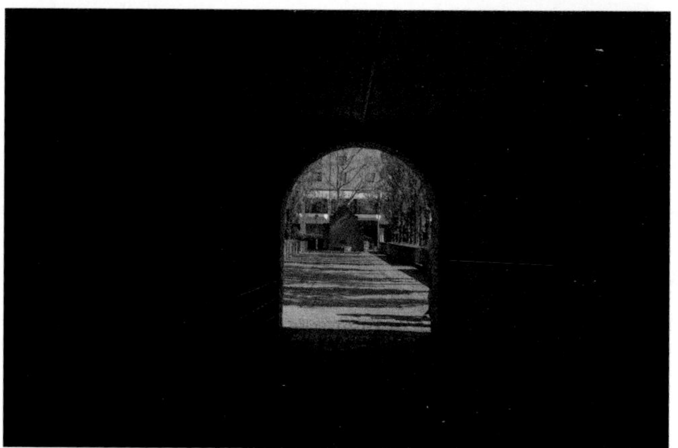

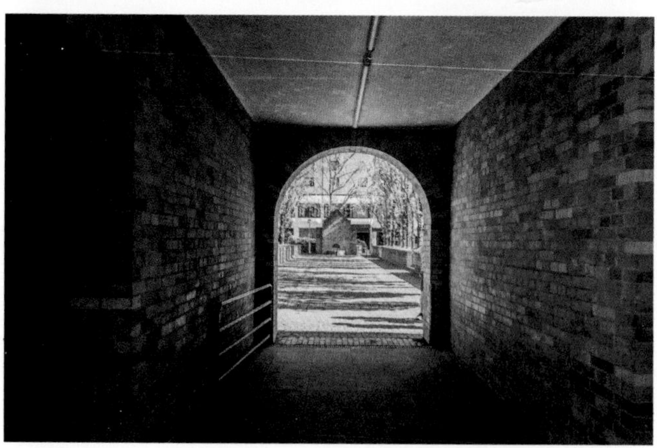

Fig. 64: These examples were all taken using the same exposure settings (ISO, aperture, and shutter speed). The exposure was geared toward the highlights of the sunlit parts behind the much darker tunnel, where the camera was positioned on a tripod.

**The image at top** shows how the live view (or JPEG) of the correctly exposed scene looks with the camera's Provia factory setting. While the sunny background is nicely lit, the dark parts of the tunnel are impossible to make out. It is really hard to frame this shot if all you can see (literally) is the light at the end of the tunnel.

**The image in the middle** depicts the same scene with the same exposure settings, but this time I used "JPEG settings for RAW shooters" (Eterna, Shadow Tone −2, Highlight Tone −2). These settings deliver a flat live view image (or JPEG) with less contrast and significantly more dynamic range than the camera's default settings. Using flat JPEG settings can be helpful when you compose high-contrast scenes. You can expose to preserve important highlights but still see what you are actually shooting. Remember: JPEG settings don't affect the RAW data—they only affect how the RAW data is processed in the live view and the resulting JPEG image.

**The image at bottom** is the final result after processing (tone mapping) the RAW file in Lightroom Classic.

You can save your "JPEG settings for RAW shooters" in a custom profile (C1 to C7) so you can quickly retrieve them and set your camera to "RAW shooter mode." To edit your custom settings, select SHOOTING MENU > IMAGE QUALITY SETTING > EDIT/SAVE CUSTOM SETTING.

<table>
<tr><td>Extending the dynamic range for JPEG shooters.</td><td>TIP 61</td></tr>
</table>

If you prefer to work with JPEGs that come directly from your camera (or want to shoot and keep RAWs *and* JPEGs), you can use Fuji's powerful DR function to capture scenes with high dynamic range. As you know, the DR function employs a two-stage process: reducing the exposure to capture critical highlights, and then lifting dark shadows and midtones to restore their brightness (exposure) back to realistic-looking levels.

You can simply set the camera to DR-Auto (not recommended), or manually set DR200% or DR400% (recommended) when you take pictures of high-contrast scenes. Remember that DR200% requires a minimum ISO setting of one stop (1 EV) above your X camera's base ISO 160, while DR400% requires a minimum ISO setting of two stops (2 EV) above base ISO. This is because the shadows and midtones in your scene will eventually be amplified by one (DR200%) or two (DR400%) ISO stops when the JPEG is created during RAW conversion. In the case of your X-T3, this means that DR200% requires at least ISO 320, and DR400% requires at least ISO 640.

What if we don't want to just *guess* what DR setting is optimal for any given scene? Can't we use the camera's metering to determine *exactly* how much DR expansion is required? Yes, we can! Here's how:

- To begin with, let's set the camera to DR100% and expose toward the critical highlights of a scene, just like a RAW shooter would do. Assuming you are shooting in one of the AE modes, this will often require you to turn the exposure compensation dial in the negative direction until the live view and live histogram display the scene without blown highlights.

- Next, turn the exposure compensation dial in the opposite (positive) direction until the shadows and midtones are displayed as bright as you want them to appear in the final image. Here's the important part: When you turn the exposure compensation dial up again, count the number of clicks it takes to reach the target brightness of your scene. One, two, or three clicks means you should set the camera from DR100% to DR200% for one stop of additional highlight dynamic range. More than three clicks means you should use DR400%. More than six clicks means that highlights may be blown even when you set DR400%, so you might want to avoid overcompensating beyond six clicks. As you know, each click of the exposure compensation dial equals 1/3 EV (or a third of a stop).

The above describes the procedure for any of your camera's auto exposure (AE) modes **P**, **A**, and **S**, including *misomatic* mode. Don't compensate with more than six 1/3 EV clicks (that's a total of 2 EV), or your resulting JPEG will be overexposed in the very highlights that you were trying to protect. Instead, try to reduce the shadow contrast by setting SHADOW TONE −1 or SHADOW TONE −2. You can also try a film simulation with less contrast, such as Pro Neg. Std or Eterna.

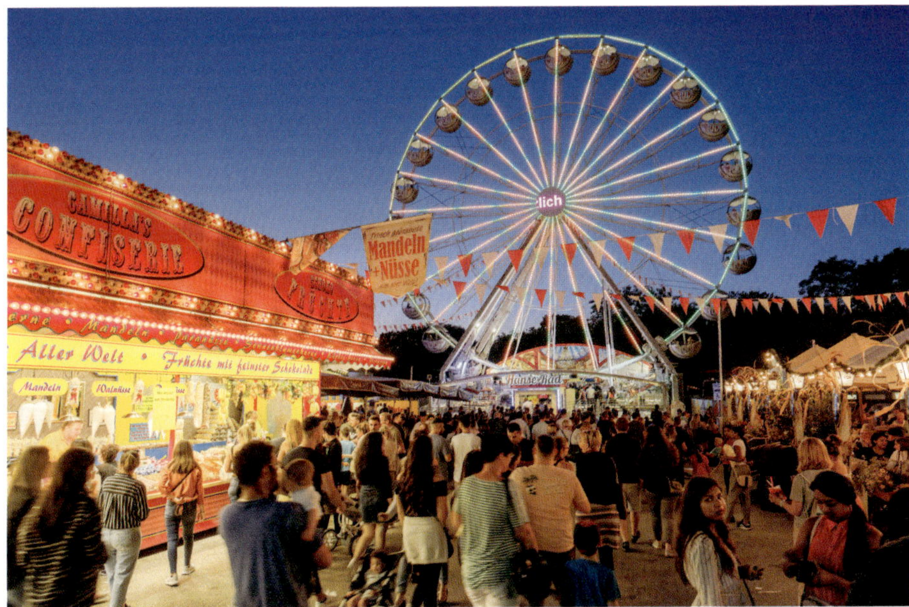


Fig. 65: **Night scenes** with bright lights and high contrast can benefit from a fixed DR400% setting to preserve color and texture in the highlights.

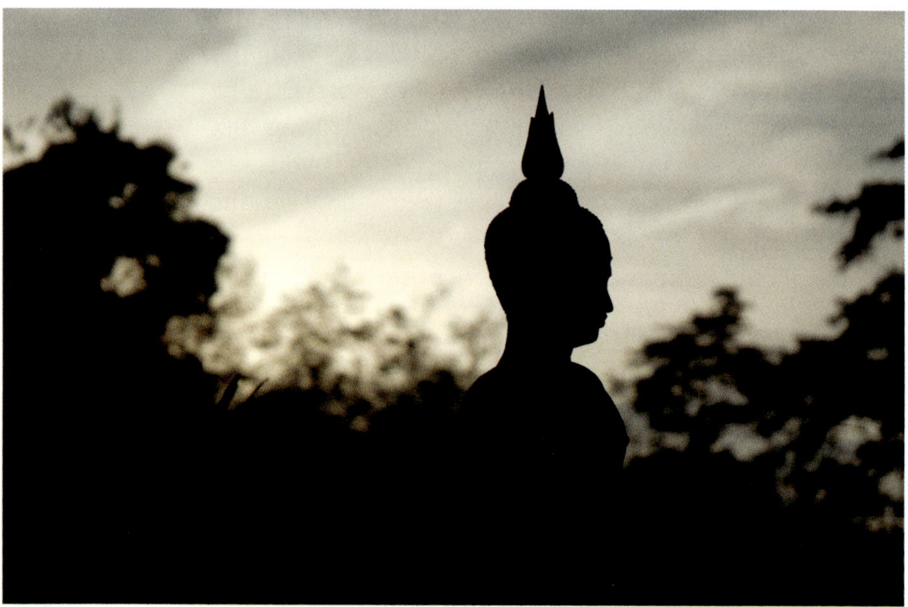

**Fig. 66:** On the other hand, there are instances where you may want to **maintain maximum contrast** and concentrate on the bright parts of a high-contrast scene. In such cases, a fixed DR100% setting is in order while you are exposing to the highlights.

The two above examples illustrate that DR-Auto is not a "smart" setting; it cannot predict what the photographer has in mind. In both cases, DR-Auto would have picked DR200%—not an optimal setting in either case.

*Important: The X-T3 simulates the effect of manually selected DR200% and DR400% dynamic range settings in the live view and live histogram. However, automatic DR expansion via DR-Auto is **not** simulated in the live view. Instead, the live view and live histogram will display a DR100% simulation, even when DR-Auto eventually decides to take the shot at DR200%.*

In extended ISO L settings, the live view and live histogram wrongly show the dynamic range of a regular ISO setting, giving you the false impression of one stop more highlight dynamic range than what is actually available. Only when you lock the exposure by half-pressing the shutter button will the live view change to display the actually recorded dynamic range. However, at this stage, there's no live histogram available.

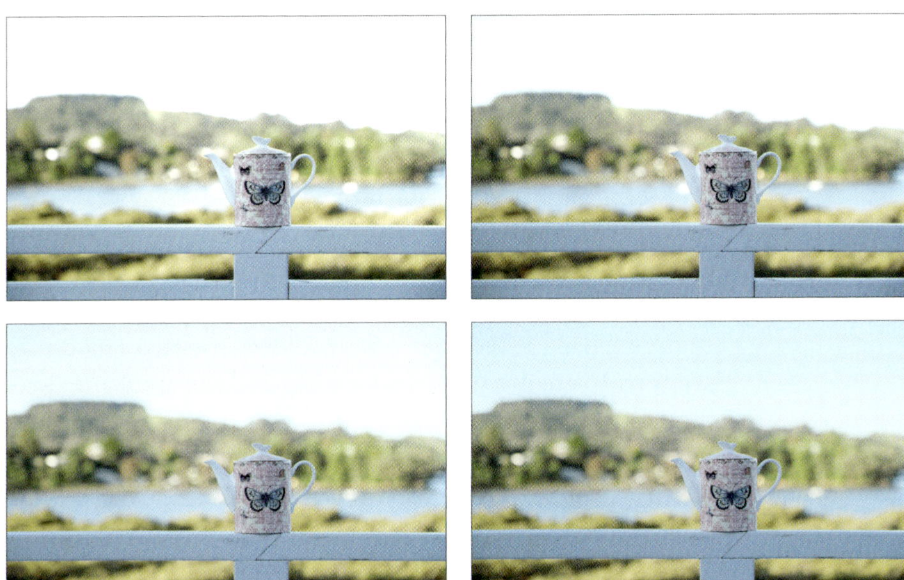

Fig. 67: **Comparing dynamic range settings:** The upper-left image shows a scene taken with extended ISO L (80), f/2.8, and 1/140 s, which is basically the missing DR50% setting of your camera. Highlight dynamic range is very poor; most bright parts of the image are blown.

The upper-right image shows the same subject shot with the camera's base ISO 160 (DR100%), f/2.8, and 1/280 s. Many parts of the shot are still without texture.

On the lower left, you can see an ISO 320 (DR200%), f/2.8, 1/550 s version of the scene, which gives us another stop of highlight dynamic range. In this example, the sky is already looking much better.

The lower-right example is an ISO 640 (DR400%), f/2.8, 1/1100 s version of our scene, which has two added stops of highlight dynamic range compared to a standard ISO 160 (DR100%) shot. Here, everything is smooth and shiny, with plenty of texture in the sky and bright areas.

These four images were captured with an X-T3 in AE mode **A**.

<table>
<tr><td>TIP 62</td><td>High-contrast scenes: Using the DR function to the benefit of RAW shooters</td></tr>
</table>

Fujifilm's DR function works by reducing the indicated ISO level of the RAW file by one (DR200%) or two (DR400%) stops. If you set ISO 640 and DR400% and take a picture, the RAW file of the image will actually be recorded with ISO 160—two stops darker than it appears in the live view or in the camera's resulting JPEG. Underexposing an image by one or two stops means that one or two stops of additional bright highlights are protected.

In other words, when the DR function is active, the camera's built-in RAW converter (which is also known as the JPEG engine) pushes the shadows and midtones of the underexposed RAW data one (DR200%) or two (DR400%) stops up to ensure that the live view and the resulting JPEG match the indicated ISO setting. It won't push the brightest highlights, though.

For example, if you set ISO 640 and DR400%, the RAW data will be recorded with ISO 160 (to protect two stops of highlights), but the built-in JPEG engine of the camera will make sure the shadows and midtones of the live view and the resulting JPEG image are pushed back up two stops to ISO 640 to compensate for the RAW file's underexposure. However, the brightest highlights of the JPEG will remain at ISO 160.

This is why the minimum ISO settings for DR200% and DR400% in cameras with a base ISO of 160 (like your X-T3) are ISO 320 and ISO 640, respectively. Remember that per definition and convention, ISO settings only apply to the JPEGs generated in the camera, not to the RAW files. It's perfectly normal for the RAW data to be recorded lower or higher than the indicated ISO level because all ISO settings apply only to JPEGs and the live view, not to RAW data.

Understanding this, it becomes clear that in the X-T3 with base ISO 160, extended ISO L (80) is doing just the opposite

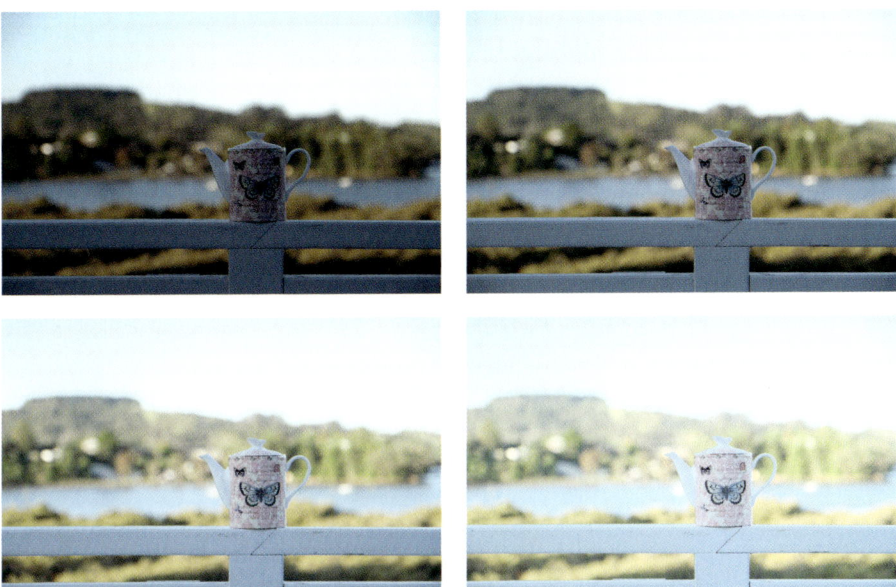

Fig. 68: In this example, I took four images using the same exposure settings: aperture f/2.8 and shutter speed 1/500 s. The only differences were four **equivalent ISO and DR settings** that neutralized each other at the RAW level: The upper-left image shows the JPEG that resulted from ISO L (80)/DR50%, while the upper-right image shows ISO 160/DR100%. The lower-left JPEG is the ISO 320/DR200% version, and in the lower right, there's the image taken with ISO 640/DR400%.

The four JPEGs are clearly different with regard to shadow and midtone brightness, because they all have to match their respective indicated ISO settings. Obviously, a JPEG taken at ISO 640, f/2.8, 1/500 s (lower right) must look brighter than one taken at ISO 80, f/2.8, 1/500 s (upper left). However, the underlying RAW data is the same in all four instances.

of the DR function: it records RAW data one stop brighter at ISO 160, while the JPEG engine pulls down (darkens) the live view and the resulting JPEG one stop to simulate and match the indicated ISO L (80) setting. Overexposing an image one stop brighter in the RAW than it appears in the live view and JPEG also means that one stop of highlight dynamic range is cut off and lost, so selecting ISO L (80) has the same effect as a DR50% setting would have (if that setting existed).

In many practical situations, correctly exposing to the important highlights of a scene results in a live view image that looks very dark in the midtones and shadows, which makes it hard to compose and focus the shot. Using "JPEG settings for RAW shooters" can mitigate this issue, but sometimes it's just not enough. If that's the case, using an equivalent ISO/DR setting can help us out.

For example, the following three exposure settings are perfectly equivalent at the RAW level:

- f/2.8, 1/500 s, ISO 160/DR100%
- f/2.8, 1/500 s, ISO 320/DR200%
- f/2.8, 1/500 s, ISO 640/DR400%

The RAW data for these three shots is the same, only the JPEGs (and hence the live view) look quite different from each other. For example, the live view and JPEG of a f/2.8, 1/500 s, ISO 640/DR400% shot looks two stops brighter than the equivalent f/2.8, 1/500 s, ISO 160/DR100% version. However, the RAW data of these two shots is the same.

This gives you additional options. For example, you can *manually* expose your scene to its important highlights at ISO 160/DR100% and then raise ISO one or two stops to 320 or 640, while at the same time changing the DR setting to DR200% or DR400%, respectively. *Increasing* RAW and JPEG ISO two stops from 160 to 640 and *decreasing* RAW ISO two stops by selecting DR400% leaves the RAW data unchanged (+2−2=0). The only thing that has become brighter is the live view and the JPEG from the camera.

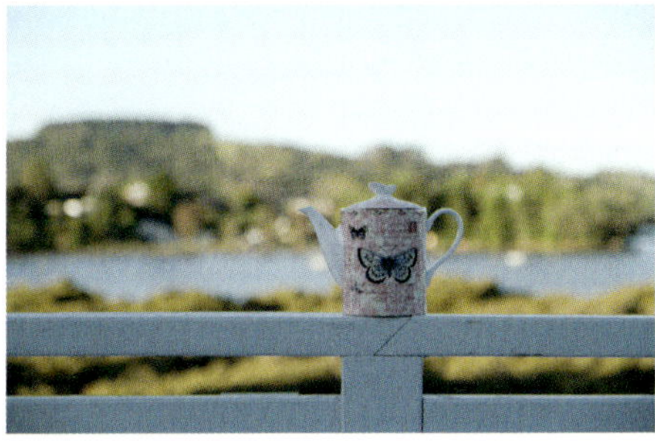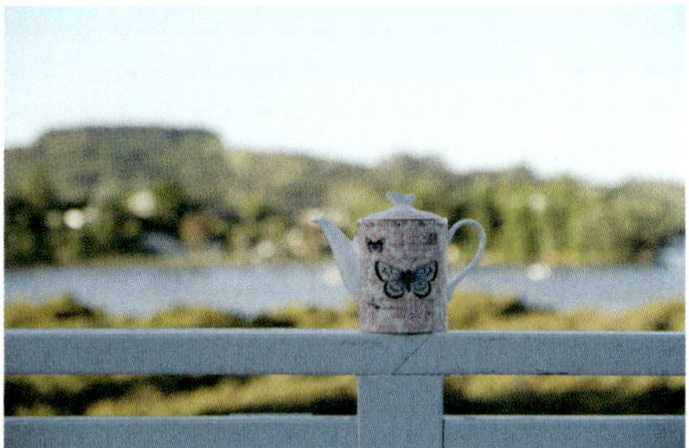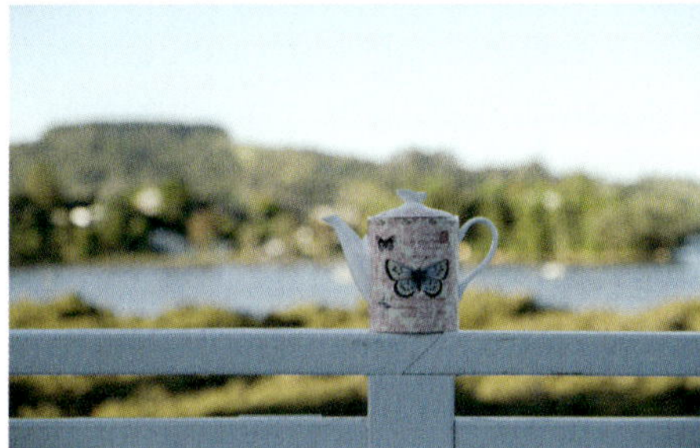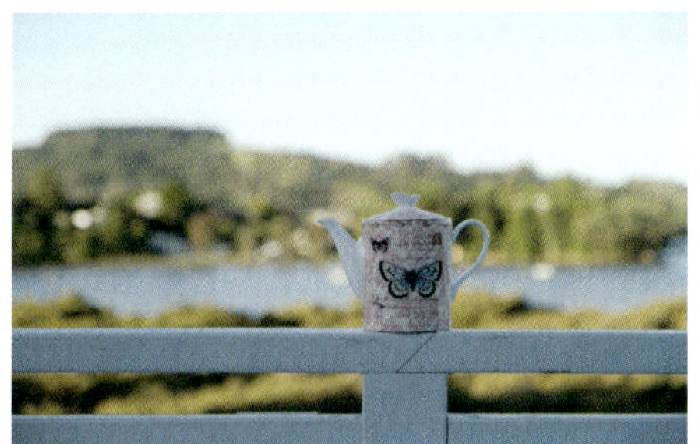

Fig. 69: This example shows the four shots from our previous illustration, all taken with the same exposure settings: aperture f/2.8 and shutter speed 1/500 s. This time, however, I processed the RAW files of the four images in Lightroom Classic and applied the same development settings to all of them—with the exception of the exposure slider, which was adjusted to compensate Lightroom's import exposure pull or push that is automatically applied to the RAW data based on the indicated ISO/DR setting.

The Lightroom-processed results from the shots taken with ISO L (80)/DR50% (upper left, Lightroom exposure slider +1 EV), ISO 160/DR100% (upper right, exposure slider 0 EV), ISO 320/DR200% (lower left, exposure slider −1 EV) and ISO 640/DR400% (lower right, exposure slider −2 EV) look exactly the same. This isn't at all surprising, because the RAW data *is* indeed the same.

This discovery can be of tremendous practical benefit if you intend to make the most of your camera's ISO-less sensor and push its dynamic range capabilities to the limits.

The best way to use the DR function for shooting scenes with very high dynamic range is to expose in manual mode **M**. Here's how to proceed:

- Set manual mode **M** and make sure the exposure preview for manual mode is enabled (SET UP > SCREEN SET-UP >

PREVIEW EXP./WB IN MANUAL MODE > PREVIEW EXP./ WB).

- Deploy "JPEG settings for RAW shooters" by selecting film simulation Eterna, Highlight Tone −2, and Shadow Tone −2.

- Set DR100% and manually expose the high-contrast scene to protect important highlights. If available, use the RGB histogram with the live overexposure warning ("blinkies") and set an exposure that is just rich enough that some of the important highlights in your scene begin to blink. Remember that this is about protecting the *important* highlights. Feel free to overexpose parts of your scene that aren't worth saving, like the sun in a backlit daylight scene.

- Now that your exposure to the scene's important high-lights is manually set and locked, the live view may look too dark to comfortably frame the scene. So, let's add the DR function to the mix. First, increase ISO as needed by either one or two full stops (1 or 2 EV). Then neutralize this ISO change by also increasing DR by the same amount (either DR200% or DR400%). For example, you can raise ISO from 160 to 640 (i.e., a two-stop ISO *increase* applied to the RAW, the live view, and the JPEG) while also raising DR from DR100% to DR400% (i.e., a two-stop ISO *decrease* that is applied only to the RAW file, but not to the live view and the JPEG).

- Having completed the previous step, the RAW remains as it was, but the live view looks either one or two stops brighter than before. That's great for demanding, high-contrast scenes, because not only can we perfectly expose to their important highlights, we can also still see what's going on in those really dark parts of the scene.

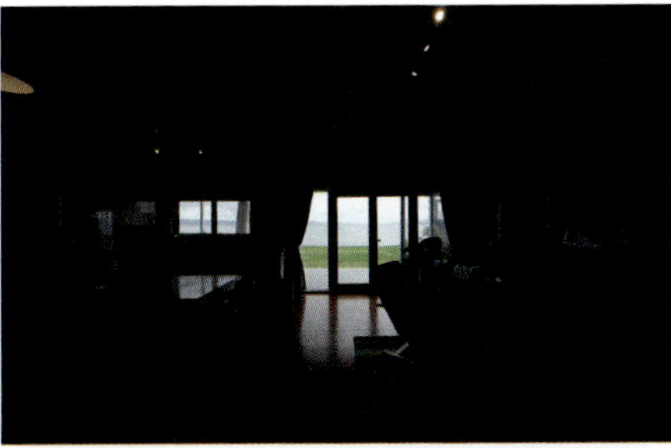 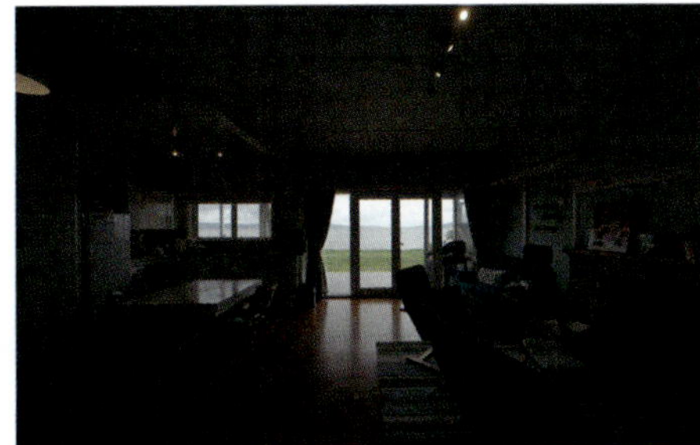

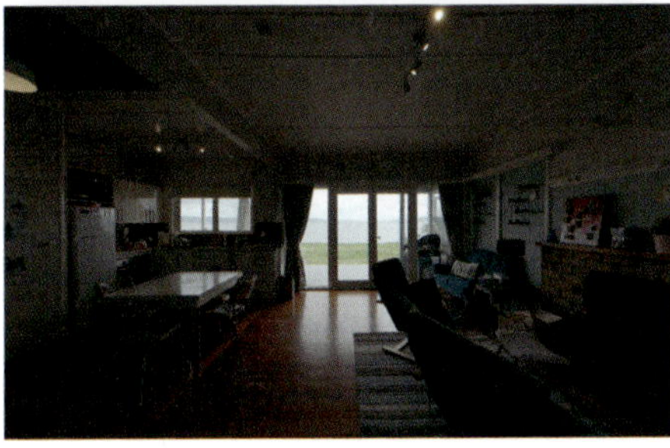 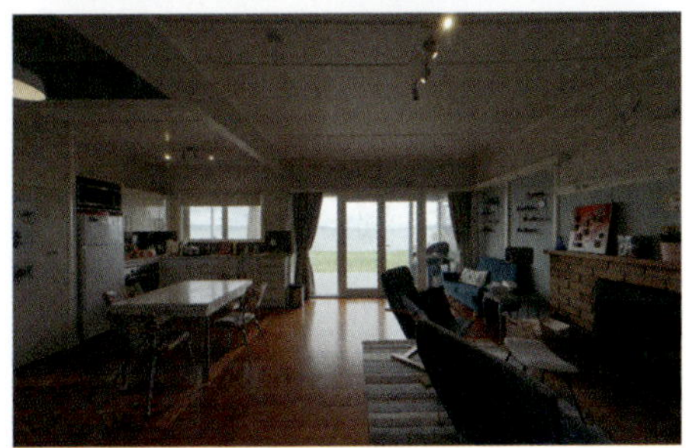

**Fig. 70:** This high-contrast interior example was shot at f/9 and 1/60 s in manual exposure mode. The upper-left image shows the scene as it looked with Provia factory settings and base ISO 160. The upper-right example shows the same image, but now with "JPEG settings for RAW shooters": film simulation Eterna, Shadow Tone −2, and Highlight Tone −2. While these are perfect settings for *exposing* a high-contrast scene toward its important highlights, the live view still looks a tad too dark to comfortably *frame* the scene. Luckily, we now know what to do. We can increase ISO/DR in tandem by one stop to ISO 320/DR200% (lower-left image) or two stops to ISO 640/DR400% (lower-right image) to get a brighter live view (and brighter JPEGs) without affecting the perfect RAW exposure that was determined and set using the base ISO/DR100% live view from the upper-left image.

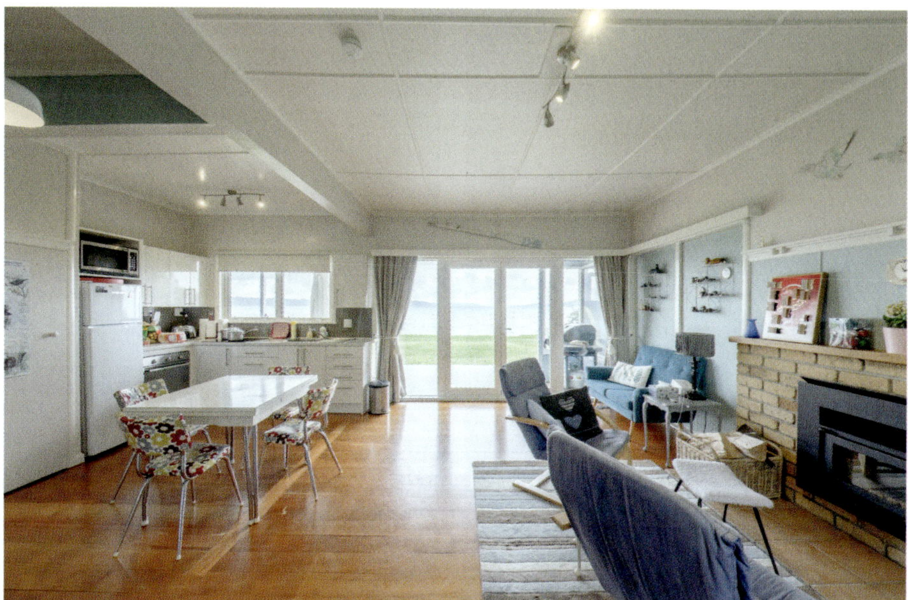

**Fig. 71:** This example shows the previous image after processing (tone mapping) the RAW file in Lightroom Classic.

Using manual mode **M** to expose high-contrast scenes is highly recommended because you can easily split the process into two stages. First, you determine and set the correct exposure to protect important highlights of the scene using DR100% and "JPEG settings for RAW shooters." After the exposure is set, you can concentrate on brightening the live view to a more useable level by increasing ISO one or two stops while also raising DR to either DR200% or DR400%. With the brighter live view, you can easily compose the scene, focus it, and take the shot at the right moment. Not only can you now see what's going on in the shadows and midtones of the scene, the camera's auto white balance will also do a better job when it's not fishing in the dark. This is an accurate, reliable, and straightforward process, and I use it frequently with great success.

As an alternative to raising ISO and DR in tandem (which brightens the live view without affecting the RAW exposure), you can also expose high-contrast scenes in manual mode **M** and then turn off the exposure preview after determining the correct exposure. Here's how it works:

- Set manual mode **M**, DR100% and turn *on* exposure preview (SET UP > SCREEN SET-UP > PREVIEW EXP./WB IN MANUAL MODE > PREVIEW EXP./WB).

- Like before, expose toward the important highlights of your scene and set a suitable exposure (ISO, aperture, and shutter speed).

- If the live view appears too dark, turn *off* exposure preview in manual mode (SET UP > SCREEN SET-UP > PREVIEW EXP./WB IN MANUAL MODE > OFF) and take your shots. The easiest way to do this is by assigning the manual exposure preview function to an Fn button. Personally, I have assigned the exposure preview toggle to the AE-L button of my X-T3, because I'm mostly shooting in manual mode, where the classic AE-Lock function is not available, anyway.

Turning off exposure preview in manual mode forces the live view to behave like it was in one of the three auto-exposure (AE) modes **P**, **A**, or **S**: the live view image will automatically change its brightness toward a middle-gray exposure (depending on the scene and the selected exposure metering method), but without affecting the actual exposure of the shot.

Using this rather simple procedure may sound quite appealing, but it has one major drawback: the JPEGs of your shots are still recorded rather dark (exposed to the highlights), making it difficult, or impossible, to immediately check critical focus and other details. You'd first have to push each image in the built-in or an external RAW converter. If you take a lot of images using this method, it can become quite a chore to browse through all your dark images and select the keepers.

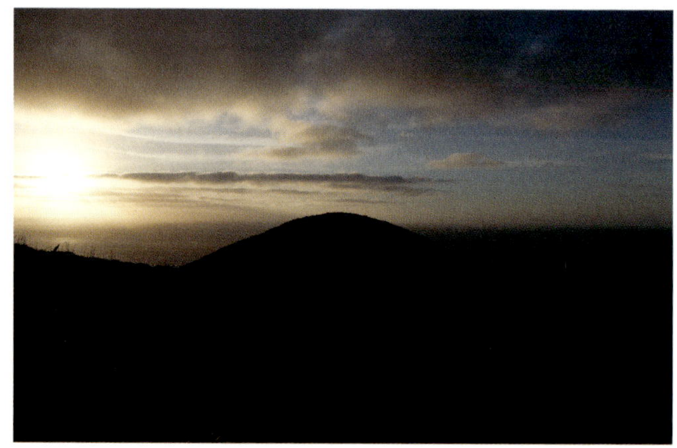

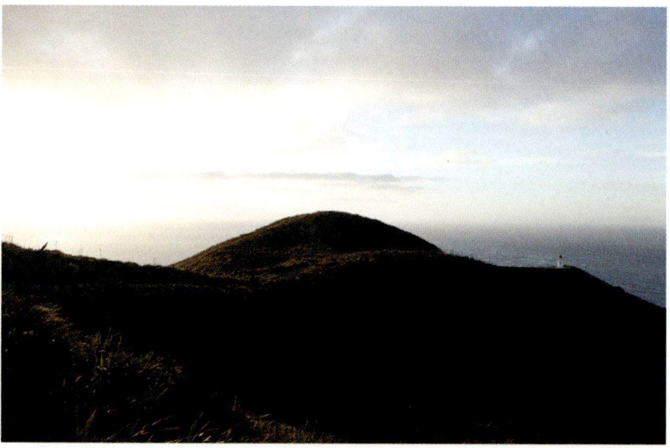

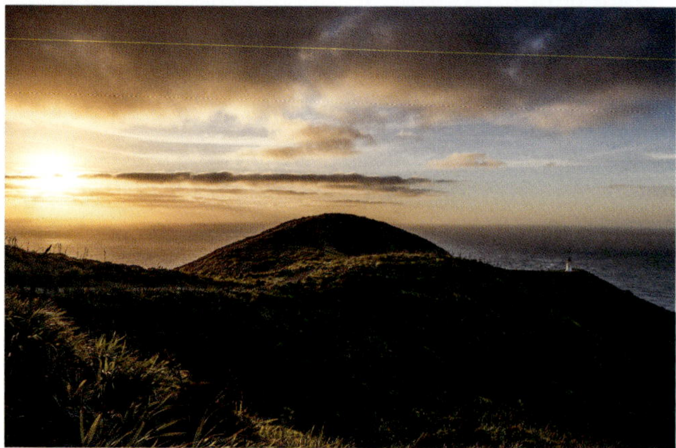

Fig. 72: This example shows a typical sunset shot with very high dynamic range. To protect the bright colored areas around the sun, I selected manual mode and exposed to the important highlights (ISO 160, f/5.6, 1/800 s). Sadly, this also resulted in a dark live view that made it very difficult to frame the scene (top). By **disabling the exposure preview for manual exposure mode,** I achieved a much more usable live view image (center) that allowed me to compose the scene. The image on the bottom shows the same shot after processing the RAW file in Lightroom Classic.

| DR versus DR-P | TIP 63 |
| --- | --- |

In addition to the DR function with its DR-Auto, DR100%, DR200%, and DR400% options, your X-T3 also features a function called DR-P, which stands for Dynamic Range Priority.

If you activate DR-P in the IMAGE QUALITY SETTING menu, it replaces the classic DR function, so you can't use both functions together. It's either the one or the other. Setting DR-P to anything but OFF automatically overrides and cancels your DR settings.

The AUTO, WEAK, and STRONG options of DR-P correspond to the DR-Auto, DR200%, and DR400% settings of the DR function, while OFF relays control back to whatever regular DR settings you have selected. This also means that DR-P WEAK and DR-P STRONG have the same minimum ISO requirements as DR200% and DR400%.

So, what exactly is the difference between DR-P and DR? It's rather mundane: DR-P *combines* regular DR settings with different contrast settings into a package that can't be untied later. For example, DR-P WEAK combines DR200% with HIGHLIGHT TONE −1 and SHADOW TONE −1. Correspondingly, DR-P STRONG results in a combination of DR400%, HIGHLIGHT TONE −2, and SHADOW TONE −2.

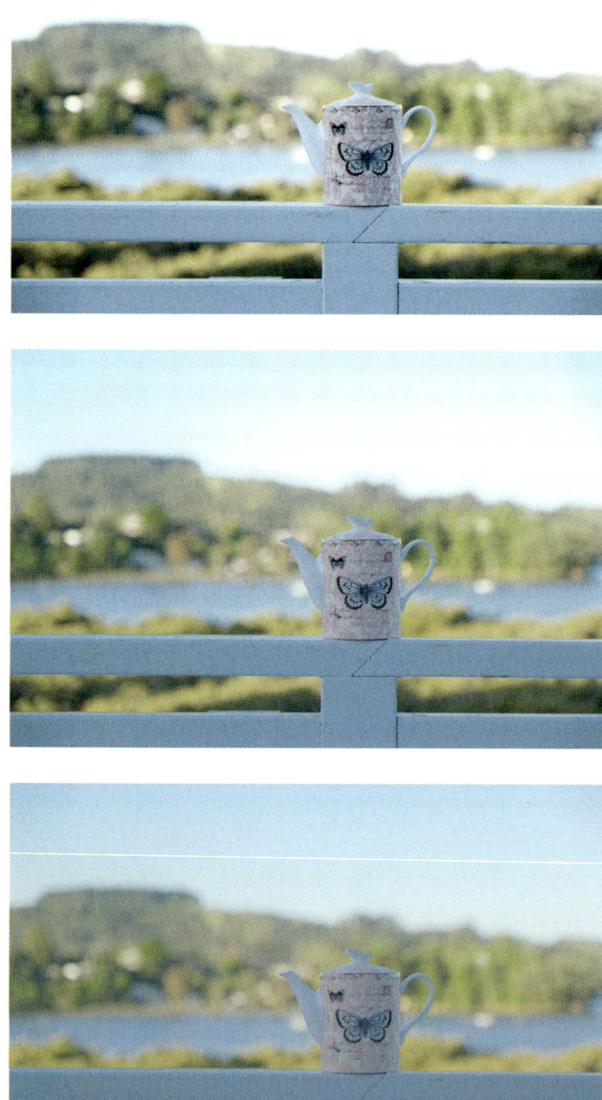

Fig. 73: This **Dynamic Range Priority** comparison shows JPEGs of the same high-contrast scene with DR-P OFF/DR100% (top), DR-P WEAK (center), and DR-P STRONG (bottom) settings.

If this sounds like a neat shortcut to you, you might want to reconsider. In fact, I do not recommend using DR-P at all, because it is blocking you from changing Highlight Tone and Shadow Tone settings independently from DR settings in the camera's built-in RAW converter.

For example, if you take a picture with DR-P STRONG and later find that HIGHLIGHT TONE –2 and SHADOW TONE –2 look too shallow for your taste, you can't use the built-in RAW converter to create a new JPEG with more contrast by adjusting Shadow Tone and Highlight Tone. You would have to live with your mistake for good.

A much better alternative is to stay in control. Set DR-P to OFF and, instead, apply DR, Highlight Tone, and Shadow Tone settings independently from one another. By doing so, you can always revisit your RAW files and create JPEGs with different contrast settings in your camera or with X RAW STUDIO.

<table>
<tr><td>Dual Conversion Gain and how to use it</td><td>TIP 64</td></tr>
</table>

We already know that your X-T3 uses a base ISO of 160. However, there's also what's called "dual conversion gain"—a second (higher) base ISO level. In our case, this additional base ISO level is automatically activated when you set ISO 800 (or higher) at DR100%.

Dual conversion gain (DCG) reconfigures the sensor for low-light use: read noise is further reduced, which means you can extract additional dynamic range in situations with very little light.

Normally, you wouldn't care about dual conversion gain, because the camera is performing everything automatically. There is no "on/off" switch or menu: simply set a minimum of ISO 800/DR100% (or ISO 1600/DR200%; or ISO 3200/DR400%) and dual conversion gain will be active.

You can make use of this second DCG ISO level in the same way you use base ISO 160 to extract as much dynamic range from high-contrast scenes as possible. However, in this case, we are talking about situations with very little light; scenes that one would usually expose with really high ISO settings such as 6400, 12800, or even 25600.

Instead of setting these high ISO values, you can just as well set the camera to ISO 800/DR100% (or to equivalent ISO-level settings of ISO 1600/DR200% or ISO 3200/DR400%) and shoot away, while protecting as many highlights as possible.

I will give you a practical example. During one of our Fuji X Secrets workshop, we organized an evening get-together in an ancient wine cellar that was illuminated by only a few candles. I shot several candid portraits of the attendees using manual mode **M** with fixed settings of ISO 800, f/2.8 (wide-open), and 1/20 s (my slowest usable shutter speed for handheld shooting of living subjects). In order to see the image I was composing, I turned *off* the exposure preview in manual mode.

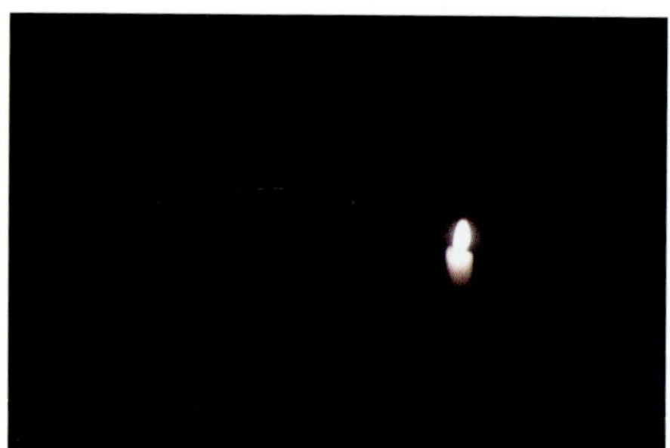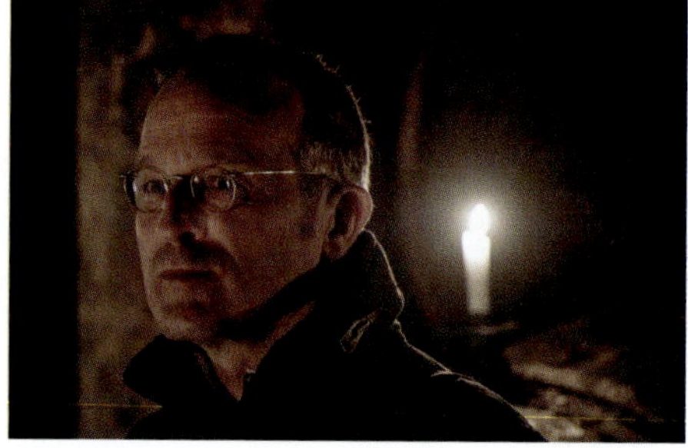

Fig. 74: This **dual conversion gain** example shows a low-light shot as it was taken with at 55 mm focal length, f/2.8, 1/20 s, and ISO 800/DR100% (the camera's additional "dual gain conversion" base ISO level). The unprocessed result on the left looks really, really dark. The only part that is clearly visible is one of the few candles that were lighting the scene.

On the right, you can see the same image after processing the RAW file in Lightroom Classic. Pushing the brightness of the face up from ISO 800 resulted in equivalents of at least ISO 12800, while the already-bright parts of the candle remained at ISO 800 to protect as much of its texture and tones as possible. It's the usual tone mapping procedure, and it gives you a glimpse of the dynamic range reserves available in Fuji's X cameras. You just have to be bold enough to unleash them.

Dual conversion gain results in a noise advantage of approximately 1/3 to 2/3 EV. This doesn't sound like much (and it really isn't, in normal situations), but it can be essential in situations where you have to push shadows up 4 or 5 stops during RAW processing (or when you need to take images at very high ISO levels like 12800 and above).

<table><tr><td>Creating HDR images with the X-T3</td><td>TIP 65</td></tr></table>

A popular method of capturing high-contrast scenes is HDR photography. HDR [56] means High Dynamic Range: multiple images of a scene are taken at various exposure levels and then they are merged into a single image with extended dynamic range. The merging process can be facilitated with specialized software, such as Photomatix Pro by HDRsoft.

Typically, HDR requires a minimum of two different exposures of a scene, but some photographers don't stop there. They take five, seven, or even nine different exposures, each separated from the other by (usually) one stop or 1 EV (exposure value).

Here's a procedure that you can use to quickly generate nine different exposures of a single scene:

- Put the camera on a tripod or a similar device.

- Connect a remote shutter release or set the self-timer to 2 seconds to avoid camera shake.

- Set the camera to aperture priority **A**, select BKT on the DRIVE dial and make sure that AE BKT is set in SHOOTING MENU > SHOOTING SETTING > DRIVE SETTING > BKT SETTING > BKT SELECT.

- Choose a low ISO setting (such as base ISO 160). Don't use extended ISO L, though!

- Deactivate any DR expansion by setting the dynamic range to DR100%.

- Select a suitable aperture for your shot and scene, and use manual focus. If you like, you can also use adapted manual focus lenses.

- Set AE BKT (auto exposure bracketing) to nine shots with a variation of ±1 EV (SHOOTING MENU > SHOOTING SETTING > DRIVE SETTING > BKT SETTING > AE BKT > FRAMES STEP SETTING).

- Select AVERAGE exposure metering.

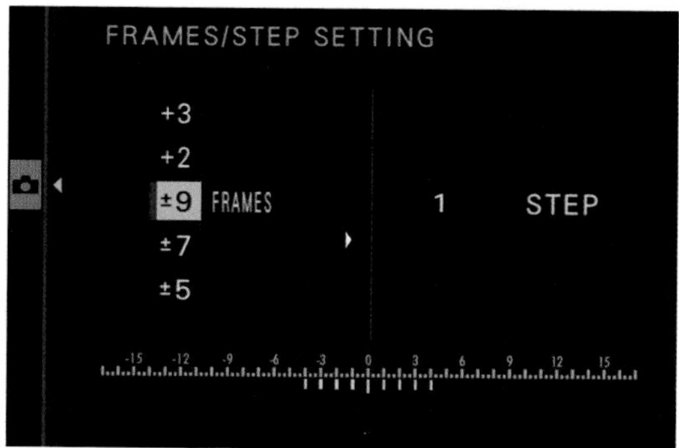


Fig. 75: In this FRAMES/STEP SETTING screen, AE BKT has already been set up to take nine images with a step of 1 EV. The images will cover exposures ranging from −4 EV to +4 EV.

Having prepared the camera for HDR, you can now capture the actual images:

- Set the exposure compensation dial to neutral (0), manually focus the scene and press the shutter release. Make sure to either use a remote shutter release or the self-timer. The camera will now record nine images ranging from −4 EV to +4 EV.

This procedure results in nine different exposures that you can merge using the HDR software of your choice. The resulting image will have an additional dynamic range of ±4 EV.

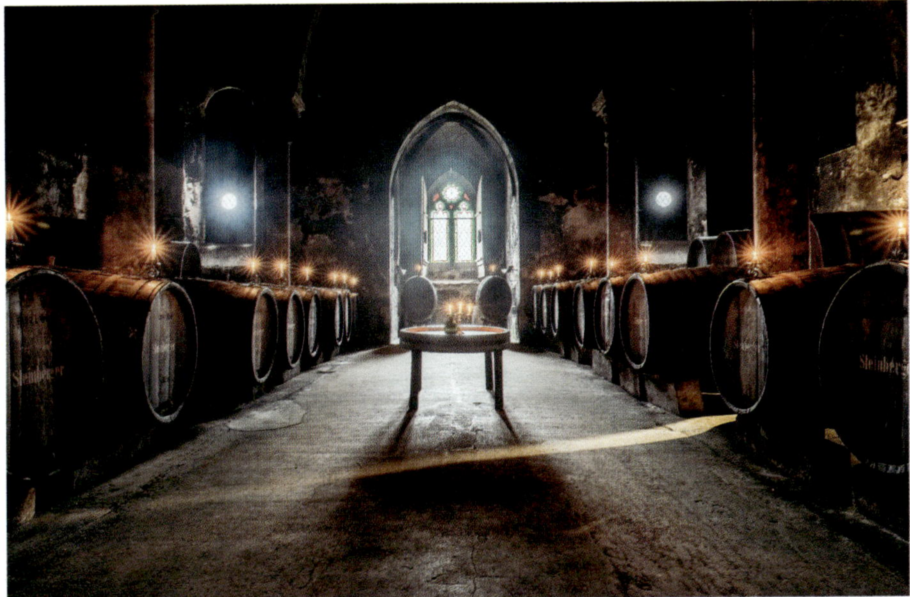

Fig. 76: This rather extreme **HDR image** consists of seven RAW shots, each taken with an exposure difference of 2 EV and merged in Lightroom Classic.

| HDR: the handheld way | TIP 66 |
| --- | --- |

Thanks to the ISO-less sensor in the X-T3, you can effectively take handheld HDR shots by combining two vastly differently exposed RAW files into one HDR-DNG file in Lightroom or Adobe Camera RAW.

Let's start with how to prepare the camera for this endeavor:

- Set the X-T3 to aperture priority **A**, select BKT on the DRIVE dial and make sure that AE BKT is set in SHOOTING MENU > SHOOTING SETTING > DRIVE SETTING > BKT SETTING > BKT SELECT.

- Select a low ISO setting, such as ISO 160. Don't set extended ISO L.

- Make sure the dynamic range is set to DR100%.

- Pre-select a suitable aperture.

- Set AE BKT with a variation of +3 FRAMES and a 2 STEP in the SHOOTING MENU > SHOOTING SETTING > DRIVE SETTING > BKT SETTING > AE BKT > FRAME/STEP SETTING menu.

- Use the "JPEG settings for RAW shooters" setup: film simulation ETERNA, SHADOW TONE −2 and HIGHLIGHT TONE −2.

Now let's take our HDR shots:

- Expose to the highlights! Using the live view and live histogram, frame your scene, and turn the exposure compensation dial until critical highlights aren't blown.

- Focus and press the shutter button to take the shot, and don't recompose the scene while doing so. Hold the camera very steady while it takes a quick burst of three consecutive AE bracketing shots (each with a different exposure).

- Import the RAW files of the three bracketed shots into Lightroom or Adobe Camera RAW, where you can merge them into a single HDR-DNG file using the HDR function. You can then process the HDR-DNG file in Lightroom like any normal RAW file.

By combining three shots with an exposure difference of 2 EV between each, we dramatically enhance the overall dynamic range of the image. Since the shots were taken in a quick burst with maximum continuous drive speed, there's also little or no motion blur in the resulting DNG composite image. This trick can even work for (slowly) moving subjects, especially since Lightroom's HDR merge tool includes automatic deghosting.

The darkest of the three shots is perfectly exposed to the highlights, while the other two exposures bring 2 EV and 4 EV less noise to the table. Since our ISO-less sensor provides very little sensor read noise, we can easily push the brightest of the three RAWs up another 3 EV without sacrificing too much image quality. This adds up to a whopping 7 EV of *additional* dynamic range, which should be enough to overcome almost every dynamic range challenge you may encounter in your photographic life. Even better, you can use this process for handheld shots—just make sure the shutter speed of the brightest shot is still fast enough to prevent blur caused by camera shake.

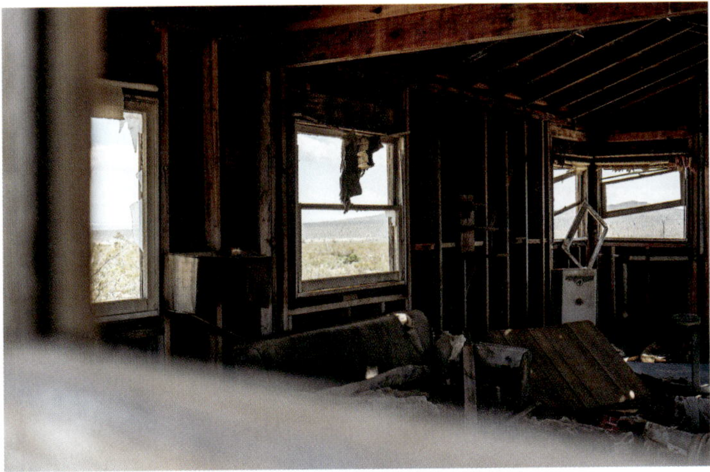

Fig. 77: This **handheld HDR** consists of the original "exposed-to-the-highlights" image, plus two additional shots that were exposed 2 EV and 4 EV brighter. Lightroom was used to merge the RAW files into a single HDR-DNG file. The result looks clean and noiseless in the shadows, with plenty of fine texture and no tonal gaps.

| Electronic shutter (ES), electronic first curtain shutter (EFCS) and flicker reduction | TIP 67 |
| --- | --- |

The electronic shutter (ES) offers three advantages: it is completely silent, it eliminates vibrations from shutter shock, and it allows shutter speeds as fast as 1/32000 s. That's great in situations where you want to be particularly stealthy, or when you want to use fast lenses (like the XF56mmF1.2 R)

with a wide-open aperture in bright light and spare yourself the hassle of attaching an ND filter.

You can set which shutter type the camera is supposed to
use in SHOOTING MENU > SHOOTING SETTING > SHUTTER
TYPE. There are six available options:

- **MS:** The camera is using only the mechanical shutter.
  This is the default setting and also my recommended
  standard setting.

- **ES:** This setting switches the camera to the electronic
  shutter with shutter speeds up to 1/32000 s. Extended ISO
  settings aren't available in ES mode, and you cannot fire
  a flash when the ES is in use.

- **EF:** This switches the X-T3 to electronic front curtain shutter (EFCS). The EFCS combines some advantages of the ES
  with some benefits of the MS: it reduces vibration and
  eliminates shutter shock by replacing the mechanical
  first shutter curtain with an electronic version. However,
  the second shutter curtain remains mechanical, thus
  avoiding issues caused by electronic rolling shutter.

- **M+E:** In this mode, the camera combines the mechanical
  (MS) and the electronic shutter (ES). It will automatically
  switch to ES for shutter speeds faster than the maximum
  mechanical shutter speed of 1/8000 s. Flash photography
  is possible, but only within the envelope of the mechanical shutter.

- **EF+M:** This mode combines the electronic first curtain
  shutter (EFCS) with the mechanical shutter (MS). The X-T3
  will generally use the EFCS, but for shutter speed faster
  than 1/2000 s, it will switch to the MS. This helps avoiding
  bokeh quality issues that occur with the EFCS at very fast
  shutter speeds.

- **EF+M+E:** This setting combines the electronic first curtain shutter (EFCS) with the mechanical shutter (MS) and
  the electronic shutter (ES). The X-T3 will generally use

the EFCS, but for shutter speed faster than 1/2000 s, it will switch to the MS. Furthermore, it will automatically switch to ES for shutter speeds faster than the maximum mechanical shutter speed of 1/8000 s. Flash photography is possible, but only within the envelope of the mechanical shutter.

To access shutter speeds beyond the camera's mechanical limit, you can set the shutter-speed dial to **T** and then browse through all available shutter speeds with the command dial in 1/3 EV steps.

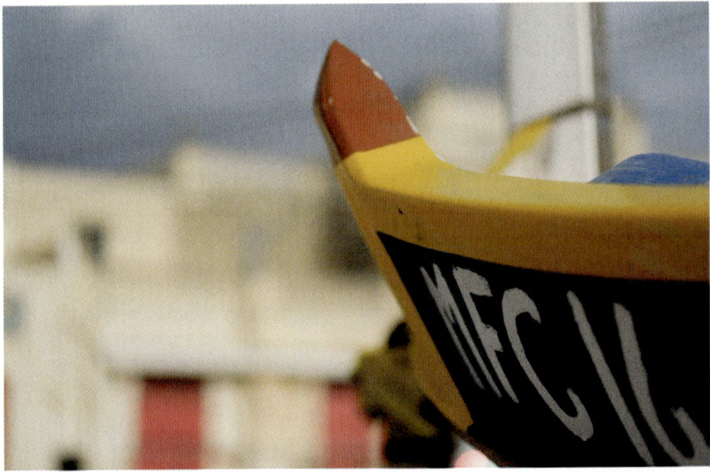


Fig. 78: The **electronic shutter** is a practical option for shots taken with fast lenses in bright light, when the maximum mechanical shutter speed simply isn't fast enough to avoid overexposure.

Please note that even at 1/32000 s, the electronic shutter needs some time (typically between 1/20 s and 1/30 s) to capture all image contents. This effect, known as *rolling shutter* [57], can lead to weird distortions when you are taking pictures of fast-moving subjects. In addition, image quality will deteriorate when the ES is used in concert with pulsing or flickering artificial light sources. The long readout time and the rolling shutter are also responsible for the restrictions regarding flash photography.

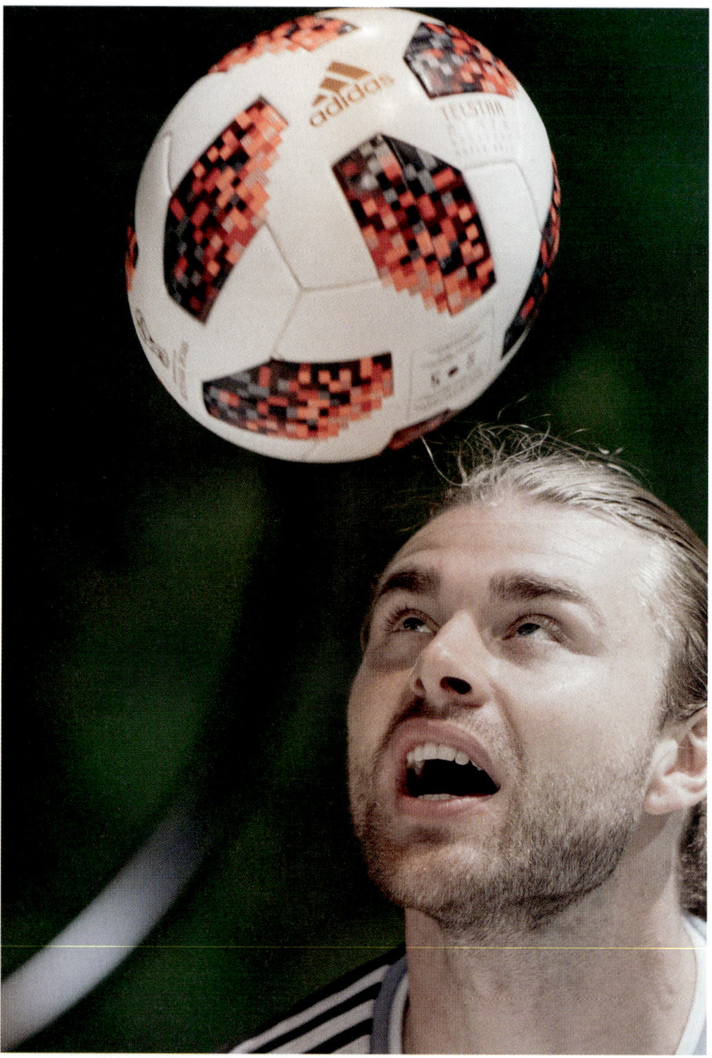

Fig. 79:  The **distortion effect** of electronic rolling shutters becomes quite visible in scenes with fast-moving subjects like this football.

The **electronic first curtain shutter (EFCS)** combines some advantages of the ES with some benefits of the MS: it reduces vibration and eliminates shutter shock by replacing the mechanical first shutter curtain with an electronic version. However, the second shutter curtain remains mechanical, thus avoiding issues caused by electronic rolling shutter. The EFCS also reduces the blackout period in the EVF and emits a subtler mechanical shutter noise.

With very fast shutter speeds, using the EFCS can potentially be detrimental to image quality (especially the bokeh). That's why there's also the EF+M setting that automatically switches back to the MS when the shutter speed exceeds 1/2000 s. Personally, I use EF+M as my default setting, manually switching to ES only when it's needed.

Please note that in the X-T3, shutter type must be set to ES (not M+E or EF+M+E) to be able to access the camera's blackout-free high-speed burst modes of 20 fps (without image crop) and 10/20/30 fps (with an image crop of 1.25x). Despite the high nominal speed of these burst modes, rolling shutter distortion and image striping due to pulsing artificial light may be an issue, so please be careful with the ES setting when you are shooting fast action, panning the camera, or shooting under artificial light.

You may wonder: Is it safe to use the mechanical shutter or electronic first curtain shutter in situations with pulsing artificial light? The answer is yes *and* no. Because pulsing light sources have the nasty habit of continuously going on and off, the scene (your subject) is illuminated with varying amounts of light that fluctuate 50 or 60 times per second along with the phase frequency of the electric AC grid. Even in manual exposure mode **M**, shooting the same scene multiple times with exactly the same exposure settings can result in inconsistently exposed images, depending on your shutter speed and how lucky you are to randomly catch a brighter or a darker portion of the pulsating light.

While this flicker phenomenon is invisible to the human eye, your camera will be affected by it as soon as you select faster shutter speeds. In such cases, the camera can record only a random portion of the light's pulsating on/off cycle.

This is where **flicker reduction** comes into play. You can find it under SHOOTING MENU > SHOOTING SETTING > FLICKER REDUCTION.

When you take a shot, flicker reduction [58] forces your camera's exposure to coincide with cyclic peaks of the AC current phase. In other words, shots are delayed until the pulsating light happens to illuminate the scene with maximum brightness. With flicker reduction, your series of exposures will look bright and uniform.

In a world of pulsing energy-saving light sources, flicker reduction is an essential feature. However, make sure to use it only in situations that actually require its magic. In natural daylight (or artificial light that doesn't pulse), flicker reduction is not only useless; it will also slow down your camera.

With firmware 3.00 and later, the X-T3 offers two options for flicker reduction: FIRST FRAME and ALL FRAMES. ALL FRAMES corresponds to the regular FLICKER REDUCTION ON setting in other X camera models, meaning the camera is synchronized with the mains frequency before every single shot it takes, even during high-speed bursts that will inevitably be slowed down because of this. On the other hand, FIRST FRAME only performs this analysis before the first shot of a burst.

## 2.4 FOCUSING WITH THE X-T3

The X-T3 features a hybrid autofocus system that combines CDAF and PDAF. CDAF, PDAF, and hybrid AF? It can be quite confusing.

- **CDAF** means **C**ontrast **D**etection **A**uto**F**ocus and is a standard in mirrorless cameras. CDAF is available throughout the entire sensor area (117 or 425 AF frames in Single Point mode or 117 AF frames in Zone and Wide/Tracking mode). It works quite precisely but is not particularly fast.

- **PDAF** means **P**hase **D**etection **A**uto**F**ocus and is the standard AF in DSLRs. Since the X-T3 is mirrorless, its PDAF works directly on the sensor and covers its entire area. PDAF is pretty fast and particularly good at tracking moving subjects. It can predict where a moving object will be a split second from now, a feature that can be quite useful when you shoot in burst mode.

- **Hybrid AF** means that the X-T3 automatically chooses and combines available AF methods (CDAF or PDAF) for the current subject and the current light conditions.

| CDAF and PDAF: what's the difference? | TIP 68 |
| --- | --- |

Both AF methods offer distinct qualities that can be useful during your daily shooting:

- CDAF focuses on surfaces and works best with areas that offer a lot of contrast. CDAF doesn't work well for a solid white or black wall, but for a checkered wall, it works great. It's the same with clothing: solid colors may be tough, but patterned clothes work wonderfully. CDAF operates with a trial-and-error approach: it keeps adjusting the focus until it finds the distance setting with the utmost contrast. CDAF doesn't directly go to the optimal focus setting. This result is heightened autofocus motor activity and visible focus hunting while the AF iterates back and forth until it finds the optimal focus position.

- PDAF loves focusing on edges, especially vertical edges (or horizontal ones if you hold the camera upright). Unlike CDAF, PDAF can directly determine the distance to an object, so there's no need for focus hunting. This is why PDAF is considerably faster.

- Both methods depend on sufficient light to work with maximum efficiency. The brighter a scene is and the more contrast it has, the better the AF will work. Bright lenses with large maximum aperture openings are beneficial because they allow the AF to work with more light and less depth of field, which helps increase the precision of the autofocus. It's worth noting that most lenses are less bright near the edges than they are at the center (this effect is called vignetting), so in poor light, the autofocus may work less efficiently with focus frames that are located far off center.

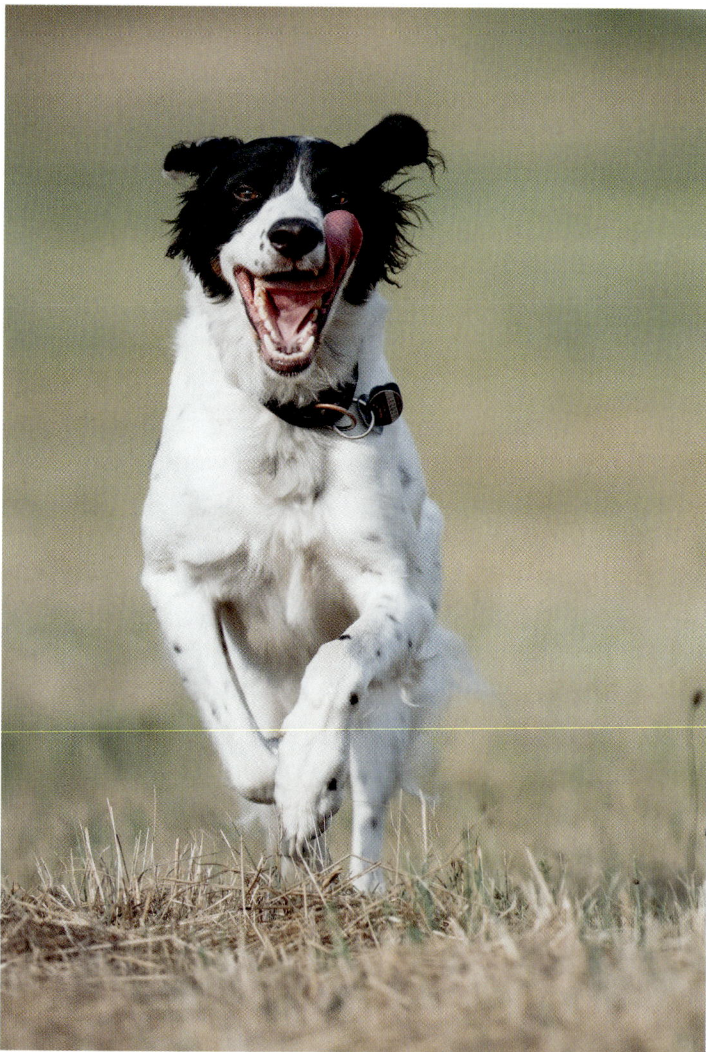

Fig. 80: Tracking fast-moving subjects like this running dog is a job for the **phase detection autofocus** (PDAF).

<table><tr><td>AF-S or AF-C?</td><td>TIP 69</td></tr></table>

Your X-T3 features two basic AF modes that can be selected with the focus selector at the front of the camera:

- **AF-S (AF Single) is meant for stationary subjects.** Once you half-press the shutter button, the camera will focus on the object covered by the active AF frame and lock the distance (as long as you keep the shutter button half-pressed). You can either fully press the shutter button to take the shot, or you can take your finger off the shutter release and try again.

- **AF-C (AF Continuous) is meant for moving subjects,** especially those that move toward or away from the camera. When you half-press the shutter button, the camera starts focusing on the object covered by the active AF frame and continuously adjusts the distance to the moving object while you keep the shutter button half-pressed.

While AF-C focuses using the set working aperture, AF-S can open the aperture beyond the working aperture to improve the AF performance in poor light. This also improves the focusing accuracy due to the reduced depth of field caused by the wide-open aperture.

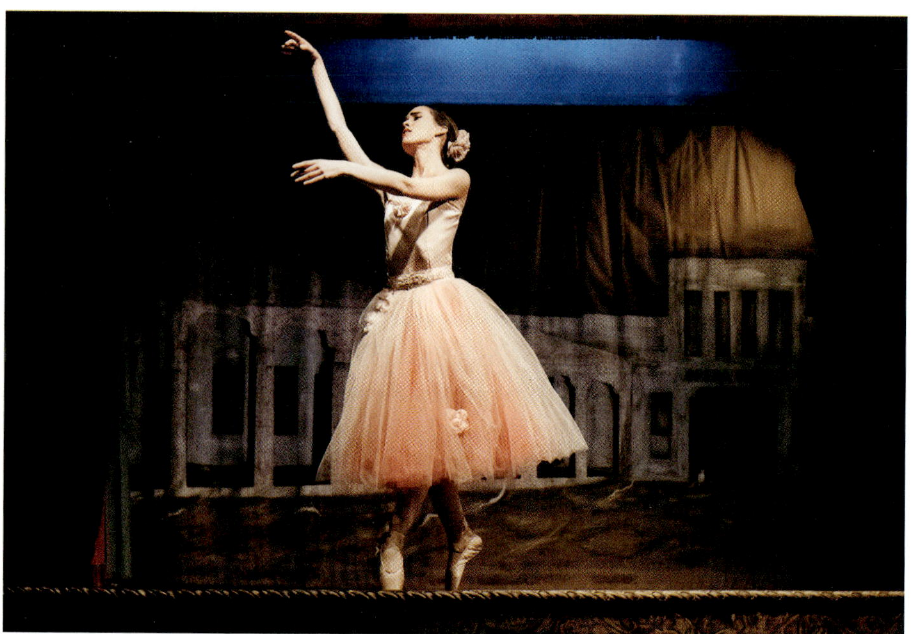

Fig. 81:  When shooting with **AF-C in poor light,** it helps to keep the aperture wide open.

| TIP 70 | Single Point AF vs. Zone AF vs. Wide/Tracking AF |

SHOOTING MENU > AF/MF SETTING > AF MODE lets you choose between SINGLE POINT, ZONE, or WIDE/TRACKING autofocus. The X-T3 also offer an ALL option, which lets you seamlessly select one of the three AF modes simply by changing the size of the focus frame or zone.

■ **Single Point AF** mode is my recommended AF setting for most applications. In this mode, you can manually select one of up to 425 available focus frames. Try to avoid old habits like using only the center frame in concert with the focus-and-recompose [59] technique. It's better to compose the shot and *then* select a suitable AF frame that covers the part of the image you want to be in perfect focus. This helps you avoid focus errors that invariably occur when you pan the focus plane. Such focus errors may be irrelevant with long focal lengths and small aperture openings (larger depth of field), but focus errors can be quite unpleasant with wide-angle lenses, a wide aperture opening (small DOF), and in situations with a short distance between the camera and the subject. Single Point AF can be used in concert with both AF-S and AF-C.

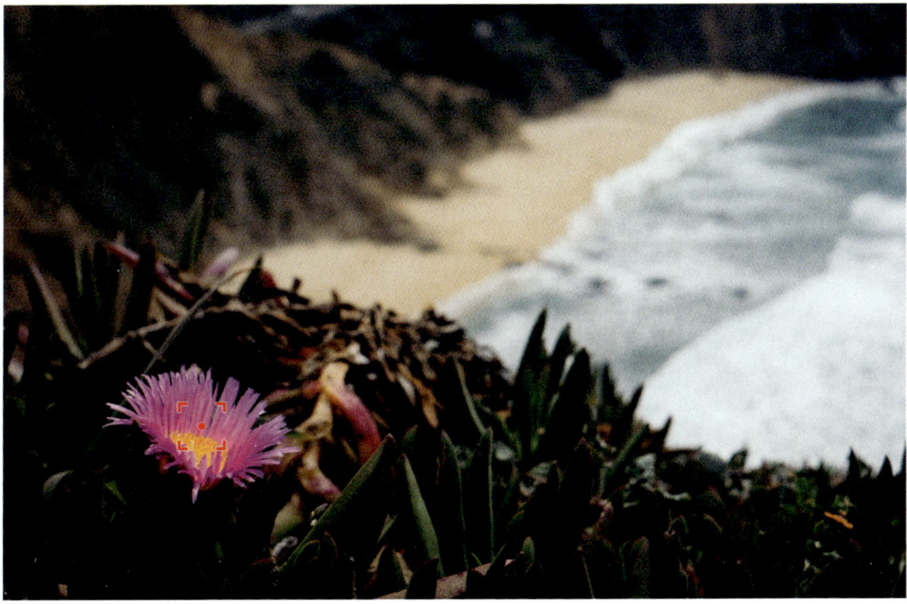

Fig. 82: Shooting with **minimal depth of field,** you can't afford to use a focus-and-recompose habit because it would quickly lead to soft results that appear out of focus. Instead, compose the shot, and then focus using a single focus frame that covers the part of the image that is supposed to be in focus.

■ You can think of **Zone AF** as an extension of Single Point AF. Basically, an AF zone is a particularly large AF frame that consists of a matrix of smaller AF points. Zones are available in sizes that cover 3 × 3, 5 × 5, or 7 × 7 out of a total of 117 AF points. Like Single Point AF frames, AF zones can be moved around within the image area. Since they are larger than focus frames, AF zones make it easier to focus on moving subjects. In Zone AF mode, the camera will usually start looking for something to focus on in the center (crosshairs) of the selected zone and will then expand its search toward the edges of the zone until it finds a target. Like Single Point AF, Zone AF works in concert with either AF-S or AF-C.

■ When you combine **Wide/Tracking AF** mode with **AF-S,** the camera scans the entire image frame and automatically selects several focus frames. It's a bit like rolling dice, since the camera is simply looking for areas it can easily focus on. It doesn't know what's important in a scene. This changes when Wide/Tracking is used in concert with **AF-C:** this combination offers real 3D tracking of moving objects; that is, objects that not only move toward or away from the camera, but also left, right, up, and down within the image frame. To track such an object, select Wide/Tracking and AF-C and pick one of the available AF points. To start the tracking process, make sure the selected point covers the moving object you want to track. Half-press the shutter button to start the tracking process. While you keep the shutter button half-pressed, the camera will automatically follow the selected subject with a cloud of small AF frames as it moves across the image area.

Please note that Fujifilm has released the *Auto Focus System Special Site* [60], which details the autofocus modes and mode combinations that come with popular X series cameras.

| TIP 71 | Selecting an AF frame or AF zone |
|---|---|

The X-T3 offers an indirect and a direct method for selecting one of its 117 or 425 available AF frames in Single Point AF and for moving an AF zone around in Zone AF:

- The *indirect* method requires you to *first* press the AF button and *then* use the selector buttons to pick an AF frame or move an AF zone. For this method, the X-T3 requires you to assign the AF button function to an Fn button. After you have done so, press it to open the FOCUS AREA screen, where you can change the sizes and positions of the focus frames and AF zones.

- The *direct* method involves either using the touchscreen or the focus stick. Make sure the touchscreen-AF interface is set to AREA mode, and then tap anywhere on the screen to select an AF area or zone. You can use the focus stick like a joystick to move the focus frame or AF zone. Press the focus stick to open the FOCUS AREA screen, where you can change the sizes and positions of focus frames and AF zones.

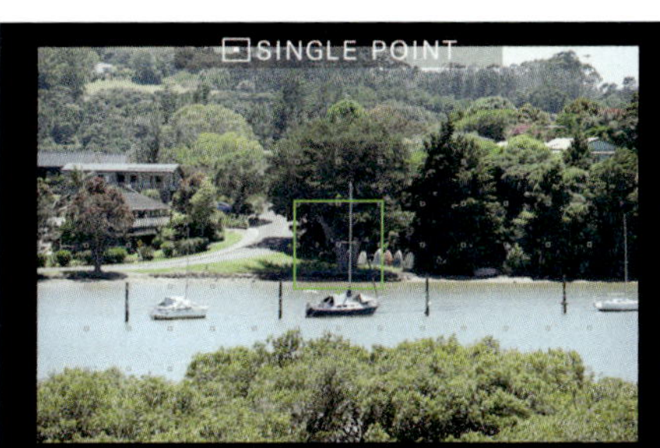


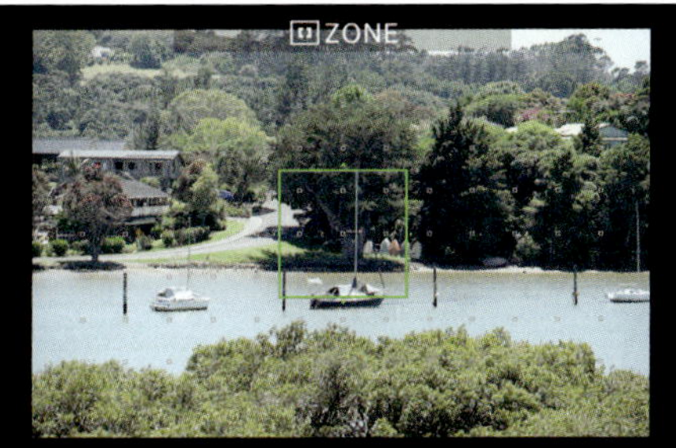


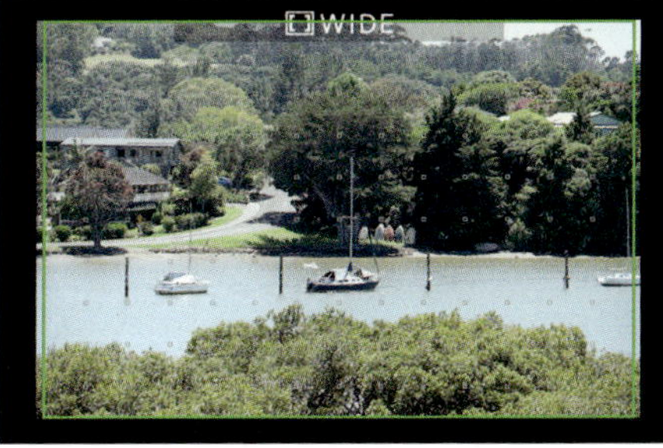


Fig. 83: Pressing the designated AF button or the focus stick opens the **FOCUS AREA screen**, where you can select a focus frame or AF Zone and change their sizes. Using the convenient AF mode ALL, changing the size cycles through AF modes Single Point AF, Zone AF, and Wide/Tracking AF.

**TIP 72**  Choosing a suitable AF frame or AF zone size

The X-T3 offers 117 or 425 different AF frames in Single Point AF, and each frame comes in six sizes. You can change the size of an AF frame by pressing the AF button (or the focus stick) and turning one of the command dials left or right to decrease or increase the frame size.

AF frame size affects the efficiency of CDAF and PDAF. A basic rule to follow is: *Make your AF frame as large as possible and as small as necessary.*

This is why:

- With a large AF frame size, the camera has more to work with and a better chance to find contrast in a target, especially when the light conditions aren't optimal. There's also a better chance the camera will be able to use the faster PDAF method. When PDAF isn't possible, the camera will fall back to the slower CDAF.

- With a smaller AF frame size, the autofocus becomes more accurate. A small AF frame gives you better control over *exactly* what the camera is focusing on. Avoid AF frame sizes that are larger than the part of your image that needs to be in focus. For example, if your AF frame is larger than the head of the person you are focusing on, there's a chance that the camera will instead focus on the background behind them, especially if that background contains a lot of contrast.

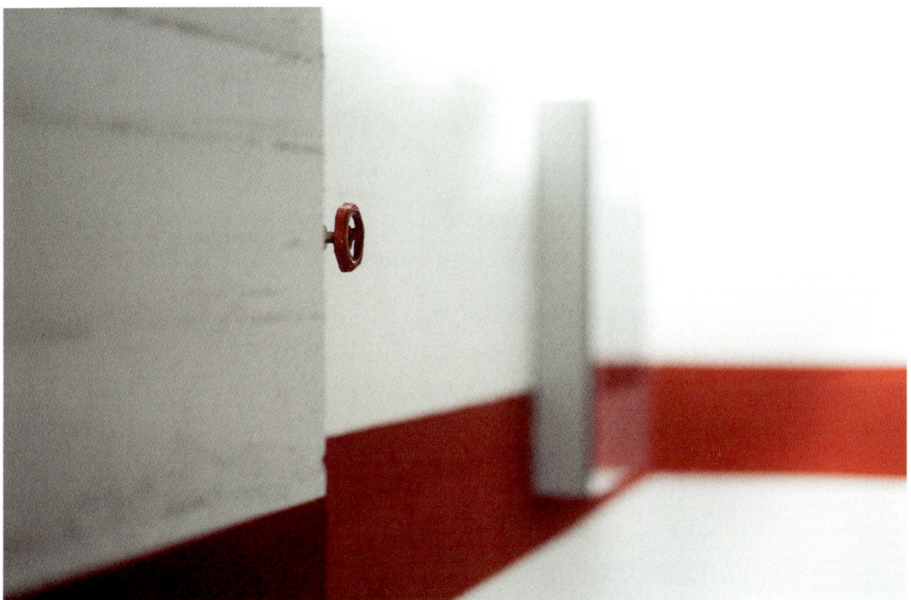

Fig. 84: To get tiny parts of an image in perfect focus, it's best to choose a **small AF frame size**.

In a similar fashion, you can change the size of AF zones by pressing the focus stick or designated AF button and then turning the command dial left or right. You have a choice of three AF zone sizes: 3 × 3 (default), 5 × 5, or 7 × 7 out of 117 frames.

Since we can regard AF zones as very large AF frames, the same rules apply: larger zones are more convenient, and they potentially offer a faster AF response, but they are also potentially less accurate than smaller zones.

| | |
|---|---|
| Manual focus and DOF zone focusing | TIP 73 |

Manual focus (MF) mode offers several focus aids:

- A magnification tool with several magnification levels.

- Focus peaking (Focus Peak Highlight) with two strength levels and optional colors.

- Digital split image.

- Digital microprism.

- An electronic distance scale with depth-of-field indicators.

- Instant AF: autofocus in MF mode that is triggered by pressing the AF-L button in manual focus mode.

The electronic distance scale can help you define a focus zone with a predetermined depth of field (DOF). The X-T3 offers two DOF scales: a *pixel-based* scale (recommended) and a *film-format based* scale (not recommended). If you opt for PIXEL BASE in SHOOTING MENU > AF/MF SETTING > DEPTH-OF-FIELD SCALE, everything inside the DOF zone will look pixel-sharp even when the image is magnified to a 100% view. Please don't confuse manual zone focusing with Zone AF—they are completely different things.

Here's a zone-focusing example using an 18 mm lens manually set a distance of 5 m and stop down to f/8. The DOF bars will show a depth-of-field zone that begins at around 4 m and ends at around 10 m. This means everything located within this zone (between 4 and 10 m) will appear equally in-focus in the final image. All you have to do is make sure your subject is within that zone when you press the shutter button.

A special case of manual zone focusing is when setting the hyperfocal distance [61]. This is the distance setting with the maximum DOF (all the way to infinity). Again, the electronic DOF scale can be very helpful: all you have to do is manually set the distance where the blue DOF bar on the right touches the infinity mark. For example, using an 18 mm lens at f/16 on, the hyperfocal distance is located at approximately 6 m, with the pixel-sharp DOF zone extending from 3 m to infinity.

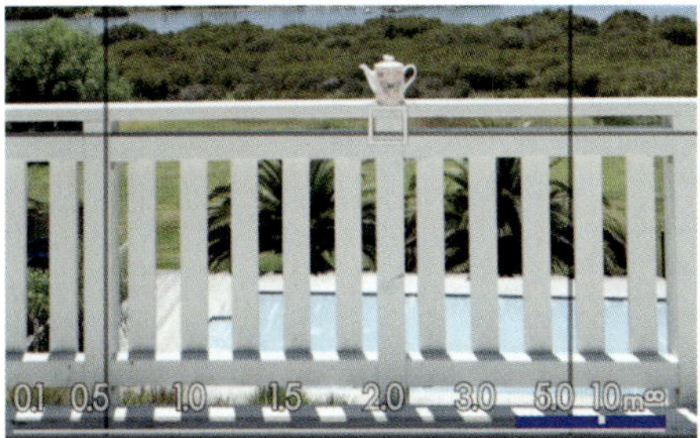
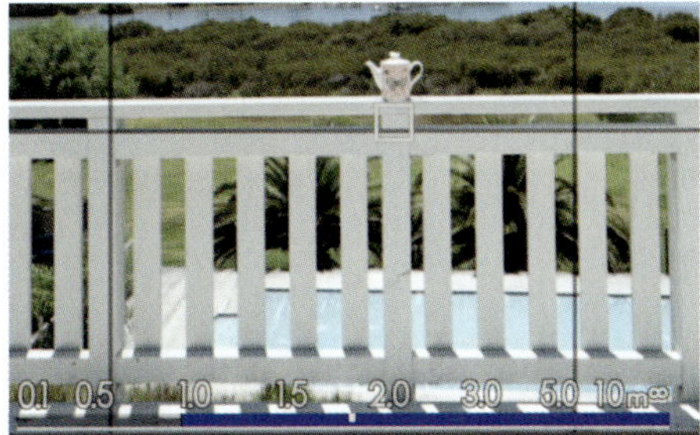

Fig. 85: Setting the **hyperfocal distance** with the electronic distance and DOF scale: instead of focusing on a predetermined distance, manually change the focus distance until the DOF bar touches the ∞ mark on the right end of the scale. This gives you the hyperfocal distance for a given aperture and focal length. This illustration shows the hyperfocal distance of a wide-angle lens (12 mm) at f/5.6 for both the PIXEL BASIS format (left) and FILM FORMAT BASIS format (right).

Please note that depth of field is very much dependent on the circle of confusion (CoC) [62]. Fujifilm uses a very conservative CoC that guarantees pixel-sharp results even when the DOF zone is viewed at 100% magnification on a computer screen. Fuji is literally using the sensor's physical resolution as a benchmark. In PIXEL BASIS mode, everything that's located inside the electronic DOF zone will be rendered as sharp as the sensor can resolve it. In the age of pixel peeping, this is as good as it can get.

It's important to know that the engraved analog distance and DOF scales on the XF14mmF2.8, XF16mmF1.4, and XF23mmF1.4 lenses follow a different rule: the FILM FORMAT BASIS option. They are based on a much less conservative circle of confusion that is several aperture stops more generous than the electronic PIXEL BASIS scale. You can change the electronic scale to FILM FORMAT BASIS (and hence use a less conservative scale with all your lenses) in SHOOTING MENU > AF/MF SETTING > DEPTH-OF-FIELD SCALE. However, I want to reiterate that I do not recommend this setting. Instead, I recommend using the PIXEL BASIS scale.

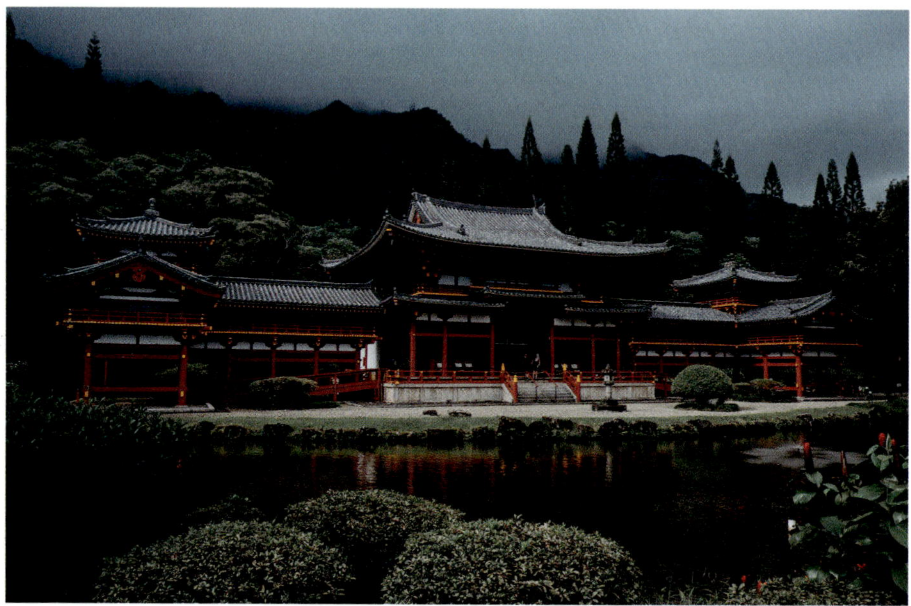

**Fig. 86:** This shot was manually focused by setting the **hyperfocal distance** for 18 mm and f/9 on the camera's electronic PIXEL BASIS focus distance scale.

| TIP 74 | Manual focus assistants |
| --- | --- |

The X-T3 features several MF assistants:

- **Focus Peaking** (or Focus Peak Highlight) emphasizes the edges of objects when they are in focus. This method is especially useful in concert with longer focal lengths and bright lenses with a tiny DOF.

- **Digital Split Image** tries to simulate the split image indicator of manual focus SLRs. It works best with vertical lines (or horizontal lines when the camera is held in portrait orientation).

- **Digital Microprism** simulates a microprism that used to be popular in the manual-focus SLR days.

To quickly switch between the available MF assistants, press and hold the rear command dial for about a second while you are in MF mode.

You can watch a short video [63] demonstrating different manual focus assistants. There's also a video demonstrating the "real thing": actual analog split image and microprism focusing in an old Minolta SLR [64].

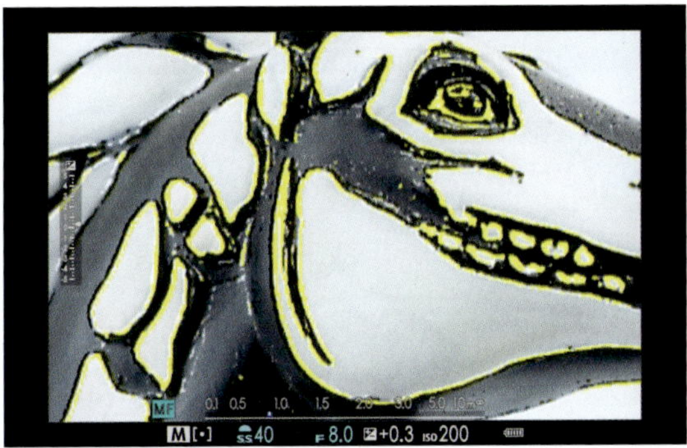

Fig. 87: **Focus peaking** is my favorite among the available manual focus aids. To make things even easier, it can be combined with the magnifier tool. In this example, I opted for yellow outlines to indicate the areas of the scene that are in focus.

| Using the Focus Check magnifier tool | TIP 75 |
| --- | --- |

The magnifier tool is helpful for checking if the current focus is spot-on. Press the rear command dial (either in AF-S/ Single Point AF or in MF mode) to magnify the area that is targeted by the selected focus frame. Of course, this assumes the rear command dial is operating with its default FOCUS CHECK Fn button assignment.

You can change the magnification level by turning the rear command dial. You can also combine focus check with any available MF assistants (focus peaking, digital split image, and digital microprism). Please note that in digital split image and digital microprism mode, only *one* magnification level is available.

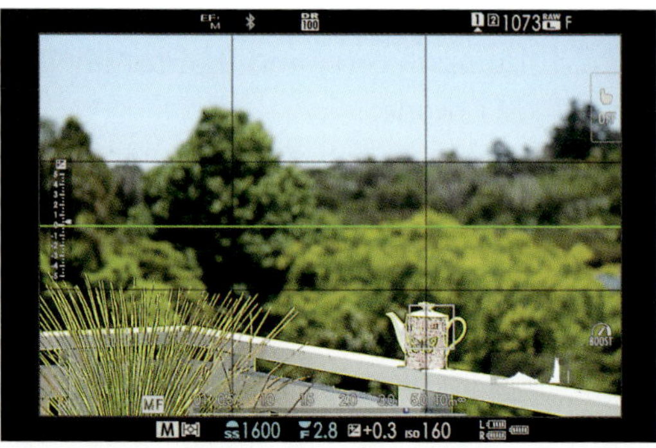

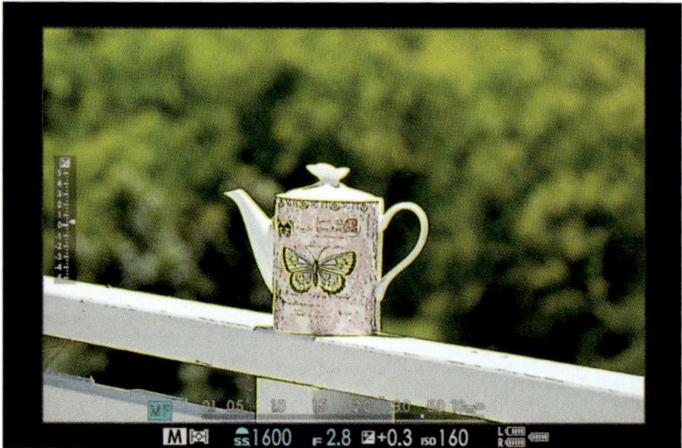

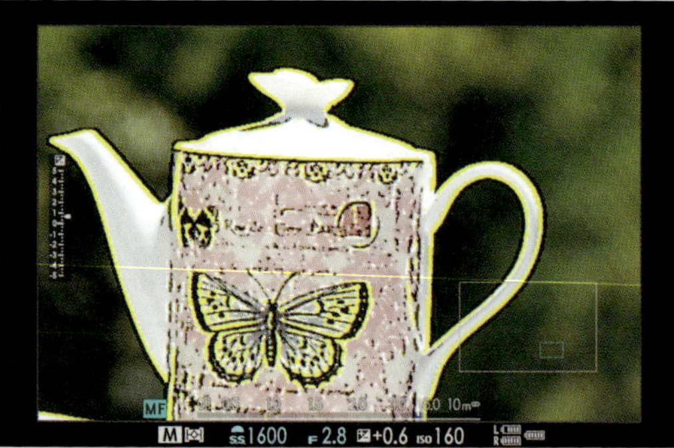

Fig. 88: The X-T3 offers two **magnification levels**. This illustration shows the full-image frame (left) as well as the lower (center) and higher (right) magnification levels of the Focus Check magnifier tool. To make things easier, the magnification was combined with focus peaking. You can also move the magnified area with the focus stick or touchscreen while Focus Check is zoomed into the frame.

By selecting SHOOTING MENU > AF/MF SETTING > FOCUS CHECK > ON, the magnifier tool is *automatically* activated when you turn the manual focus ring of a lens in MF mode. You can immediately cancel any automatic focus check by half-pressing the shutter button.

There are up to 425 different focus frames available in manual focus mode. The active frame indicates which part of the image will be magnified when focus check is activated. As usual, you can change the active frame by pressing the focus stick or designated AF button and then moving the focus frame around with the selector keys or focus stick.

Please note that Focus Check is not available in AF-C mode.

| Using Instant AF-S and Instant AF-C | TIP 76 |
| --- | --- |

Instant AF allows you to autofocus the X-T3 in manual focus mode by pressing the AF-L button. Instant AF always works with a wide-open aperture. Like the regular autofocus, its efficiency depends on the size of the selected focus frame.

Instant AF is the most precise AF method available, but it is a bit slower than the camera's normal autofocus. It can be combined with conventional manual focusing: you can use Instant AF to quickly autofocus on an object, and then manually fine-tune the focus by turning the focus ring and using MF assistants like the magnifier and focus peaking.

Sadly, this convenient method of fine-tuning Instant AF with manual focus is *not* available when you are using lenses with manual focus clutches (e.g., XF14mmF2.8, XF16mmF1.4, and XF23mmF1.4).

Instant AF normally functions like AF-S, but you can also set it to continuous focus with SHOOTING MENU > AF/MF SETTING > INSTANT AF SETTING > AF-C. In this mode, Instant AF will track the subject distance with AF-C as long as you keep the AF-L button pressed in manual focus mode.

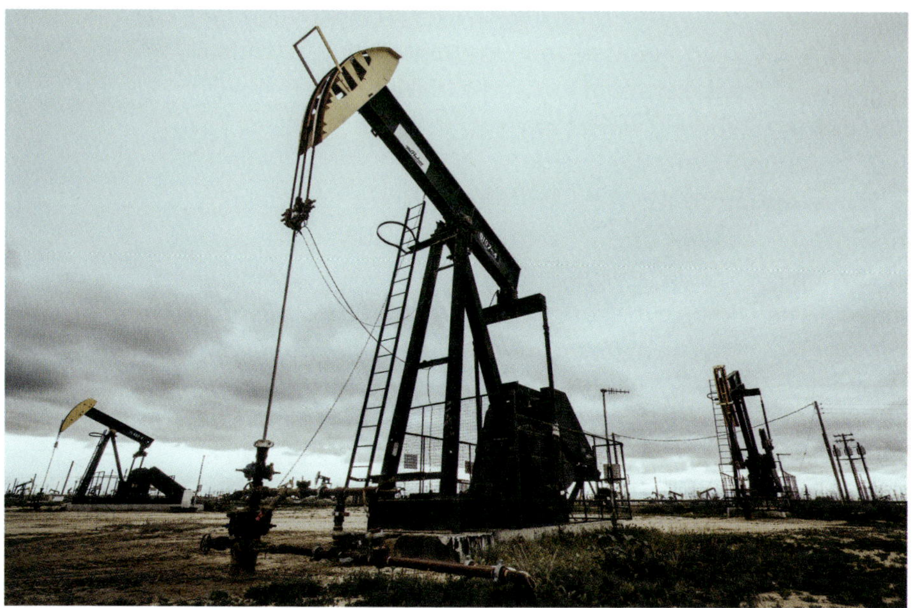

Fig. 89: **Instant AF** forces the lens to focus with a wide-open aperture. This AF method is particularly accurate when you shoot with a stopped down wide-angle lens.

Unlike normal AF-C (that focuses with the working aperture), Instant AF-C can focus with a wide-open aperture, making it an option for stage and concert photography with moving subjects in poor light, where you want to shoot with AF-C and a stopped-down lens. Just keep the AF-L button pressed for continuous instant autofocus as you press the shutter button at the right moment.

Note that Instant AF-C stops focusing as soon as you half-press the shutter button. To avoid unnecessary time lags between focusing and shutter release, it's best to first activate Instant AF-C by pressing and holding the AF-L button (or any other designated Instant AF button) to continually focus and then *fully press* the shutter button to take a shot.

<table><tr><td>Using AF+MF</td><td>TIP 77</td></tr></table>

AF+MF allows you to manually focus in AF mode by turning the focus ring, all while holding the shutter button half-pressed. Select SHOOTING MENU > AF/MF SETTING > AF+MF > ON to enable this feature. To use AF+MF, your camera needs to be in AF-S autofocus mode.

Here's how it works:

- Autofocus on your subject as usual in AF-S mode by half-pressing the shutter button.

- Once the autofocus has been confirmed (green square[s]) or not confirmed (red AF warning), keep the shutter button half-pressed and rotate the focus ring of your lens to *manually* adjust the focus distance until you are satisfied. If focus peaking is enabled, it will automatically engage as soon as the focus ring is rotated and manual focus (MF) kicks in. You can also use the Focus Check function (AF/MF SETTING > FOCUS CHECK > ON) to automatically magnify the focus area as soon as you turn the focus ring. For this to work, make sure that AF-S and Single Point AF are set. You can also combine Focus Check magnification with focus peaking. Turn the rear command dial to change the magnification factor and press the rear command dial to manually enable/disable the live view magnification. Remember that all this has to be performed while you hold the shutter button half-pressed, so this might require some practice.

- When you are happy with your manual focus adjustments, fully press the half-pressed shutter button to take the shot.

I see three main applications for AF+MF:

- **Manual focus in situations when autofocus fails:** Instead of losing time by changing the focus mode from AF to MF, you can immediately focus manually when the camera's

AF fails to acquire the subject. Simply adjust the focus manually using the focus ring.

- **Correcting the camera's autofocus:** There are instances when you might want to fine-tune the autofocus of your camera by adjusting it manually. Again, focus peaking is available to make things easier, and you can enable Focus Check to automatically show a magnified view of the focus area when you turn the focus ring.

- **Shifting the depth-of-field (DOF) zone or setting the hyperfocal distance:** After half-pressing the shutter button, AF+MF lets you quickly shift the DOF zone toward or away from the camera by turning the focus ring. The electronic distance scale on the screen can be quite helpful here. For example, you can set the hyperfocal distance [65] by shifting the right tip of the DOF bar to touch the infinity mark of the electronic distance scale.

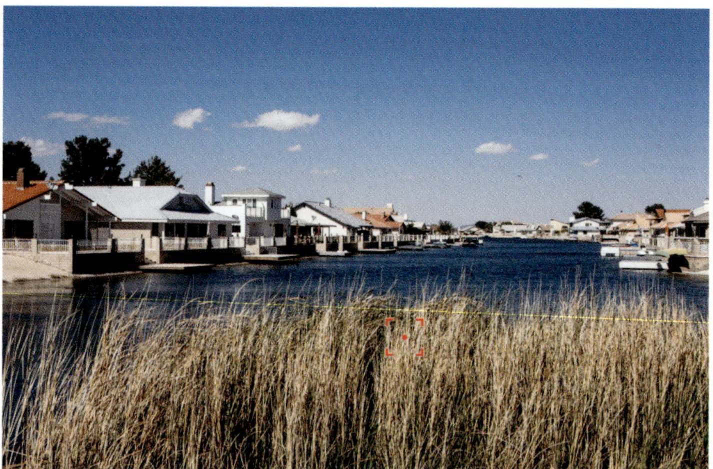

Fig. 90: In this example, I autofocused on the reeds by placing the AF frame right over them. I used a small aperture of f/9 for a decent amount of depth of field (DOF). Since the portion of the DOF zone that extends in front of the reeds toward the camera is useless in this case, I manually shifted the DOF zone away from the camera using **AF+MF**. The resulting DOF zone starts at the reeds and extends all the way back.

At first glance, the MF component of AF+MF may look like your regular manual focus, but it's not. While genuine MF is performed at a wide-open aperture, the MF part of AF+MF is performed at the selected working aperture. That's because the shutter button is half-pressed, so the camera has already been primed to take the shot with minimal shutter lag.

This also means the EVF/LCD will display a live view image that shows the actual depth of field of the resulting image, and focus peaking will show a larger zone as being in focus when you stop down the lens. This can make it more difficult to nail your manual focus adjustment.

AF+MF also works with clutch-type lenses such as the XF14mmF2.8, XF16mmF1.4, and XF23mmF1.4. These lenses feature a clutch to mechanically switch between MF and AF mode. Since the focus ring of these lenses can be turned only when the clutch is in the MF position, you need the following configuration to get AF+MF to work:

- Enable AF+MF in SHOOTING MENU > AF/MF SETTING.

- Select AF-S on the camera and MF on the lens (by pulling the clutch mechanism toward the camera).

- Use AF+MF as described above.

Here are a few tips regarding AF+MF and clutch lenses:

- Make sure the manual focus ring of the lens has sufficient play to the left and right so you can make the necessary MF adjustments.

- The distance and DOF markings on your clutch lens are meaningless when in the AF+MF configuration. Instead, use the electronic distance/DOF scale that's displayed in the camera's viewfinder or on the LCD.

- To use clutch lenses in manual focus mode when AF+MF is set to ON, both the lens *and* the camera must be set to MF.

## TIP 78 — Pre-AF: a relic of the past

Pre-AF brings the AF-C of older Fujifilm X cameras (like the X-Pro1) to more recent models like your X-T3. With Pre-AF set to ON, the camera will always focus on whatever is covered by the active AF frame, even when the shutter button is *not* half-pressed.

Pre-AF burns plenty of power because the autofocus in the lens is always working. On the other hand, using it can potentially result in a quicker AF response. When you are shooting action with telephoto lenses, Pre-AF may be helpful—remember to pack a few extra batteries. I usually set this option (SHOOTING MENU > AF/MF SETTING > PRE-AF) to OFF.

## TIP 79 — Using face detection, eye detection and Face Select

Face detection is a combined autofocus and exposure metering mode. It even affects auto white balance. You can activate it with SHOOTING MENU > AF/MF SETTING > FACE/EYE DETECTION SETTING > FACE DETECTION ON and picking one of the four eye detection options.

Here's what it does:

- The camera scans the scene and detects human faces. It automatically focuses on one of the detected faces when the shutter button is half-pressed. When more than one face is detected, the camera tends to focus on the face that's closest to the center. That face will be highlighted with a green frame. The other detected faces will be highlighted with a white frame.

- Face detection uses a custom version of weighted multi metering that puts an emphasis on the selected face. The goal is to deliver an exposure with correct skin tones. It may also influence the camera's auto white balance.

Face detection is both a blessing and a curse. It's a blessing when it works because it focuses directly on a face and makes sure that it's "correctly" exposed. It's a curse when the detection goes wrong, because it doesn't just mean the focus might miss its mark; it may also mess up your exposure metering.

The good news is that in many cases, face detection works, even with people who only show their profiles to the camera. The bad news is that face detection may not work well on folks wearing glasses.

The performance of face detection has been significantly improved in the X-T3 compared to previous models.

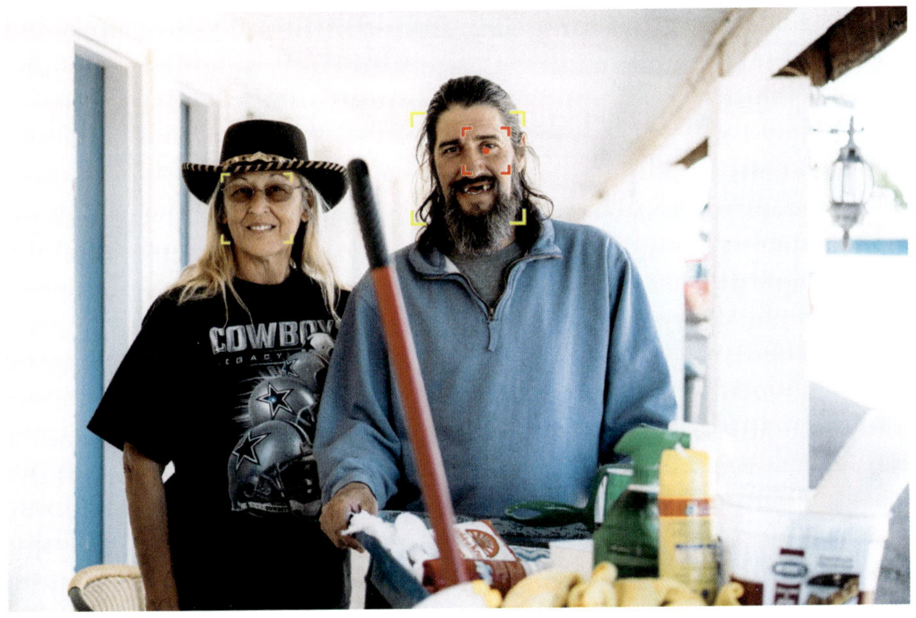

Fig. 91: **Face detection** is great for stationary scenes with one or more people looking at (or showing their profile to) the camera.

Here are a few helpful tips regarding face detection:

- If you want to take face detection exposure metering out of the equation (and I highly recommend that you do), you can set the camera to manual exposure mode **M**.

While the *metering* will still be affected in this mode, the *exposure* itself will not. Alternatively, you can use the AE-L button to meter and lock the exposure and prohibit face detection from interfering with it while AE-L is active. You can still adjust your locked exposure with the exposure compensation dial.

- Spot, center-weighted, and average metering aren't available when face detection is active. The camera is always using a derivate of multi metering.

- When face detection fails to detect a face in the scene, the camera will automatically fall back to the selected regular AF mode: Single Point, Zone, or Wide/Tracking. At the same time, exposure metering reverts to regular multi metering.

- Face detection can be assigned to any function (Fn) button. Personally, I have assigned it to Touch-Fn4.

Face detection accuracy can be improved with the optional eye detection feature. To activate it, select either LEFT EYE PRIORITY or RIGHT EYE PRIORITY. You can also select EYE AUTO to make the camera focus on the eye that's closest to the camera, or select EYE OFF to deactivate eye detection during face detection.

In the viewfinder, the camera will highlight a detected eye with a small square and will focus on it when you half-press the shutter button. In my experience, it doesn't hurt to leave this feature on all the time. I usually set it to EYE AUTO.

**Fig. 92:** For people who are moving around, the X-T3 is fast enough to track their faces with **AF-C and face/eye detection.**

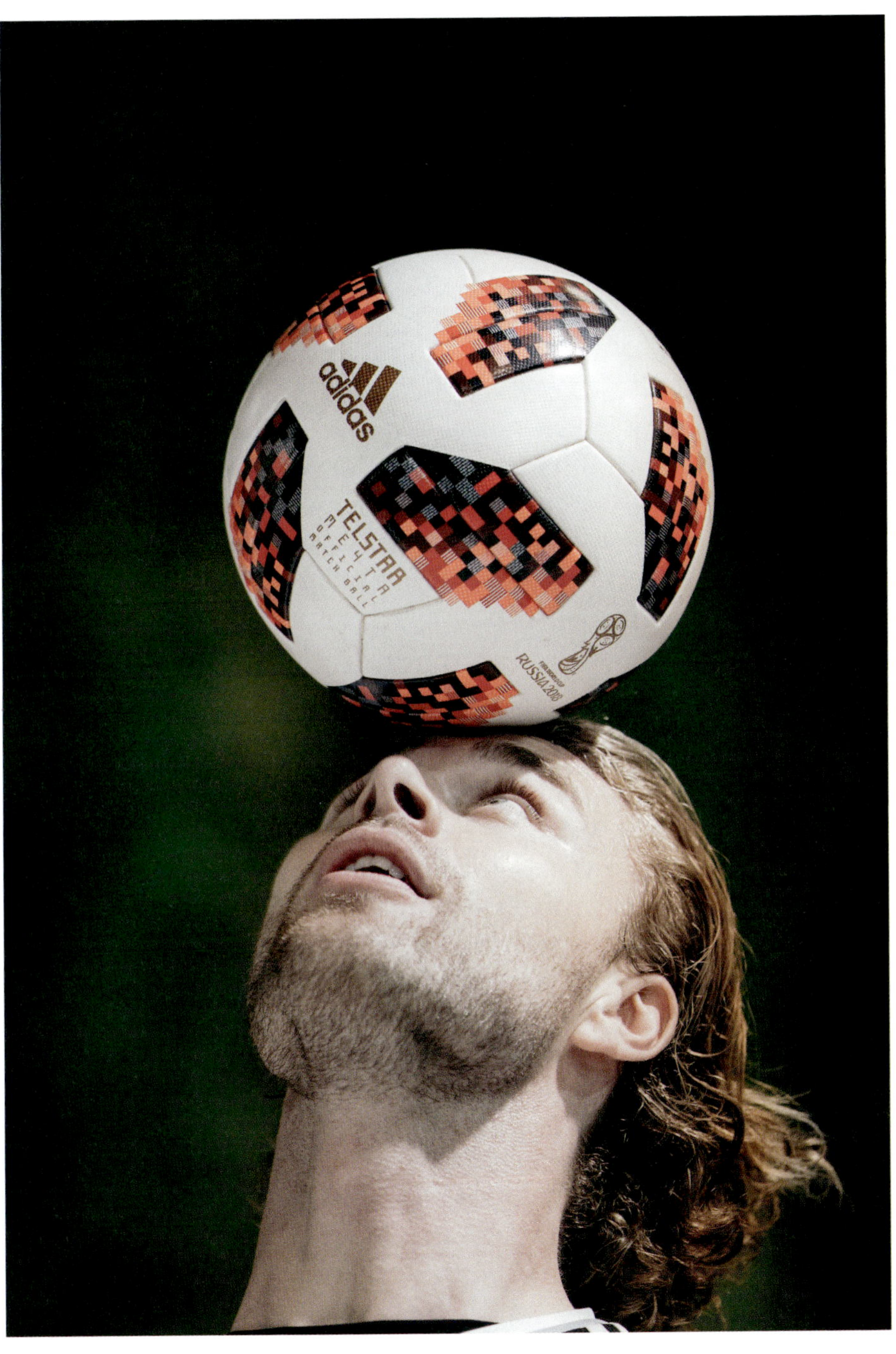

With current firmware, the X-T3 also features a FACE SELECT function, which can only be accessed via an appropriately configured Fn- or Touch-Fn button. Personally, I put this function on Fn5. After activating FACE SELECT, you can use the focus stick or the touch screen to switch between multiple detected faces and focus on a specific person within a group. If necessary, engaging FACE SELECT will automatically activate FACE DETECTION.

| TIP 80 | Using AF-Lock and AE-Lock |
|--------|---------------------------|

In AF-S or AF-C mode, pressing the **AF-L** button locks the current distance setting. In SET UP > BUTTON/DIAL SETTING > AE/AF LOCK MODE, you can configure the button to function as an on/off switch (which is always my choice) or to work only as long as it is being pressed.

When AF-Lock is active, the camera won't refocus when the shutter button is half or fully pressed. Instead, it will keep the focus at the previously locked distance. This is convenient when you want to take multiple shots of a non-moving subject in quick succession. With AF-Lock, you don't have to refocus every time to take another image. AF-Lock decouples autofocus and exposure metering: while AF-Lock is engaged, half-pressing the shutter button will only meter and lock the exposure, not the focus. Of course, this only applies if SHUTTER AF (in the SET UP > BUTTON/DIAL SETTING menu) is in its default ON position for AF-S and AF-C.

You can also use an indirect form of AF-Lock that doesn't involve a dedicated AF-L button. Start as usual by taking one shot in AF-S mode. However, after taking the shot, do not *fully* release the shutter button, but only release it back to its *half-pressed* position. This will lock the focus of the previous shot (indicated by a tiny AF-L symbol in the live view), so when you next press the shutter button (going from half press to full press), the camera won't refocus. Rinse and repeat as long as you want to take additional shots without refocusing.

In a similar fashion to AF-L, you can use the designated **AE-L** button to meter and lock exposure: in this case, half-pressing the shutter button will only change the focusing. You can even combine both AE-Lock and AF-Lock, so half-pressing the shutter will only set the working aperture and prime the camera.

| Using AF-ON (back-button focusing) | TIP 81 |
| --- | --- |

AF-ON brings genuine back-button focusing to your X-T3. Back-button focusing is a common practice among DSLR users. Simply put, AF-ON assigns the camera's autofocus to a function button. Press that button, and the camera starts focusing. Release it, and the focusing stops at the current focus position—until you press the AF-ON button again.

In other words: AF-ON performs the same autofocus function as half-pressing the shutter button (assuming that SHUTTER AF ON is set in the SET UP > BUTTON/DIAL SETTING menu). In AF-S mode, pressing AF-ON will perform a single focus search and lock the distance. In AF-C mode, AF-ON will continuously focus on a target as long as the button is kept pressed (just like half-pressing the shutter button).

In the X-T3, AF-ON must be assigned to an Fn button. To keep things simple and comfortable, it's best to replace the AF-L button with AF-ON. To do so, press and hold the DISP/BACK button until the Fn setting page appears. Scroll down to AF-L and select AF-ON from the list of available functions.

You can press and hold AF-ON while you simultaneously press the shutter. In AF-S, pressing and holding AF-ON will focus the camera and lock that focus while AF-ON is held, so simultaneously half-pressing or pressing the shutter button won't interfere with your locked focus. In AF-C, pressing AF-ON means that the camera keeps tracking your target as long as AF-ON is pressed and held.

If you are a "religious" back-button-AF user (some DLSR converts are), you may find it more comfortable to entirely disable the shutter button's AF functionality by selecting SET UP > BUTTON/DIAL SETTING > SHUTTER AF > OFF for AF-S and/or AF-C, so AF-ON will be the only available method to autofocus in AF-S or AF-C mode.

In manual focus (MF) mode, AF-ON turns into Instant AF, just like the normal AF-L button.

<table>
<tr><td>TIP 82</td><td>Focusing in poor light</td></tr>
</table>

Low light can lead to poor contrast along with more photon noise, making it more difficult for the camera to find and lock the correct autofocus distance. However, the amount of light (and hence noise) that reaches the sensor depends not only on the brightness of a scene, but also on the brightness of the lens. The XF56mmF1.2 is 3.5 stops or EVs (exposure values) brighter than the XF18–55mmF2.8–4 kit zoom in its 55 mm position. In other words, with the XF56mmF1.2 lens, the same scene can look 3.5 stops brighter to the camera's autofocus system. You can guess which lens will perform better when the lighting gets tough.

Don't be confused by appearances—it's true that the live view image in the viewfinder will look equally bright with both lenses, but that's only because the camera is electronically amplifying the live view display. However, the autofocus needs *actual* light and contrast. When the light is poor, it's vital to target surfaces with contrast and, if possible, use a larger AF frame size.

One way of tackling a tough lighting situation is by using fast lenses, like the XF56mmF1.2, XF35mmF1.4, or XF23mmF1.4. You can also generate light—the camera's AF assist lamp can illuminate a subject to help the autofocus find better contrast. Be aware that the AF assist lamp can be easily blocked by an attached lens hood. Watch out for this and remove the lens hood if necessary. Since the AF assist lamp tends to concentrate on the center of the image, it works best in concert with one of the more central AF frames. To use the AF assist lamp, make sure to set SHOOTING MENU > AF/MF SETTING > AF ILLUMINATOR > ON.

An alternative to using the AF assist lamp is using a flashlight to temporarily illuminate a subject. If you are indoors, you can try turning on the lights in the room for a moment and using AF-Lock to lock the focus. Just make sure to meter and set the exposure *after* the lights are off again.

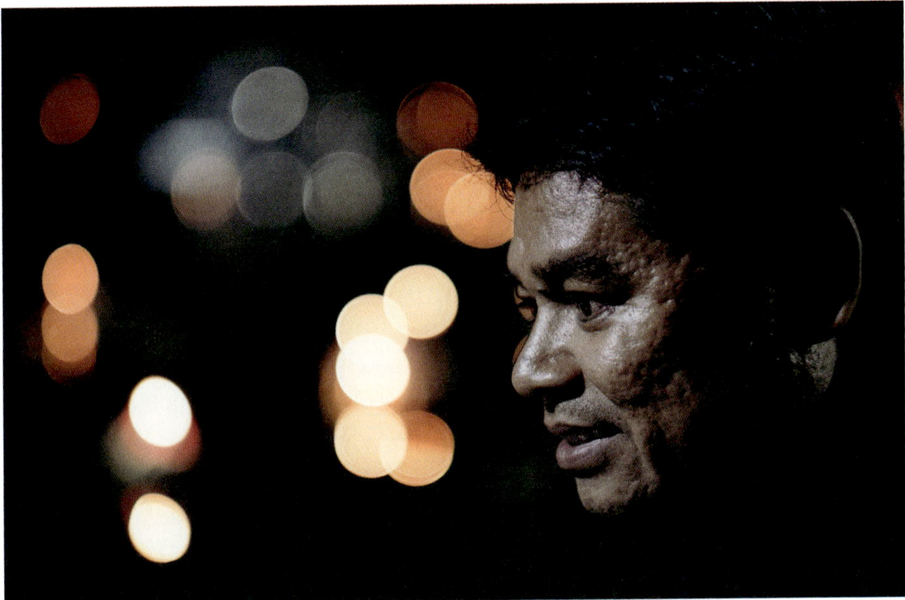

Fig. 93: In this **low-light shot,** the fast XF56mmF1.2 R lens made it easier on the autofocus system to find its target in AF-S mode. In AF-S mode, low-light AF performance isn't related to the actually set working aperture, but to the maximum wide-open aperture that is available. In this particular example, it wouldn't have made a difference if I had set the aperture to 1.2 or 5.6 or 8, because in AF-S mode, the focusing system can temporarily open up to the widest lens aperture.

*Important: If you intend to stop down the aperture of your lens in poor lighting, make sure to use either AF-S or manual focus with Instant AF-S or Instant AF-C as your focusing mode. Why? Because Instant AF always focuses wide open. Try to avoid regular AF-C, because this mode will usually focus with (or closer to) your stopped-down working aperture, which will make things more difficult for your camera since less light will reach the sensor.*

| **TIP 83** | Macro: focusing at close distances |
| --- | --- |

The biggest challenge with shooting macro is the lack of depth of field (DOF). The slightest movement may cause the shot to be out of focus. That's why macro photography is usually performed using a tripod and manual focus, often with Instant AF, Focus Check (magnifier tool), and focus peaking. It's vital not to recompose after the focus has been set. To get a visual impression of the current DOF, you can half-press the shutter (make sure SHUTTER AE is ON) or assign PREVIEW DEPTH OF FIELD to one of your Fn buttons.

Macro shots usually require you to stop down the lens to increase the DOF. Since this can result in slower shutter speeds, it's important to make sure the subject isn't moving too fast or out of the focus plane. Shooting a close-up of a flower in the wind may not yield excellent results.

If you don't want to use manual focus in macro mode, you can also focus automatically. Here's how:

- Set AF-S and Single Point AF and select a small AF frame size.

- Reposition the small AF frame to exactly cover the part of the image you want to be in focus. Quickly take the shot after you half-press the shutter—don't recompose.

- You can check your focus with the magnifier tool before taking a shot by pressing the rear command dial. After doing so, you can change the magnification factor by turning the command dial.

- Try not to shoot handheld; it's better to use a tripod.

- Stop down the lens and visually check the depth of field by half-pressing the shutter button or using the DOF preview function (remember that function can be assigned to any Fn button).

- Make sure there is sufficient light and try to shoot subjects that don't move in and out of the focus plane.

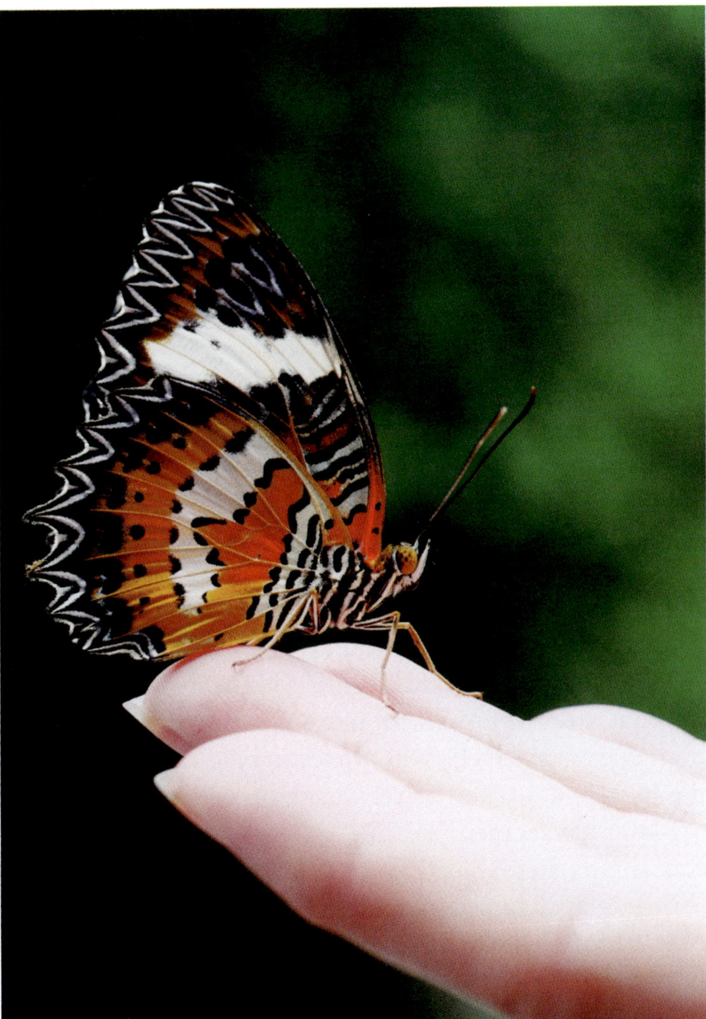

Fig. 94: **Macro shots** can be quite challenging due to their lack of DOF. This is why a tripod is highly recommended. With a little bit of luck, handheld shots like this example are possible, as well.

You can add macro capability to many of your existing XF and XC lenses by using Fujifilm's electronic macro extension tubes MCEX-11 and MCEX-16. You can download a PDF file [66] from Fujifilm's website that provides a chart that shows how these extension tubes enhance the magnification factor of compatible lenses. Please note that the camera's electronic DOF/distance scale doesn't reflect the use of macro extension tubes.

| TIP 84 | Focus Bracketing |

The need for greater depth of field (DOF) [67] is a common issue for macro and landscape photographers. With increasing sensor resolution, diffraction blur [68] becomes a serious limitation. To avoid visible diffraction with your 26 MP APS-C sensor, you should avoid stopping down your lenses beyond f/9.

Even worse, many lenses have their "sweet spot" (the critical aperture delivering the best resolution and sharpness) [69] about two stops down from their maximum wide-open aperture. For example, my XF27mmF2.8 pancake delivers its maximum resolution around f/5.6.

For macro and landscape photographers, stopping down the lens to f/16 or f/22 often isn't an option due to quality considerations. Not to mention that even at f/22, depth of field would still not be sufficient in many macro situations.

What to do? There is a popular solution among ambitious photographers called *focus bracketing* [70], in which multiple images are taken at various focus distances and they are later are merged (i.e., *stacked*) into a single image that contains an increased depth of field. The series of individual source images can be merged in Photoshop or in other specialized software such as Helicon Focus [71]. This technique is referred to as *focus stacking*.

Focus bracketing helps you automate the generation of the source material you need for focus stacking. To configure focus bracketing in your X-T3, select SHOOTING MENU > SHOOTING SETTING > DRIVE SETTING > BKT SETTING > FOCUS BKT.

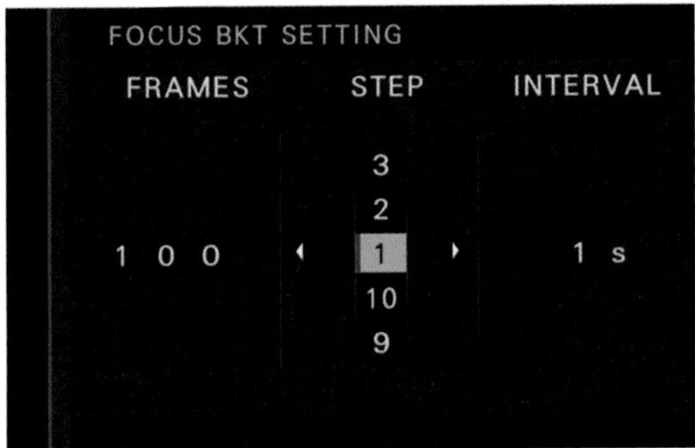


Fig. 95: The **focus bracketing** configuration screen allows you to set the number of frames the camera should automatically take (FRAMES), the focus difference between individual shots (STEP), and the pause between individual shots (INTERVAL). The latter is useful so that the camera can settle down after each shot to avoid shutter-induced vibration. It's also recommended to activate the electronic first curtain shutter (EFCS) or even the electronic shutter (ES).

To initiate focus bracketing, it's best to select MF and manually focus on the nearest point of your subject you want to have in perfect focus. It's also recommended to stop down the lens to its "sweet spot." With macro lenses this is typically two stops down from their maximum aperture; while wide-angle lenses often deliver peak performance three or four stops down.

Depending on your needs and time restraints, you can experiment with various step settings. To start the sequence, make sure the camera is in BKT mode (DRIVE dial) and that FOCUS BKT is selected as the BKT MODE, and then press the shutter button. The camera will take the set number of images or stop when it reaches infinity—whatever occurs first.

When the camera has finished recording the source images, you can merge them in Photoshop or in specialized focus-stacking software like Helicon Focus.

**TIP 85** | Focusing on moving subjects (1): the autofocus trick

Consider these "rules:" use AF-S (Single) for stationary subjects; use AF-C (Continuous) for subjects that move toward or away from the camera. However, as usual, there are no rules without exceptions. Meet the so-called "autofocus trick" or "shutter mash" technique. It employs AF-S to focus on moving subjects. Here's how:

- Set the camera to AF-S and single shot drive mode (S).

- Make sure that Boost mode is switched on.

- Use Single Point AF or Zone AF. Select an AF frame or zone position and size that cover the part of the moving subject you want to be in focus.

- Set a suitable exposure and make sure the shutter speed is fast enough to avoid unwanted motion blur. Most action shots require shutter speeds of at least 1/1000 s.

- Follow the moving subject in the viewfinder, making sure the selected AF frame or AF zone always covers the part of the subject that needs to be in focus. Do *not* half-press the shutter button!

- *Fully* press the shutter button in one swift motion when you want to take the shot. The camera will need some time to focus, so make sure the focus frame remains positioned on the moving subject while the camera is focusing. As soon as the camera can lock the focus, it will automatically take the shot.

The AF trick, also known as *shutter mash,* is based on the camera's autofocus priority logic. When you release the shutter, the camera *first* attempts to lock the focus and *then* takes the shot. Since the delay between having locked the focus and releasing the shutter is very short, the moving subject ends up being in focus most of the time. This means the AF trick works best with aperture settings that offer sufficient depth of field, and with subjects that don't move too quickly toward the camera.

A negative aspect of this method is the delay between fully pressing the shutter button and the camera taking the shot. This makes it challenging to hit decisive moments and requires some amount of foresight from the photographer.

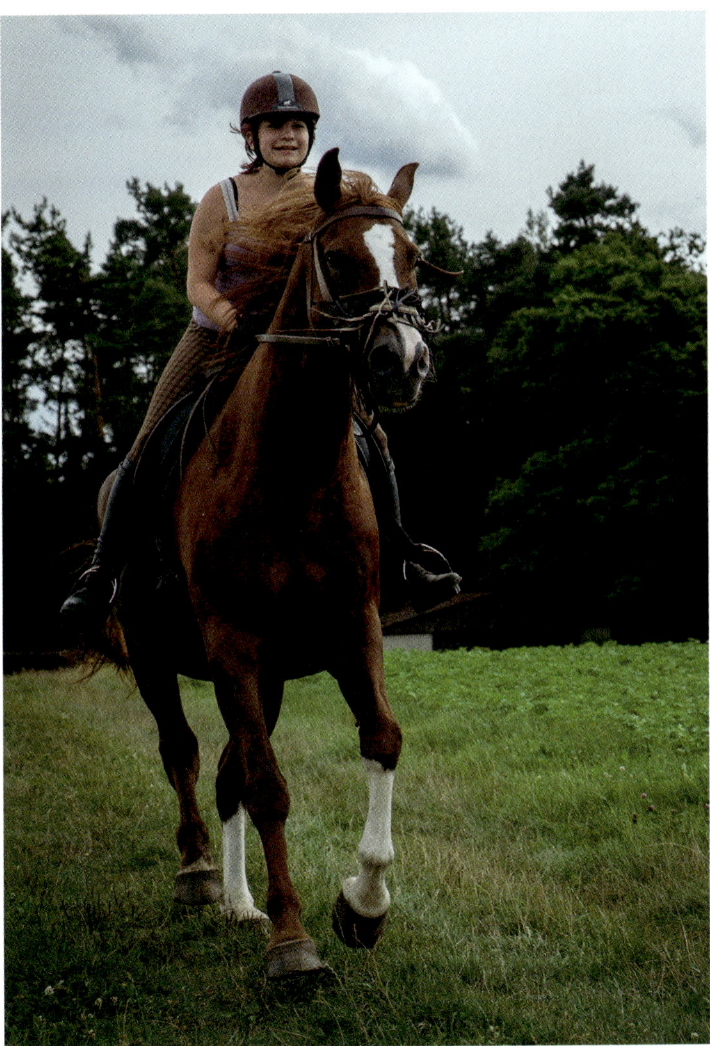

Fig. 96: A running horse captured using the **autofocus trick** or **shutter mash technique**.

| TIP 86 | Focusing on moving subjects (2): the focus trap |

Setting up a focus trap is about pre-focusing on a location that a moving object will eventually pass through. This method can be useful with sports and other action that runs along a pre-determined course (track, street, trail, etc.).

This is how it works:

- Set the camera to manual focus (MF).

- Pre-focus on the location where you want to capture the moving subject. Select an aperture with sufficient depth of field (DOF) to make sure all relevant parts of the object will be in focus.

- Half-press the shutter button when the moving subject is approaching the location you have in focus. The camera will lock the exposure and set the working aperture (assuming SHUTTER AE is ON).

- Fully press the shutter button as soon as the subject is about to cross the in-focus location.

There's only a very small shutter lag between half-pressing and fully pressing the shutter button. Depending on how fast the subject is moving, it may be necessary to fully press the shutter button a split second before it is in the optimal position.

Alternatively, you can set the camera to high-speed burst mode, increasing the chance that one or two frames will successfully capture your fast-moving subject as it crosses your focus trap.

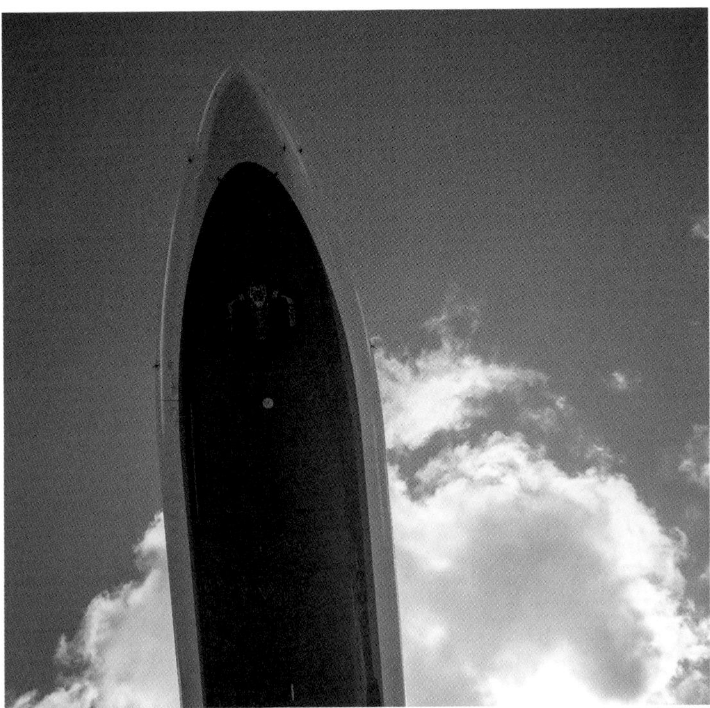

Fig. 97: **Focus trap:** To capture this landing Airbus A330 as it was flying over me at a distance of only a few meters, timing was essential. Instead of using autofocus, I pre-focused the 18 mm lens with sufficient depth of field and waited for the right moment with my camera primed and the shutter half-pressed. At the decisive moment, I fully-pressed the shutter button.

You can also trap moving subjects in a preset focus zone. Stop down your lens enough to create a sufficiently large DOF zone, and then wait until a subject enters the zone. This method is often used by street photographers with wide-angle lenses (typically 16–23 mm) who can't afford to miss the decisive moment.

A variant of this method is panning [72] the camera with a slow shutter speed and a small aperture (plenty of DOF). The slow shutter speed makes sure that the background is blurred while the subject remains in focus.

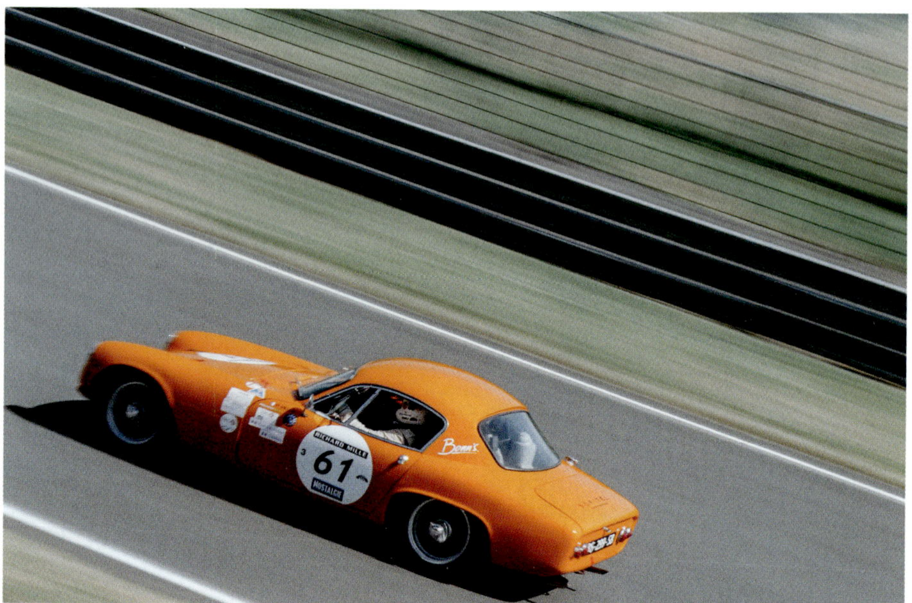

Fig. 98: **Panning** the camera at 1/60 s in synch with a racecar. The slow shutter speed resulted in f/18 and there was more than sufficient DOF using a focal length of 50 mm.

| TIP 87 | Focusing on moving subjects (3): Autofocus tracking using Single Point AF, Zone AF, or Wide/Tracking AF |
| --- | --- |

Predictive PDAF (phase detection autofocus) allows you to track moving subjects in three-dimensional space. Since the camera can calculate the movement of the subject, it can automatically pre-focus on its predicted distance and compensate for any inherent shutter lag.

Unlike previous X camera models, the X-T3 features predictive PDAF that covers the entire sensor area, so you don't have to restrict AF frames or zones—the entire sensor is the PDAF area!

Let's start with the **Single Point AF** and **Zone AF** modes:

- Set the focus to AF-C and make sure Boost mode is set.

- Set the camera to burst mode. I recommend a CL setting of 5.7 fps that displays a real-time live view image between shots. I also recommend using the EFCS to minimize the blackout time in the live view.

- Select a suitable autofocus frame or zone size. Since PDAF covers the entire sensor area of the X-T3, there are no restrictions in regard to size and position of the AF frame or zone.

- Position the selected AF frame or AF zone to directly cover the subject or the part of the subject you want in focus. Half-press the shutter button, and the camera will start tracking the subject covered by the AF frame or AF zone.

- Keep the shutter button half-pressed as you follow the moving subject with the selected AF frame or AF zone.

- Fully press the shutter when you want to start taking the series of exposures. The actual burst speed (frame rate) depends on how well the camera can track the subject. As the camera is taking pictures, keep the selected AF frame or AF zone on the part of your image that is supposed to be in focus. This may be challenging at first, so practice is important.

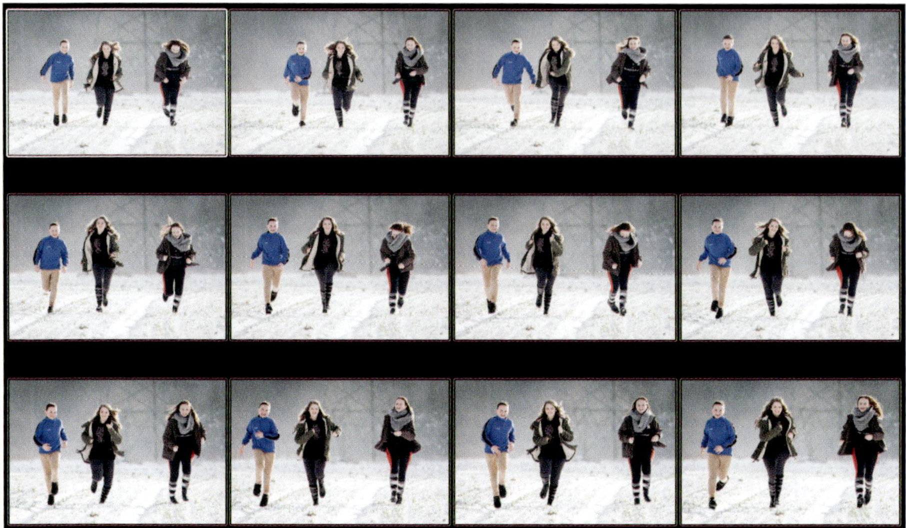

Fig. 99: **AF tracking** with AF-C and burst mode: The predictive autofocus was tracking one of the kids with the selected AF zone while they were running toward the camera. To make this kind of shot work, it's vital to follow the subject with the active AF frame or AF zone, making sure it's always covering the part of the subject that is supposed to be in focus.

In principle, AF-C tracking also works in single shot mode (DRIVE mode **S**—not to be confused with the AF mode **S**). In this case, the camera takes a single frame when the shutter button is fully pressed and then ends the tracking.

As an alternative to tracking moving subjects using Single Point and Zone AF, you can use **Wide/Tracking AF** mode in concert with AF-C. This mode enables real 3D tracking; meaning the camera isn't merely tracking a subject's changing distance from the camera (z-axis), but it also tracks its left/right (x-axis) und up/down (y-axis) movements inside the image frame.

Here's how it works:

- Set the focus mode to AF-C and make sure that Boost mode is active.

- Set the camera to **Wide/Tracking AF** and select a slow burst mode.

- Select one of the available tracking AF points. The point you select will serve as a starting point for your tracking action, so position it in a way that suits your composition.

- To identify your target, make sure the selected AF point covers the object you want to track and then half-press the shutter button. While you keep the shutter button half-pressed, the camera will use pattern recognition to automatically follow the object as it moves around in the frame (or as you move the camera), where you will see a "cloud" of small green AF frames.

- Fully press the shutter button and keep it pressed to take pictures at the selected burst rate. The camera will continue exposing images until you release the shutter button.

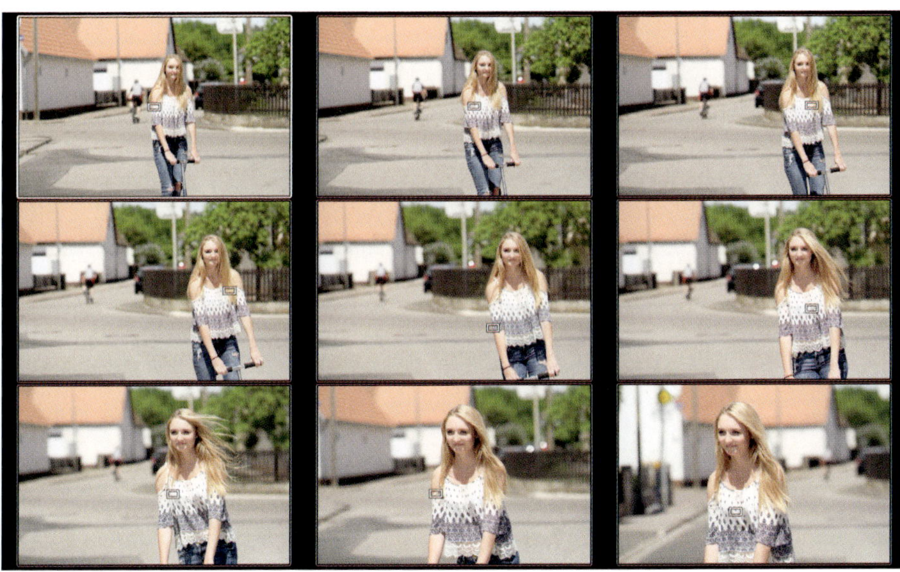

Fig. 100: AF-C in concert with **WIDE/TRACKING** and burst mode can track a subject in 3-dimensional space. To accomplish this, the camera is using pattern recognition to follow the designated subject as it moves.

Performance-wise, AF-C tracking mode has long been a weakness with many X cameras. This has changed for the better with the X-T3. The same is true for AF-C tracking with face detection. The X-T3 offers much-improved AF-C subject tracking in concert with face and eye detection.

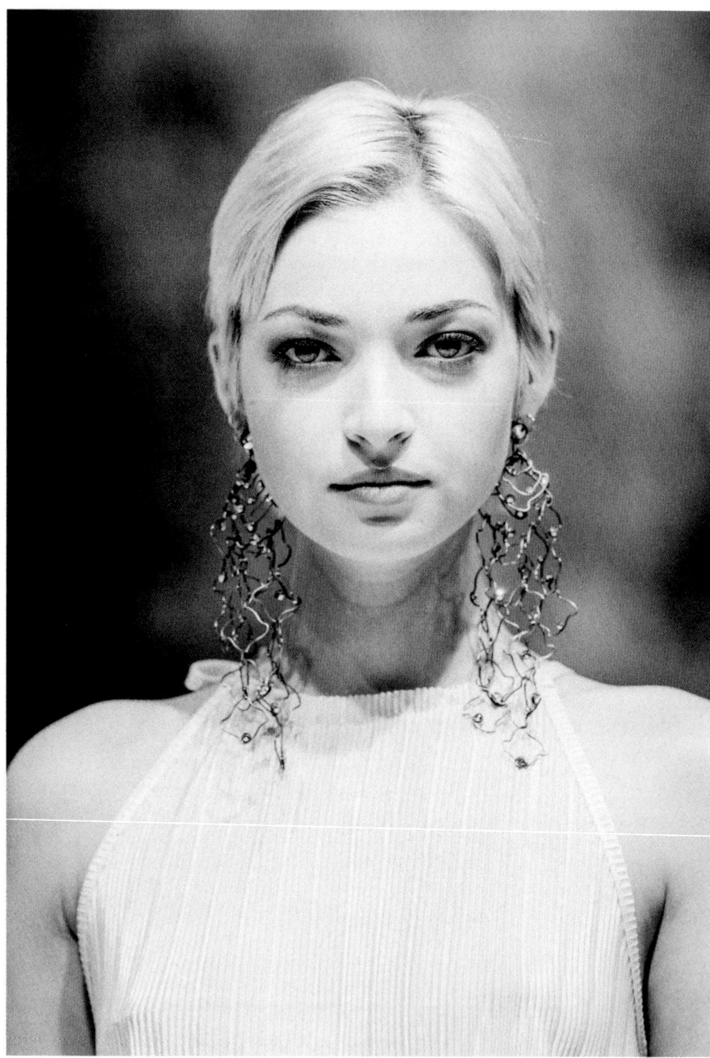

Fig. 101: **AF-C in concert with face detection** has traditionally been a weakness of X series cameras. This changed with the X-T3, which offers fast face- and eye-detection tracking. This catwalk demonstration was shot wide open with the XF200mmF2 R LM OIS WR telephoto lens.

<table><tr><td>Using AF-C custom settings</td><td>TIP 88</td></tr></table>

The X-T3 features three parameters that allow you to customize the AF-C's behavior for a specific task or application:

- **Tracking Sensitivity** (TS) specifies whether the camera should switch its focus to a different subject or retain its current focus to wait for the subject to reappear. This control is useful when the subject you are tracking disappears behind an obstacle or goes out of the frame, or when you aim at a new target with a different distance. Selecting 0 (zero) makes the camera switch its focus immediately, while choosing 1–4 progressively extends the time it will retain focus. Technically speaking, tracking sensitivity 0 will not predict an autofocus target's position when it's temporarily lost or obscured by something else. Tracking sensitivity settings of 1, 2, 3, and 4 will predict a lost or obscured target's position for another 0.4 seconds, 0.7 seconds, 1.0 second, and 1.3 seconds, respectively, before the AF-C locks on a new tracking target.

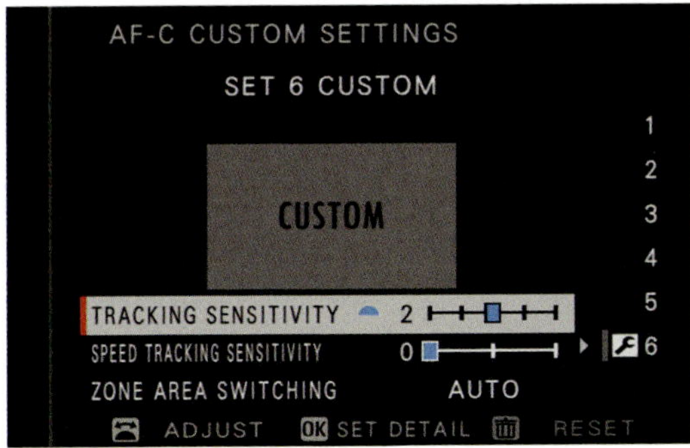


Fig. 102: By selecting a higher **TS** setting, the camera will wait a moment or two before it switches the continuous autofocus to a new target distance. The default setting is 2, which means the camera will give you about 0.7 seconds to re-aim the focus frame or zone back on your subject after you have lost sight of it. Higher TS settings are useful in situations where you want to track a specific subject with as little interference as possible.

- **Speed Tracking Sensitivity** (STS) controls the camera's tracking characteristics based on changes to the subject's speed. Selecting 0 (constant speed), the camera expects a steady movement when it predicts the subject's distance. Select 1 or 2, and the camera takes speed changes more and more into account when it's predicting subject movement, making it suitable for suddenly accelerating or decelerating targets, like race cars.

- **Zone Area Switching** (ZAS) is available only in the Zone AF mode and specifies which part of the focusing zone should be given focusing priority. CENTER maintains focus on the center of the zone. FRONT switches the focus to the closest subject (or the closest part of a subject) anywhere inside the zone, which (in concert with a TS setting of 0) is great for immediately capturing new targets that suddenly move into a zone. AUTO tracks the subject you first focused on.

Fig. 103: By selecting FRONT as your **ZAS** setting, you can force the camera to focus on whatever part of the image inside your selected AF zone happens to be closest to the camera. In the case of the vulture that was flying toward the camera (above), a ZAS FRONT setting allowed me to focus on the bird's head and beak instead of the more prominent wings. However, using the same settings in a fly-by situation (below) only shifted the focus toward the left wing, which was closest to the camera within the 3 × 3 zone I had selected.

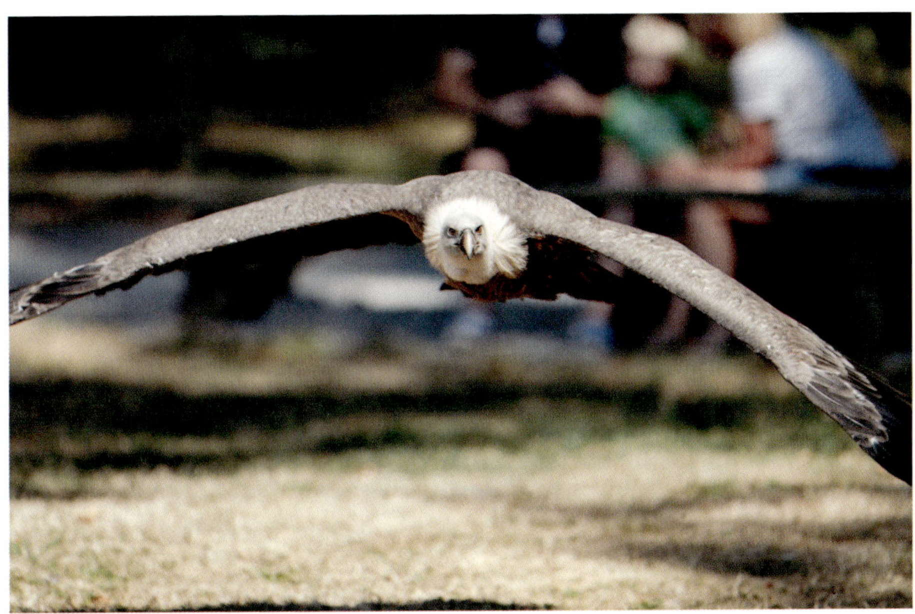

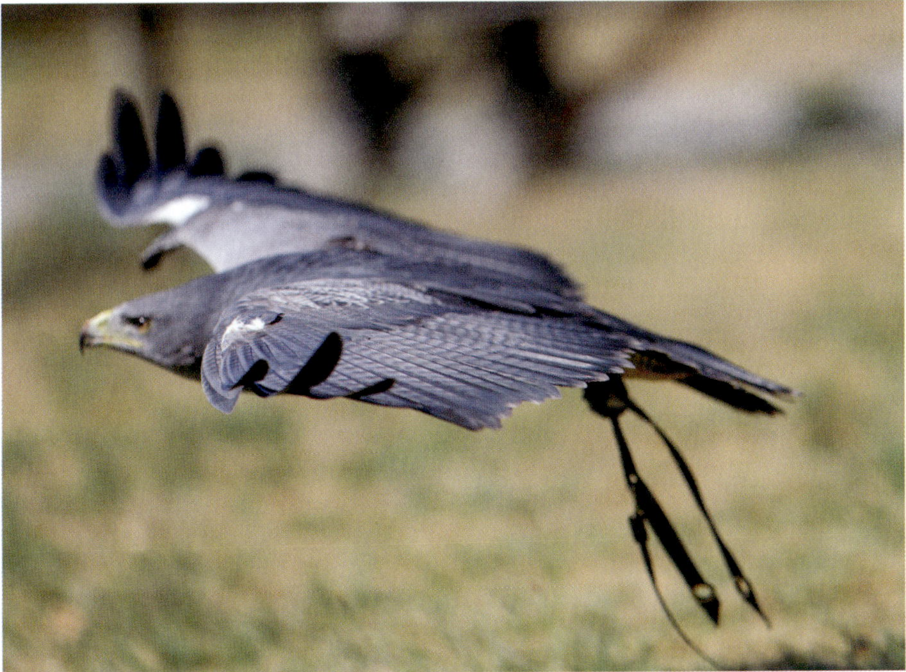

The X-T3 offers several presets that cover typical AF-C shooting scenarios. Select SHOOTING MENU > AF/MF SETTING > AF-C CUSTOM SETTINGS, and then pick one of the following available parameter sets:

- SET 1: MULTI PURPOSE is the default setting and is our general AF-C setting. It's a great choice for situations where you don't have a clear understanding of how a specific custom setting could improve the AF-C performance. Its parameter settings are TS 2, STS 0, and ZAS AUTO.

- SET 2: IGNORE OBSTACLES & CONTINUE TO TRACK SUBJECT keeps the focus on a subject even when it has temporarily gone out of the frame or has been obscured by obstacles. This can be useful for following a specific target with the camera and ensuring that the target isn't lost when it's temporarily obscured by people, trees, or other obstacles that pass through the line of sight. Its parameter settings are TS 3, STS 0, and ZAS CENTER.

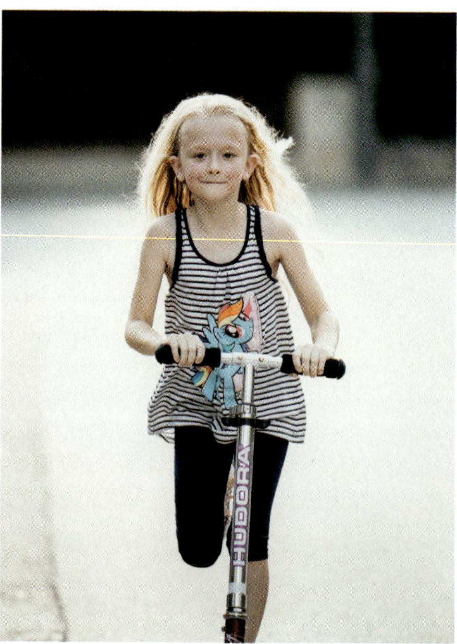

Fig. 104:
**Set 2** is a good choice when you want to track a specific, steadily moving subject without interference, like this girl riding a scooter through the shot.

- SET 3: FOR ACCELERATING/DECELERATING SUBJECT is your typical racetrack mode. It takes changing relative speeds of subjects moving toward the camera into account. Whenever you have targets that rapidly accelerate or decelerate, this mode can be useful, especially in concert with XF lenses featuring high-speed linear autofocus motors. Its parameter settings are TS 2, STS 2, and ZAS AUTO.

- SET 4: FOR SUDDENLY APPEARING SUBJECT allows the camera to instantly focus on a subject that enters the focusing area, with priority given to any object (or any part of it) that is closest to the camera. It is ideal for subjects that suddenly appear in the focusing frame. Its parameter settings are TS 0, STS 1, and ZAS FRONT.

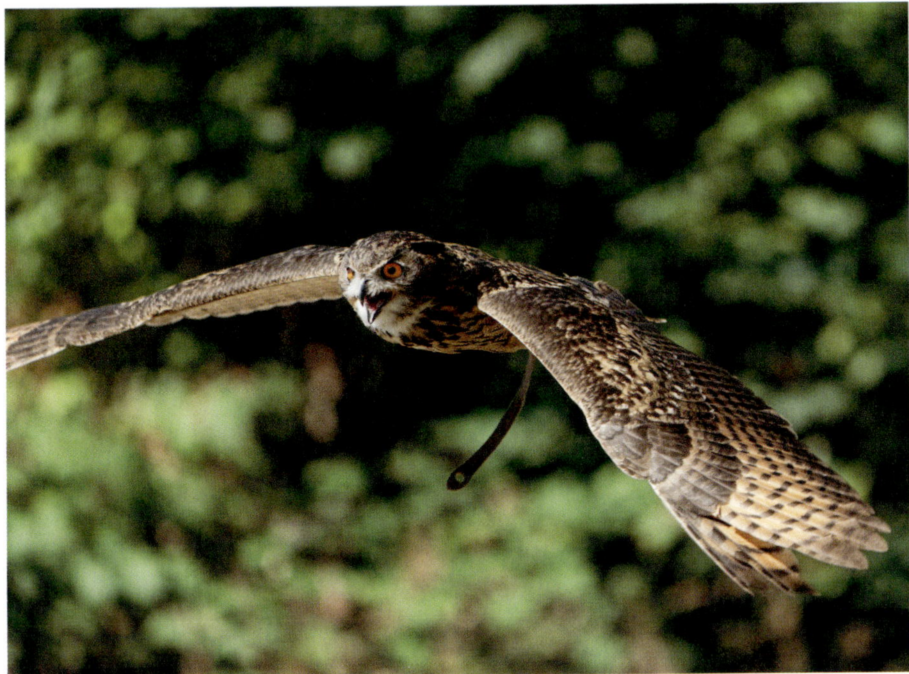

Fig. 105: **Set 4** makes sure that the AF-C immediately focuses on what's closest to the camera (as long as it's located anywhere inside the selected AF zone).

- SET 5: FOR ERRATICALLY MOVING & ACCEL./DECEL. SUB-JECT is suitable for subjects that are moving at varying speeds in different directions, coming in and out of the focusing area. It is optimized for shooting field sports like soccer or tennis. Its parameter settings are TS 3, STS 2, and ZAS AUTO.

- SET 6: CUSTOM stores your chosen setting for the three AF-C subject-tracking parameters: TRACKING SENSITIV-ITY (TS), SPEED TRACKING SENSITIVITY (STS), and ZONE AREA SWITCHING (ZAS). Use this preset to manually create optimized settings for the specific movement characteristics of your subject.

| TIP 89 | Focus Priority vs. Release Priority |
| --- | --- |

The autofocus in your camera will *always* try to focus on a subject before it takes the shot. In this context, release priority vs. focus priority only refers to how the camera behaves when the AF *fails* to lock on a target.

By selecting focus priority for AF-S and AF-C you can reduce the number of out-of-focus pictures on your memory card. Here is how to set it up:

- Set SHOOTING MENU > AF/MF SETTING > RELEASE/FOCUS PRIORITY > AF-S PRIORITY SELECTION > FOCUS to prevent the camera from taking a picture when the autofocus (AF-S) cannot lock onto a target (red AF warning).

Set SHOOTING MENU > AF/MF SETTING > RELEASE/FOCUS PRIORITY > AF-C PRIORITY SELECTION > FOCUS to make sure the camera takes pictures in AF-C mode (particularly in concert with burst mode) only when the autofocus can lock onto something. By default, the camera is set to release priority, following the motto, "better a misfocused shot than no image at all." Since I am no fan of misfocused shots, my cameras are set to focus priority for both AF-S and AF-C.

Please note that when AF+MF is active in AF-S mode, the camera will always use AF-S Release Priority.

<table><tr><td>Using Pre-Shot ES</td><td>TIP 90</td></tr></table>

Pre-Shot ES is a "time machine" that allows you to capture moments you just missed. It only works in concert with the electronic shutter (ES) and high-speed burst mode (CH). It takes advantage of the X-T3's improved electronic shutter and processor, which allow for faster read rates—especially with fast burst mode settings (10, 20 or 30 frames per second) that work with a 1.25x crop.

Pre-Shot ES compensates for the lag time between recognizing a sudden event and actually pressing the shutter release button. With extremely quick subjects, that delay can cause you to miss your ideal moments.

In Pre-Shot ES mode, the X-T3 starts recording and buffering images as soon as you half-press the shutter release button. As long as you keep your finger pressed halfway down, the camera keeps recording images into its buffer. It will continue to refresh the buffered content (FIFO: first in, first out) so that you always have several frames stored in the buffer.

When a sudden event happens and you fully press the shutter to capture it, the camera will not only take new images from that moment on, it will also write the previously buffered images onto the memory card. It will continue to capture and write new images to the card as long as you hold the shutter release all the way down.

In effect, Pre-Shot ES allows you to go back in time and capture the moment or moments right before you fully pressed the shutter release button. Normally, those moments would be lost due to the inevitable reaction time of the photographer and camera. You can activate Pre-Shot ES with SHOOTING MENU > SHOOTING SETTING > PRE-SHOT ES > ON, but only when the camera is set to ES-only and CH high-speed burst shooting.

Since Pre-Shot ES only works in concert with the electronic shutter, it is subject to rolling shutter artifacts such as object distortion (when you are panning the camera or with subjects that move very fast) and an uneven exposure (banding) under pulsing artificial light.

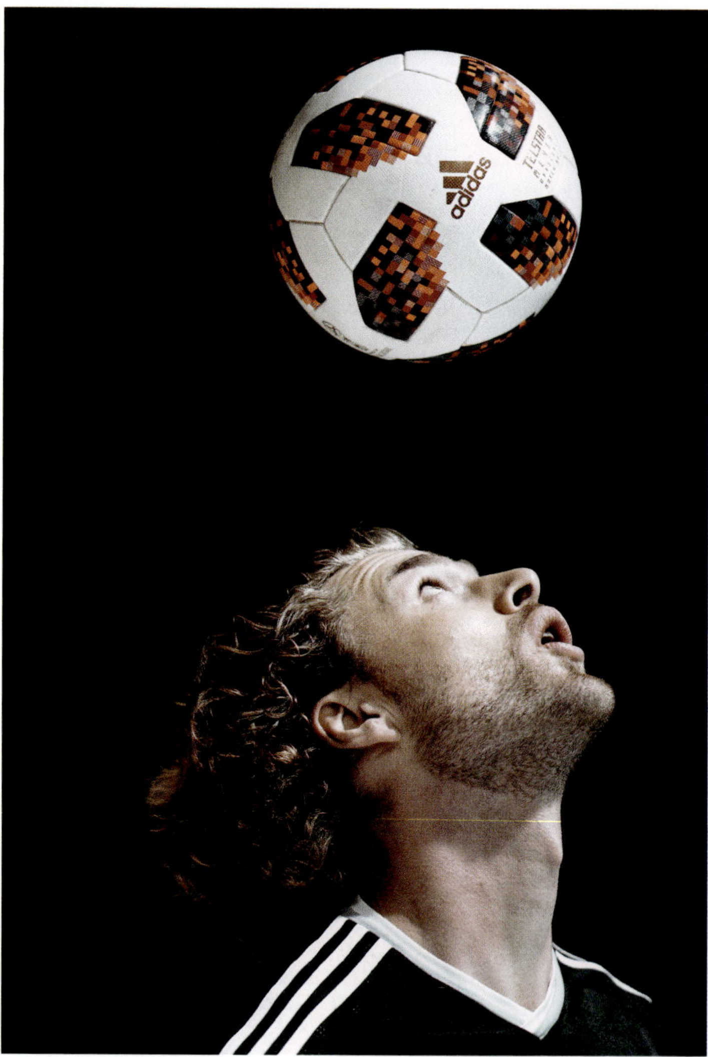

Fig. 106: Missing a decisive or sudden moment? **Pre-Shot ES** allows you to go back in time and capture it.

| Using Sports Finder Mode | TIP 91 |

Sports Finder Mode adds a 1.25x crop to your resulting image. The crop is indicated through a bright white frame in the live view. The cropped images have a resolution of approx. 16.6 MP.

Sports Finder Mode only works in concert with the mechanical shutter (MS) or electronic first curtain shutter (EFCS). It can help you reduce your reaction time in situations with moving objects that suddenly appear in the live view, because it allows you to see beyond the final image frame. This is similar to the bright frame in the optical viewfinders of the X100 or X-Pro series.

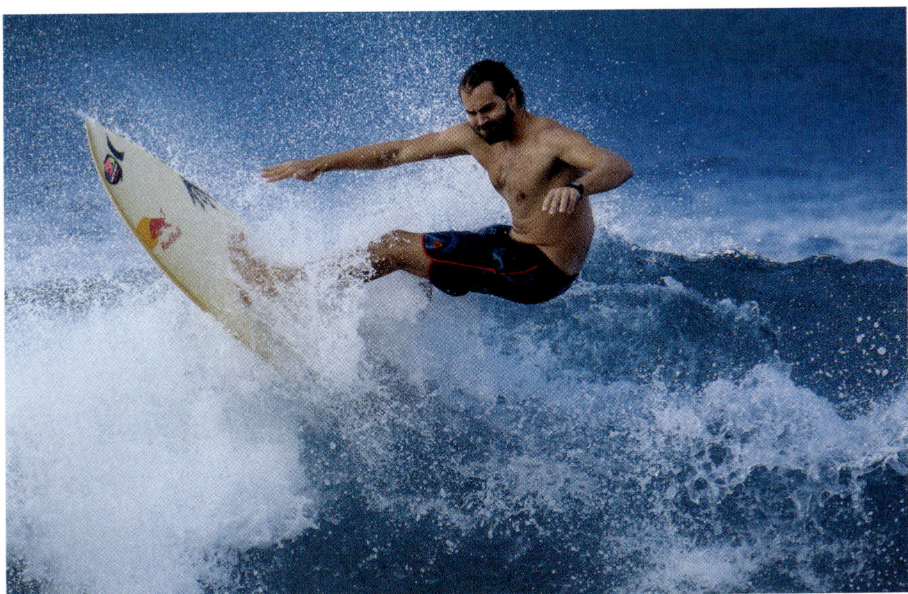

Fig. 107: **Sports Finder Mode** adds a 1.25x crop to the image. In this example, it transformed my 400 mm lens into an effective focal length of 500 mm. The downside is a decrease in resolution from 26 MP to approx. 16.6 MP. Since the effect is the same as cropping an image in post-processing, the actual benefit of Sports Finder Mode is its ability to let you see beyond the final (cropped) image borders and to allow the autofocus to track subjects beyond these borders.

In Sports Finder Mode, the camera's AF tracking extends beyond the indicated bright frame, making it possible to track objects that are outside the active image area. This is also why I am covering this feature here in the focus section of this book and not in the section about the viewfinder.

You can activate Sports Finder Mode with SHOOTING MENU > SHOOTING SETTING > SPORTS FINDER MODE > ON.

## 2.5 WHITE BALANCE, JPEG PARAMETERS, AND RAW CONVERSION

A great feature of all X series cameras is their ability to set white balance [73] and JPEG parameters before *and* after you take a shot, thanks to the built-in RAW converter. This gives you full control over the JPEGs that are generated in your camera.

It's not necessary to anticipate and set the perfect settings for each shot in advance because you can always generate different JPEG versions of a shot with the internal RAW converter. For example, you could create a version with bold Velvia colors, or a black-and-white version with strong contrast and minimal noise reduction. As long as you have access to the RAW file, you can change all JPEG parameters after the fact and you can use the RAW file to create as many different-looking JPEGs as you want.

Using the built-in RAW converter in the playback menu is quite easy because it offers the same functions that are available in shooting mode.

| IMAGE QUALITY SETTING menu | RAW CONVERSION menu |
| --- | --- |
| (Exposure Comp. Dial) | PUSH/PULL PROCESSING |
| DYNAMIC RANGE | DYNAMIC RANGE |
| FILM SIMULATION | FILM SIMULATION |
| WHITE BALANCE | WHITE BALANCE |
| (incl. WB SHIFT) | WB SHIFT |
| COLOR | COLOR |
| SHARPNESS | SHARPNESS |
| HIGHLIGHT TONE | HIGHLIGHT TONE |
| SHADOW TONE | SHADOW TONE |
| NOISE REDUCTION | NOISE REDUCTION |
| GRAIN EFFECT | GRAIN EFFECT |
| COLOR CHROME EFFECT | COLOR CHROME EFFECT |
| D RANGE PRIORITY | D RANGE PRIORITY |
| B&W ADJUSTMENT | B&W ADJUSTMENT |
| LENS MODULATION OPTIMIZER | LENS MODULATION OPTIMIZER |
| COLOR SPACE | COLOR SPACE |

Notable differences between shooting mode and after-the-fact RAW conversion in playback mode affect only the first two items in this list:

- **Exposure corrections** made *before* you take a picture can affect aperture, shutter speed, and ISO. **Push/pull processing** applied *after* you have taken a picture affects only the ISO amplification. Effectively changing the ISO via push/pull processing also doesn't change the nominal ISO value in the EXIF data [74] of the JPEGs. Instead, Push/Pull processing in the internal RAW converter has the same effect as moving the exposure slider in external RAW conversion software, such as Lightroom, Silkypix, or Capture One.

- *Before* you take an image, you can select from four **dynamic range** options: AUTO, DR100%, DR200%, and DR400%. DR200% exposes the RAW file one ISO stop darker than indicated; DR400% exposes it two ISO stops darker. DR-Auto automatically selects either DR100% or DR200%. *After* you have taken an image, you can still select different DR settings in the internal RAW converter. However, you can only *reduce* the DR after the fact; you cannot increase it. If you are working on a RAW file that was recorded with DR400%, you can reprocess it to create JPEGs with DR400%, DR200%, or DR100%. A DR200% RAW file can be reprocessed with DR200% or DR100%, but not DR400%. And a DR100% RAW file can only be reprocessed with DR100%. The same restrictions apply to the D RANGE PRIOITY settings STRONG, WEAK, and OFF.

The correct **white balance** ensures that neutral (white or gray) areas of an image appear without color tints, regardless of the light conditions. At the same time, the results are usually not supposed to look clinically neutral. Your X camera masters this task quite well, so you can rely on the Auto white balance setting to get it right most of the time.

However, "most of the time" is not "all the time." There are instances when the white balance is off, or when you *want* it to be off. For example, you may want to emphasize a sunset with a warmer white balance. In such cases, it makes perfect sense to manually set the white balance in advance or after the fact.

The X-T3 offers a variety of options to manually set the white balance, as follows:

- Several white balance presets for typical situations, such as sunny weather (Fine), cloudy skies (Shade), and tungsten light (Incandescent).

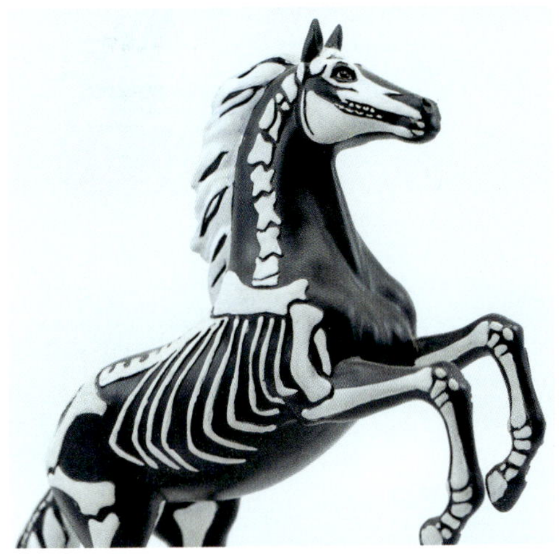

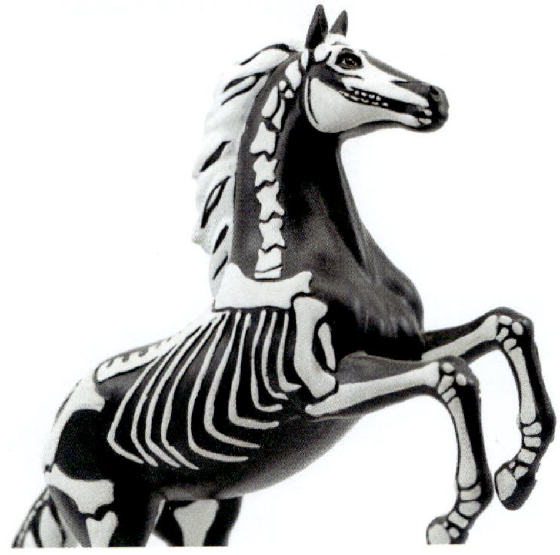

Fig. 108: AUTO white balance isn't always right. However, you can always adjust white balance later with the built-in, or an external, RAW converter. In this case, a simple **white balance preset** change from AUTO (top) to FLUORESCENT LIGHT-1 (bottom) did the job.

■ A Kelvin option to manually set the color temperature.

■ Custom white balance that meters a white or neutral surface (like a white wall) under the current light conditions. This way, the camera can adjust the white balance to make the surface appear neutral.

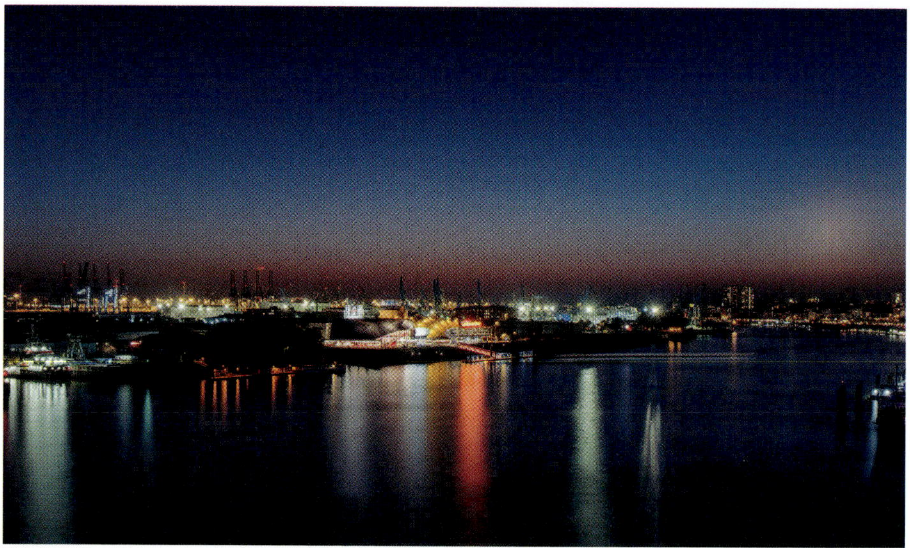

Fig. 109: Two versions of the same shot processed with **different white balance settings**. The image above shows the WB Auto setting without further corrections; the image below shows the same shot after a manual white balance adjustment in Lightroom. While white balance can also be adjusted with the camera's built-in RAW converter, extensive changes like this one are easier to accomplish with external RAW conversion software.

---

**Custom white balance: a little effort can go a long way.**    **TIP 92**

---

This useful function is only available *before* you take a shot, because you are metering the white balance of the actual scene. Custom white balance allows you to calibrate the camera's white balance toward a part of your scene you want to appear neutral in the final image.

Here we go:

- Select SHOOTING MENU > IMAGE QUALITY SETTING > WHITE BALANCE > CUSTOM. The X-T3 allows you to set and save three different custom white balance settings at the same time (CUSTOM 1–3).

- Point the camera toward a surface you want to use as a neutral reference—for example a white wall or a gray card [75]. Make sure the surface is large enough to be fully covered by the white balance metering frame in the viewfinder. Move closer to your subject or zoom in if you need to.

- Fully press the shutter button to meter and set the new custom white balance. The live view will change accordingly and will simulate the adjusted color temperature. If you are happy with the result, confirm it by pressing the OK button.

You can use the same procedure with a firing flash unit. In this case, the custom white balance will meter the mix of light from the flash with the ambient light that hits your neutral reference surface.

Don't worry! You are under no obligation to use the custom white balance later during RAW conversion. It's simply one of many options, and you can always adjust it later as you please. For example, you can use the built-in RAW converter with a manual KELVIN setting or select one of the white balance presets (usually FINE, SHADE, FLUORES-

CENT LIGHT 1–3, INCANDESCENT, and UNDERWATER). You can even apply AUTO white balance anytime later because the camera will always save its automatic white balance reading for later use by the internal RAW converter.

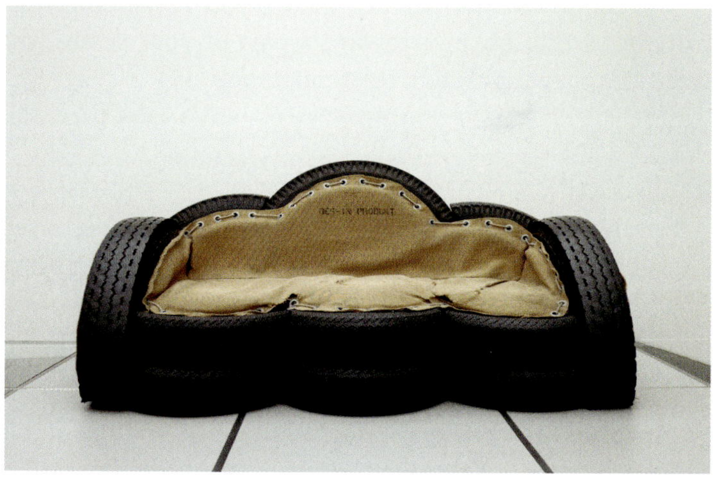

Fig. 110:  A **custom white balance** setting was used to take this shot. The wall behind the sofa served as a neutral reference.

| TIP 93 | Changing color tints with WB SHIFT |
|---|---|

WB SHIFT offers the opportunity to correct (or introduce) a color tint in any shot. You can adjust the color tint as an addition to any white balance setting—either before you take a shot, or in the built-in RAW converter.

You can individually set a *different* white balance shift for each of the camera's white balance options (Auto, Kelvin, WB presets, and Custom white balance settings). You can do this by adjusting the setting between green and red on the X-axis and between yellow and blue on the Y-axis of the display that automatically appears when you select one of the white balance options.

I recommend a neutral setting here to avoid confusion. As mentioned before, there's a different white balance shift setting for each of the white balance options, meaning the camera can store up to a dozen white balance shift settings at once. This makes it too easy to forget a previously set correction, which is why I recommend introducing white balance shift only during RAW conversion.

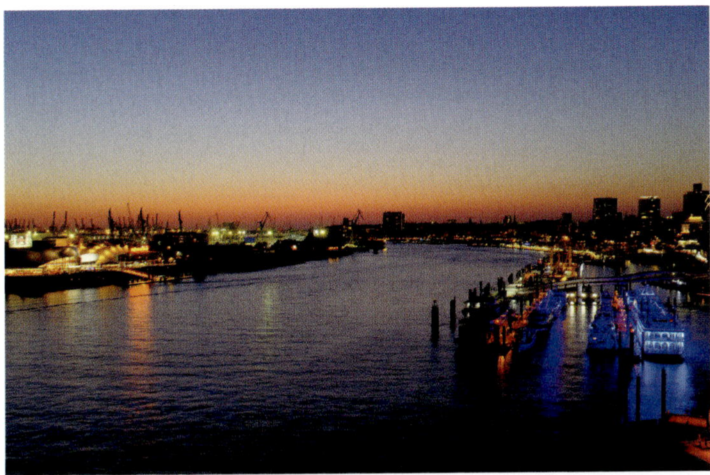

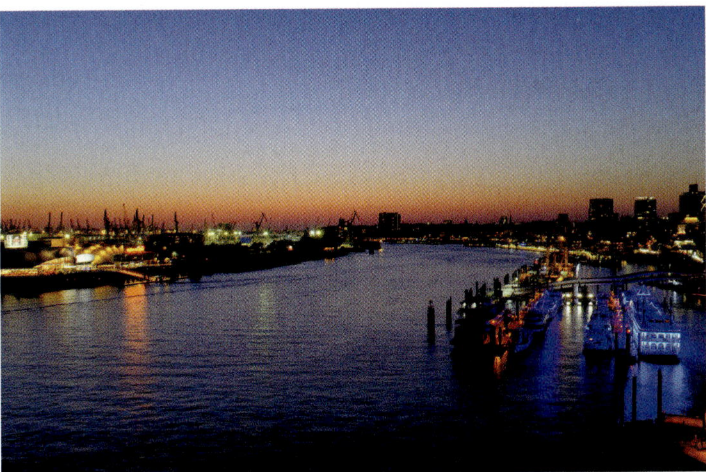

Fig. 111: **WB SHIFT in action:** The example at top shows a straight-out-of-camera image (SOOC JPEG) with the AUTO white balance settings. At bottom, you can see the same image, again straight out of camera and with AUTO white balance, but with an additional WB SHIFT of BLUE +3 and RED −3 to make it look cooler than the original.

*Important:* WB Shift works with in-camera JPEGs from the built-in RAW converter. When you process a RAW file externally with Lightroom or similar software, any WB Shift settings that were active when you took the image will usually be disregarded. However, Capture One is an exception to this rule and honors WB Shift settings automatically.

**TIP 94** | White balance and monochrome images

You may think white balance adjustments don't affect black-and-white images because monochrome shots only consist of neutral shades of gray. In reality, your white balance settings still affect the *underlying* color information that your monochrome conversion is based on.

Black-and-white photography is color photography with an additional dimension of difficulty. This added dimension is determining how particular grayscale levels are assigned to particular colors. Since your white balance settings affect the colors of the underlying shot, they also affect the grayscale tones of the color-to-monochrome conversion.

Black-and-white images can be created either in-camera (with the MONOCHROME and ACROS film simulations) or externally with RAW conversion software such as Lightroom, Capture One, or Silkypix. When you set your X-T3 to ACROS or MONOCHROME, it is still recoding RAW *color* images, which are then converted into black-and-white JPEGs.

Knowing this, you can manipulate the look of your black-and-white conversions by changing the white balance during RAW conversion—either in-camera or externally in your post-processing software. In-camera with the built-in RAW converter, you can use one of the white balance presets, or you can select a manual Kelvin setting between 2500K and 10000K.

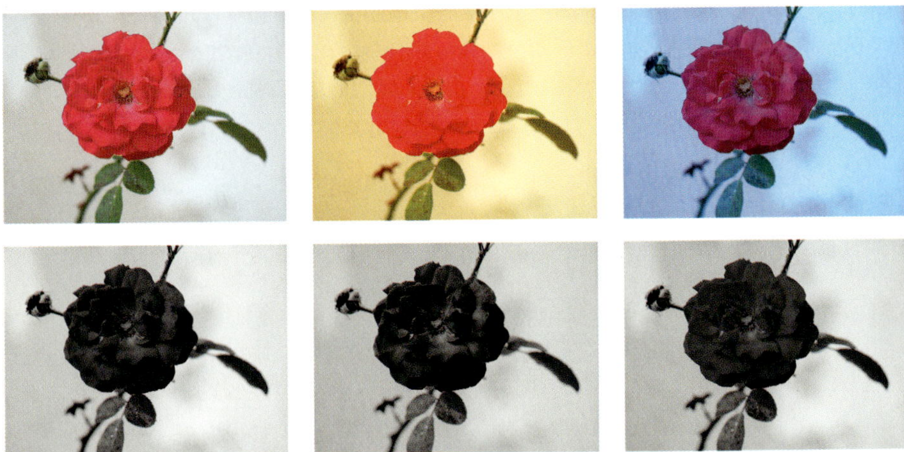

Fig. 112: **White balance and monochrome:** In the upper row, this illustration shows the same color image with Auto white balance (left), a 2500K setting (center) and a 10000K setting (right). The lower row exhibits monochrome conversions of the above images; all three made with a MONOCHROME+G FILTER film simulation and a SHADOW TONE +4 setting. The various underlying white balance settings have a visible impact on the appearance of the monochrome conversions.

| Using film simulations | TIP 95 |
| --- | --- |

The importance of film simulations for the overall look of a JPEG is often underestimated. Film simulations influence color grading, color saturation, dynamic range, and contrast in the resulting JPEGs. Picking a film simulation should always be the first step when adjusting JPEG parameters. As with all JPEG settings, film simulations have no effect on the actual RAW file (the digital negative). They only affect the JPEGs that are generated in the camera (the digital prints).

Here are the available film simulation options:

■ PROVIA is the standard, all-purpose setting. The name reminds us of Fuji's popular Provia slide film.

- ASTIA is another color slide film derivate with softer highlights and pleasing skin tones. It's often used for portraits but can also work with landscape shots that feature vegetation and blue sky.

- VELVIA is a very contrast-heavy, color-saturated derivate of the legendary Fuji Velvia slide film. It's mostly used for landscape and nature shots and is rather unsuitable for portrait work.

- CLASSIC CHROME reminds us of the golden era of *LIFE* magazine color photography. The distinctive look of Classic Chrome is equally suitable for landscapes and portraits.

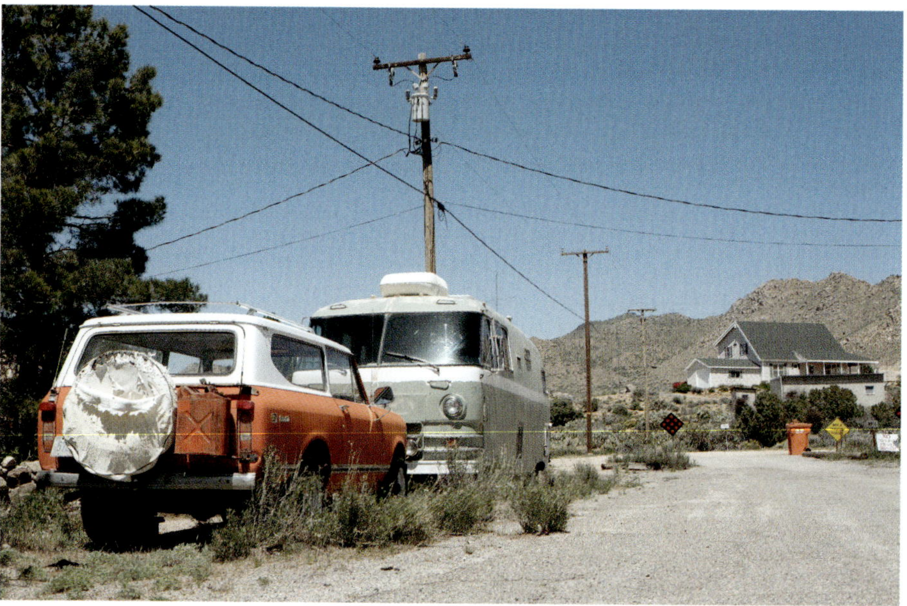

Fig. 113:  The distinctive look of **CLASSIC CHROME** has earned it much popularity in a very short time.

- PRO NEG. HI is derived from a professional color negative film that was specifically made for portraits. It delivers accurate and pleasing skin tones with nice contrast, and adds some punch to the image without adding too much color to faces.

- PRO NEG. STD is a rather neutral film simulation. Featuring flat contrast, subdued colors, and high dynamic range, it can look dull at first, but the JPEGs are usable for further post-processing. Fuji recommends this film simulation for studio portraits in a flash setup.

- CLASSIC NEG. is a new film simulation that was introduced with the X-Pro3. It resembles Fujifilm's classic Superia negative film, and it is supposed to be made available in the X-T3 via a free firmware upgrade.

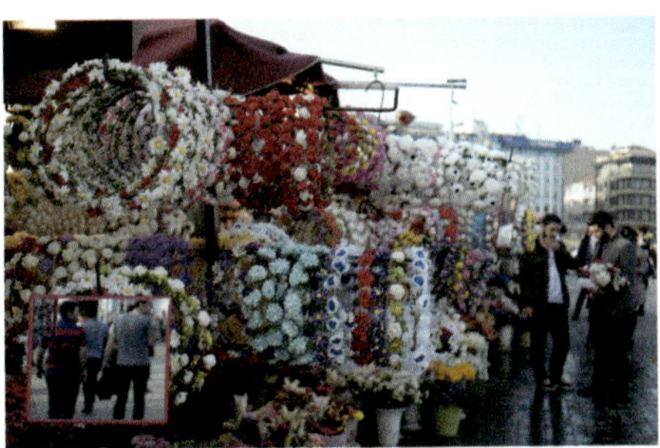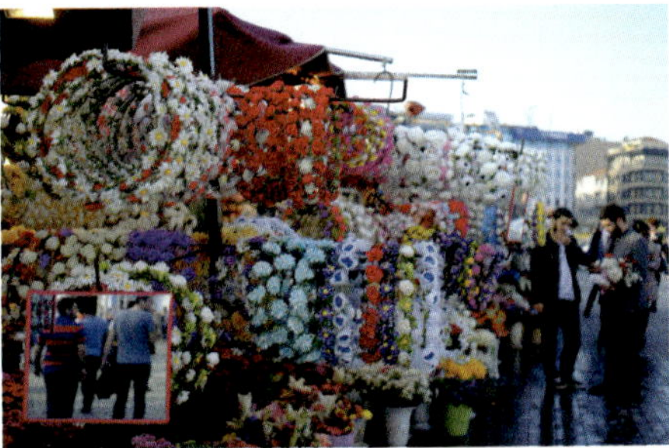

Fig. 114: **Antagonists:** PRO NEG. STD and VELVIA illustrate the spectrum of Fuji's various film simulation modes. On the left you can see the PRO NEG. STD version of a shot, and on the right its VELVIA cousin.

- ETERNA is the most neutral film simulation. Though Eterna was designed as a flat and desaturated film simulation for video production, it's also our preferred low-contrast, high dynamic range profile for RAW photography.

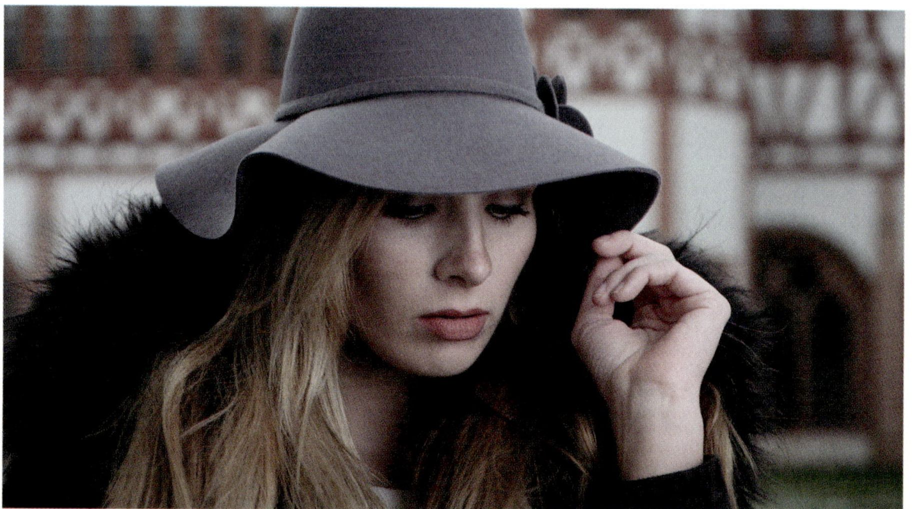

**Fig. 115:** ETERNA is a flat film simulation profile with a cinematic look. It is named after Fujifilm's discontinued Eterna motion picture film. With low contrast, high dynamic range and desaturated colors, it's ideal for video production work. That said, it can also be used as a flat RAW shooter profile (along with Highlight Tone −2 and Shadow Tone −2 settings), or for neutral, cinematic JPEGs like this sample image.

- MONOCHROME is Fuji's standard black-and-white conversion. Black-and-white photography is based on assigning particular gray levels to particular colors of a scene. To increase the contrast, many photographers combine MONOCHROME with increased SHADOW TONE and HIGHLIGHT TONE settings. Additionally, noise reduction is often decreased to reveal more detail and display more noise, which gives the appearance of film grain.

- MONOCHROME+Ye FILTER adds a digital yellow filter to the black-and-white conversion. This typically results in a slight increase of contrast because yellow parts of the scene will be represented by brighter gray tones.

- MONOCHROME+R FILTER adds a red filter to the black-and-white conversion. This means that skin tones will become brighter, which will camouflage reddish skin impurities. Conversely, blue skies will be darkened, adding contrast between clouds and the sky.

- MONOCHROME+G FILTER adds a green filter to the black-and-white conversion. This filter will add texture to skin tones and can potentially emphasize imperfections.

- SEPIA results in a sepia-toned monochrome JPEG for a vintage-looking touch.

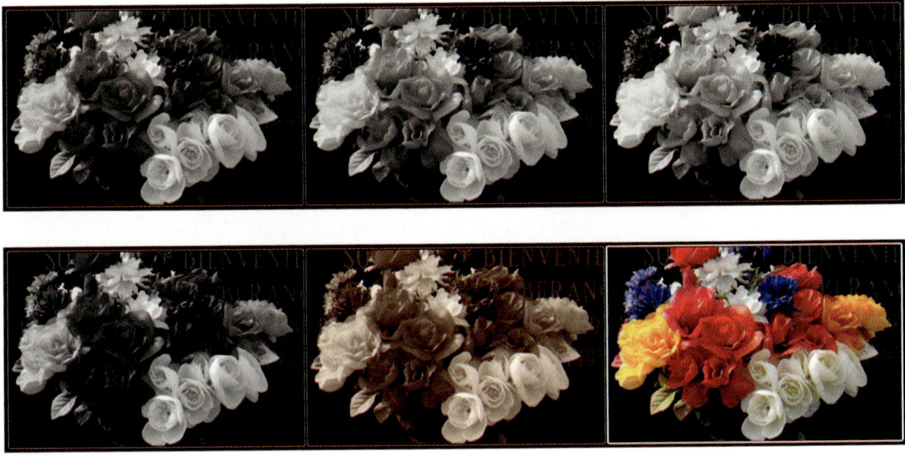

Fig. 116: **Comparing B&W options:** From left to right, top row: unfiltered B&W, yellow filter, and red filter. Bottom row: green filter, sepia, and the original shot in color.

- ACROS is a more sophisticated alternative to the regular MONOCHROME settings and is available in four versions: no filter, or with either a yellow, red, or green filter. It reminds us of Fujifilm's analog Acros film and offers a quite cinematic look. This is partly because ACROS includes a noise-dependent analog film grain simulation that transforms regular image noise into analog-looking grain.

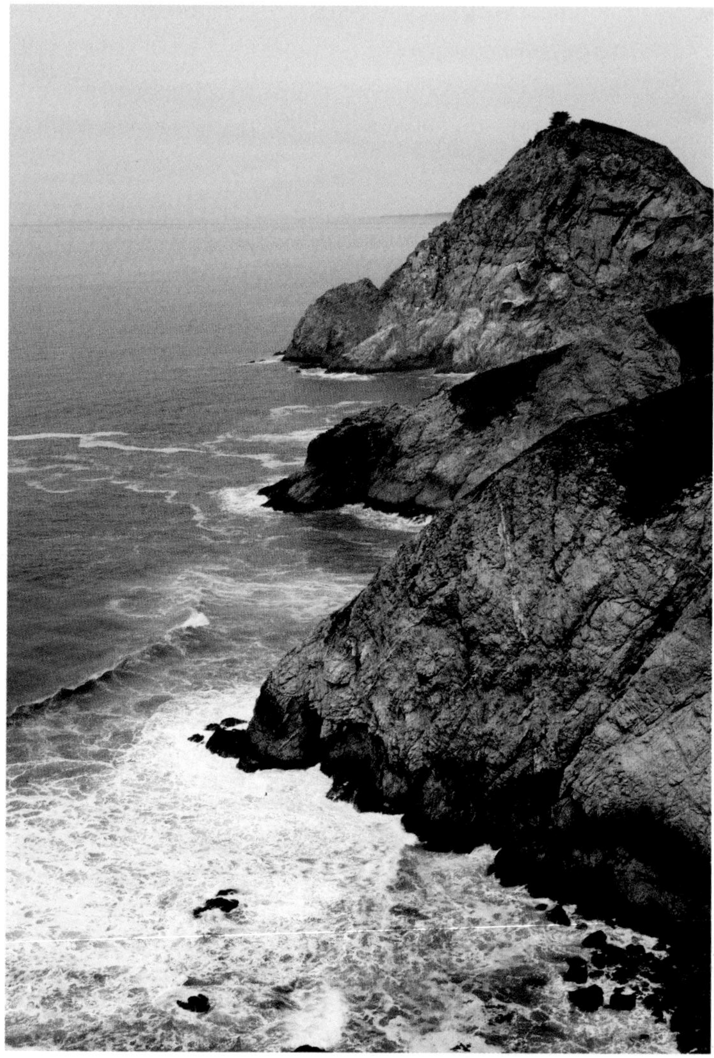

Fig. 117: ACROS has quickly become a favorite among X series users. Due to its high processing requirements, this sophisticated monochrome film simulation is currently available only in cameras that are equipped with X-Processor Pro or X-Processor 4.

The noise-dependent analog film grain simulation of ACROS is based on innovative noise shaping. To make the grain visible, your image must contain some noise, so it's best to set in-camera noise reduction to a minimum. Even at base ISO, there's already a subtle difference between ACROS and the regular MONOCHROME film simulation—as long as you set noise reduction to −4 in order to give the noise-shaping algorithm something to work with.

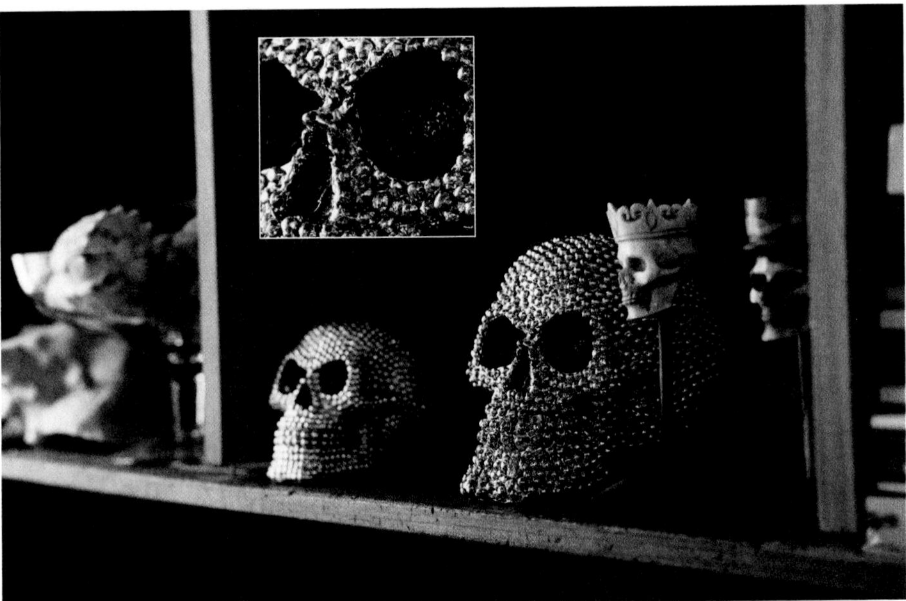

Fig. 118: Even at ISO 25600, the noise shaping of the **ACROS film simulation** delivers a natural-looking result with high resolution and fine details.

The best way to learn about film simulations is to experiment and compare the various options for yourself. The easiest way to do so is with the camera's internal RAW converter. Take one RAW file and process it with all available film simulations, and then import the JPEGs into your computer and compare the results on your monitor.

You can also use X RAW STUDIO [76] to conveniently remotely control your camera's built-in RAW converter from your Mac or your Windows PC.

| TIP 96 | Using the GRAIN EFFECT |

Fujifilm is all about great film simulations with an organic look. For example, adding "analog film grain" to a digital image can be useful to achieve a more natural look with enhanced micro contrast.

GRAIN EFFECT offers three settings: OFF, WEAK, and STRONG. It adds a layer of randomized, simulated film grain to the image and can be used with all film simulations.

Please note that I do *not* recommend using GRAIN EFFECT in concert with the ACROS film simulation—it would mix two different grain effects. After all, ACROS already brings its own noise-dependent grain to the table.

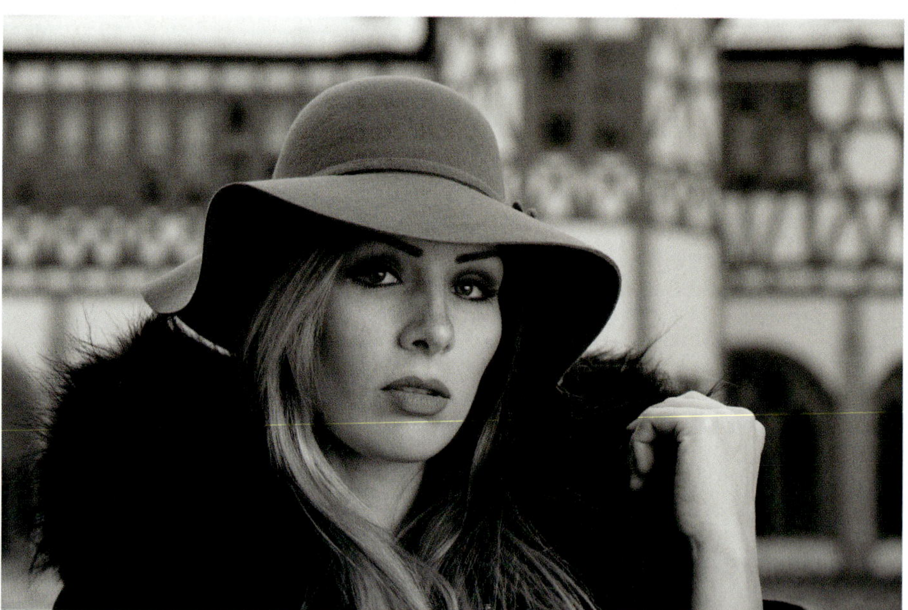

Fig. 119: Even at base ISO, using the ACROS film simulation in concert with minimal noise reduction (−4) results in a subtle grain effect that adds organic texture to the image.

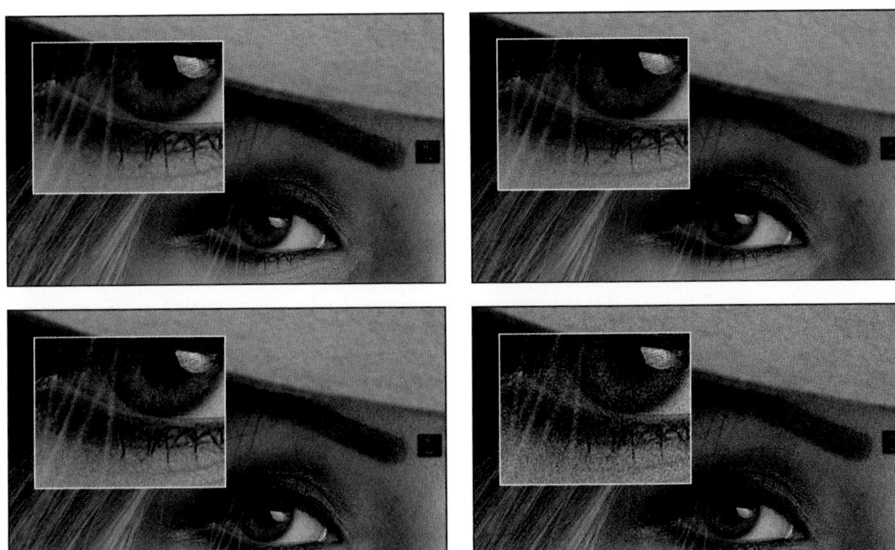

Fig. 120: GRAIN EFFECT adds natural-looking analog grain to all film simulations, providing extra texture and micro contrast for an organic look. These zoomed-in samples show the same image as before in four variations, all processed in-camera with minimal noise reduction: MONOCHROME with GRAIN EFFECT OFF (top left), ACROS with GRAIN EFFECT OFF (top right), MONOCHROME with GRAIN EFFECT WEAK (bottom left), and MONOCHROME with GRAIN EFFECT set to STRONG (bottom right). As you can see, the built-in noise shaping of ACROS holds its own without adding another layer of artificial grain via the GRAIN EFFECT setting.

Adding artificial grain may not be necessary for shots that were taken with ISO settings of 800 or higher. Instead, you can reduce the NOISE REDUCTION setting to −4 to preserve as much noise (and detail) as possible and allow the camera to do its magic.

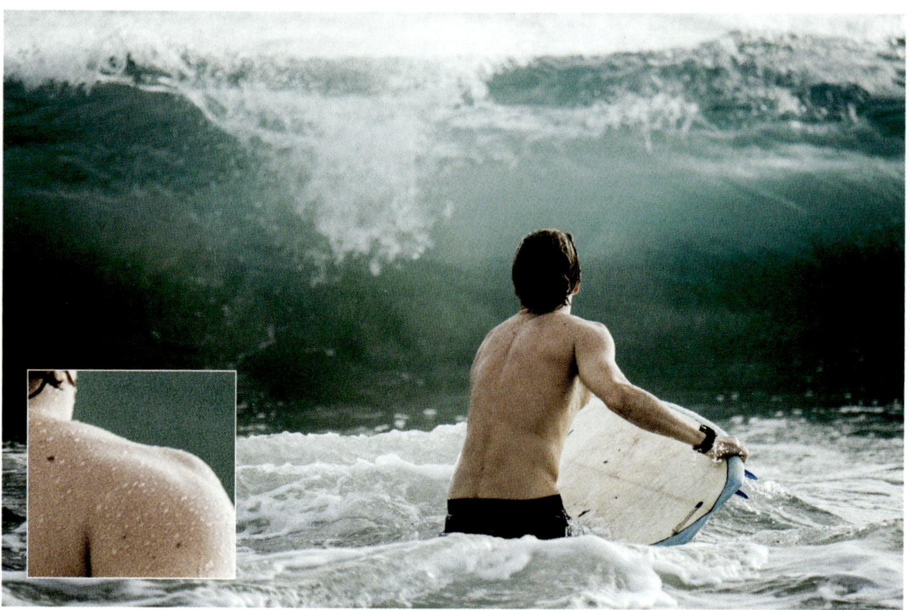

**Fig. 121:** Grain effects are also available in some external RAW converters and post-processing software. This sample shows an image processed in Lightroom with a subtle grain effect. Artificial grain is primarily about adding texture and micro contrast to an image. In most cases, the grain itself will be invisible at normal viewing distances. Subtle extra grain can also be used to trick hosting services and websites into applying less JPEG compression to out-of-focus areas when you upload images to share online. Less compression means larger files and smoother tonal transitions with fewer artifacts.

| TIP 97 | Contrast settings: adjusting highlights and shadows |
|---|---|

A useful feature of the X-T3 is its ability to independently set the contrast [77] for dark and bright parts of a JPEG image using the HIGHLIGHT TONE and SHADOW TONE settings. These settings can also be used to extend a JPEG's dynamic range by lifting dark shadows or darkening bright highlights. To increase the overall contrast of a shot, you can increase both parameters in tandem by choosing a setting on the plus side. To reduce the overall contrast, pick a negative setting for both parameters.

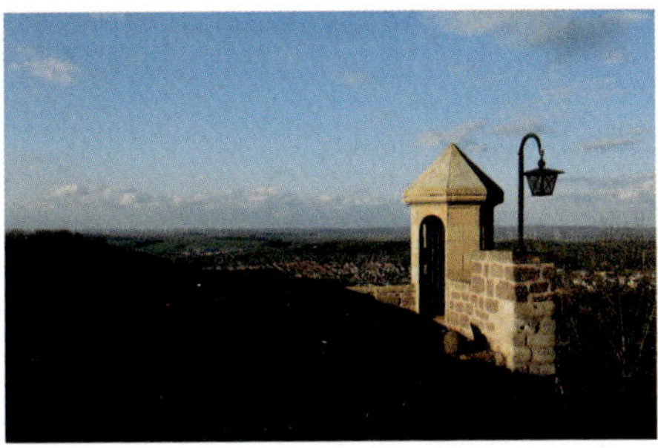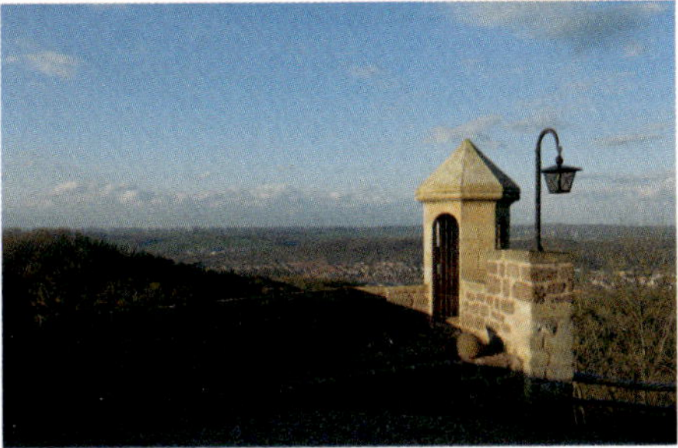

Fig. 122: Comparing **Shadow Tone** settings: The image on the left shows a SHADOW TONE +2 version; the image on the right shows the same RAW file processed with SHADOW TONE −2. Shadows and dark midtones were lifted by the reduction of the JPEG's shadow contrast, while the highlights remained untouched.

It's worth mentioning that increased contrast also enhances the impression of image sharpness and color saturation. This demonstrates that JPEG parameters always work in concert with each other.

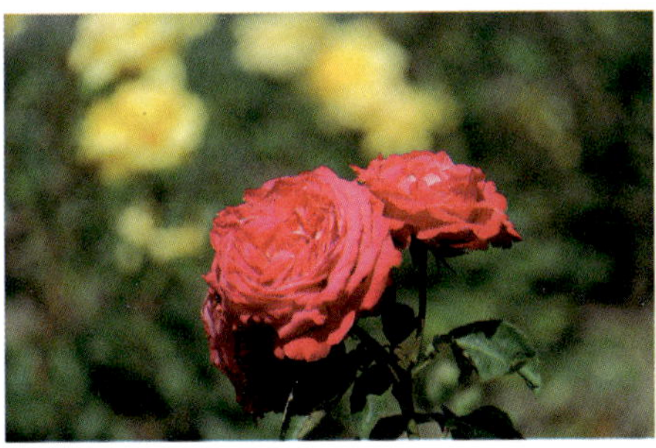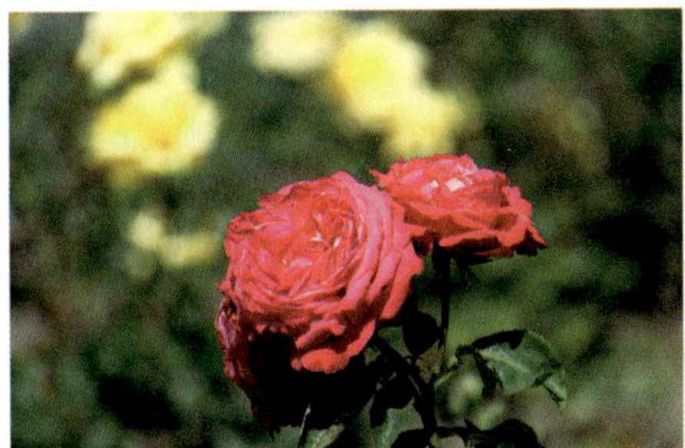

Fig. 123: Comparing **Highlight Tone** settings: The image on the left shows the HIGHLIGHT TONE −2 version of a shot; the image on the right shows the same RAW file processed with HIGHLIGHT TONE +2. Increasing the highlight contrast leaves the shadows and darker midtones untouched.

| Color saturation | TIP 98 |
| --- | --- |

After picking a suitable film simulation mode, you still might want to change the color saturation [78] of an image. You can do so with the COLOR setting.

Too much color saturation can obscure texture and details. For example, VELVIA is a very saturated film mode that may sometimes require a reduction in color saturation.

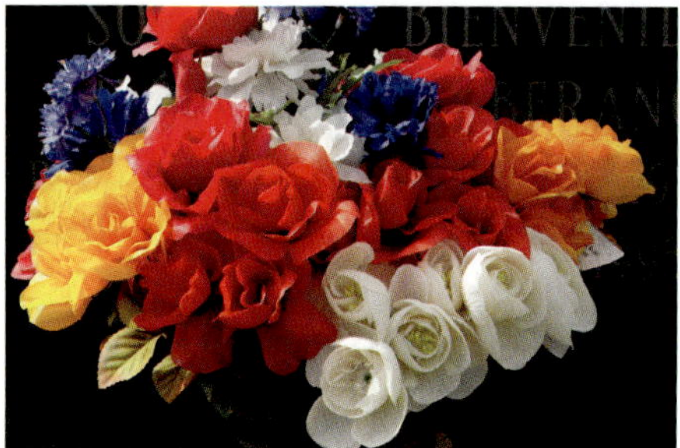 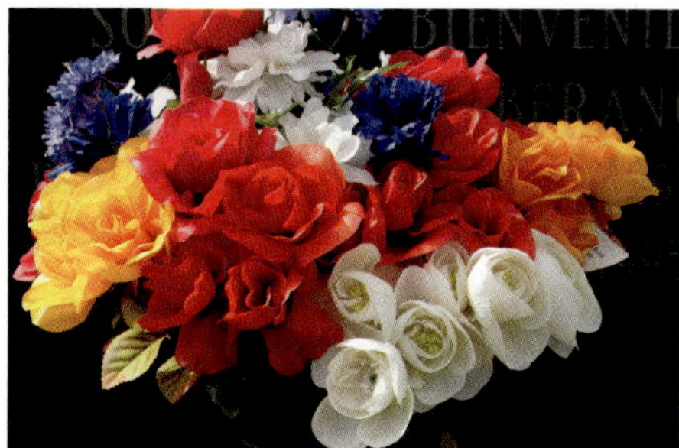

Fig. 124: **Color saturation:** The left image shows a PROVIA version with COLOR −4; the right image shows the same RAW file processed with COLOR +4.

<table>
<tr><td>TIP 99</td><td>The COLOR CHROME EFFECT</td></tr>
</table>

Color Chrome Effect is a calculation-heavy process that adds depth to saturated colors in an image. I don't recommend using this setting in shooting mode. Instead, apply it as needed after the fact with your camera's built-in RAW converter.

COLOR CHROME EFFECT offers three settings: OFF, WEAK and STRONG. It can be applied in concert with any film simulation.

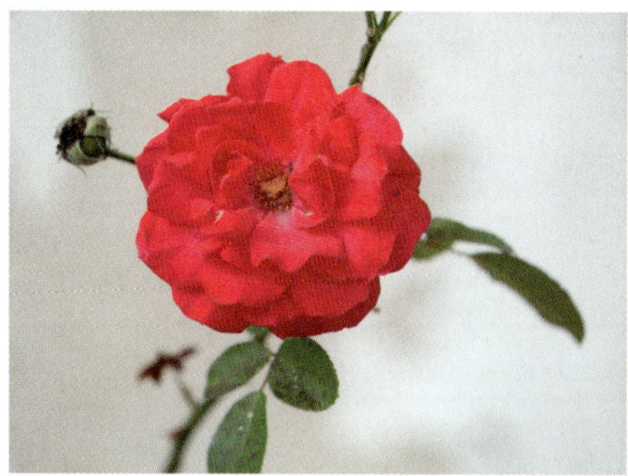 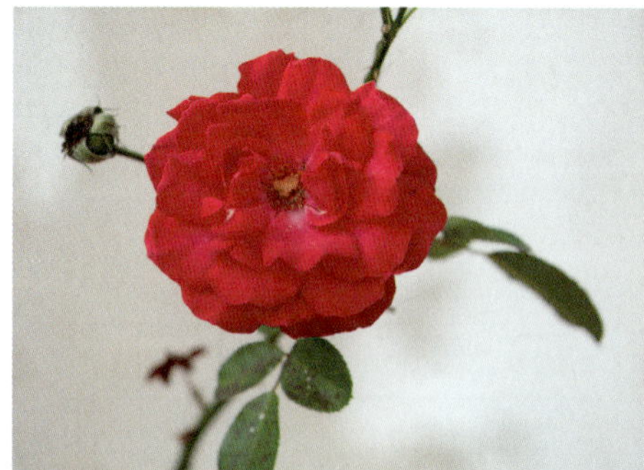

Fig. 125: This example illustrates how a regular Provia image (left) is changed by adding a COLOR CHROME EFFECT > STRONG setting (right).

| B&W ADJ.: adding color tints to monochrome images | TIP 100 |

In many cases, printed black-and-white photos aren't just black and white, but they contain a warm or cool color tint. Even in photographic books, it's a common printing practice to add at least one color to monochrome pictures in order to increase the range of tones that can be realized during the printing process.

The X-T3 is Fujifilm's first X camera that allows adding a warm or cold color tint to ACROS and MONOCHROME images. With the B&W ADJ. setting, you can change the neutral look of black-and-white images with a Warm/Cool adjustment in ±9 steps.

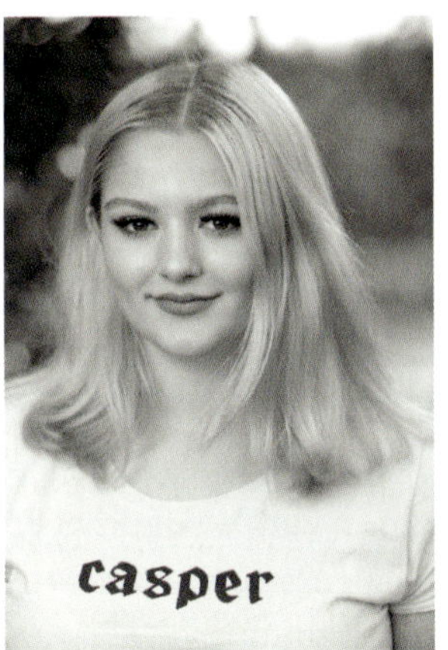

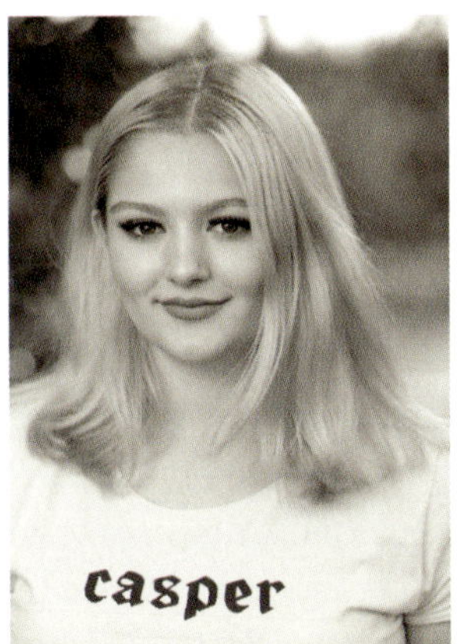

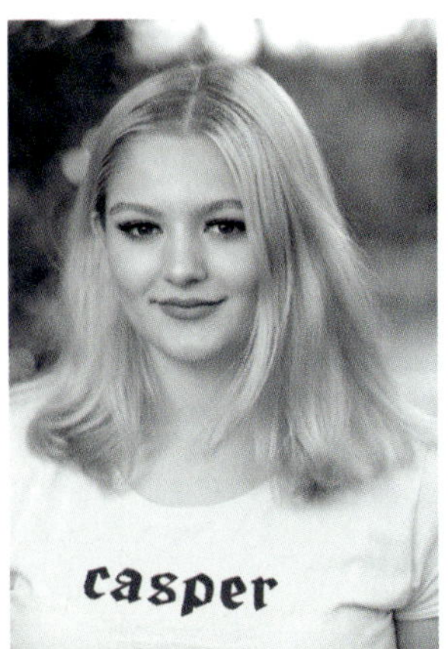


Fig. 126: This example illustrates the effect of the B&W ADJ. setting on monochromatic JPEGs: The sample at left shows an ACROS image with a neutral Warm/Cool setting of 0. The center sample is the same shot, but with Warm/Cool set to +4. On the right, we have the image with a Warm/Cool −4 setting.

| Color space: sRGB or Adobe RGB? | TIP 101 |

A color space [79] is a way of organizing available colors. The X-T3 offers two options: sRGB [80] and Adobe RGB [81]. Both color spaces contain the same *number* of colors, but not the *same* colors—their gamuts [82] are different.

Adobe RGB covers a larger gamut than sRGB because its colors are optimized for CMYK printing. On the other hand, sRGB is optimized for computer monitors and all kinds of high-resolution displays, such as HD and UHD TVs, smartphones, and tablets. Since Adobe RGB encompasses a wider gamut than sRGB, the gaps between neighboring colors and tones are wider because both color spaces contain the same number of colors. Adobe RGB must spread this number over its larger gamut. This larger gamut (compared to standard sRGB) is why Adobe RGB is also known as an extended color space.

Users often misunderstand and assume that "extended" means "better." It does not. The additional colors in Adobe RGB are only useful if you intend to print your JPEG or TIFF files with a commercial CMYK printer. This requires a calibrated workflow and a wide-gamut monitor that can display the entire Adobe RGB gamut. However, most computer monitors are capable of displaying only the sRGB gamut. Using Adobe RGB on such a monitor would be like working with half-closed eyes because you wouldn't be able to see many of the colors you are using.

For most users (including me), sRGB is the best choice of color space. Images rendered in this color space can be viewed, processed, and printed on a wide variety of devices without unpleasant surprises. In any case, you should calibrate your computer monitor with hardware like Datacolor's Spyder and X-Rite's ColorMunki. Uncalibrated screens will not give you an accurate representation of the colors in your images.

| TIP 102 | Using custom settings (usage profiles) |
| --- | --- |

The X-T3 offers seven custom settings (C1 to C7) that can hold sets of camera settings for quick access. The available settings are:

- Dynamic Range
- D-Range Priority
- Film Simulation
- B&W Adjustment
- Grain Effect
- White Balance
- Highlight Tone
- Shadow Tone
- Color
- Color Chrome Effect
- Sharpness
- Noise Reduction

Basically, custom settings are comprised of your camera's JPEG parameters with the addition of dynamic range settings.

Custom settings (or usage profiles) are not camera modes. They are storage spaces for sets of settings that can be quickly retrieved (usually via the Quick menu) to replace the currently active camera settings with new ones. Custom settings are mere shortcuts—time-savers that allow you to quickly change several of your camera's current settings at once instead of changing parameters one by one.

The best way to select a custom setting is via the Quick menu:

- Pull up the Quick menu by pressing the Q button and then select one of the available custom settings (C1 to C7).

- At this point, you can make changes to individual items of the retrieved parameter set using the Quick menu. Once you change a parameter, it is marked with a red dot.

- When you are happy with your settings and changes, you can make them your new *current* settings by pressing the OK button or by half-pressing the shutter button. In the upper-left section of the Quick menu, the currently active settings are always marked with the word BASE. It also displays the custom setting that was last retrieved; for example, C1.

What kind of custom settings may be useful? Here are a few suggestions:

- Make sure to save your favorite all-purpose default settings in one of the user profiles (such as C1). This enables you to quickly revert to your standard settings.

- RAW shooters can use a RAW shooter profile with dynamic range set to DR100%, HIGHLIGHT TONE –2, SHADOW TONE –2, and ETERNA film simulation. The C7 custom setting is traditionally the spot where I keep my "RAW Shooter" settings. To help you remember what each of the (up to) seven custom settings does, you can assign them memorable labels such as "RAW Shooter."

- You could create a profile for black-and-white shooting. It could contain one of the eight B&W film simulations, minimal noise reduction, and additional highlight and shadow contrast.

| TIP 103 | Working with the built-in RAW converter |
| --- | --- |

The RAW converter in your X-T3 serves two main purposes:

- You could create various versions of a shot; for example, a colorful Velvia version and a gritty black-and-white version of the same image. Not sure what's best or what you want? Quickly create multiple versions with different film simulations and varying JPEG parameters, and then sort them out later on your calibrated computer screen.

- You can improve your JPEGs after the fact. Since it's hard (if not impossible) to guess and set the perfect JPEG settings for each shot in advance, it's more convenient to adjust these parameters later when you have time to look at your results. You can easily change parameters like white balance, color saturation, contrast settings, sharpness, or noise reduction. You can also adjust the exposure and try various film simulations.

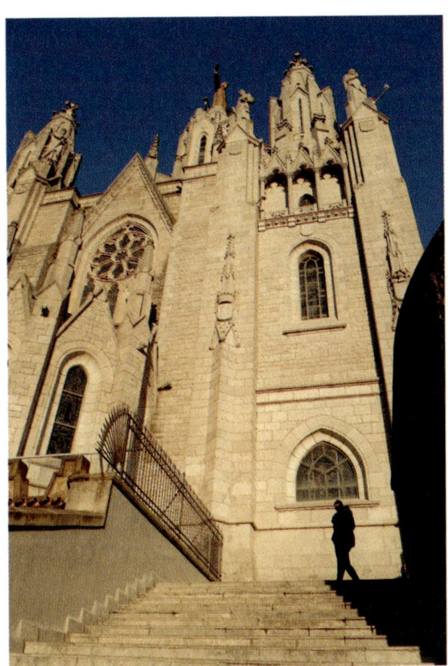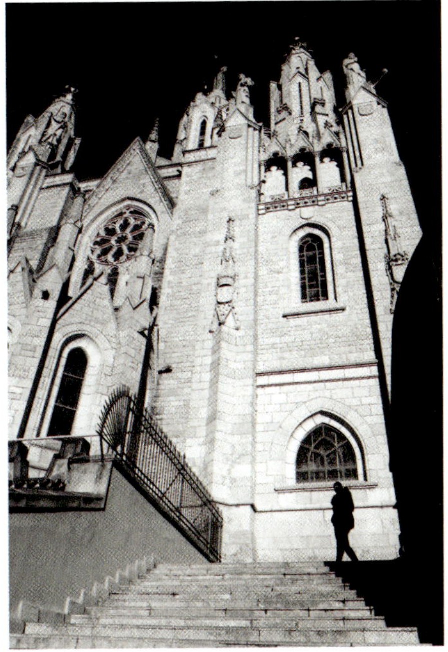

Fig. 127: Using the **built-in RAW converter** to change the look of a shot: the left image shows the scene as it was recorded with the camera's default settings. On the right, you can see the same shot processed with ACROS+Red Filter and maximum contrast (SHADOW TONE +4 and HIGHLIGHT TONE +4).

Here are a few things you can accomplish with the built-in RAW converter:

■ Use PUSH/PULL processing to brighten (*push*) underexposed shots or darken (*pull*) overexposed images.

■ Use the contrast settings (SHADOW TONE and HIGH-LIGHT TONE) to selectively adjust the contrast of dark or bright parts of your image. It's perfectly adequate to combine these functions with PUSH/PULL processing. To generate JPEGs with maximum dynamic range for further post-processing on your computer, it may be useful to set both contrast parameters (shadows and highlights) to −2 and use a neutral film simulation like PRO NEG. STD or ETERNA.

- Adjust the color saturation of your JPEGs with the COLOR parameter. Reducing the color saturation can recover texture when one or more of the color channels appear oversaturated.

- Use SHARPNESS and NOISE REDUCTION in opposition with each other: increase sharpness while diminishing noise reduction to preserve more texture in high-ISO shots.

- Adjust the white balance using one of the presets or a Kelvin value to make your shot look warmer or cooler. Use WB SHIFT to correct or introduce a color tint.

- Want to know what the Lens Modulation Optimizer (LMO) is doing? Take a RAW sample and process JPEGs with and without LMO in the internal RAW converter. Then, compare the results on a computer screen. Happy pixel peeping!

- Picked the wrong color space? No problem! Just reprocess the shot with the correct color space.

To process RAW files that have already been transferred to a computer, you can use the free X RAW STUDIO application as a remote control interface for your camera's built-in RAW converter.

By the way: Your X-T3 cannot process RAW files from other X series models. For example, the built-in RAW converter of your camera cannot process RAW files that were taken with an X-T20. However, you can process RAW files that were shot with a different X-T3 camera.

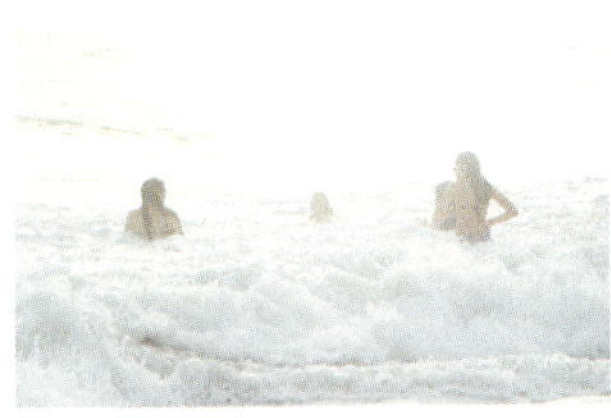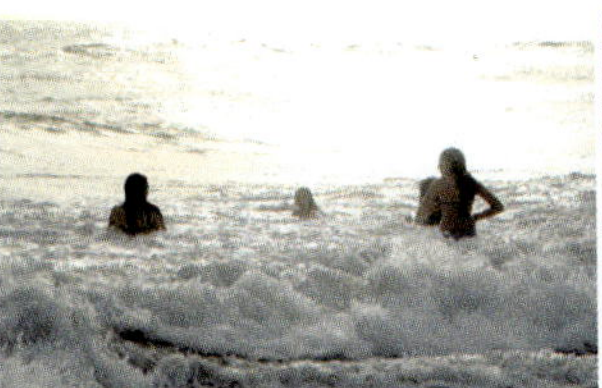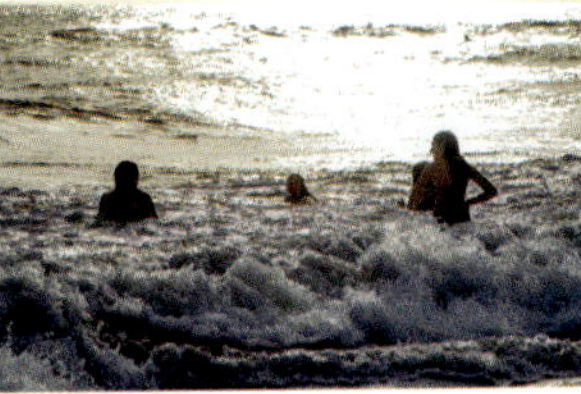

Fig. 128: You can also use the **built-in RAW converter** to correct a shot. The left image shows an overexposed sample shot that was recorded with default settings and DR400%. In the middle, you can see the same shot processed in-camera with a PULL of −2 EV, maximized shadow contrast (SHADOW TONE +4), and the VELVIA film simulation. To complete the comparison, the version on the right was created in Lightroom.

<table>
<tr><td>Working with X RAW STUDIO</td><td>TIP 104</td></tr>
</table>

The built-in RAW converter of X series cameras is a practical tool for on-the-fly RAW conversions while you are in the field. You can use your camera's LCD or EVF display (I recommend the latter) to create new and improved JPEGs from RAW files that are saved on the SD card in your camera.

But what if your RAW files have already been transferred from the SD card to a computer? Instead of copying them back to a card and processing them in-camera, there's a better and more comfortable way: FUJIFILM X RAW STUDIO.

X RAW STUDIO is a free download for Windows and macOS [83]. Don't confuse it with a stand-alone RAW converter, though. Basically, X RAW STUDIO is a PC/Mac-based remote-control and user interface for the built-in RAW converter of your X-T3. This means that X RAW STUDIO doesn't work without your camera, which must be tethered to your Mac or PC via USB.

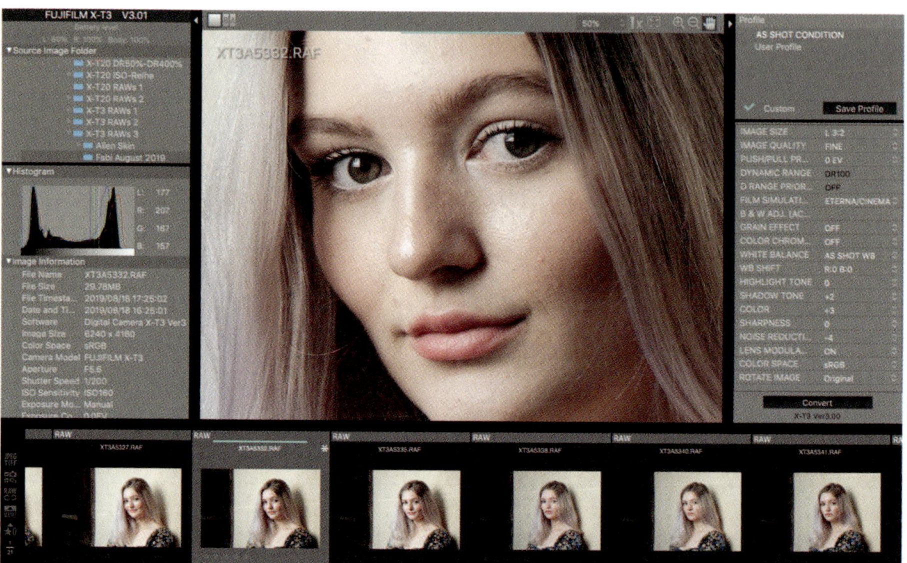

Fig. 129: **FUJIFILM X RAW STUDIO** is a simple way to remotely control the built-in RAW converter of your camera and use it to process RAW files that are stored on your Windows PC or Mac. The free app sends RAW files from your computer to the camera via a USB-C connection, where they are processed to "in-camera JPEGs" that are immediately returned to your PC. You get the best of both worlds: the ease of use of a computer interface (with a large display and convenient storage for all your images) is combined with the processing power and image quality of your camera's internal RAW converter.

Set-up your camera to work with X RAW STUDIO by selecting SET UP > CONNECTION SETTING > PC CONNECTION MODE > USB RAW CONV./BACKUP RESTORE, and then connect it to your Mac or PC via USB while X RAW STUDIO is running. Operating the software is mostly self-explanatory, but feel free to consult Fuji's online manual [84].

Since it runs on a computer, X RAW STUDIO offers a more comprehensive user interface than the stand-alone converter in your camera. You can copy and paste development settings from one image to others, and you can set-up and save development presets for later use. Batch processing of multiple RAW images is also no problem.

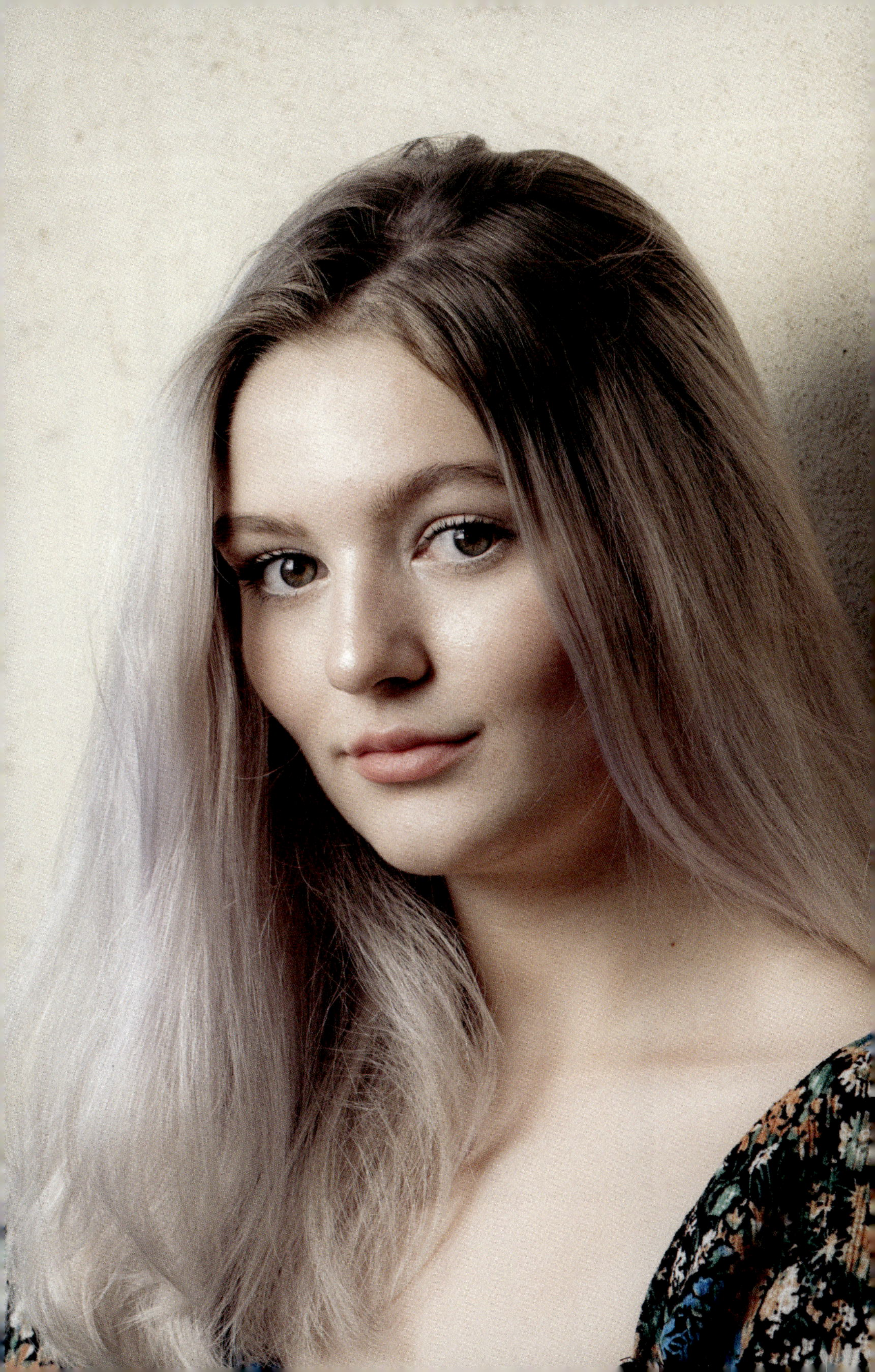

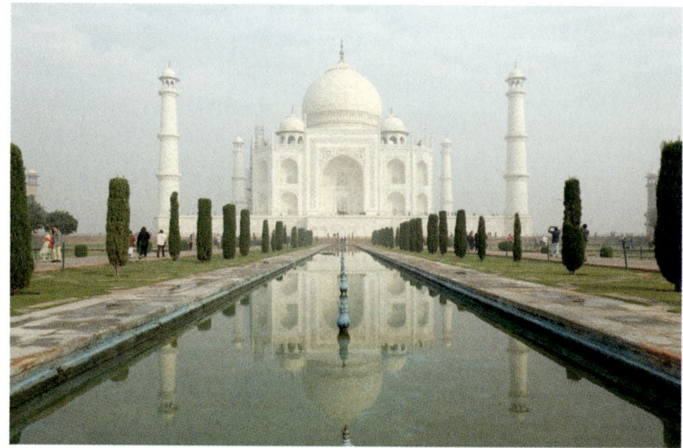

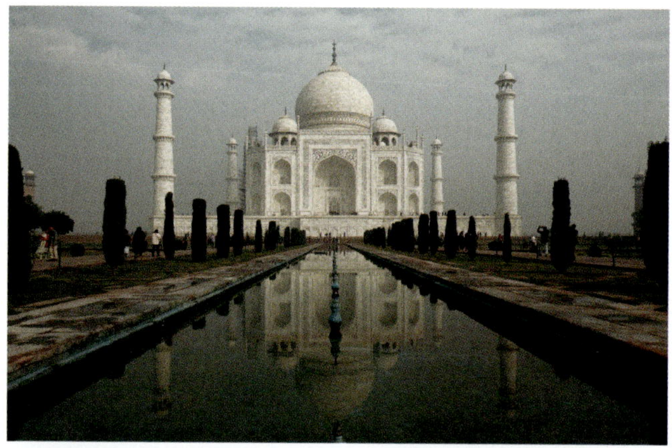

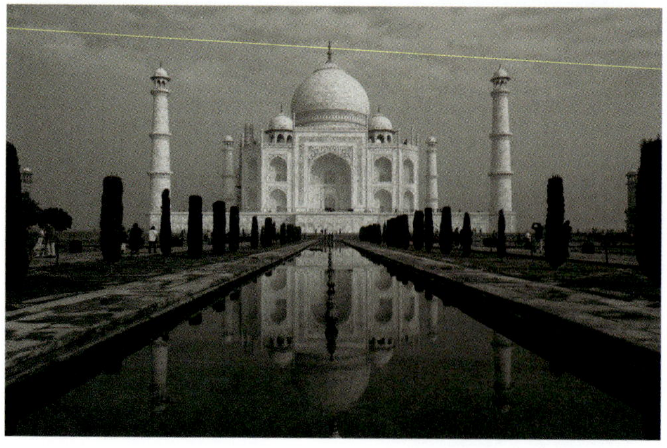

Fig. 130: **X RAW STUDIO** offers a straightforward workflow. You begin with selecting a RAW image from your computer's hard drive. In this case, I chose a shot of the Taj Mahal, which I took with an XF18–55mm kit zoom. The image was automatically processed and displayed with the camera settings that were active when I took the shot (top image). I used the camera's factory defaults with PROVIA.

The center image is the same RAW file after processing it with different settings. After changing the film simulation to CLASSIC CHROME, I lowered the exposure by applying a PULL of −1.33 EV, raised HIGHLIGHT TONE to +4 for brighter highlights, reduced NOISE REDUCTION to −4 to reveal maximum detail, and applied SHARPENING +3, because I was unlucky enough to bring a soft XF18–55mm lens copy with me to India. After clicking on the Convert button, the app saved the new-and-improved JPEG on my Mac, using the same directory as the underlying RAW file.

The image below is a second processing variant of the same shot, this time using MONOCHROME+R FILTER, PULL −1.33 EV, HIGHLIGHT TONE +4, SHADOW TONE +1, NOISE REDUCTION −4, and SHARPENING +3. I also changed the white balance to 4500K and applied a WB shift of R: −5 and B: +7 to add a bit more drama.

# 2.6 SHOOTING VIDEO WITH THE X-T3

Your X-T3 doesn't just shoot great stills, it is also a powerful video camera with a plethora of features and options that can at first be overwhelming. Let's take a walk through many of the functions, options, codecs, and settings.

| What you should know about the codecs of the X-T3 | TIP 105 |
|---|---|

**Codec** is a portmanteau of **co**der and **dec**oder. It describes an algorithm that encodes and decodes digital video, often compressing it to reduce file size. The X-T3 is the first X-series camera that allows you to choose between two different codecs:

- MPEG-4-AVC/H.264, named "H.264" in the camera menu
- MPEG-H HEVC/H.265, named "H.265(HEVC)" in the menu

HEVC, short for "High Efficiency Video Codec," was developed to reduce file size while maintaining high video quality [85]. It uses efficient compression and is meant to produce acceptable file sizes even with high-resolution video at high frame rates. When using the H.265 (HEVC) codec, the X-T3 saves files with 10-bit color depth. The combination of H.265, 10-bit color depth, and bit rates of up to 400 Mbps offers the highest quality available.

You can select one of the two available codecs with SHOOTING MENU > MOVIE SETTING > H.265(HEVC)/H.264.

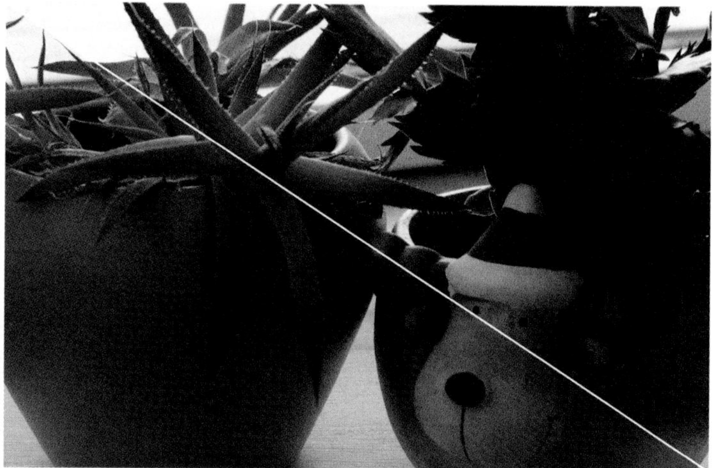

Fig. 131: Comparing a heavily edited H.264 8-bit recording (lower-left half) with a H.265 10-bit recording (upper-right half) we can spot the differences in color information, especially in the shadow areas.

H.265 delivers better image quality than H.264 without producing larger files [86]. However, H.265 also comes with a few drawbacks: While H.265 is a great acquisition codec, it is harder to decode on a computer, thus resulting in higher hardware requirements. If you are running into problems working with H.265 files, the following points might help you with troubleshooting:

- Update or upgrade your software and your operating system. MacOS offers hardware acceleration of HEVC on a system level with version 10.13 (High Sierra) and higher. The free version of the non-linear editing software Da-Vinci Resolve officially does *not* support HEVC or High 10 Profile H.264. However, it does so in its paid studio version.

- Use an intermediate codec for editing. Best known are ProRes and DNxHR.

*Important: Due to the large number of combinations of hardware components, operating systems and software used, even systems that work on paper might run into problems. Always check compatibility before working on important projects!*

Which codec to choose? This may help:

- The H.264 codec has become a universally used codec for everything from recording (acquisition codec) to output (delivery codec). If you are just getting started with video or want to upload or share your clips without much post-processing, the H.264 codec is a great choice. In concert with inter-frame compression and a moderate bitrate of 100 Mbps, you can get files with very good quality and an acceptable size that can be viewed on almost every device.

- If you want to record the best image quality the camera is capable of, use the H.265 codec. Furthermore, H.265 is a prerequisite for higher frame rates (50p or 60p) in the 4K DCI 17:9 format.

| Compression: ALL-Intra Versus Long GOP | TIP 106 |
| --- | --- |

The X-T3 is Fujifilm's first camera to offer intraframe compression (ALL-Intra). Before, the only option was interframe compression, known as Long GOP. Long GOP stands for "long group of pictures." These pictures are compressed across frames, hence the term *interframe*. This kind of compression allows a lower bitrate with smaller file sizes, while at the same time delivering high image quality.

On the other hand, intraframe compression doesn't analyze and compress multiple pictures, but does so isolated for every single frame, hence the name *intraframe*. To get the same image quality as you would with Long GOP, the bitrate has to be higher, resulting in larger files [87].

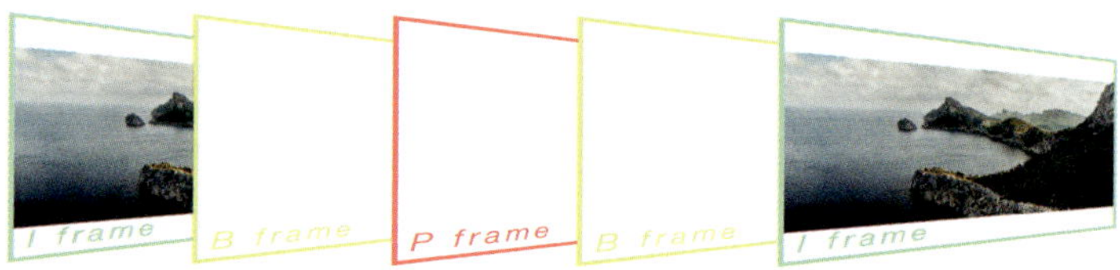


Fig. 132: With *interframe* compression (also known as IPB), not all frames are kept. Starting with a complete image (i-frame), only changes to this frame are saved. This way, high image quality and small files are possible.

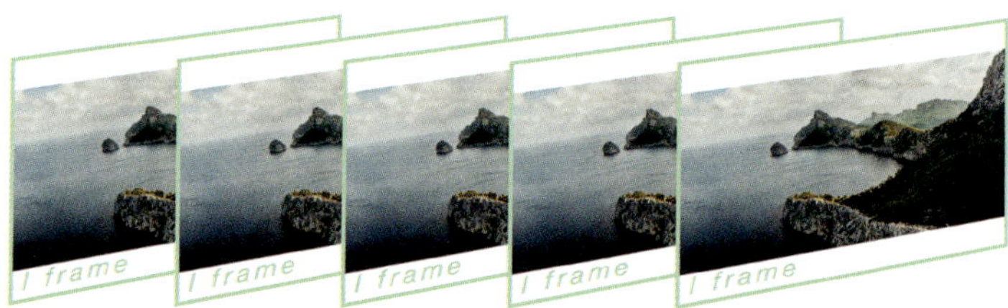


Fig. 133: With *intraframe* compression, each image is stored as a complete image (i-frame), hence the name ALL-Intra (meaning "only i-frames").

At first glance, Long GOP sounds like the better option, but ALL-Intra has two major advantages:

- For complex movements such as waterfalls or camera pans, ALL-Intra leads to fewer artifacts and therefore higher image quality.

- Since only complete images are stored and therefore no additional calculations are necessary, the hardware demands for processing ALL-Intra footage are significantly lower.

For non-moving subjects, Long GOP (with the same maximum bit rate of 400 Mbps) should theoretically provide better quality. However, differences at such high bit rates are very difficult to detect, even with extreme post-processing and strong magnification. You can select your choice of compression under SHOOTING MENU > MOVIE SETTING > MOVIE COMPRESSION.

Long GOP compression is mandatory in concert with the following settings:

- 4K recording with more than 30p is only available with Long GOP compression. If your camera grays out the 50p and 59.94p options, check if Long GOP compression is selected.

- 4K DCI 17:9 recording requires Long GOP compression in combination with the H.265 codec to record in 50p or 59.94p.

- Full-HD high-speed recording also requires Long GOP compression. The camera automatically changes the compression setting to Long GOP when you activate high-speed recording.

Interframe compression provides good image quality at a relatively low bit rate. The camera offers bit rates of 100–400 Mbps for 4K/UHD recordings, and 50–200 Mbps for Full-HD recordings. Due to the larger number of full-image frames, a higher bit rate is required for ALL-Intra compression to achieve comparable quality. With ALL-Intra, the camera records video at either 400 Mbps (4K/UHD) or 200 Mbps (Full-HD) and does not allow any further data rate reduction.

Keep in mind that 400 Mbps generate 50 MB of video data per second, which corresponds to 1 GB every 20 seconds, or 3 GB per minute. That's why ALL-Intra requires large and fast storage media.

| **TIP 107** | 24p, 25p, 29.97p: choosing your frame rate |

Your X-T3 offers a variety of frame rates—but which one is right for you? It depends primarily on where you live, where you want to film, and what your output medium is supposed to be. The different frame rates have a historical background. While the PAL format [88] is used in large parts of Europe, Asia, and Australia, the NTSC format [89] is mainly used in North America.

- Due to different AC voltages, different frame rates are used in **broadcasting**. In the PAL area, 25 frames per second (or a multiple thereof) is standard, while the NTSC parts of the world use 30 frames per second. To be precise, the exact frame rate is 29.97 frames per second, but for the sake of simplicity it's often called just 30p [90]. Double that and you get 59.94 frames per second, often just called 60p. To avoid interference like banding, it is recommended to work with a frame rate that corresponds to the local power frequency.

- 24p has its roots in the world of **cinema,** where this frame rate was established as the standard in 1929. The number 24 is divisible by many other integer values such as 2, 3, 4, 6, 8 and 12, which helped with analog editing. In concert with corresponding shutter speeds, the popularity of 24p as the standard frame rate has formed our viewing habits and established a look that many refer to as "cinematic." However, this frame rate plays a subordinate role in concert with digital recording devices like your X-T3.

- 23.98p (to be precise: 23.976 frames per second) is the digital video equivalent to 24p. It can be synchronized at 60 Hz (23.976 × 2.5 = 59.94).

In the Fujifilm X-T3, all available frame rates [91] can be directly selected anytime and anywhere around the globe, without having to restart the camera or reformat the SD card, as is the case with some other cameras. If you use the X-T3 in combination with other cameras, make sure that they all use the same frame rate or a multiple of it.

To sum it up:

- Use 24p if you are going for a cinematic look and are targeting digital movie projectors or Blu-ray discs for distribution. 24p is also becoming more popular on the web, as it is supported by YouTube, Vimeo and an increasing number of mobile devices. Do watch out for banding in concert with artificial light sources, though!

- Use 23.98p if you are going for a cinematic look but are targeting over-the-air television distribution.

- Use 25p/50p if you are recording in the PAL region and are either shooting indoor scenes under artificial light or want to use a DVD as your delivery medium.

- Use 29.97p/59.94p if you are recording in the NTSC region and are either shooting indoor scenes under artificial light or want to use a DVD as delivery medium.

- You can use 29.97p/59.94p in a PAL region if there is no artificial lighting and if you want to distribute your movie via online video streaming services.

The X-T3 is Fujifilm's first camera to allow 4K shooting in 50p and 59.94p. However, this feature is only available in concert with certain other settings:

- To record in 4K 16:9 with 50p or 59.94p, you must use Long GOP compression. Either H.264 or H.265 can be selected as the codec.

- To record 4K DCI 17:9 with 50p or 59.94p, you must select Long GOP compression and H.265 as the codec.

*Important: If you record in 4K with fast frame rates and change one of the prerequisite settings, the frame rate automatically drops to 29.97p. This is indicated by the menu options being displayed in yellow.*

<table><tr><td>**TIP 108**</td><td>Picking an aspect ratio</td></tr></table>

After you have determined the appropriate frame rate, you should decide on an aspect ratio. In addition to the 16:9 UHD format, which is familiar from TVs and computer monitors, the camera also offers the wider 17:9 DCI format [92].

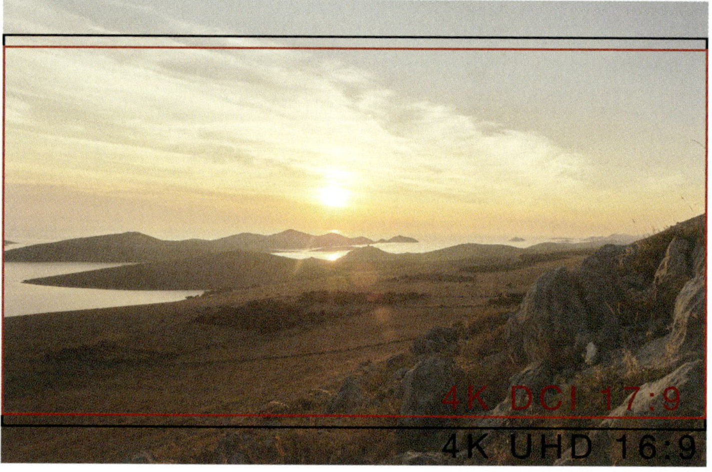


Fig. 134:  Since the X-T3 reads the full sensor width for 4K recordings up to 30p, the 17:9 format is simply a trim of the 16:9 format.

With the 16:9 UHD format, 6240 × 3510 pixels (22.1 MP) are sampled in the sensor; with the 17:9 format, 6240 × 3303 pixels (20.6 MP) are used. The camera downsamples this data to the actual recording resolution, resulting in better detail and reduced aliasing effects.

The DCI 17:9 format resolution of 4096 × 2160 pixels suggests that it contains more information than the UHD 16:9 format with "merely" 3840 × 2160 pixels. However, the opposite is true, because standard 16:9 is based on a better acquisition resolution with higher oversampling than 17:9 DCI.

Shooting 4K at high frame rates of 50p or 59.94p (or with Full-HD high-speed recording), your X-T3 no longer reads the full width of the sensor: an additional trim is introduced.

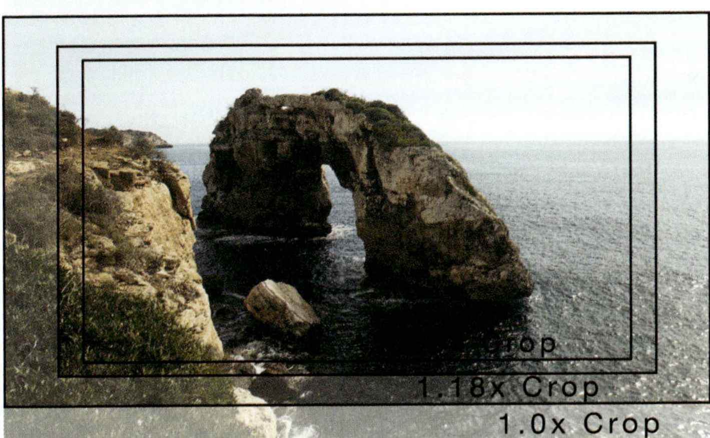


Fig. 135: Different frame rates result in different trims: The 4K 50p and 59.94p options are trimmed (cropped) by an additional factor of 1.18x, and the Full-HD high speed image receives a crop of 1.29x. With firmware 2.0 and later, the X-T3 displays the current trim factor in the upper-left corner of the live view.

This additional trim must be taken into account when you select a lens. For example, the angles of view of a Fujinon XF16mmF1.4 R WR without crop and a Fujinon XF14mmF2.8 R with a crop of 1.18x are almost identical.

The same crop factor of 1.18x is also introduced when differing (i.e., not matching) settings for internal (SD) and external (HDMI) recording have been selected (SHOOTING MENU > MOVIE SETTINGS > F-Log/HLG RECORDING), even when no external output device is actually connected. You can also use this extra trim as a digital in-camera zoom.

Similar to 4K shots with 23.98p, 24p, 25p, or 29.97p, Full-HD shots capture the full width of the sensor. The image is oversampled as well, which means that considerably more pixels are read out than would be necessary for Full-HD. However, some pixels are left out (line skipping), which leads to the funny fact that in 4K mode, the X-T3 can produce recordings with less noise and higher dynamic range than in Full-HD.

Recording Full-HD therefore primarily makes sense if your playback device does not support 4K, if a 50/59.94p video without any additional crop factor is required, or if you want to avoid the higher hardware requirements of 4K post-processing.

| TIP 109 | Full-HD high speed recording |

The X-T3 offers a Full-HD high-speed mode with up to 120 frames per second. Unlike regular frame rates, this mode is implemented as a separate menu item and it automatically changes the compression method to Long GOP.

High-speed recordings are captured with either 100 or 120 fps, during which the files are already slowed down and saved as slow-motion recordings in one of the six regular frame rates (23.98, 24, 25, 29.97, 50, 59.94 fps), so they can be played back directly as slow-motion videos. Since the actual recordings still have 100 or 120 fps, you can easily adjust the final nature of the slow-motion effect in a video editing app.

Full-HD high-speed mode operates with a crop factor of 1.29x and uses less oversampling than other modes. This can lead to higher noise levels and more artifacts, such as moiré. Since Full-HD high-speed mode is a separate menu item and works independently of other frame rates, it can also be placed in the Quick menu or on Fn buttons for faster access.

***Important:*** *No sound is recorded in Full-HD high-speed mode.*

| TIP 110 | Aperture, shutter speed, and ISO in movie mode |

In video mode, the X-T3 offers you the same tools to control exposure and brightness that you already know from still photography: aperture, shutter speed, and ISO. The aperture setting controls the depth of field, and shutter speed controls the motion blur. However, since video is not about a single image but a sequence of frames, there are some limitations.

A larger **aperture** (i.e., a lower f-number) will reduce the depth of field, resulting in fewer parts of your image being in focus. If you need to change the aperture during a video sequence, remember that native autofocus lenses for the X system only allow this in 1/3 f-stop increments. This can cause visible brightness jumps in the video footage.

If you want to avoid these jumps, I recommend using Fujifilm's MK cine-zoom lenses for the X-mount, or manual lenses from third-party manufacturers that feature a stepless (or "clickless") aperture. Korean manufacturer Samyang offers several such lenses for the Fujifilm X-mount, and many more can be connected via adapters. Samyang lenses can also be found under brand names such as Rokinon or Walimex Pro.

**Shutter speed** controls motion blur. Unlike stills photography, motion blur is often welcome in video because it helps emphasize motion and at the same time makes the image appear more harmonious. Fast shutter speeds (and the staccato effect that is often associated with them) interfere with a smooth flow and are often associated with amateur and smartphone footage.

It is a common practice for filmmakers to synchronize the shutter speed with the frame rate to create videos with "cinematic motion blur". The best-known rule for this is the "180-degree shutter angle rule". It says that the shutter speed should be set to one over two times the selected frame rate [1/(2 × frame rate)]. Examples: For a video recorded in 30p (29.97p), select a shutter speed of 1/60 s; for footage recorded in 25p, select 1/50 s; and so on.

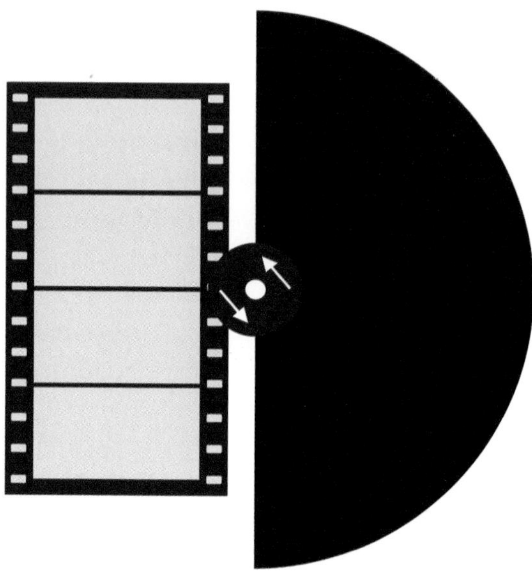

**Fig. 136:** Like many things in photography, the 180-degree shutter rule has a historical background: the rotating shutter of analog film cameras usually covered 180 degrees. Like with 24p, our viewing habits were conditioned to this look over decades of movie-making.

You should keep in mind that the 180-degree shutter rule is just a rule of thumb. Nobody will stop you from using different shutter speeds. In some instances, faster shutter speeds can help improve your shots, like when you are shooting fast movement. In scientific recordings, motion blur might not be desired, either.

In stills mode, setting the shutter speed to "A" will automatically change the speed in 1/3-stop increments. In movie mode, the shutter speed is automatically adjusted in finer 1/10-stop differentials, resulting in smoother brightness transitions.

**ISO** is used to control the brightness of the image by amplifying the signal. If you can't or don't want to decrease the shutter speed and also can't or don't want to open the aperture any further, you can still increase ISO to achieve the desired image brightness.

Like in still photo mode, the native ISO setting range of your X-T3 extends from 160 to 12800. Extended ISO L cannot be set in video, and only Extended ISO H (25600) is available as an ISO high profile. Please note that the ISO H (25600) option is *not* available in any of the following cases:

- Dynamic range is set to DR200% or DR400%

- F-Log or HLG recordings (internal or external)

If you select Auto-ISO in video mode, the camera will use a range of:

- ISO 160–12800 for shooting with a film simulation and DR100%

- ISO 320–12800 for shooting with a film simulation and DR200%

- ISO 640–12800 for shooting with a film simulation and DR400%, or for recording in the F-Log format

- ISO 1000–12800 for recording in the HLG format

Unlike stills mode, video Auto-ISO isn't adjusted in 1/3 f-stop increments, but in much finer and smoother steps to keep brightness fluctuations at a minimum.

Learn how to deal with the limitations that arise! If your video looks too dark with the selected aperture and shutter speed, you can increase ISO. In the opposite scenario, if your video is too bright, you face a problem. In stills photography, you would just select a faster shutter speed. In video, you are limited if you want to preserve a specific amount of motion blur, like adhering to the 180-degree shutter rule. If that's the case, ND filters can help. They diminish the light falling onto the sensor and darken the video.

Once you've selected the appropriate aperture and shutter speed, using ND filters or additional light sources to provide the desired brightness is preferable to increasing ISO. Only if these options aren't available, you should increase ISO as a last resort.

To avoid having to constantly think about different filters in situations with ever-changing light conditions, it may be a good idea to use a slightly stronger filter and let Auto-ISO regulate the brightness instead. This way you can focus on the composition and camera work.

| TIP 111 | Finding the correct video exposure |

The X-T3 saves compressed 8-bit or 10-bit files. Since the absence of RAW data in video mode limits your post-processing leeway, a correct exposure is essential. To evaluate the exposure, the X-T3 supports two types of histograms. The first one is a smaller histogram that can be permanently displayed.

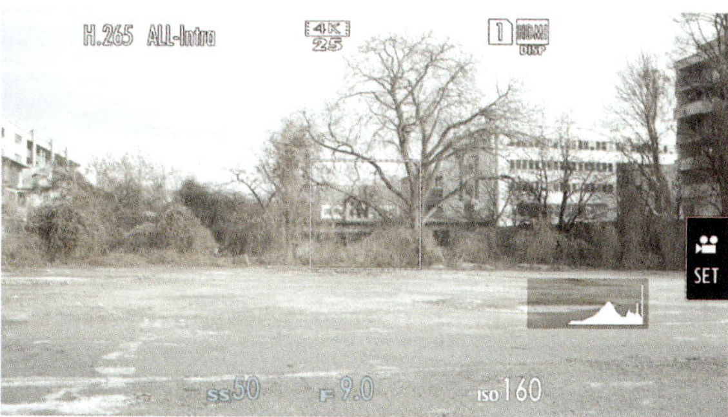


Fig. 137:  The smaller standard histogram can be activated in the SET UP > SCREEN SET-UP > DISP. CUSTOM SETTINGS menu. It displays the distribution of the brightness values in a shot.

Additionally, a more sophisticated RGB histogram can be assigned to any Fn or Touch-Fn button. The RGB histogram is larger and also displays the channels red, green, and blue separately. This makes it easier for you to see which color channel of your image overshoots. Function buttons can be assigned with SET UP > BUTTON/DIAL SETTING > FUNC-TION (Fn) SETTING or by pressing and holding the DISP/BACK button for several seconds.

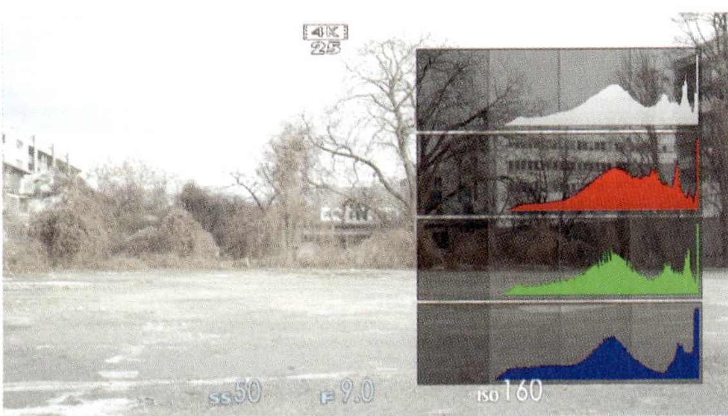

**Fig. 138:** The larger RGB histogram shows the brightness distribution in each color channel. As with the regular histogram, a pileup of bars at the right edge means that a color channel has overflowed. The RGB histogram can be assigned to any Fn or Touch-Fn button and can also be quickly activated and deactivated during recording.

Use histograms to determine the appropriate brightness in the video and pay particular attention to important highlights. Unlike RAWs in still photography, compressed video offers less room for adjustments in post-production. Since the latitude for recovering blown highlights or boosting very dark shadows is limited, your shots should have the appropriate brightness from the get-go.

*Important: Both histograms are calculated from the live view contents. They also reflect manually set dynamic range settings (DR200%, DR400%). If you use the NATURAL LIVE VIEW function, the histogram provides incorrect values and the live view doesn't represent the recorded video image.*

The **Zebra** function (SHOOTING MENU > MOVIE SETTING > ZEBRA SETTING) is another exposure aid that displays an optical warning when a preset brightness threshold has been passed. The striped/hatched warning pattern is reminiscent of a zebra—hence the cute name.

In the X-T3, the zebra threshold range can be set between 50% and 100% in 5% increments. The percentage amount corresponds to the so-called IRE value, which is a unit to measure video signals [93]. Absolute black equals 0 IRE, while peak white equals 100 IRE. Zebras can be assigned to a function button and then cycled between ZEBRA RIGHT, ZEBRA LEFT, and OFF. The threshold value reflects the brightness of the scene. If you know how bright you want your subject to appear, you can use this function to determine the appropriate exposure.

Here are some typical and popular zebra threshold settings:

- **55%.** Middle gray is located just below this value. If you use a gray card, increase the exposure until the card displays the zebra pattern and then reduce the exposure so the effect just disappears.

- **65%–70%.** This is considered the correct exposure of faces with Caucasian skin tones. Therefore, this threshold is relevant for filming people. Proceed as in the previous example.

- **100%.** This value is right below the sensor saturation with the currently active JPEG settings. Use this zebra setting to prevent relevant highlights of your image from blowing out. You can also set the Zebra function to only **95%.** This gives you more time to react to sudden lighting changes.

- **46%.** Since a logarithmic curve is used in log profiles, middle gray is located at a different IRE value. In the case of F-Log, middle gray is located at 46 IRE. Since the camera doesn't allow you to set thresholds below 50% (50 IRE), you can proceed as follows: set 55% as the threshold value for your zebras while increasing ISO by one stop. Then adjust the exposure (aperture, shutter speed, and ND filters) according to the zebras. Finally, reduce ISO by one stop again. Since F-Log has a logarithmic curve, this is only an approximation.

Since the Zebra function in the X-T3 hatches all brightness values above the set threshold, it's hard to evaluate brighter regions above the threshold. That's why I recommend using a function button to enable zebras, so you can quickly switch them on and off. Sadly, zebras can currently only be enabled or disabled between shots and not during an ongoing recording.

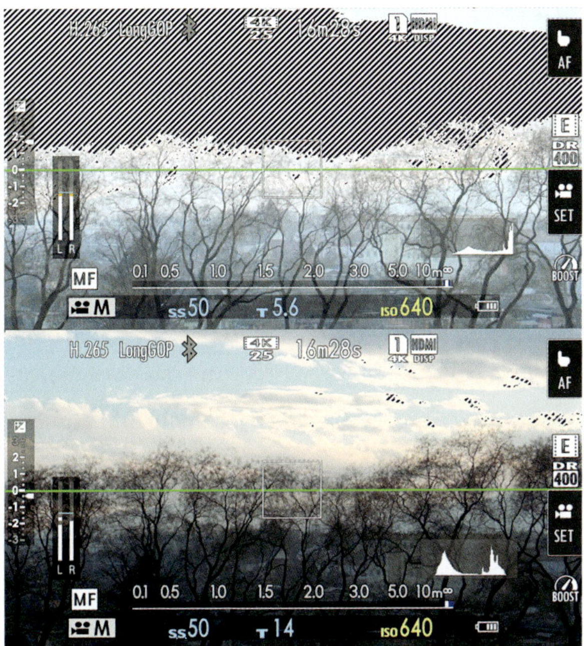

Fig. 139: These two pictures show how the Zebra function can help you protect critical highlights. The threshold value was set to 100% and the shutter speed to 1/50 s at 25p. The aperture was then closed just to the point where the highlights in the image displayed only minimal zebra striping.

*Important: Just like the standard histogram, the Zebra function is based on the overall brightness of the scene. This means that individual color channels may overflow or exceed the set threshold before the zebra pattern is displayed. This is why I recommend using zebras in combination with the RGB histogram.*

**TIP 112** | JPEG settings for video

The X-T3 offers the same film simulations and JPEG settings for video as you already know from taking stills. However, the settings for video are kept in a separate menu and can be adjusted independently. Carefully adjust these settings—there is no RAW option. Since the X-T3 oversamples the image in most video modes, a much larger number of pixels is captured and scaled down to the final recorded image, resulting in a very detailed picture. Therefore, you should pay particular attention to the sharpening setting.

To avoid oversharpened video files, I recommend reducing the value of the SHARPNESS setting. I also recommend applying less NOISE REDUCTION, especially at low ISO values. This helps avoiding loss of details in your video.

Of particular importance is the film simulation ETERNA, named after Fujifilm's discontinued Super 35 and Super 16 motion picture film stocks. ETERNA features a flat contrast profile with high dynamic range, and it is particularly famous for its beautiful reproduction of skin tones. ETERNA is an interesting starting point for quick post-processing requirements: good results can be achieved with little effort. ETERNA can therefore be considered the first choice for beginners in the field of video post-production.

Along with film simulations and other JPEG settings, the white balance is also "burned" into your video footage. Since bold changes in post-production can lead to posterization or other unpleasant artifacts, it is important to select the correct white balance from the start. As long as you record video under stable lighting conditions, I recommend manually setting a fixed white balance. Automatic white balance can cause color changes in the video, which are difficult to correct later.

<table><tr><td>JPEG settings for a post-production workflow</td><td>TIP 113</td></tr></table>

If you plan to edit your videos on your computer, I recommend the following settings:

- Reduce sharpness (SHOOTING MENU > MOVIE SETTING > SHARPNESS). You can always sharpen later during post-processing, but it is very difficult to remove artifacts from over-sharpened footage.

- Reduce noise reduction to a negative value (SHOOTING MENU > MOVIE SETTING > NOISE REDUCTION). If noise reduction is set too high during recording, details may be lost. Noise can always be removed later during post-processing.

- "Expose to the right." By adding a tonal curve adjustment, the image can be easily darkened in post. On the other hand, bringing up the shadows introduces noise and might lead to color issues. However, make sure not to blow out important highlights.

<table><tr><td>Maximizing dynamic range during video recording</td><td>TIP 114</td></tr></table>

In order to record as many tonal values as possible and use them in post-processing, these points may be helpful:

- Use flat film simulations (SHOOTING MENU > MOVIE SETUP > FILM SIMULATION) such as ETERNA and PRO NEG. STD that inherently offer more dynamic range.

- Protect the black and white points by setting SHADOW TONE and HIGHLIGHT TONE to –2.

- The DYNAMIC RANGE function offers three settings: DR100%, DR200% and DR400%. This function adds one (DR200%) or two stops (DR400%) of usable highlight dynamic range to the footage.

- Alternatively, you can use the logarithmic curve of the so-called F-Log function. F-Log allows you to record the maximum dynamic range that the X-T3 has to offer for video purposes. With F-Log, any additional adjustments such as film simulation or dynamic range modes are ignored, because F-Log is already designed for maximum dynamic range. However, using F-Log requires post-processing and is therefore not always the ideal choice—especially if you are still a novice.

- The HLG option offers similar dynamic range to F-Log and doesn't allow any further JPEG adjustments either.

Note that the dynamic range, F-Log, and HLG functions cause the camera to automatically adjust the available ISO range. Here are the minimum ISO requirements for each setting:

- ISO 160 with DR100%
- ISO 320 with DR200%
- ISO 640 with DR400%
- ISO 640 with F-Log
- ISO 1000 with HLG

Don't worry too much about the higher base ISO values. Using the same exposure settings, footage recorded with DR400% and ISO 640 usually produces better results than footage of the same scene that is recorded with DR100% and ISO 160—assuming that both versions are adjusted to the same look in post-processing.

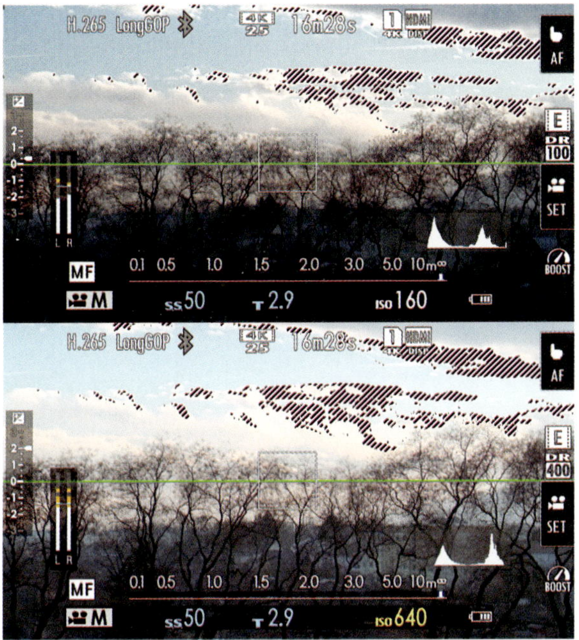

Fig. 140: These two images were taken with the same exposure: shutter speed 1/50 s and aperture f/2.8. The upper image was recorded with ISO 160 and DR100%, the lower image was recorded with ISO 640 and DR400%. Despite the two stop ISO increase, the highlights remain almost unchanged and are still located just below the saturation limit of the sensor (Zebra 95%). The higher ISO only raised the shadows and mid-tones by two stops and didn't affect the highlights, because DR400% added two stops of highlight dynamic range. This effect can also be seen in the histogram.

| Noise reduction and interframe NR | TIP 115 |
|---|---|

Like the other JPEG settings, noise reduction for video can be set independently from noise reduction settings for still photography. The NOISE REDUCTION function analyzes each frame and removes both luminance and color noise. Since this comes at the expense of detail, I recommend to keep noise reduction at a low level. Especially at low ISO values, a setting of −4 is preferable. I recommend to selectively carry out the noise reduction in post-processing.

Unlike the regular noise reduction, interframe noise reduction (INTERFRAME NR) is not limited to a single image during image analysis, but also includes frames that were recorded before and after. This allows the camera to better detect noisy areas.

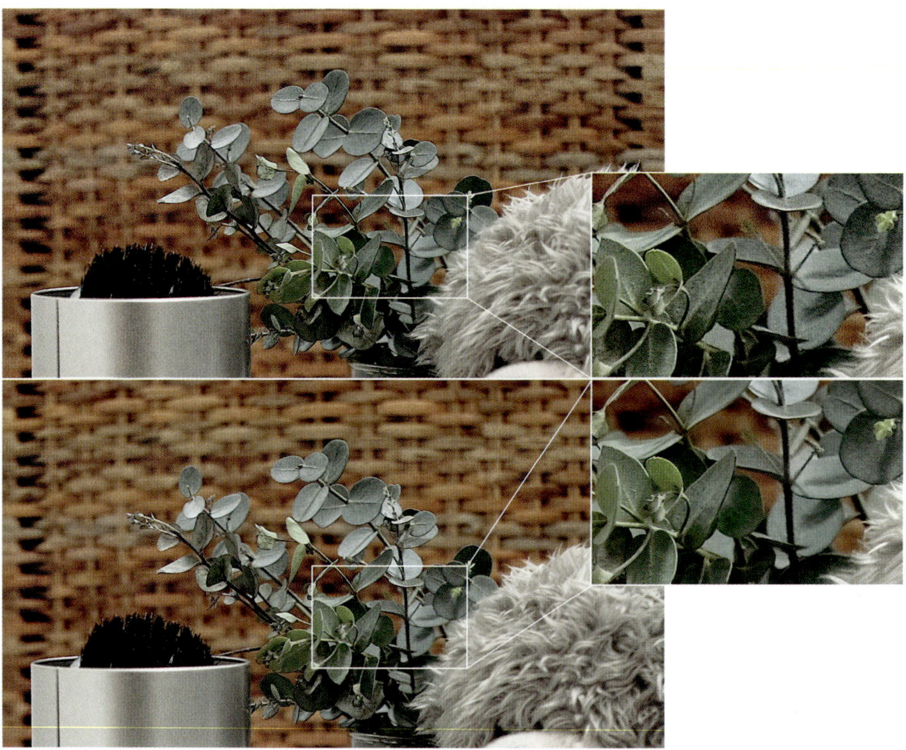

Fig. 141: These two images, both shot at ISO 800, illustrate how interframe noise reduction leads to less noise (bottom). However, interframe noise reduction also results in a slight loss of detail. Both images have been greatly magnified and edited to better show the differences.

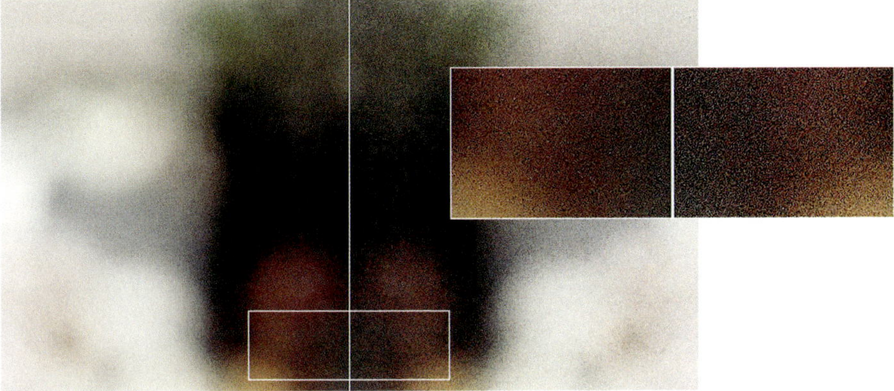

Fig. 142:  At higher ISO values, interframe noise reduction can lead to a significant reduction of noise especially in image parts with fewer details, such as the bokeh. In the image on the left, interframe noise reduction was turned on. Both images were shot at ISO 12800, heavily processed, enlarged and sharpened for demonstration purposes.

The intensity of interframe noise reduction cannot be adjusted, so it should only be used selectively, because it leads to a loss of detail. Since successive frames are analyzed, interframe noise reduction works particularly well with a fixed camera position and only little movement in the video.

Interframe noise reduction can be especially helpful in these situations:

■ Shooting from a tripod or fixed camera position at medium ISO values.

■ Shooting at very high ISO values, where interframe noise reduction can make an otherwise useless video useable.

■ If you are are very sensitive to noise and are shooting with DR400%, where noise becomes visible in the brightened shadows.

■ If you want to post-process your videos, you should apply noise reduction on the computer rather than in-camera. This is especially true for recordings in F-Log format. The changed gamma curve, which is expressed by a higher base ISO, makes the shadow noise visible and may tempt you to increase the noise reduction setting. However, since F-Log requires post-processing and a gamma correction, this noise reduction can be better performed during post-processing. Lost details due to an overly high noise reduction setting during recording cannot be recovered.

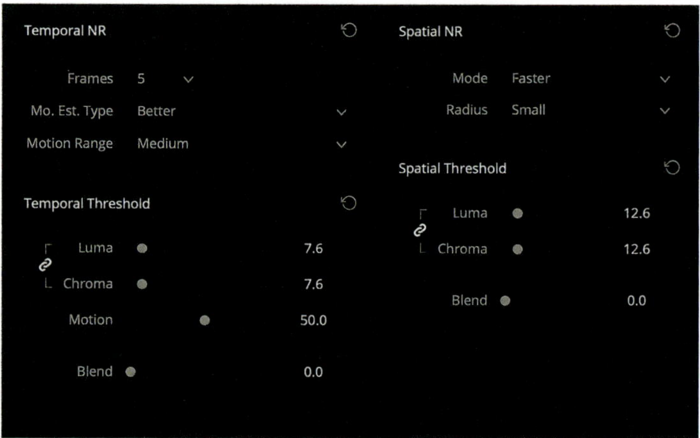


Fig. 143:  Modern video editing software like DaVinci Resolve is usually much better at reducing noise than the camera—and it can also apply it selectively. Therefore, I recommend that you keep the noise reduction inside the camera to a low value.

<table>
<tr><td>TIP 116</td><td>Using F-Log</td></tr>
</table>

Like the X-T2 and X-H1, the X-T3 allows you to record with a log profile, the so-called F-Log. However, the X-T3 is Fujifilm's first camera to also allow F-Log recording in 10-bit instead of only 8-bit. To understand what a log profile is, it helps to know how modern digital cameras work: The sensor has an analog-to-digital converter with a bit depth of up to 14 bits. The way data is saved in digital files, the highlights are finely graduated with hardly any differentiation in the shadows.

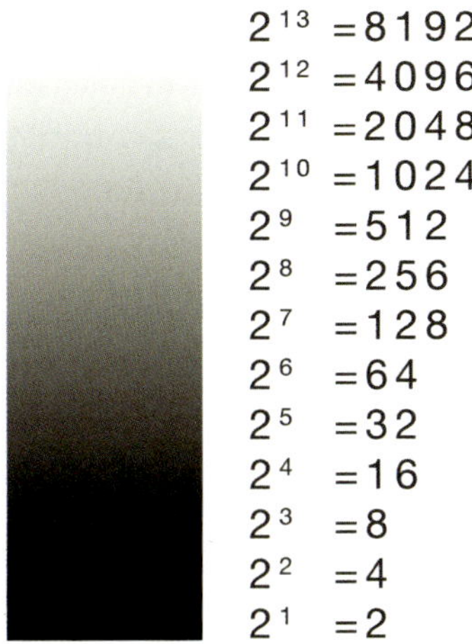

$$2^{13} = 8192$$
$$2^{12} = 4096$$
$$2^{11} = 2048$$
$$2^{10} = 1024$$
$$2^{9} = 512$$
$$2^{8} = 256$$
$$2^{7} = 128$$
$$2^{6} = 64$$
$$2^{5} = 32$$
$$2^{4} = 16$$
$$2^{3} = 8$$
$$2^{2} = 4$$
$$2^{1} = 2$$

**Fig. 144:** Of the 16384 displayable tonal values of a 14-bit RAW, half (i.e., 8192) are designated to the brightest f-stop or EV level. On the other hand, there's little tonality differentiation in the shadows.

This can result in unusable, crushed shadows, limited dynamic range and restricted post-processing options. With log profiles, a logarithmic curve is used to reduce these problems and give shadows a higher priority.

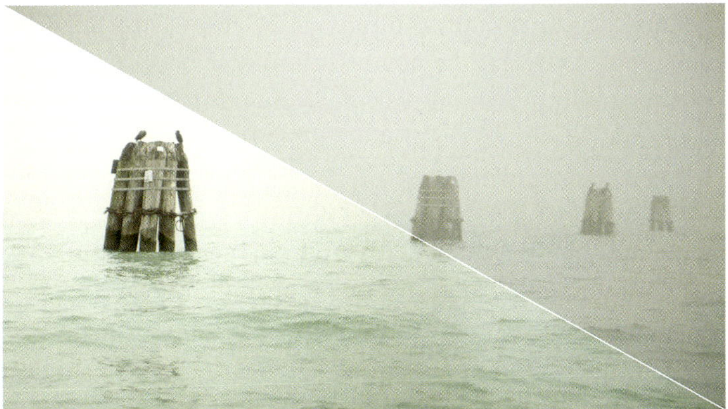

**Fig. 145:** The F-Log image on the top-right appears extremely flat. The logarithmic curve makes the shadows appear much brighter as intended. However, this offers more possibilities in post-processing, as it captures as much dynamic range as possible. The picture at the bottom-left shows the edited image.

To turn flat F-Log recordings into attractive-looking footage, you can use the corresponding LUTs. A LUT, short for Look-Up Table, is an inverted log curve that is used to transform flat log clips back to video with higher contrast. LUTs provided by Fujifilm for the X-T3 can be downloaded from Fujifilm's website [94].

Various other LUTs can be applied. Some are camera-specific (like those for the popular FilmConvert software [95]); others are generic but still deliver interesting results. Alternatively, video can also be manually adjusted and corrected. This process of color correction encompasses not only colors but also contrast, saturation, and many other parameters, and is known as *color grading* [96].

***Important:*** *Unlike many other manufacturers, Fujifilm does not provide a generic LUT for all their cameras with F-Log profiles. Instead, it offers camera-specific profiles. Make sure to use only X-T3 LUTs in concert with X-T3 video files.*

The Fujifilm X-T3 is Fujifilm's first camera (and one of the first consumer cameras ever) to allow saving 10-bit log recordings internally. The higher bit-depth is particularly useful in cases with heavy post-processing. Compressing the maximum dynamic range of 14 stops into an 8-bit file can quickly lead to posterization and banding during post-processing. Therefore, I recommend using F-Log with 10-bit color-depth in concert with the H.265 codec.

If you are interested in the technical background of F-Log, you can find a white paper on Fujifilm's website [97].

## BUT DO YOU ABSOLUTELY NEED F-LOG?

You don't need F-Log if you are already getting close to your desired look with the camera's JPEG settings. Even though F-Log—in combination with 10-bit files—offers a finer gradation and more post-processing potential, it also involves a more cumbersome workflow. The H.265 codec is tougher on the hardware, and the necessity of color grading results in additional time spent in front of a computer.

The F-Log gamma correction and curve adjustments lead to increased shadow noise. This is already indicated by the higher base ISO value of ISO 640. In order to keep the noise low, you should try to collect as much light as possible during recording. To do this, you should optimize the exposure by using the RGB histogram and the Zebra function.

The NATURAL LIVE VIEW function allows you to better estimate the look of the final result before you start an F-Log recording. However, remember that this function also affects histograms and zebras, that's why the exposure settings should already be fixed before using the Natural Live View.

Since a log profile isn't a RAW recording, some settings will be "burned" into the finished video. These include the white balance setting and settings for sharpening and noise reduction.

| How to use HLG (Hybrid Log Gamma) | TIP 117 |
|---|---|

Hybrid Log Gamma (HLG) is a High Dynamic Range (HDR) standard developed by the BBC and the NHK, the Japanese Broadcasting Corporation. The standard is intended to enable playback on high dynamic range (HDR) *and* standard dynamic range (SDR) devices. For this purpose, a logarithmic curve is used in the highlights, while the midtones and shadows are set on the SDR gamma curve.

HDR recordings in the HLG format are well suited for playback on HDR televisions. The camera automatically uses the H.265 codec in this format, as the standard officially requires the use of 10-bit or 12-bit formats [98].

With Hybrid Log Gamma, the X-T3 records dynamic range similar to F-Log. However, unlike F-Log, HLG footage is suitable for direct playback without LUT post-processing.

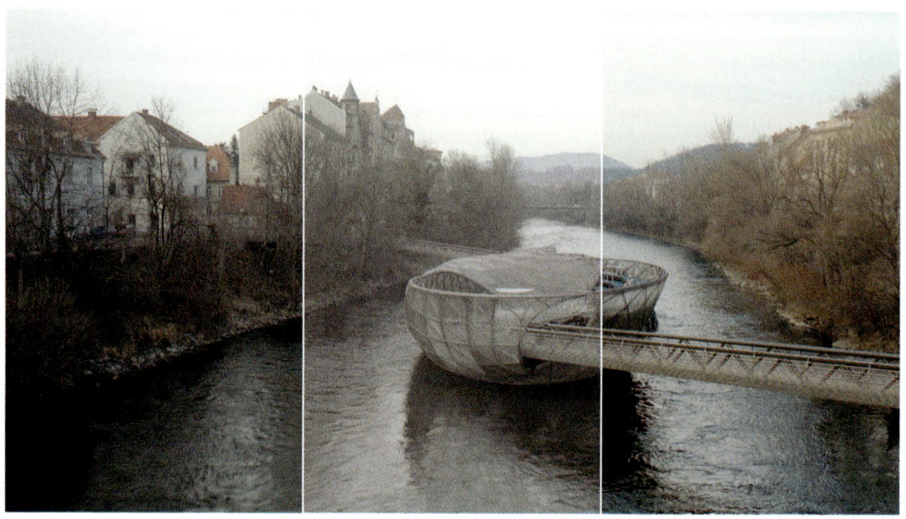

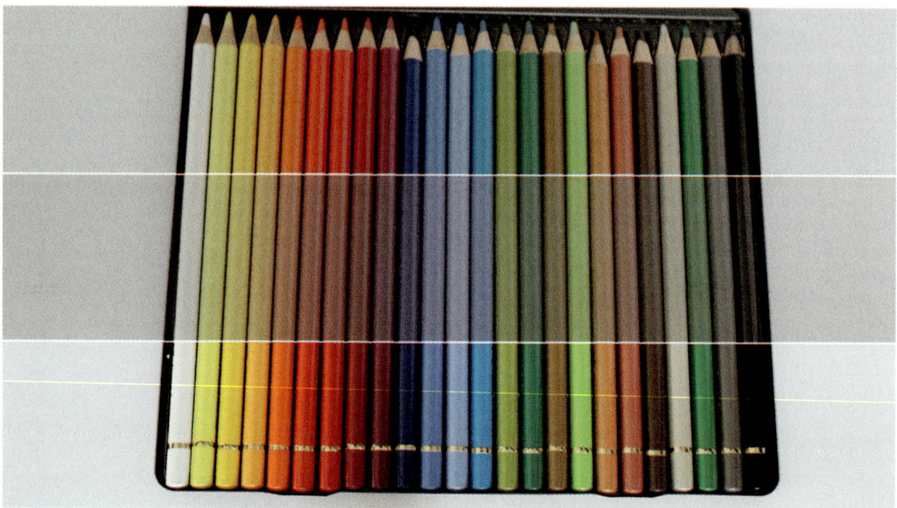

**Fig. 146:** These two comparisons show the Hybrid Log Gamma format as an SDR export (left and top), the unprocessed F-Log format (center), and the graded F-Log (right and bottom). HLG and F-Log offer very similar dynamic ranges.

Even though Hybrid Log Gamma is intended as an output format, you can also use it as a starting point for your own post-processing workflow. The SDR gamma curve makes it easier to evaluate the overall exposure than F-Log. HLG delivers high dynamic range in a high-contrast image and comes with its own color profile. In an SDR (Standard Dynamic Range) workflow, Hybrid Log Gamma can therefore be used like just another film simulation. However, consider the following points:

- Hybrid Log Gamma is very sensitive to under- and overexposure, so pay attention to the important highlights and shadows. Use zebras with 100% to check the exposure.

- Due to heavy manipulation and processing, the best available recording quality should be used. Use H.265 10-bit with 400 Mbps (respectively 200 Mbps for 50p and 59.94p recordings) or an external recorder.

- Hybrid Log Gamma in Fujifilm cameras places middle gray much lower than other modes. A field monitor with LUT support can help you evaluate the image contents by boosting the shadows.

Before making any color adjustments, I recommend using a LUT in post-production to convert the videos from BT.2020 HLG to the BT.709 gamut [99]. Most NLEs (non-linear editing software) [100] offer pre-installed profiles. If that's not the case, you can create a corresponding LUT with the online tool LUTCalc [101].

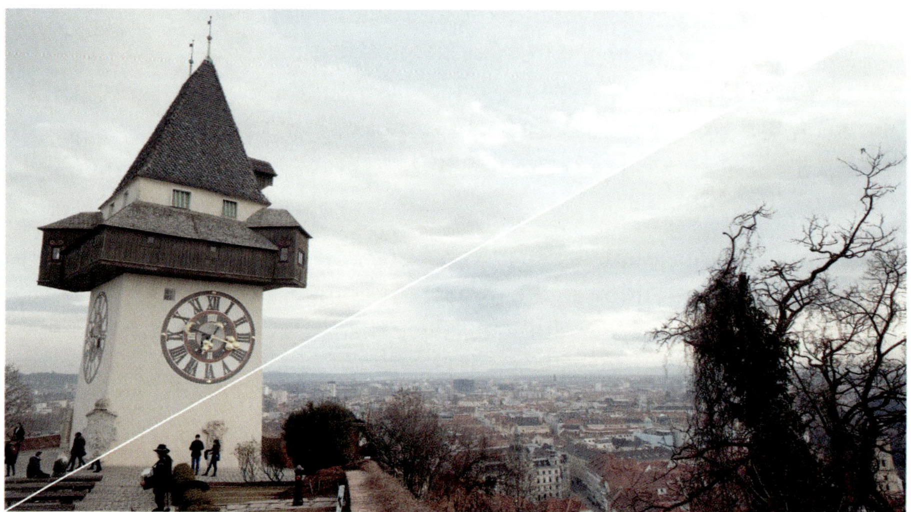

Fig. 147: A direct comparison of F-Log on the top-left (F-Log to Eterna BT.709 LUT and minimal color correction) and HLG on the bottom-right (BT.2020 HLG converted to BT.709 with minimal color correction) shows that HLG can be used as another film simulation. The brightness curve differs, as do the colors. HLG also provides artifact-free blue regions in the sky, while F-Log tends to produce occasional magenta blocks.

When you post-process your clips, consider which output devices you are targeting. Hybrid Log Gamma is designed first and foremost to look good on HDR TVs and deliver an acceptable picture on SDR devices at the same time. Note that very few computer monitors provide wide dynamic range. Therefore, the image on your PC or notebook may look very different from what's displayed on an HDR output device. Most manufacturers of video editing software offer corresponding guides for an HDR workflow [102].

| TIP 118 | Setting up the autofocus for video |
| --- | --- |

The autofocus settings in video mode are very similar to those in still mode. Both single AF (AF-S) and continuous AF (AF-C) are available. Selecting an autofocus frame can be left to the camera (MULTI AF), or you can do it yourself (AREA AF). However, video mode offers only one focus frame size. If you use the touchscreen in MULTI AF mode to select a focus frame, the camera automatically switches to AREA AF mode.

- In **AF-S** mode, the camera focuses only once. During recording, you can refocus by pressing the shutter release button halfway, by using the AF-ON function, or with the touchscreen in its "AF" setting. When you are using AREA AF, you can move the focus frame with the focus stick or touchscreen (with the touchscreen set to "AREA"). I recommend using AF-S when you do not want to change the focus plane, or in situations where AF-C is too inconsistent. With sufficient depth of field, changing focus is often not necessary even with minimally moving subjects. In these types of situations, a fixed focus setting can lead to better results than continuously tracking and refocusing the subject. Please note that the AF-C CUSTOM SETTING parameters also affect refocusing in AF-S mode. The speed at which refocusing takes place is influenced by the AF SPEED setting.

- **AF-C** constantly adjusts the focus position, which makes it particularly interesting for moving subjects. In videography, the process of focusing is recorded and therefore affects the video. That's why the X-T3 offers independent AF-C custom settings in the movie menu. To prevent the camera from constantly trying to adjust the focus, you can increase the TRACKING SENSITIVITY in the AF-C CUSTOM SETTING menu. The AF-L function is also available to prevent unwanted refocusing.

Your X-T3 offers custom focus adjustments for AF-C (SHOOTING MENU > MOVIE SETUP > AF-C CUSTOM SETTING). Two parameters can be adjusted:

- TRACKING SENSITIVITY. This setting controls the locking duration on the current subject before the camera focuses on a new subject at a different distance. Use a higher value to keep the focus in your original subject, even if it is temporarily obscured by other objects. Keep in mind that this setting can delay deliberate focus transitions to new subjects.

- AF SPEED. This setting controls the speed at which the camera changes focus. Higher values are especially important for fast-moving subjects such as animals or at sports events. Slower speeds allow smoother transitions.

While it makes sense to set high values for TRACKING SENSITIVITY and AF SPEED for fast-moving subjects, I recommend lower values for most other subjects.

| TIP 119 | Pulling focus using autofocus |
| --- | --- |

Shifting the focus plane in video is often used as a stylistic means. It's called "pulling focus" or "racking focus" [103]. As an example, set the focus on a subject in the foreground and then move the focus to another subject with a different distance to the camera. This can be used as a means to direct the viewer's attention, or as a transition between sequences. The focus should be changed at a steady pace without overshooting or "pumping" movements.

To perform a focus pull with the X-T3's autofocus system, you must select AREA AF. If MULTI AF is selected, the camera automatically switches to AREA AF as soon as you touch the touchscreen.

I recommend changing the focus point with the touchscreen. Using the focus stick in concert with AF-C may cause the camera to temporarily focus on other parts of the image, resulting in an uneven transition.

Please note:

- If TRACKING SENSITIVITY is set too high, the camera may not start the focus pull until a certain amount of time has passed.

- If TRACKING SENSITIVITY is set too low, the camera may want to carry out a correction of the focus position at the end of the focus pull.

- If AF SPEED is set too high, it can cause the focus to overshoot the target. This will result in a noticeable correction of the final focus position.

- If AF SPEED is set too low, it can cause a single focus pull to extend over several seconds.

Personally, I start with TRACKING SENSITIVITY at 1 and AF SPEED at about −1 and then adjust the settings according to the situation.

| Using face and eye detection | TIP 120 |
| --- | --- |

The X-T3 offers face and eye detection in video mode, and unlike still mode, it automatically uses continuous focus (AF-C) when face or eye recognition is activated.

The following face and eye detection settings are available:

- FACE DETECTION ON/EYE OFF. In this mode, the focus area is placed on the entire face.

- FACE DETECTION ON/EYE AUTO. The camera automatically tries to focus on the eye closest to the camera.

- FACE DETECTION ON/RIGHT EYE PRIORITY. The camera will attempt to focus on the right eye of a detected face.

- FACE DETECTION ON/LEFT EYE PRIORITY. In this mode, the camera tries to focus on the left eye of a detected face.

- OFF. Face and eye detection are disabled.

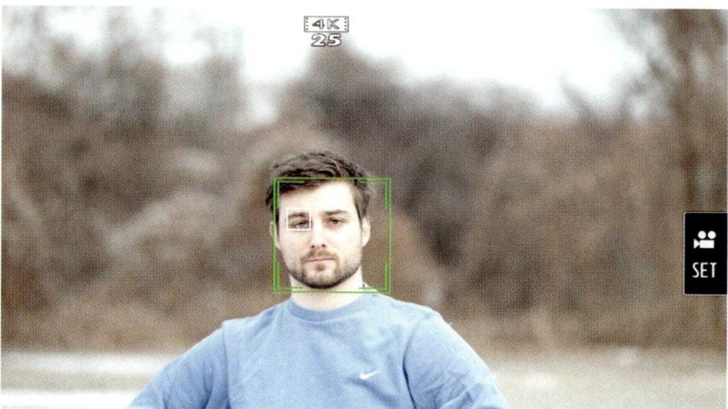

Fig. 148: With firmware 3.0 and later, eye detection displays only a white square around the selected and detected eye. If the camera is not able to detect an eye (e.g., because the distance increases too much or the person turns sideways), the camera falls back to regular face detection, which usually works well in these situations.

Note that in situations where the focus position needs to be as steady as possible, face detection *without* eye detection may sometimes produce better results than the combination of both. By prioritizing the small area of an eye, even tiny movements (or a switch between the recognized eyes in EYE AUTO mode) can cause slight focus changes.

Face and eye detection respect the values set in the AF-C CUSTOM SETTING menu. In situations where people are at rest, do not set high values for AF SPEED. For fast-moving subjects, increase the speed accordingly. With long focal lengths and very fast lenses, I recommend stopping down by one or two f-stops.

The FACE SELECT function allows you to switch between different faces. You can use the focus stick or touch the desired face on the active touchscreen. If there are multiple faces in the frame and the camera loses the selected face, it will focus on another face. The AF-L function can be used to lock the focus, even when face/eye detection is active.

The FACE SELECT function activates and deactivates face and eye detection. When activated, the last-used face detection mode is used. To set up face/eye detection, you can follow these steps:

- Set SHOOTING MENU > MOVIE SETUP > FACE/EYE DETECTION SETTING > FACE DETECION ON > EYE AUTO. Then set FACE/EYE DETECTION SETTING to OFF. Make sure that you are using the MOVIE SETUP menu and not the AF/MF SETTING menu.

- Make sure that FACE SELECT has been assigned one of your function buttons. Pressing this button activates face detection with eye detection and allows you to choose between more than one detected faces in the frame.

- If you still want to switch between face detection autofocus (FACE DETECTION ON > EYE OFF) and eye detection autofocus (FACE DETECTION ON > EYE AUTO), or if you want to select a preferred eye to focus on, you can put the FACE/EYE DETECTION SETTING function into the Quick Menu or My Menu. When you set up the My Menu, note that the face/eye detection function can be found in both the photo and movie menu. If you are hybrid video/still shooter, you might end up with two different face/eye detection settings inside your My Menu. The camera will indicate what version you are using by displaying a video camera icon next to the movie-related face/eye detection item.

If no face or eye is recognized, the camera will revert to the selected autofocus mode.

*Important: Neither FACE SELECT nor FACE DETECTION (FACE DETECTION ON/OFF) can be activated or deactivated during shooting. These settings must be set before recording starts.*

<table>
<tr><td>TIP 121</td><td>Using manual focus</td></tr>
</table>

In videos, it's not just about the subject being in focus—it's equally important that focus changes aren't abrupt and distracting. This is why manual focusing still plays an important role in videography. While autofocus systems can track subjects well and focus very quickly, pumping movements might occur. To make manual focusing as easy as possible, the X-T3 offers several adjustment aids:

- **Focus magnification**. The X-T3 allows you to zoom into the selected focus frame either by pressing a designated function button (usually the rear command dial), or by double-tapping on the touchscreen. For the latter to work, SET UP > BUTTON/DIAL SETTING > TOUCH SCREEN SETTING > DOUBLE TAP SETTING must be set to ON. The magnification factor can be changed by turning the rear command dial. During magnification, the focus frame can be moved with the focus stick or by touching the edges of the touchscreen.

- **Focus peaking** (SHOOTING MENU > MOVIE SETUP > MF ASSIST > FOCUS PEAK HIGHLIGHT). This function highlights edges with high contrast to make it easier to determine the position of the focal plane. You can choose between four colors and two intensities. Focus peaking is also available in the magnified view.

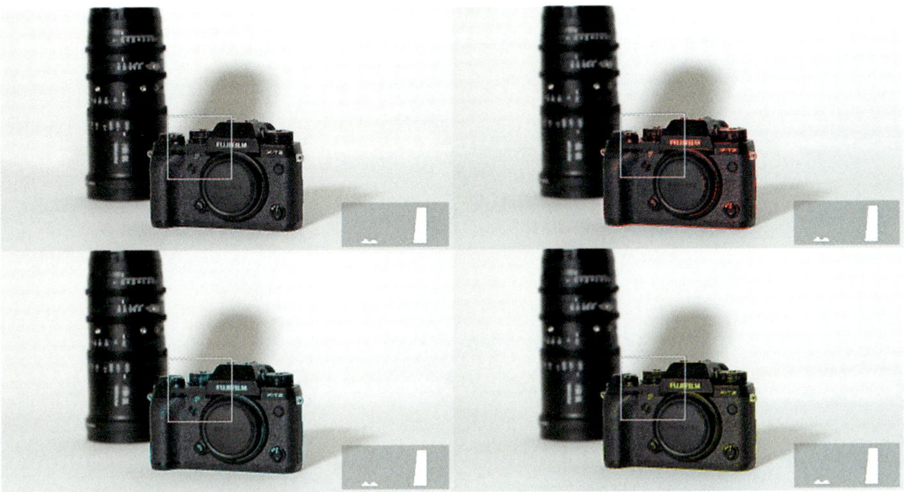

Fig. 149: This illustration shows the four available focus peaking colors in high intensity. It's best to use a color that contrasts with the subject's color.

Focus peaking is based on the contents of the live view. You can take advantage of this fact by activating the Natural Live View when working with F-Log to get a higher contrast image and thus better focus peaking. However, using the Natural Live View is only possible before you start recording.

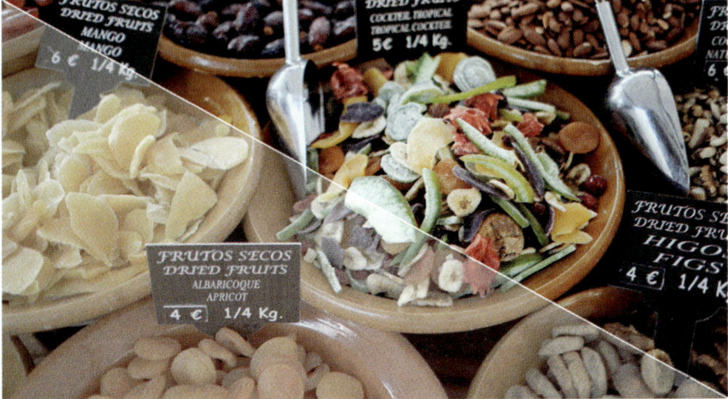

Fig. 150: F-Log vs. a high-contrast film simulation: The better contrast of selected film simulations and JPEG settings can be helpful in concert with focus peaking.

Fujifilm's autofocus lenses for the X series are so-called "focus-by-wire" lenses. Their focus ring is not mechanically linked to the focus group inside the lens. Instead, a sensor records the rotation of the focus ring and transmits the data to the camera. The camera then tells the focus drive the position it has to move to.

There are also two different types of focus-by-wire lenses:

- Lenses with mechanical clutch mechanisms (XF14mmF2.8, XF16mmF1.4, XF23mmF1.4). These lenses can be switched to manual focus by actuating the mechanical clutch. The focus ring rotation is mechanically locked at the minimal focus distance (MFD) and at infinity. Focusing is linear, and the lenses also feature engraved depth-of-field scales that correspond with the FILM FORMAT BASIS setting of your camera's electronic depth-of-field scale.

- Regular lenses without clutch mechanisms. With these lenses, the focus ring can be freely rotated without hard bookends. To enter MF mode, the focus selector switch on the front of the camera must be set to the "M" position.

Lenses without clutch mechanism allow accurate *and* fast focusing, because they consider the speed at which the focus ring is rotated to determine the extent of the focus change. Fast movements result in wider focus adjustments, slow movements allow more precise focusing.

However, this behavior is often undesirable in videography, because the effect of a specific focus ring rotation angle becomes unpredictable. As a remedy, the X-T3 offers a linear focus mode (SET UP > BUTTON/DIAL SETTING > FOCUS RING OPERATION > LINEAR). This setting affects both photo and video operation. With FOCUS RING OPERATION set to LINEAR, the focus always shifts by the same amount for any given ring rotation angle, regardless of the ring's rotation speed. This option is especially important when you are using a follow focus system. Please note that the pull angle of most lenses is noticeably above 360°, which can make direct hand operation somewhat difficult.

Regardless of whether you focus your lenses directly or use a follow focus, the linear focus mode allows reproducible results. However, manual focusing is a quite demanding task. For larger productions of feature films or TV shows, it is usually performed by an assistant. This "first assistant camera (1st AC)" or "focus puller" is solely responsible for the exact guidance of the focus.

Don't let yourself be demotivated if your initial manual focusing attempts turn out disappointing—keep practicing! You can practice at home, by repeatedly focusing from one object to another. Get to know your lenses and their different rotation angles. Practice trains your muscle memory. You should also try the different focus aids.

If you use a follow focus, relevant focus positions can be marked to enable precise switching between these positions. The X-T3 allows you to change the direction of the focus ring rotation (SET UP > BUTTON/KEY SETTING > FOCUS RING) of native X-mount lenses without a manual focus clutch.

<table>
<tr><td>Suggested Fn button assignment and menu options for video</td><td>TIP 122</td></tr>
</table>

The X-T3 offers three types of customization:

- **Quick menu:** You can use the Quick menu to change simple settings that are not to be changed during recording.

- **My Menu:** You can copy menu items into the My Menu for expedited access. My Menu is great for settings with more complex submenus that don't have to be changed during recording.

- **Function buttons.** The X-T3 offers 13 customizable Fn buttons. Four of them are so-called Touch-Function buttons (T-Fn) that are activated by flicking gestures on the four touchscreen edges.

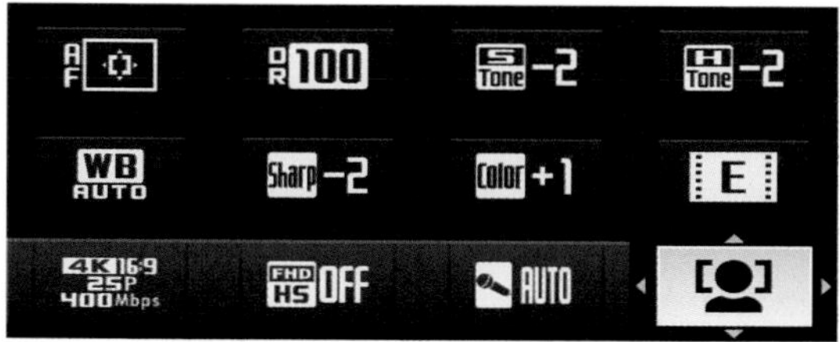

Fig. 151: The Quick menu is useful for settings that you don't need to access during recording, such as Full HD high-speed mode, face and eye detection mode, JPEG fine-tuning, or focus peaking color and intensity.

Think practical when you assign video functions to Fn buttons. For example, T-Fn buttons operate completely silent, which can be useful when you are using the built-in microphone. Mounted on a gimbal, buttons placed further up and on the front of the camera are easier to reach.

Here are some useful video functions that can be assigned to Fn buttons:

- **RGB histogram**. Activate and deactivate the larger RGB histogram to better judge your exposure.

- **Zebras**. During shooting, the Zebra function can be used to check the exposure. However, it cannot be toggled, nor can the threshold be changed once recording has started.

- **Focus check**. In AF-S or MF mode, you can zoom into the image to check focus. This feature is also available during recording and is usually assigned to the rear command dial.

- **Internal/external microphone**. Assign this function to a function button for sound level adjustments during recording.

- **Natural Live View**. When you are recording with the F-Log profile, the Natural Live View can be useful as it displays a higher-contrast image that makes it easier to focus manually. While the Natural Live View cannot be used during F-Log recording, it can be helpful to quickly toggle it on and off before the recording starts.

- **Face Select**. With Face Select, you can switch between multiple detected faces using the focus stick or touchscreen. Sadly, Face Select cannot be activated or deactivated during shooting. Since only FACE/EYE DETECTION but not FACE SELECT can be placed inside the Quick Menu or My Menu, I recommend that you assign FACE SELECT to a function button.

You might want to use the "T" position on the shutter speed dial to control the shutter speed via the front or rear command dial (adjustable in the SET UP > BUTTON/DIAL SETTING > COMMAND DIAL SETTING menu). This setting facilitates quick and silent shutter speed changes during video recording.

<table>
<tr><td>Movie Silent Control</td><td>TIP 123</td></tr>
</table>

To quickly transit between stills and video modes, the X-T3 offers the so-called Movie Silent Control (SHOOTING MENU > MOVIE SETTING > MOVIE SILENT CONTROL). This feature allows you to save some of the video settings separately—and automatically recall them when movie mode is activated.

For example, you can set a suitable 180-degree shutter speed and the ETERNA film simulation in movie mode, while using different settings for still photography. You can change the Movie Silent Control settings by pressing the video icon labeled SET on the right side of the touchscreen. In the MOVIE SILENT CONTROL menu, you can navigate with swipe gestures, the focus stick, or the selector buttons.

*Important: Your special movie mode settings will be lost when you deactivate the Movie Silent Control function. When you activate it again, the current camera settings will be applied.*

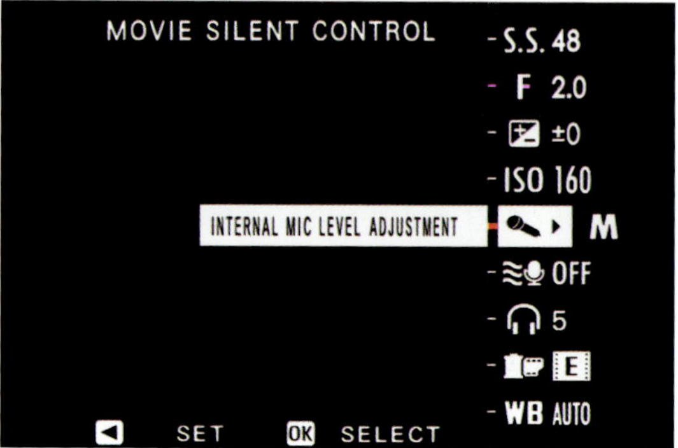


Fig. 152: Movie Silent Control allows you to change important video settings via an overlay menu. They are automatically recalled when the movie mode is activated.

| TIP 124 | Limitations of XF and XC lenses for video use |
|---|---|

In optical terms, the entire range of Fujifilm autofocus lenses is ideal for 4K video recording. However, since most of the lenses have primarily been designed for photography rather than videography, there are some limitations:

- Turning the aperture ring generates a clicking noise. To avoid that, you can adjust the aperture with a command dial. Change SET UP > BUTTON/DIAL SETTING > APERTURE RING SETTING(A) to COMMAND and assign the aperture function to one of the command dials with the SET UP > BUTTON/DIAL SETTING > COMMAND DIAL SETTING menu. Alternatively, you can also use MOVIE SILENT CONTROL.

- The aperture can only be adjusted in 1/3 f-stop increments, so any aperture change results in a visible brightness change of the video footage.

- The lenses use focus-by-wire. While the manual focusing operation can be switched to linear mode (SET UP > BUTTON/DIAL SETTING > FOCUS RING OPERATION), the focus rotation of some lenses is well above 360°, which can be challenging for single operators.

■ Some focus motors produce an audible sound, especially in older lenses (e.g., the XF18mmF2.0 R, XF35mmF1.4 R, or XF60mmF2.4 R). Since these lenses are working with a focus-by-wire system, the noise also occurs during manual focusing. If you notice noise from the lens, better use an external microphone to record audio further away from the lens. Luckily, many newer Fujifilm lenses use almost silent focus motors. These include all lenses models with linear motors bearing the "LM" label and lenses with stepper motors used in the current range of weather resistant compact primes (XF16mmF2.8 R WR, XF23mmF2 R WR, XF35mmF2 R WR, XF50mmF2 R WR). The new XF16–80mmF4 R OIS WR also features silent focus motor operation.

If you feel limited by one of these factors, consider using Fujifilm's specialized MK cine-zoom lenses for the X-mount.

| MK cine-zoom lenses | TIP 125 |
|---|---|

Fujifilm's MK cine-zoom lenses are high-quality cine lenses at a reasonable price. They offer optical features and benefits that can otherwise only be found in much more expensive products.

The MK18–55mmT2.9 and MK50–135mmT2.9 lenses have the same dimensions and weight. Their front diameters, filter thread diameters and gear positions (for aperture, zoom and focus control) are also identical. This facilitates using the same accessories and allows quick lens changes in a rig that consists of a matte box and follow focus system.

The focus ring of the MK cine-zoom lenses has a rotation angle of 200°—a good compromise for both direct manual focusing and using a follow focus.

***Important:** Even though the two lens hoods of the Fujinon MK18–55mmT2.9 and Fujinon MK50–135mmT2.9 lenses have the same dimensions, they differ slightly to deliver optimal performance with their respected lenses. Mixing up the lens hoods can lead to vignetting and increase the risk of flare.*

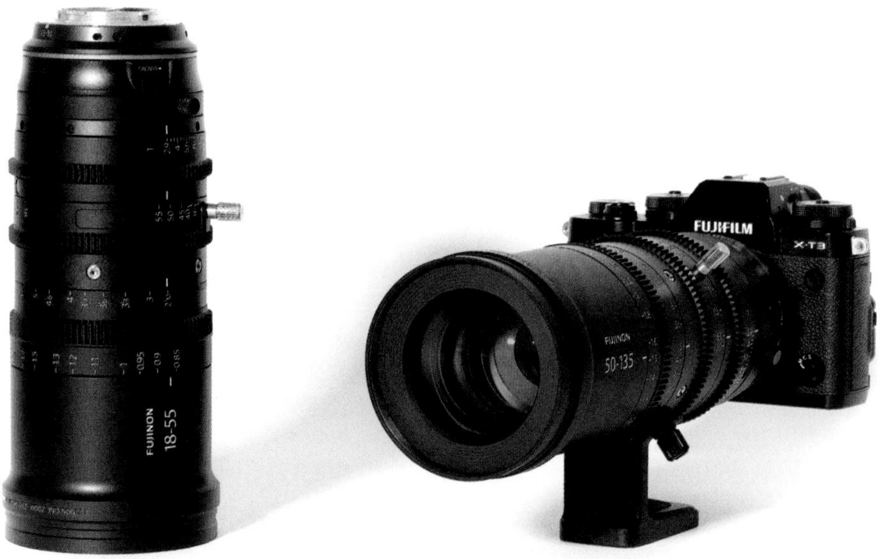

**Fig. 153:** Fujifilm's dedicated cine-lenses MK18–55mmT2.9 and MK50–135mmT2.9 for the X-mount are rather compact and light-weight cinema zooms.

Lenses that were built for still photography often change their field of view (FOV) during focusing. This behavior is known as *focus breathing*. When the focus is changed during filming, such FOV changes are undesirable. For this reason, Fujinon MK lenses feature an optical design that eliminates focus breathing.

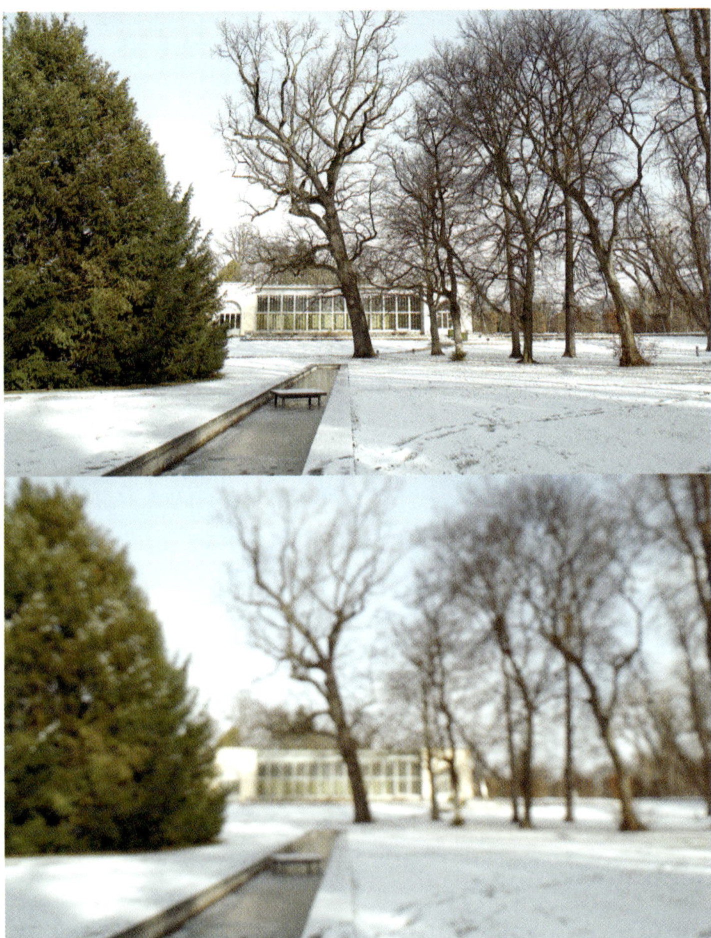

**Fig. 154:**  Throughout their zoom range, the Fujinon MK18–55mmT2.9 and MK50–135mmT2.9 lenses project the exact same image section at every focus position. This allows you to pull focus without being distracted by focus breathing.

Another important feature of the Fujinon MK lenses is their *parfocality*, which is essential for cinema lenses. A parfocal zoom lens doesn't change the position of the focal plane during zooming. For stills photography, parfocality isn't very important. However, parfocal lenses have clear advantages for video recording:

- When you zoom during filming, your subject stays in perfect focus.

- You can achieve maximum sharpness by manually focusing on the subject using the highest available focal length, then reducing the focal length to the desired value.

While some lenses for stills photography are referred to as parfocal, tests have shown that they are a far cry from the performance of genuine cine lenses [104]. Additionally, MK lenses allow back focus adjustments to ensure parfocal operation in all situations, such as different climates and temperatures [105].

The overall optical performance of the Fujinon MK lenses is outstanding. Both lenses are characterized by beautiful contrast and consistently high sharpness over the entire frame. In addition to their great optical performance, the MK lenses feature an extremely uniform look. Both lenses deliver results with the same colors and a very similar amount of aberrations.

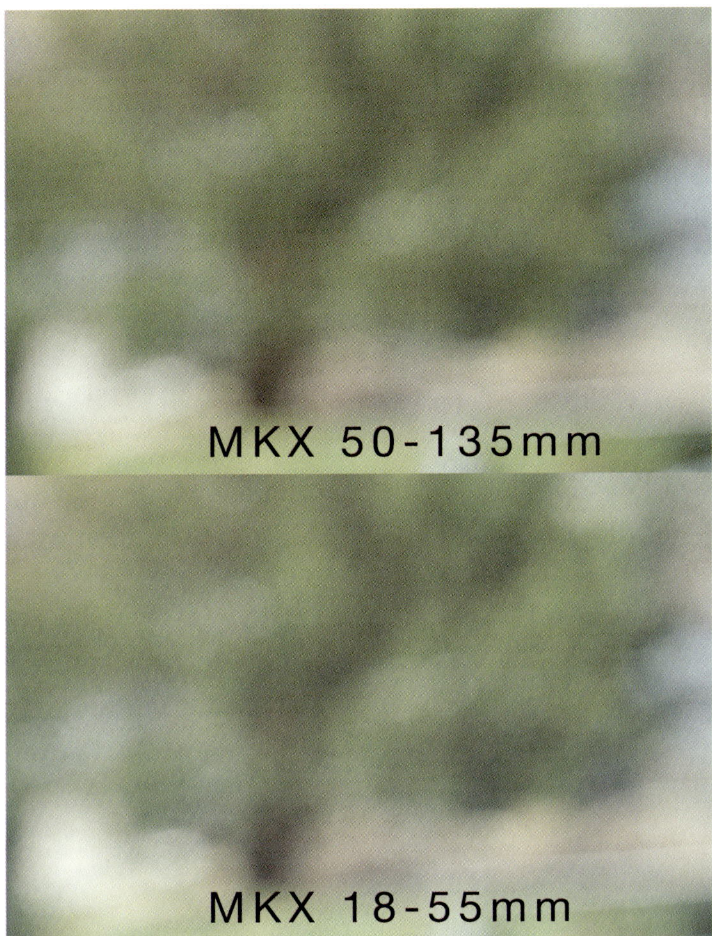


Fig. 155: In the overlapping focal length range of 50–55mm, there are hardly any differences in bokeh and general rendering, even at high magnifications of 100% and more.

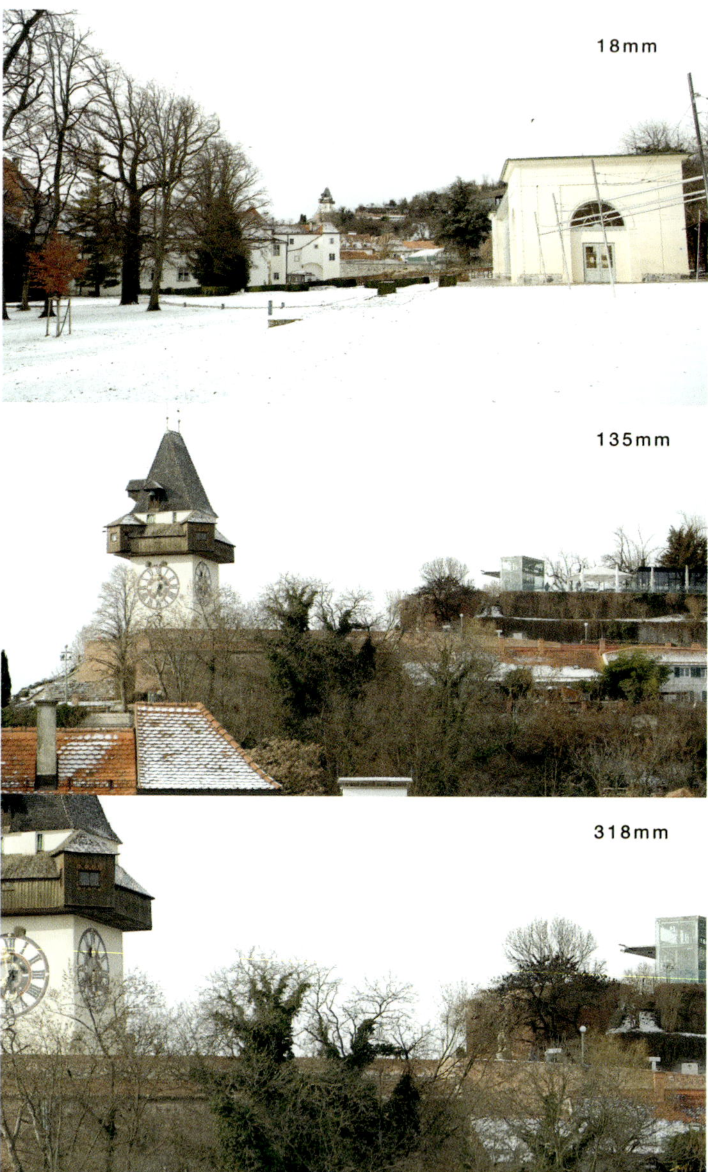


Fig. 156: This picture illustrates the range that can be covered with the MK18–55mmT2.9 and MK50–135mmT2.9 lenses. The last shot shows a 1080p detail of a 4K 60p (1.18x crop) shot. This corresponds to a focal length equivalent of 318 mm. Even with such extreme trimming, the quality is still outstanding.

Fujifilm MK lenses are available for Sony E, Micro Four Thirds and the Fujifilm X-mount. While the lenses for the Sony and Micro Four Thirds bayonet are so-called "dumb" lenses (i.e., without any communication between lens and camera), the X-mount versions of the MK lenses are equipped with electronic contacts that give them many characteristics of regular XC and XF autofocus lenses.

For example, a combination of optical and digital lens corrections can be used. The slight distortion of the Fujinon MK18–55mmT2.9 is automatically corrected by the camera during recording. As usual, this also works for still photography: JPEGs are automatically corrected, and RAW files contain lens correction metadata that can be used by built-in or external RAW converters.

In addition to the correction of aberrations, the communication between camera and lens enables the camera's digital depth-of-field scale.

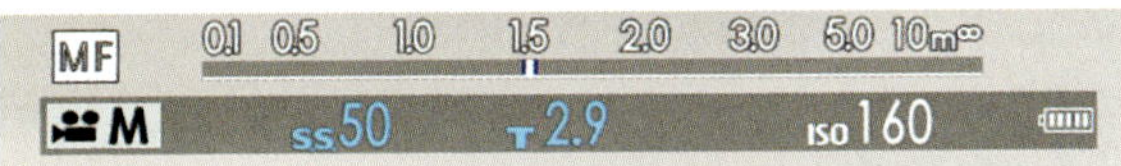

Fig. 157: The digital distance and depth-of-field scale can help you determine which parts of the image will be in focus. However, it is based on the same PIXEL BASIS or FILM FORMAT BASIS settings as for stills photography. This means that PIXEL BASIS is way too conservative even for 4K recordings, so better use the FILM FORMAT BASIS scale.

The MK cine-zooms for X-mount cameras also work perfectly in concert with the IBIS of the X-H1—and possible future X-camera models with In Body Image Stabilizers. Knowing the exact focal length is a prerequisite for stabilizing the first three axes (roll, yaw, tilt), while knowing the focus position allows stabilization of the remaining two axes (x- and y-shift). Since MK lenses for the X-mount know and transmit all this information to the camera, they inherently support in-body stabilization of all five axis.

Aperture settings are also transmitted from the lens to the camera. Since videographers are often more interested in the actual amount of light that reaches the sensor (the transmission or "t-stop") rather than the physical size of the aperture opening (the "f-stop"), the X-T3 allows you to choose between both formats.

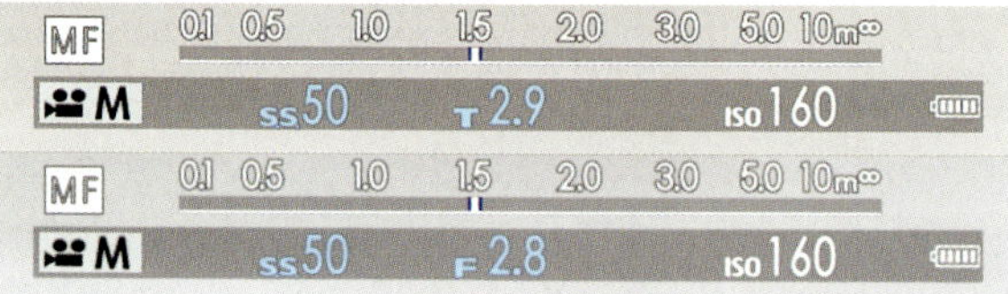

Fig. 158: Select SET UP > SCREEN SET-UP > APERTURE UNIT FOR CINEMA LENS to switch between f-stop (F NUMBER) and t-stop (T NUMBER) displays. However, the t-number will only be displayed when a Fujinon MK lens is attached. With other lenses, the camera reverts back to displaying the f-stop.

| TIP 126 | Useful video accessories |

With the right additions, you can turn your small camera into a larger rig. In this tip, we cover some popular and useful accessories.

**Neutral-density (ND) filters** [106] reduce the amount of light that falls onto the sensor and are useful in bright shooting situations. In general, there are two types of ND filters:

- Standard/constant ND filters

- Variable ND filters

I recommend buying filters that match the front diameter of your largest lens. On lenses with smaller diameters, the same filters can then be attached using appropriate step-up rings.

A **standard neutral-density filter** is a colored plate of glass. You can either get it enclosed in a metal housing with a filter thread, or in a rectangular shape to be used in plug-in filter systems.

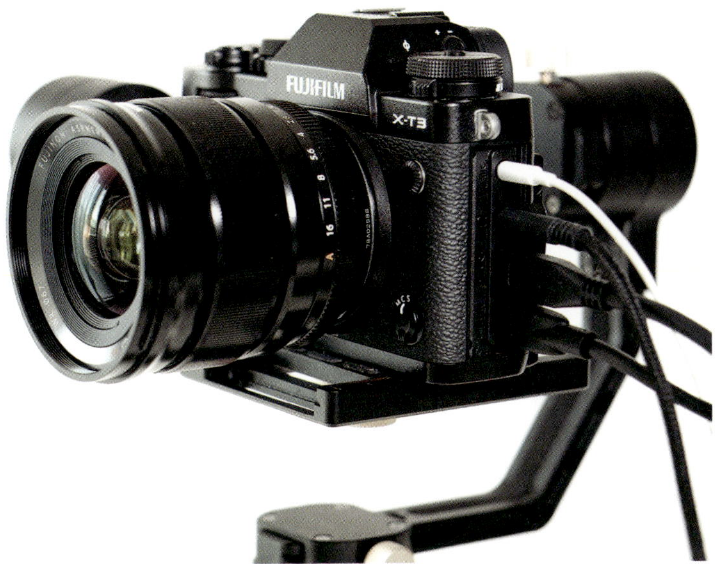

Fig. 159: The flap on the left side of the Fujifilm X-T3 can be removed for better access to the ports.

If you work with standard ND filters under changing light conditions, you have two options:

- Replace the ND filter every time the light changes.

- Use a strong ND filter and let the camera adjust the brightness by increasing the ISO. This can lead to increased noise.

While it's possible to stack multiple ND filters on top of each other, this should only be done in rare cases. Filter stacking can lead to color shifts, loss of resolution and increased artifacts such as reflections.

Unlike standard ND filters, **variable ND filters** are not colored glass, but two opposing polarization filters. Variable ND filters allow you to seamlessly control the strength of light transmission.

There are obvious benefits to using variable ND filters: They allow you to change the image brightness without changing filters, and they allow fine changes that are significantly smaller than a full stop (which is usually the gradation of constant ND filters).

However, variable ND filters also have some drawbacks:

- Variable ND filters are usually considerably thicker than standard ND filters.

- The higher number of glass surfaces can lead to more reflections and a loss in resolution.

- A so-called cross-effect pattern can occur.

- High-quality variable ND filters are much more expansive than standard ND filters.

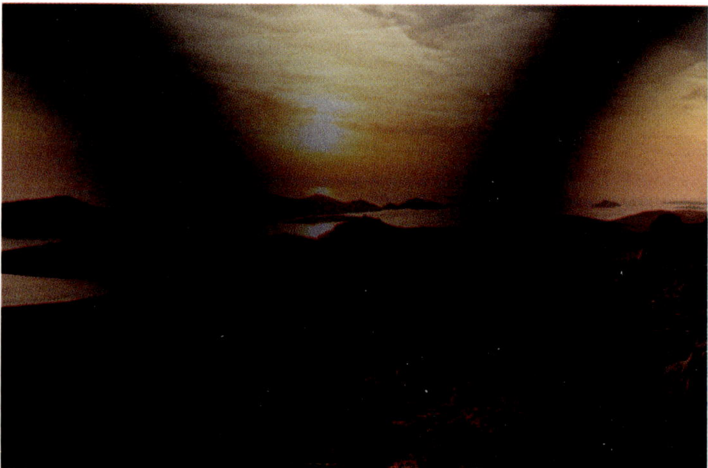

Fig. 160: In this example, you can see the cross-shaped pattern that can occur with variable ND filters. This effect can be particularly prominent with wide-angle lenses and cheaper variable ND filters.

High-quality variable ND filters are available from B+W, Nisi, SLR Magic, and others. These higher-end models usually have a more limited adjustment range in exchange for better image quality. Due to that limited range, you might have to stack a standard ND filter underneath the variable filter when you are working with very fast lenses such as the XF56mmF1.2 R.

Please note that even cheap standard ND filters deliver better optical performance than very expensive variable ND filters. Therefore, a set of standard ND filters combined with a quick-change filter system is often preferred.

Video users find it important to **stabilize** their recordings to compensate for trembling hands or walking and running movements. Three types of video stabilization are particularly popular in concert with mirrorless cameras:

- Lenses with OIS (optical image stabilization)
- Gimbals
- Tripods

Many native Fujifilm lenses offer a built-in optical stabilizer (OIS). While an **OIS** can compensate for the trembling of your hands, it is ill-suited for compensating camera shake caused by walking or running.

With a **motorized gimbal,** the camera can be moved smoothly in different directions [107]. Please note that a gimbal only corrects the axes for pan, roll, and tilt movements. Vertical movements generated by fast walking or jumping cannot be compensated. I recommend practicing a calm, gentle walking style with the gimbal. This may be unfamiliar at first, but it helps you better stabilize your videos [108].

Before using a gimbal, the camera and lens have to be balanced. This makes it easier for the electric motors, saves energy, and avoids vibrations [109]. Many gimbals come with quick release plates where you can mark the appropriate positions for different camera and lens combinations to speed-up the balancing process.

*Important: As of fall 2019, most gimbals offer only limited direct camera control functions in concert with Fujifilm cameras. Before purchasing, find out whether such functions are available or if the manufacturer plans to supply them in the near future.*

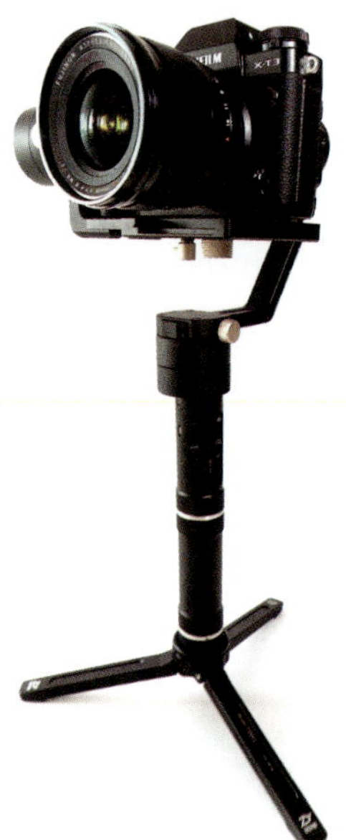

Fig. 161:
Due to its low weight and small dimensions, the X-T3 works well with smaller gimbals such as the Zhiyun Crane Plus. This setup with the X-T3 and a Fujifilm XF16mmF1.4 weighs less than 2 kg (excluding mini tripod).

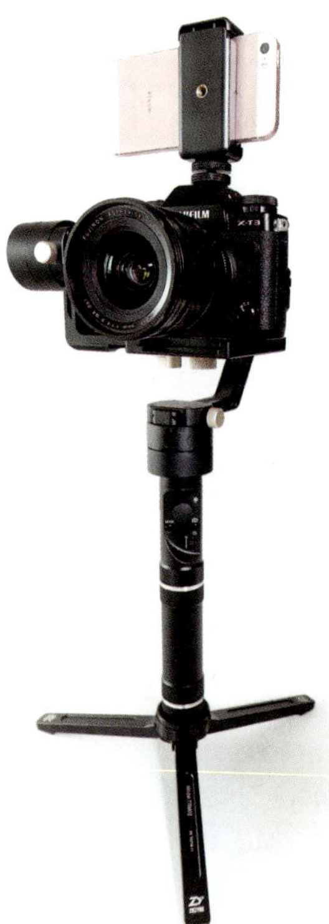

Fig. 162:
A smartphone that is mounted to the hot shoe of the X-T3 can enable new functions. For example, the gimbal can communicate with the smartphone and use its camera and processing power to track subjects. With stationary subjects and a moving gimbal, this provides quite good results, but with fast-moving subjects, the results are usually inadequate with jerky movements and overcompensation.

A **classic tripod** is one of the most popular forms of stabilization. When it comes to precise panning or tracking of moving subjects from a fixed position, a tripod provides very good results and easy handling. In combination with a compact camera like the X-T3, even tripods primarily designed for photography can deliver the goods. Dedicated video tripods are even more stable, but they are also bulkier and heavier. In any case, I recommend using a video head (fluid head) instead of a ball head. A fluid head allows smoother and more accurate movements.

In videography, a **cage** refers to a metal housing with plenty of screw threads that allow mounting different accessories at various positions, e.g.:

- Microphones
- Grips
- Field monitors or external recorders
- Lighting equipment
- Rail systems for follow focus, matte boxes or lens support
- Battery packs

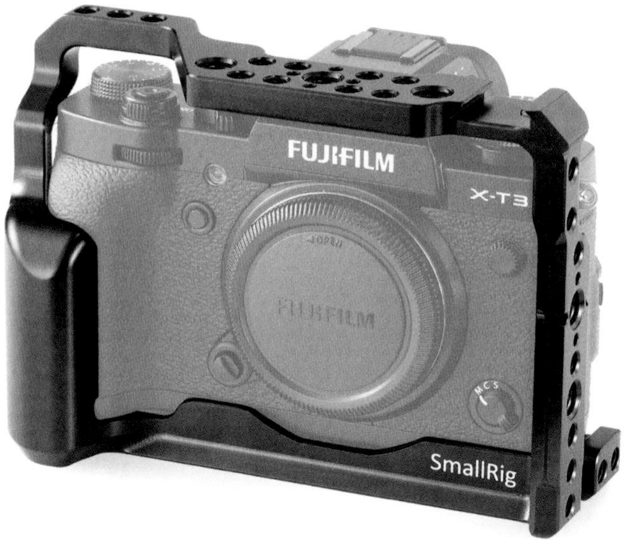

Fig. 163: Manufacturers like SmallRig and 8Sinn offer cages with a precise fit for the X-T3.

| TIP 127 | External recorders |
|---|---|

An external recorder can display the video signal of the X-T3 externally and record it if necessary. Prices start around several hundred dollars and often exceed $1000. This may seem high at first, but external recorders offer benefits that aren't available with in-camera recording: They can record in ProRes or DNxHD/DNxHR, they use cheaper recording media, they come with brighter and larger monitors, they offer various aids to determine the correct exposure, they don't suffer from the typical camera recording time limits, they can record up to 10-bit 4:2:2, and they offer additional accessory options.

The ProRes and DNxHD/DNxHR codecs deliver high quality without posing high demands on post-processing hardware. While smooth processing of H.265 requires powerful hardware, ProRes and DNxHD/HR can usually be displayed and processed even on older and less sophisticated systems.

External recorders are usually operated with SSDs that cost only a fraction of similar-sized UHS-II SD cards. They usually offer a large and bright screen that greatly simplifies monitoring. With the appropriate equipment, the recorder can be mounted on the camera's hot shoe, a cage, a gimbal, etc.

Most external recorders offer focusing aids like different levels of magnification and focus peaking with different colors and shapes, and it's often possible to display image aspect ratios such as 2.41:1, 2.35:1, 1.9:1, or 1.85:1 that can't be set or displayed in-camera.

External recorders offer a variety of additional options (like vectorscopes, false color, or waveform displays [110]) that can help you achieve the correct exposure. External recorders can also be used to apply and display LUTs. This can help you to better estimate the final look, especially with F-Log or HLG.

Video specifications often include information such as 4:4:4, 4:2:2, or 4:2:0, which describe different forms of chroma subsampling [111]. With internal camera recording, the X-T3 only supports 4:2:0 color subsampling. Recording externally, you get 4:2:2. In concert with strong post-processing, 4:2:0 might lead to problems such as color issues on contrast edges, or banding in large, color-graded areas like a blue sky. 4:2:2 color subsampling is especially important with visual effects work like green or blue screens.

In SHOOTING MENU > MOVIE SETTING > F-LOG/HLG RECORDING, you can specify which type of footage (film simulation, F-LOG, HLG) should be recorded internally and externally. Note that a mild crop factor of 1.18x will be introduced if you don't select identical settings for internal and external recording (e.g., film simulation + F-Log).

Use the 4K MOVIE OUTPUT and FULL HD MOVIE OUTPUT menu items to select the resolution (4K/Full HD) that you want to record internally and externally. It is also possible to output to an external device without internal recording.

The HDMI OUTPUT INFO DISPLAY option allows you send the full display contents to the external recorder, not just the video signal. This will record all the information that is shown on the display, including histograms or zebras.

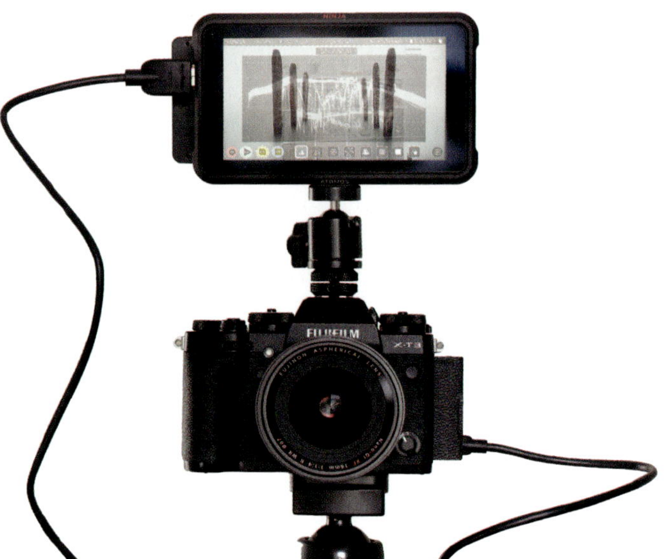

Fig. 164:  The **Atomos Ninja V** supports all frame rates of the Fujifilm X-T3 and allows 4K recording with up to 60p at 10-bit color depth. It can be mounted on the camera's hot shoe, on a cage, or on a gimbal or rig. In this example, it was mounted on a small ball-head that allows me to freely rotate the monitor.

If your recorder officially supports 4K recording with 50p or 60p and you are running into problems, please check your HDMI cables. Only cables with at least HDMI 2.0 allow 4K recordings with 50p and 60p. HDMI cables that meet the 2.0 standard are called "HDMI Premium High Speed." Cables that support the new 2.1 standard are called "HDMI Ultra High Speed." Alternatively, you can also look at to the transmission rate, which should be at least 18 Gbps.

| TIP 128 | Increasing your recording time |
| --- | --- |

There are limits to the maximum recording time:

- 20 minutes when shooting in 4K 50p or 60p

- 29 minutes and 59 seconds per shot when recording in any other format

The artificial per-shot recording restriction of less than 30 minutes is due to an old European Union regulation.

With higher frame rates and increasing resolution, the camera limits the recording time to protect itself from overheating. However, the 20-minute limit does not mean that the camera won't be able to record video beyond this threshold. In most cases, you can keep shooting without problems. The number of possible successive recordings depends on factors like the ambient temperature, the type of power supply used, camera settings such as display brightness, etc.

You can bypass the recording limits with an external recorder. It allows you to exceed the 30-minute limit, and it also keeps the temperature lower, so you can record longer with high frame rates. Note that if you are simultaneously recording internally and externally, all recording limits still apply.

If you want to record long sequences without interruption, the power supply plays an essential role. As you know, the X-T3 uses the NP-W126S battery that was developed for better heat dissipation. Older NP-W126 and third-party batteries may lead to faster overheating. However, the capacity of this type of battery is limited: the maximum recording time is about 45 minutes in 4K. There are three ways to extend your recording time:

- The vertical battery grip VG-XT3 extends the capacity of the X-T3 to a total of three batteries. This prolongs the total usable video recording time to about 120 minutes. In contrast to older X-camera models, the switch between empty and full batteries is fluid and should not interrupt the recording.

- The X-T3 offers two ways to be operated via mains power: You can either use the vertical battery grip and its included power supply, or you can get a CP-W126 DC coupler.

- You can also power the camera via USB when it is switched on. However, this requires an inserted battery that has not been completely drained. When the camera is powered via USB, the battery still discharges, albeit at a much slower rate. Fujifilm specifically recommends Anker PowerCore Speed 20000 PD and Power-Core+26800 PD power banks. For optimal results, make sure that your power bank supports USB-C Power Delivery (PD) with at least 24W.

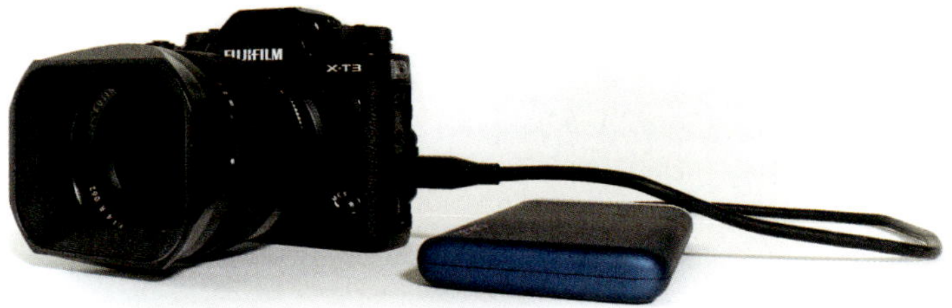

Fig. 165: Even with external power banks, the battery life of the Fujifilm X-T3 can be significantly extended. The 18W power bank in this example extends the battery life to about 2.5 hours.

| TIP 129 | Pros and cons of using the Camera Remote app |
|---|---|

The Fujifilm Cam Remote app grants limited control over the camera. For example, you can use the app with its Bluetooth connection as a remote shutter release to simply start and stop the recording. Alternatively, the camera can be remote-controlled via Wi-Fi.

However, this option has some limitations: When you use the Wi-Fi control of the smartphone app, the camera will ignore most of your settings. Recording with the Camera Remote app has a resolution limit of 1080p and a maximum bitrate of 100 Mbps—even if you have set 4K and higher bit rates in the camera menu.

If you use an autofocus lens in manual focus mode, the smartphone app forces the camera back to autofocus.

Furthermore, the camera is forced into AF-C and MULTI focus mode.

The smartphone app bases its settings on the settings of the mechanical dials and ignores settings made in MOVIE SILENT CONTROL. To choose your settings manually, you have to make sure that the dials for aperture and shutter speed are not set to "A."

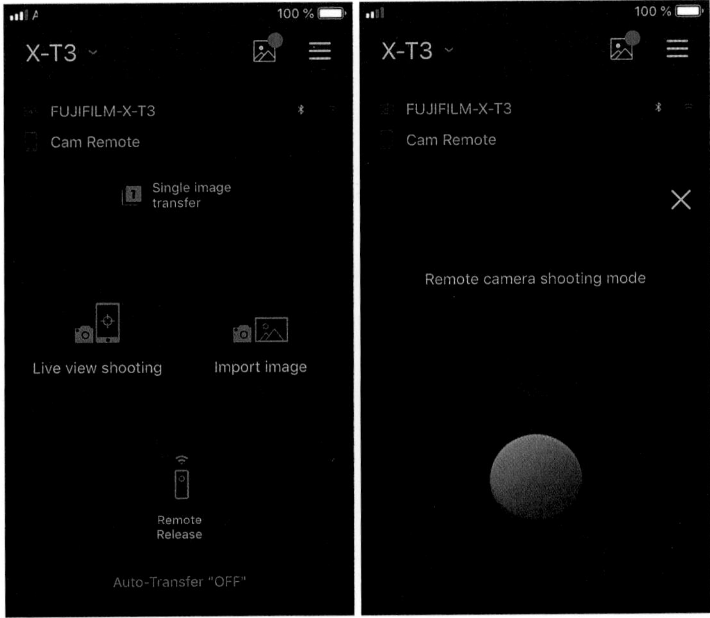

Fig. 166: The Camera Remote app allows you to control the camera. With the Bluetooth remote shutter release (right), the recording is started and stopped when the onscreen button is pressed. The live view shooting mode (left) overwrites all in-camera settings.

## 2.7 FLASH PHOTOGRAPHY

Flash photography means taking a double exposure. The lighting in a flash shot always consists of two components: **surrounding light** and **flash light**.

- The **surrounding-light** component is metered like a regular exposure. Your camera is metering the scene with multi, average, center-weighted, or spot metering, while the auto exposure mode (**P**, **A**, or **S**) automatically selects suitable exposure parameters based on your adjustment of the exposure compensation dial. As usual, the live view and live histogram are your friends. You can also set the exposure of the surrounding-light component manually in mode **M**, which is my preferred method in almost all situations. Basically, exposing for the surrounding-light component works exactly like exposing a scene without flash.

- The **flash-light** component can be automatically metered and adjusted by the camera to match the overall exposure. To accomplish this, the camera employs a so-called TTL metering system [112]. TTL stands for Through The Lens. It means the flash light is entering the camera through the lens before it's metered with the image sensor. This happens with the help of a weaker pre-flash that is emitted solely for metering purposes. You can bias the strength of the automatic flash-light component either on the FLASH FUNCTION SETTING page, or directly on external Fujifilm TTL flash units like the EF-X20 and EF-X500. Please note that while the live view and live histogram provide a preview of the surrounding-light component, they completely ignore the flash-light component that will be added to the final image.

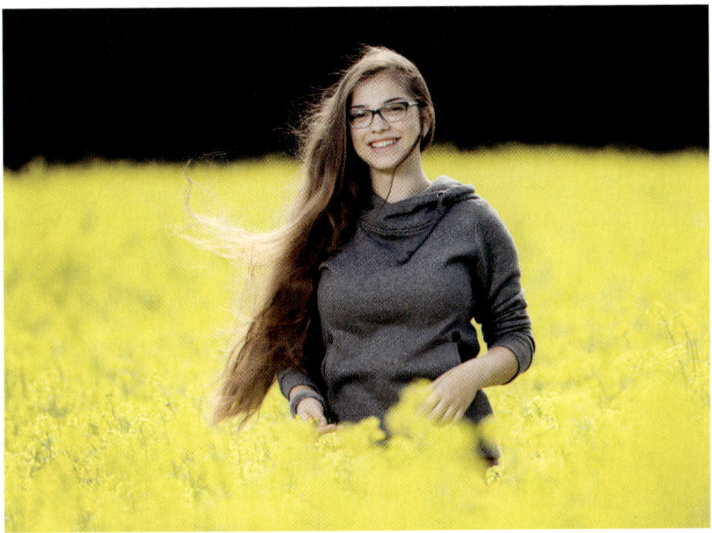

Fig. 167: In many cases, **flash photography** is about balancing the natural surrounding light and the artificially added flash light.

In addition to Fujifilm-branded or Fujifilm-compatible TTL flash units, you can use generic third-party flash units. Pretty much everything that will fit onto the hot shoe will work. Using generic third-party flash units means that TTL flash metering is no longer available, so you must manually set the flash's power output. You can also use automatic flash units that use their own built-in light sensors to automatically measure and adjust the flash output independently from the camera.

The TTL flash logic in your X-T3 supports several flash modes that can be selected in the Quick menu or on the SHOOTING MENU > FLASH SETTING > FLASH FUNCTION SETTING page:

- TTL FLASH AUTO is available only in auto exposure mode **P**. It automatically fires an available flash unit if the camera decides it's necessary. It's a silly mode, since you probably know better than your camera whether or not you want to use a flash. When the flash is firing, it works just like regular TTL, which is our next mode.

- TTL STANDARD (formerly known as FORCED FLASH) always fires an active flash unit. This setting is available in all four exposure modes (**P**, **A**, **S**, and **M**).

- TTL SLOW SYNC works like standard TTL but allows shutter speeds as slow as 1/8 s to better capture the surrounding-light component. This can be helpful when the light is poor, and you still want to capture more of the background. This setting is only available in exposure modes **P** and **A**.

- MANUAL FLASH works like TTL SLOW SYNC but allows you to manually specify the light emission power. This setting is available in all four exposure modes (**P**, **A**, **S**, and **M**).

- COMMANDER is a trigger flash that optically releases external flash units (or slaves) that feature an optical trigger sensor (like Fuji's EF-X20 and several third-party flash units). Please note that you must *manually* adjust the power output of the triggered slave flash. Don't forget that the commander flash is also emitting flash light that can affect the overall exposure of your scene, especially when you are shooting with high ISO settings. COMMANDER is available in all four exposure modes (**P**, **A**, **S**, and **M**).

- OFF makes sure no flash is fired, even when the flash is switched on and connected to the camera.

- In the FLASH FUNCTION SETTING page, there is an option to specify whether the flash is supposed to fire on the FRONT (1st) or REAR (2nd) curtain. This option is available in all flash modes, and it is relevant for shooting moving subjects at slow shutter speeds. Since flash photography is a double exposure, it makes a difference whether the flash is fired at the beginning or at the end of a longer exposure. With the higher-end EF-X500 flashgun, there's also an option called FP, which stands for Focal Plane. This is Fuji's version of High-Speed Synchronization (HSS), which allows firing the flash at all mechanical shutter speeds up to 1/8000 s.

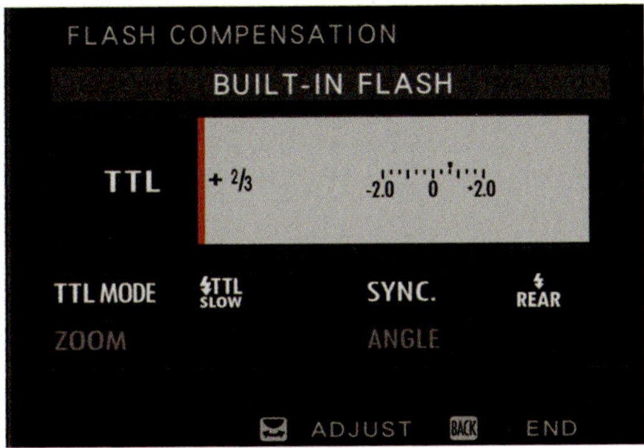


Fig. 168: The FLASH FUNCTION SETTING page lets you control flash parameters such as flash mode, sync. mode, and flash exposure compensation.

<table>
<tr><td>Flash photography in modes P and A:<br>slow shutter speed limits</td><td>TIP 130</td></tr>
</table>

In exposure modes **P** and **A**, the camera automatically selects suitable shutter speeds to capture the surrounding-light component of the scene.

- In flash modes TTL AUTO, TTL STANDARD, and COMMANDER, the slowest available shutter speed is 1/60 s. No matter what focal length is in use, the camera will not use a slower shutter speed than that. This limit marks the point where the surrounding-light component (usually the scene's background) can end up underexposed.

- TTL SLOW SYNC and MANUAL FLASH allow the camera to use slower minimum shutter speeds with flash photography. There's only one hard limit of 1/8 s, which is independent from the focal length or an active OIS. To achieve even slower shutter speeds, you should use mode **S** or **M**.

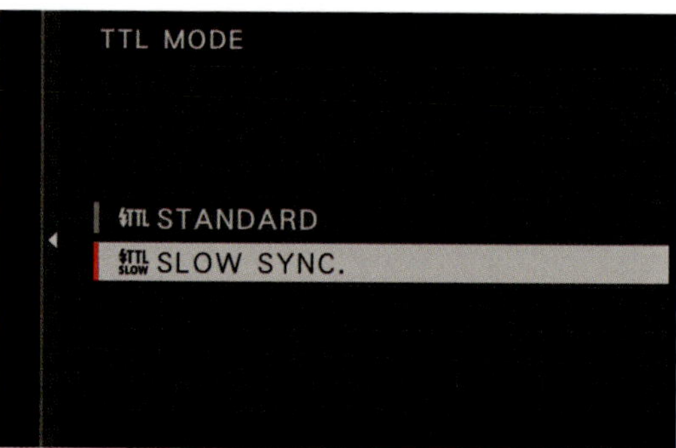


Fig. 169: If you insist on using the AE modes **P** or **A** to automatically expose the surrounding-light component of your flash image, selecting TTL SLOW SYNC will reduce the minimum shutter speed the camera can use to sync with the flash to 1/8 s. Please note this may still be too fast to properly expose the background in low-light situations. This is another reason I highly recommend exposing the surrounding-light component in mode **M**. Of course, the main reason is maintaining full control over the look of the picture and the balance between surrounding light and flash light.

*Important: Using Auto-ISO in combination with flash can lead to unexpected results in exposure modes* **A** *and* **P** *because the camera can generate shutter speeds that are faster than the minimum shutter speed limit set in the Auto-ISO configuration, or the slow-sync limit of 1/8 s. For this reason, I recommend you turn off Auto-ISO when using flash in the* **A** *and* **P** *exposure modes. Instead, set the desired ISO value manually.*

**TIP 131**   Controlling the surrounding-light component

When you are metering a scene with your X-T3, you will quickly realize it makes no difference whether the flash function is turned on or off while doing so. The metering result will always be the same. In other words, the camera is metering the surrounding-light component always in the same way, with or without flash. In case you choose to use a flash, the flash-light component will simply be *added* to the surrounding-light component.

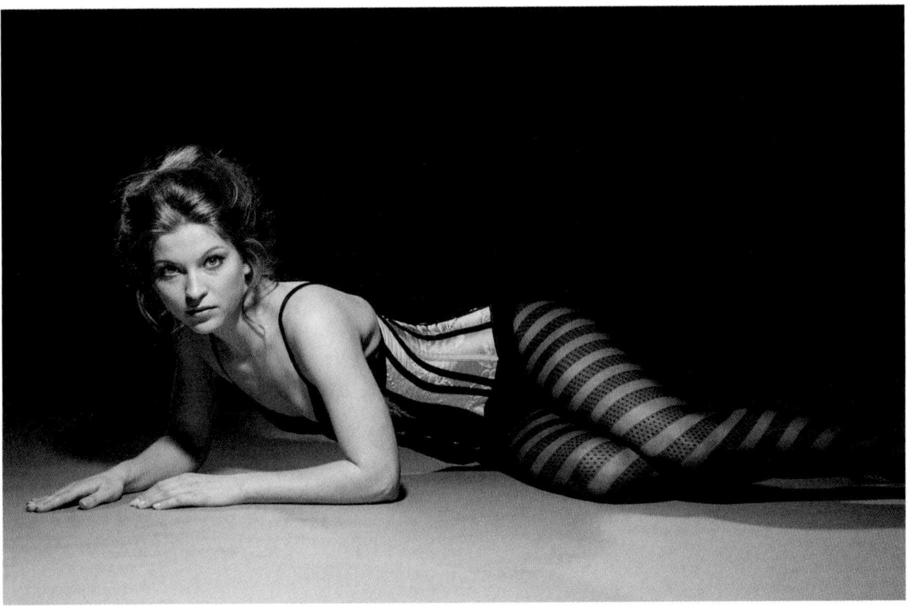

Fig. 170: **Reducing the surrounding-light component** to darken the background leaves more room for the flash-light component. This is particularly easy in a studio, where you have full control over the intensity of both light components.

This is important because it tells us we don't have to fear some camera voodoo that may or may not influence the metering of the surrounding light as soon as we switch on a flash. Instead, we can be certain the camera's metering will always deliver consistent results. This also means it's *our* job to balance both light components; for example, we can reduce the surrounding-light component to make room for more flash light in the composite exposure.

If you want to use the TTL flash as a fill light to brighten a dark foreground (such as a backlit person), the flash-light component will brighten the foreground by filling in the light that's missing. However, if you use the flash on a scene that's already fully exposed by natural light, the camera's TTL flash metering will probably conclude that no additional light is needed. A forced flash would still fire, but with minimal output; it would probably be almost invisible in the resulting shot. To emphasize the flash-light component, you must reduce the exposure of the surrounding-light component.

Here's how it works:

- You can control the exposure of the surrounding-light component either with the exposure compensation dial or by setting an appropriate manual exposure (ISO, aperture, shutter speed). Less surrounding light will prompt the TTL flash metering to add a stronger flash-light component, since the TTL flash system will always try to deliver balanced results. Changing the exposure compensation dial has no effect on the flash component of the shot; it only affects the exposure of the surrounding-light component.

- To control the surrounding-light component in manual mode **M** using the live view and the live histogram, make sure the exposure preview in manual mode is enabled by selecting SET UP > SCREEN SET-UP > PREVIEW EXP./WB IN MANUAL MODE > PREVIEW EXP./WB.

- In a studio setting, you often want to minimize the surrounding-light component and illuminate your subject entirely with flash light. In such cases, I recommend smaller aperture settings (larger aperture numbers), base ISO 160, and a fast shutter speed. The fastest official flash synchronization speed of the X-T3 is 1/250 s. To compose a studio scene with very little surrounding light in mode **M**, make sure the exposure preview in manual mode is disabled by selecting SET UP > SCREEN SET-UP > PREVIEW EXP./WB IN MANUAL MODE > OFF. Otherwise, it will be hard for you to see anything in the viewfinder other than a dark or black image.

- Sometimes the fastest available flash sync speed will still overexpose the surrounding-light component, even at base ISO. Yes, you could stop down the aperture, but this might negate the purpose of achieving a nice subject-to-background separation with a shallow depth of field. In such a case, it's useful to attach a neutral density filter [113] to the lens to reduce the amount of light that hits the sensor by 3 to 6 stops. Alternatively, you can use a Fuji-compatible flash that supports high-speed sync (HSS).

■ Like the DR function, flash light is often used to reduce the contrast between a darker foreground-subject and a brighter background. You can combine both features (flash and the DR function), which may be useful if the background—when viewed isolated from the foreground—still contains so much contrast that DR expansion is required. Think of a night scene with city lights, street lamps, and bright billboards in the background. In such a scenario, a flashgun could illuminate a person standing in the foreground, while the DR function (DR400%) would help capture the bright colors and textures of the city lights. DR400% is also useful when you are illuminating scenes with subjects that expand deep into space and don't have an equal distance to the camera. In such cases, DR400% will give subjects that are closer to the flash light an additional overexposure protection of 2 EV, which can be retrieved during external RAW conversion of your shot.

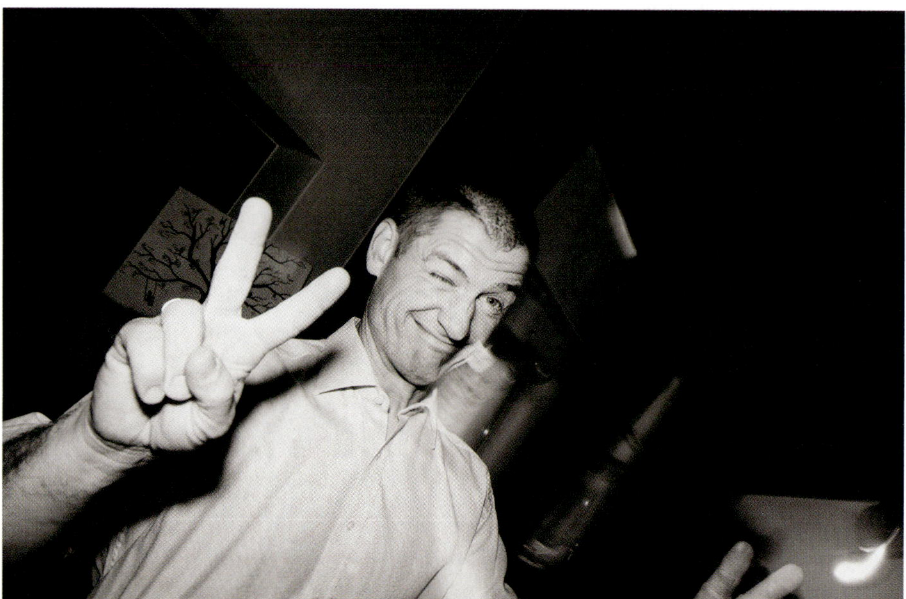

Fig. 171: Shooting close-ups with **a hot shoe flash and a wide-angle lens** can make things tricky. For this snapshot, I used a XF16mmF1.4 lens at f/6.4, 1/6 s, and ISO 800/DR400% in exposure mode **M**. The hand of the party guest happens to be much closer to the camera (and hence to the TTL flash) than his face, so with every "normal" camera, the hand would either be overexposed, or the face would be underexposed by the flash light. Not with Fujifilm, though. The DR function comes to the rescue. By manually setting DR400%, the guest's hand can be overexposed up to 2 EV by the TTL flash—and we can still fully recover it during external RAW conversion. In this case, I used Lightroom.

- The previously discussed hard limits for minimum shutter speed in modes **P** and **A** can lead to an underexposed surrounding-light component. However, these limits can be somewhat useful because they prevent blurred backgrounds in handheld shots. This isn't an issue when using a tripod, so you could circumvent the limits by selecting TTL SLOW or by manually setting a slow shutter speed in **S** or **M** mode. I personally recommend using **M** mode.

- Surrounding light and flash light frequently exhibit different color temperatures, which makes it difficult to find a white balance setting that suits all parts of the image. Luckily, some RAW converters (like Lightroom) allow selective white balance editing in an image. Another method is to use a gel filter in front of the flash unit to warm or cool the flash light to better match the surrounding light.

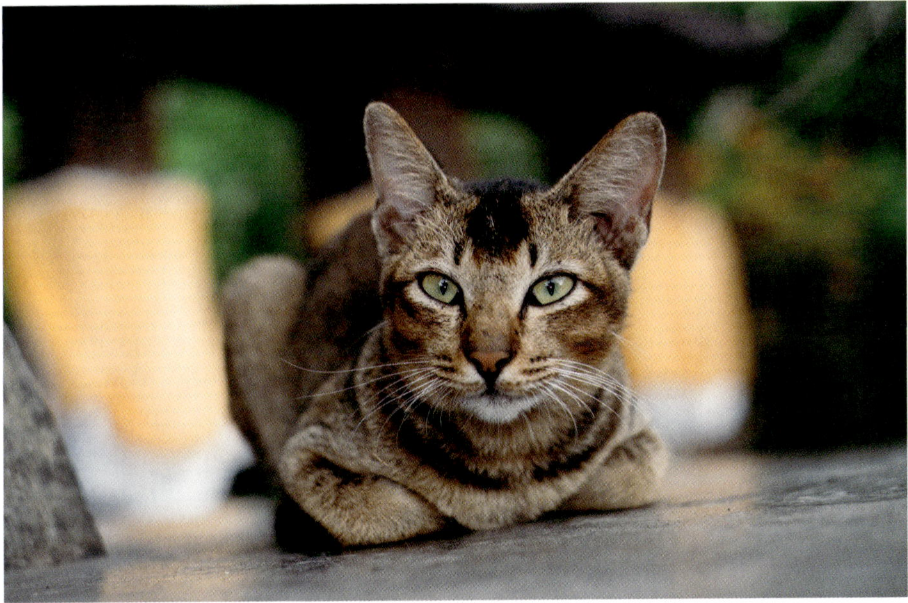

Fig. 172: With plenty of **surrounding light,** the flash-light component takes a backseat. In this example (taken with an EF-20), it simply added a spark to the cat's eyes. The best flash shots are often those that are hard to identify as flash photography.

| Controlling the flash-light component | TIP 132 |
| --- | --- |

If the flash-light component of your image turns out too bright or dark, you can bias the camera's TTL flash system:

- To bias the flash-light component of your shot, you can adjust the flash exposure compensation in the camera on the SHOOTING MENU > FLASH SETTING > FLASH FUNC-TION SETTING page or on many external TTL flash units. Combining the in-camera flash compensation with an additional compensation setting on the flash unit itself will simply combine both corrections (the EF-X500 and Metz M400 are exceptions to this rule).

- You will often get nicer-looking results by bouncing the flash off the ceiling, as this softens the harsh flash light. Of course, bouncing the flash light requires more power, so you may need a stronger flash. It's also worth noting that bouncing the flash from a colored surface will tint the light accordingly.

- To add a tint or to change the color temperature of your flash light, you can attach colored gel filters in front of your reflector. The color temperature of unfiltered flash light usually corresponds to regular daylight.

- The range of your flash unit depends on the set aperture, the ISO setting, and (of course) the power setting. In TTL mode, the camera is automatically adjusting the light output of your flash, but many flash units can also be set to manual. This way, you are the one setting the power output of the flash. In manual mode **M**, changing the shutter speed doesn't affect the brightness of the flash-light component of your shot, as long as you remain at or below the official maximum sync speed of 1/250 s. Hence, changing the shutter speed is a quick way to adjust the exposure of the surrounding-light component without messing with your carefully balanced manual flash-light setup.

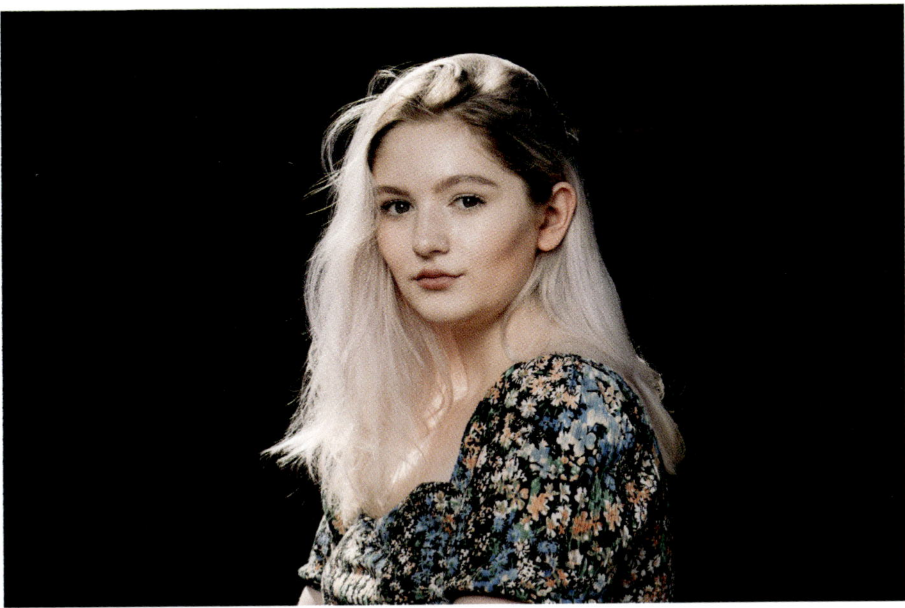

Fig. 173: Having **full manual control over both light components** is my preferred and recommended way of merging flash light and surrounding light—as long as there's enough time to make the necessary adjustments.

- Don't forget that when using an on-camera hot shoe flash, large lenses and lens hoods might block parts of the flash light, resulting in unpleasant shadows. It's better to remove the lens hood or to use an off-camera flash.

- Some wide-angle lenses cover a larger angle of view than the reflector of your flash can handle. This results in unpleasant vignetting. In such cases, bouncing the flash light off the ceiling can be helpful. Alternatively, you can attach a diffusor to the flash reflector. Many flash units feature built-in diffusors—just don't forget to flip them on.

<table><tr><td>TIP 133</td><td>Front- versus rear-curtain flash synchronization</td></tr></table>

Flash photographs are double exposures consisting of surrounding light and flash light. When you shoot the surrounding light with a slow shutter speed, there is the question of when the flash (with its much faster speed) should fire. Normally, the flash is fired along with the shutter opening its FRONT (or 1st) curtain at the *beginning* of an exposure. However, if the REAR (or 2nd) curtain has been selected, the flash fires at the *end* of the exposure when the rear shutter curtain closes.

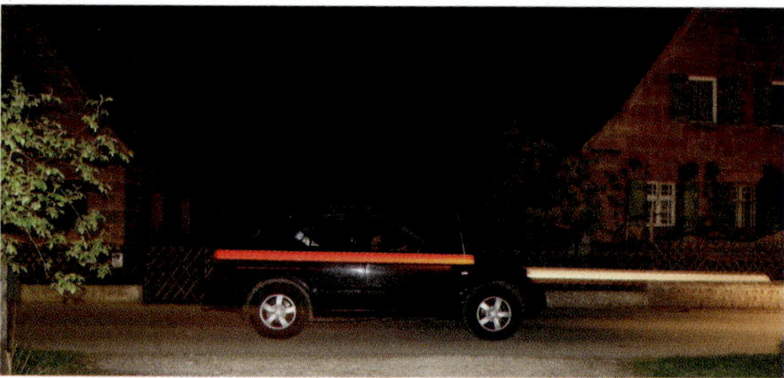

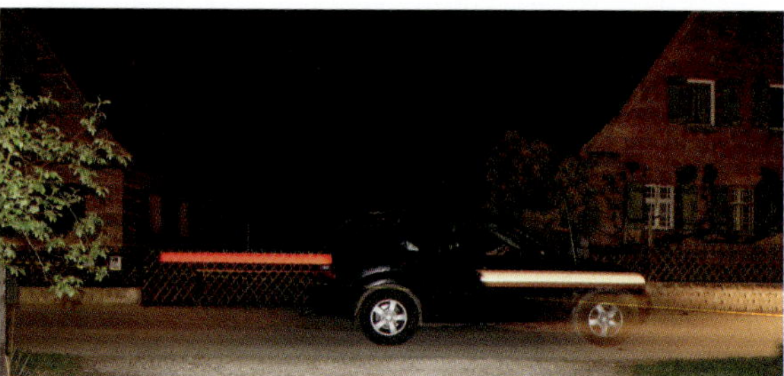

Fig. 174: **Front- versus rear-curtain sync:** This example shows the same scene photographed with front-curtain sync (above) and rear-curtain sync (below). The shot above shows how the flash freezes the moving vehicle at the beginning of the exposure, while the shot below shows it being frozen at the end of the exposure. The rear-curtain version looks more natural and avoids the false impression of the car moving backward. This is also a good example to examine the nature of flash photographs as double exposures. You can see how the slow shutter speed captures the moving vehicle as a blurry trail of light, while the fast flash instantly freezes parts of it.

Naturally, moving objects change their position during the exposure of a shot. Synchronizing the flash with the rear curtain ensures that moving objects are frozen where they are located at the end of the exposure as opposed to at the beginning. This often results in the moving object appearing more natural in the image.

| Flash synchronization: what's the limit? | TIP 134 |
| --- | --- |

The maximum official flash sync [114] speed of the X-T3 is 1/250 s.

- In exposure modes **P** and **A**, the camera will never offer a shutter speed faster than the official maximum sync speed. If this is too slow for the current light conditions, the surrounding-light component will be overexposed. In this case, the shutter speed will be displayed in red. To avoid overexposure, stop down the lens, reduce ISO (but never below base ISO 160), or use a neutral density (ND) filter [115] in front of the lens.

- In exposure modes **S** and **M**, you can select shutter speeds faster than the maximum sync speed. Your camera will honor these settings in flash mode, but there is a price to pay: the resulting images will display some partial shadowing of the flash. It's often possible to use shutter speeds that are a little bit faster than the official maximum sync speed without visible negative effects — it depends on the type of flash you are using. Its power setting plays a role, as well. Proceed at your own risk!

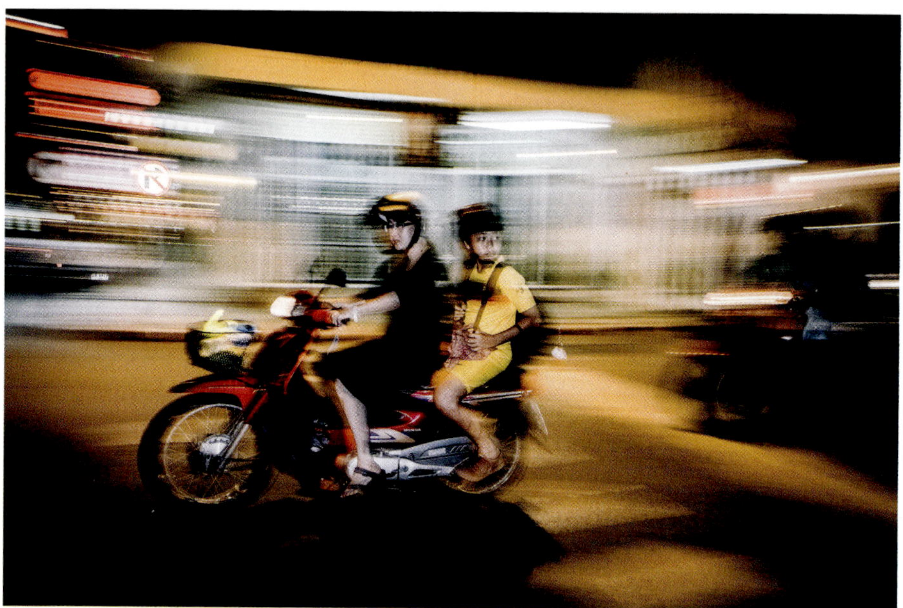

Fig. 175: Many photographers wish to use a **flash sync speed** faster than the maximum sync speed of their camera. That said, it's also possible to deliberately use very slow synch speeds to create a blurry background behind a more contoured flash-lit foreground. This shot was taken with an EF-X500.

- High-speed synchronization (HSS, also known as FP mode) up to 1/8000 s is officially supported by the X-T3. As of fall 2019, the only HSS-compatible flash from Fujifilm was the EF-X500. Luckily, several Fuji-TTL-compatible third-party flashguns and systems (Godox, Metz M400, etc.) support HSS, as well.

- HSS/FP consumes more flash power, so you may need a more powerful flash unit to compensate HSS-related losses. Depending on the brand and type of your flash, the effective power reduction that occurs at the transition point between normal sync and high-speed sync can vary between 2/3 EV (Godox AD200 or AD600) and almost 2 EV (some speedlights).

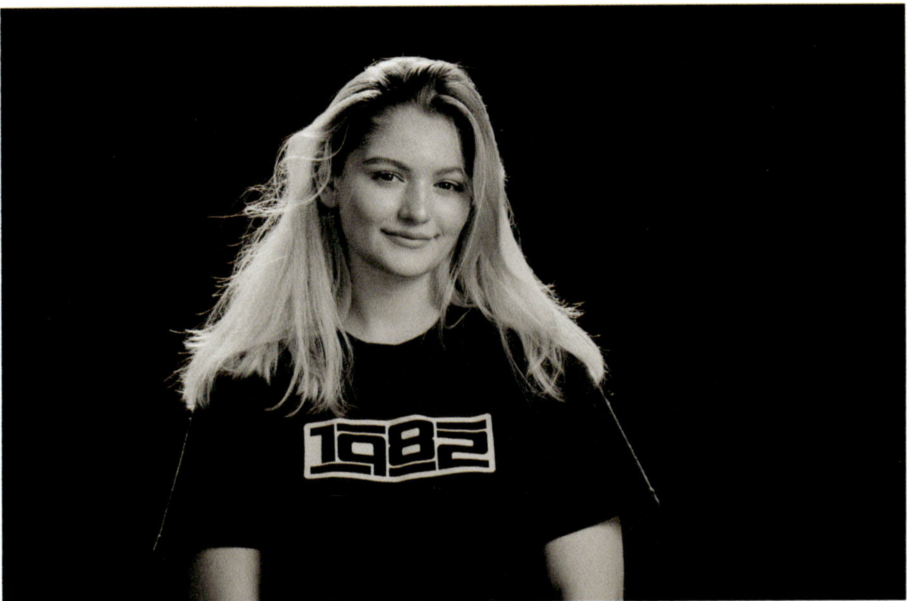

**Fig. 176:** This manually controlled **HSS** shot was taken at a shutter speed of 1/4000 s, using a Godox V1 in a small softbox and a Godox X2T-F radio controller.

| Red-eye removal: a two-step affair | TIP 135 |
| --- | --- |

If the flash and your subject share almost the same optical axis (a frequent occurrence with the built-in flash or with a clip-on flash), it can lead to the red-eye effect [116]: an unpleasant red reflection in the eyes.

- If you pull up SHOOTING MENU > FLASH SETTING > RED EYE REMOVAL and then select either FLASH or FLASH+REMOVAL, the camera will emit a pre-flash prior to each shot that forces your subject's pupils to contract, thus reducing or eliminating the red-eye effect.

- In addition to the pre-flash, there's *another* red-eye removal tool available: selecting REMOVAL (or FLASH+RE-MOVAL) in the FLASH SETTING > RED EYE REMOVAL menu will detect and remove unpleasant red-eye effects in a JPEG after the fact. This function is also available in PLAYBACK MENU > RED EYE REMOVAL in case you decide to use it later. If you want to keep a copy of the unretouched JPEG, select SET UP > SAVE DATA SET-UP > SAVE ORG IMAGE > ON. The RAW file isn't affected by this variant of red-eye removal.

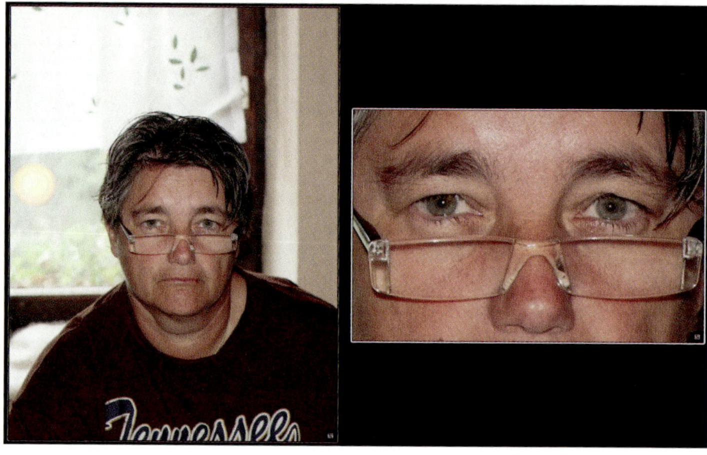

Fig. 177: The **red-eye removal** function emits a pre-flash that is bright enough to prompt your subject's pupils to contract.

| TIP 136 | Using TTL-Lock |

TTL-Lock works like AE-Lock, but where AE-Lock locks the exposure of the surrounding-light component, TTL-Lock locks the exposure of the flash-light component. To use TTL-Lock, you have to first assign it to one of your camera's Fn buttons.

TTL-Lock can work in one of two ways:

■ Keep and lock the exposure of the most recent flash exposure when you press the TTL-Lock button (SHOOTING MENU > FLASH SETTING > TTL-LOCK MODE > LOCK WITH LAST FLASH).

- Meter the flash exposure with a metering flash when you press the TTL-Lock button and immediately lock the metered result (SHOOTING MENU > FLASH SETTING > TTL-LOCK MODE > LOCK WITH METERING FLASH).

TTL-Lock is practical in situations where you want to take more than one picture of the same scene and maintain a consistent flash output for the entire series. A typical method involves setting the LOCK WITH LAST FLASH option, and then taking a few test shots of the scene and applying flash exposure compensation until the result looks great. Now press TTL-Lock to lock and maintain this "perfect" flash exposure while you take additional pictures of the scene.

| Tiny slave: the Fujifilm EF-X20 | TIP 137 |
| --- | --- |

Fuji's TTL system flash EF-X20 was specifically made for retro-style cameras like the X-Pro1, but it also works perfectly with the X-T3. In addition to using it as a TTL flash, you can set its output power manually. You can even trigger it wirelessly with another flash, such as the camera's Commander flash.

- Set the flash mode in your X-T3 to COMMANDER.

- Move the mode switch on your EF-X20 to the N position.

- Manually set the desired flash output on your EF-X20. There are seven levels, from 1/1 (full power) to 1/64.

With this setup, the flash on your X-T3 will wirelessly trigger the EF-X20. Please note that the light emitted by the commander flash can still affect your image.

Fig. 178:  An optically triggered **EF-X20** slave flash

| TIP 138 | Grand master: the Fujifilm EF-X500 |

The EF-X500 is Fuji's version of a professional flashgun, with wireless TTL control of several flash units (organized in up to three independent groups) and stroboscope flash. It has a secondary LED reflector that can be used as a catch light [117], a more powerful AF assist lamp, or a video lamp. It also features FP high-speed sync to support shutter speeds of up to 1/8000 s.

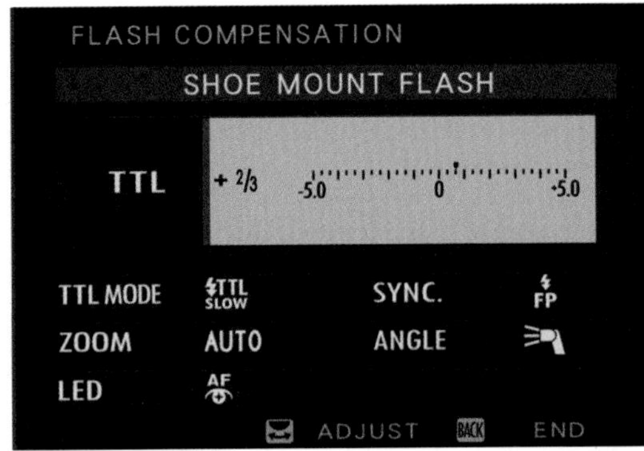


Fig. 179: With the fully featured **EF-X500** attached, the FLASH FUNCTION SETTING page adds several new items, including high-speed sync (FP), zoom settings, a reflector angle control, and control of the secondary LED, which can be used as an AF assist lamp and/or a catch light.

You can use the EF-X500 as a single clip-on flashgun or as a master/slave in setups with multiple wireless flash units. Communication between master and slave units is light based.

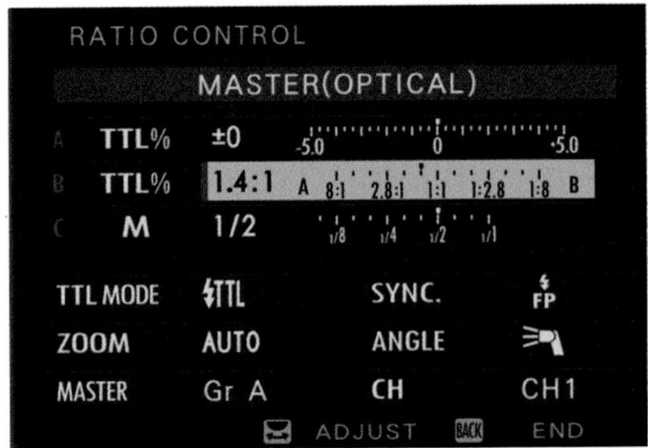


Fig. 180:  In **TTL master mode,** one EF-X500 can control several compatible flashguns in three independent groups (A, B, C) via a light communication protocol. Each group can be controlled via direct TTL or as a ratio of another TTL group, or it can be manually controlled.

While the EF-X500 has many great features and delivers good quality, there are also a few negative aspects to it:

- The flash is quite large, heavy, and expensive.

- Wireless TTL control is realized with outdated light signals instead of state-of-the-art radio transmission.

- Users must purchase and attach either a heavy and expensive EF-X500 or a Metz M400 as a wireless master controller. The included EF-X8 cannot be used as a master control flash.

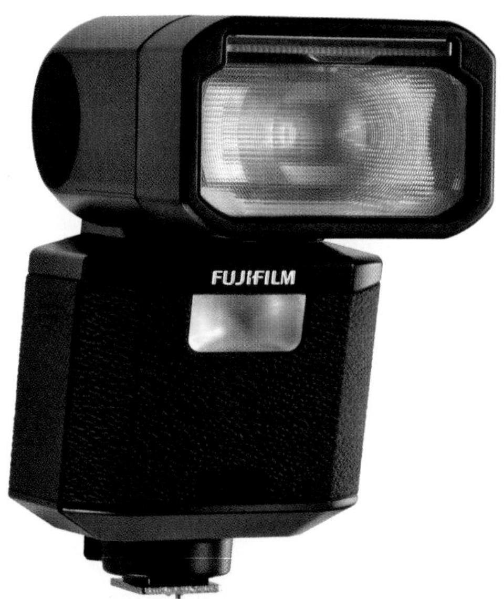

Fig. 181: The **EF-X500** is Fujifilm's pro speedlight. It leans a bit to the large, heavy, and expensive side. At this level, one would expect wireless TTL based on radio transmission instead of the outdated light signals it still uses.

A growing number of independent manufacturers are offering Fuji-compatible flash solutions with wireless radio TTL, multi-group support, and HSS/FP high-speed-sync. I can particularly recommend options from Godox and the Metz M400.

| A good alternative: the Metz M400 | TIP 139 |

Metz was one of the first flash manufacturers to support Fujifilm's new flash system, including HSS/FP high speed sync, the AF assist lamp, and convenient control via the camera's flash configuration page. This makes the Metz M400 [118] an interesting alternative to the larger and more expensive EF-X500.

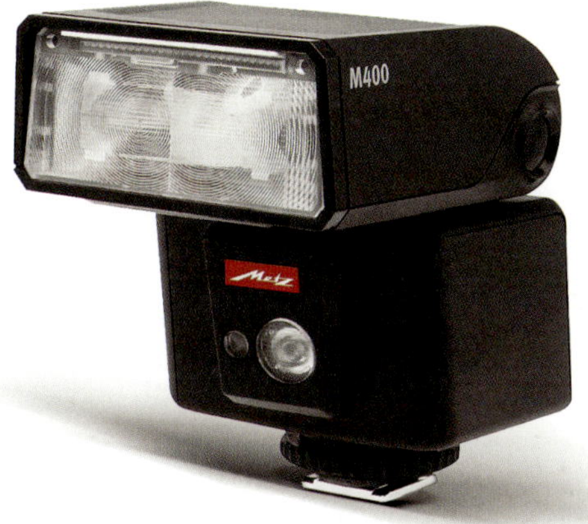


Fig. 182: If you are looking for a fully compatible shoe-mount flash that is more affordable and less bulky than the Fujifilm EF-X500, the Fujifilm edition of the **Metz M400** might be just right for you.

The M400 is based on a "fly-by-wire" user interface that doesn't feature dials with fixed markings. Instead, there are four generic control buttons and an LCD display that can be read day and night. Thanks to this flexible user interface, the M400's firmware can be fully compatible with any camera. Also, there are never any discrepancies between flash settings made in the camera and those made directly on the flash unit. Most flash functions can be conveniently accessed and changed on the flash configuration page and in the menus of your camera.

In addition to this, Metz keeps improving its flash firmware and provides free updates that can be applied by the user via the flash unit's built-in USB interface. This ensures compatibility with upcoming Fujifilm cameras and future feature changes.

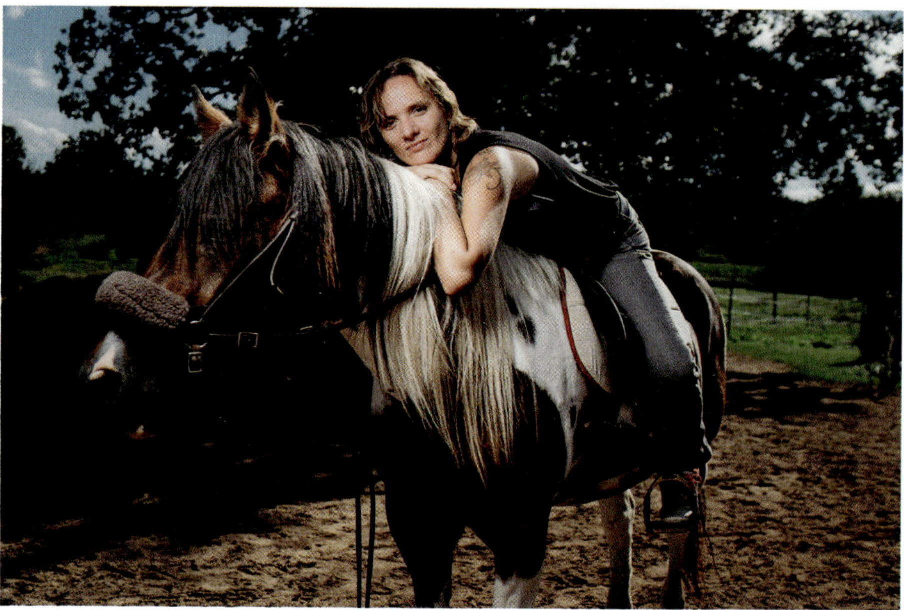

Fig. 183: Despite its compact size, the **Metz M400** packs enough punch to be used with small light modifiers. In this example, I put it in a 40 × 40 cm softbox and triggered it remotely with an EF-X500.

| TIP 140 | Generic third-party flash units |
| --- | --- |

Basically, you can use any modern flashgun from any vendor with your X-T3, as long as you are prepared to set its power manually. You can connect third-party flash units directly to the camera's hot shoe or use a cable or a wireless (radio) triggering device.

The camera's TTL modes are not available when you are using generic third-party flashes because the camera isn't *metering* the flash light, it's only *triggering* the flash. There's also no HSS support.

This makes using generic flash equipment possible but inconvenient. Luckily, major flash brands like Broncolor, Profoto, and Elinchom are now supporting Fujifilm with dedicated transmitters for the Fujifilm X series. They also support HSS.

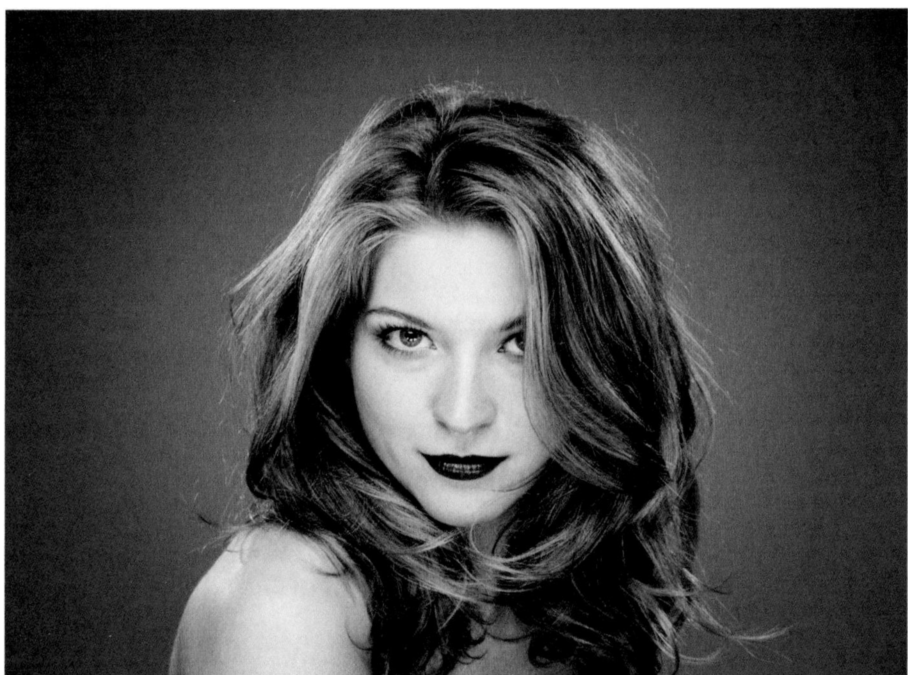

Fig. 184:  A manually controlled **studio flash shot**.

***Important:*** *Attaching Canon-compatible TTL flash equipment to the hot shoe could result in the camera overheating and performing an emergency shutdown. While Fujifilm and Canon share the same type of hot shoe contacts, the protocols are not compatible. In this case, either tape off the TTL contacts of your device or use an adapter that only loops the sync signal from the camera to the flash.*

## 2.8 USING ADAPTED LENSES

Thanks to its short flange-back distance, the X-mount system is able to host almost every existing full-frame, medium format, cinema (Super 35 and larger), or APS-C lens. All you need is an appropriate adapter ring. This means that in addition to more than two-dozen native lenses, you have access to hundreds of additional modern and legacy lenses.

**TIP 141**    Finding the right lens adapter

X-mount lens adapters are available for many old and current lens mounts. Here are a few tips to help you find the right adapter for your third-party lens:

■ Adapters are available at a wide range of price and quality levels, and, as usual, you get what you pay for. Don't try to skimp too much or you may end up buying twice. The German manufacturer Novoflex has set the benchmark here, but even their simple, mechanical adapters could cost more than the lens you are adapting. Manufacturers like Kipon or Metabones enjoy good reputations and they offer adapters for a wide variety of lens mounts.

■ With merely mechanical adapters, third-party lenses can only be used as manual focus lenses with manual mechanical aperture control. Smart electronic adapters can translate between Fuji's AF protocol and the AF protocols of popular brands like Canon, and they can also control the aperture of the lens. Some even support the OIS of the third-party lens.

■ With mechanical adapters, adapted lenses always operate with a manually set working aperture. This means that when you are stopping down the lens, the live view and live histogram of your camera must contend with the smaller aperture's reduced amount of light. It also means that mechanically adapted lenses can only be used in exposure modes **A** or **M**. With smart adapters, all exposure modes should be available.

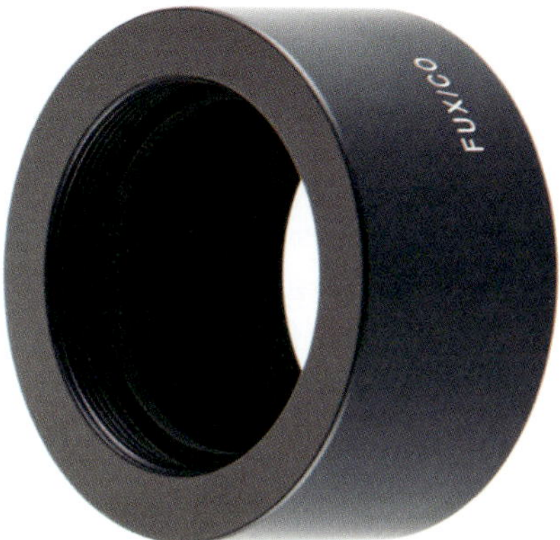


Fig. 185: Mechanical **M42 adapters** like this high-end model from Novoflex allow you to connect legacy M42 screw-mount lenses to X-mount cameras.

- Many modern third-party lenses that don't feature a manual aperture ring can still be mechanically adapted to your camera, but you can't change their apertures while they are connected via a mechanical adapter. This is why some of these adapters feature a mechanical replacement aperture; nevertheless, the results produced by these devices will differ from the results created by the original lens. If available, use a smart adapter for such lenses.

- Modern electronic features like optical image stabilization (OIS) aren't supported by mechanical adapters since there is no communication or power transfer between the camera and the adapted lens. In fact, the camera believes that there's no lens attached at all. Some smart adapters do offer OIS support.

- Speed Booster Ultra from Metabones offers the fascinating possibility to attach full-frame legacy lenses from Contax/Zeiss, Canon FD, Nikon G, Minolta MD, and Leica R to X-mount cameras without changing their original angle of view or cropping the image on your camera's smaller APS-C sensor. With Speed Booster, your APS-C camera sees what a full-frame (35mm format) camera would see. Speed Booster is a focal reducer—basically the opposite of a teleconverter [119]. It reduces the focal length of the adapted lens by a factor of 0.71. At the same time, the brightness (speed) of the lens is increased by about one stop. At $400 to $600 apiece, Speed Booster adapters aren't cheap. However, they offer better quality than knock-off products like the Lens Turbo II by Zhongyi Mitakon.

- Fujifilm offers its own X-mount adapter for Leica M-type full-frame lenses. This is a regular adapter (no Speed Booster), but it features electronic contacts, so your camera will recognize the adapter when it's mounted. It also features an Fn button that provides direct access to the camera's MOUNT ADAPTOR SETTING menu. With all other mechanical adapters, to take a picture you must set SET UP > BUTTON/DIAL SETTING > SHOOT WITHOUT LENS > ON.

- Caution: don't use cheap macro lens adapters with electronic contacts. These knock-off adapters are designed to serve as macro spacer rings for native X-mount lenses. They promise full AF functionality thanks to their electronic contacts, but in reality, these adapter rings can be a poor fit and can damage your camera and lenses. Instead, I recommend using Fujifilm's own electronic macro extension tubes.

- If possible, don't combine more than one adapter. Stacking adapters leads to a measurable and visible loss in quality. Instead, get the right adapter for your lens.

<table><tr><td>Adapting third-party lenses</td><td>TIP 142</td></tr></table>

When you connect third-party lenses to your camera via a mechanical adapter, the camera won't notice it due to the lack of electronic contacts. It will think there is no lens.

- To make the camera work with mechanically adapted lenses, select SET UP > BUTTON/DIAL SETTING > SHOOT WITHOUT LENS > ON.

- Enter the focal length of your adapted lens in the SHOOTING MENU > SHOOTING SETTING > MOUNT ADAPTOR SETTING menu. You can enter the focal lengths of up to six different lenses. Always enter the actual focal length of the adapted lens (the number that is printed on the lens), not its full-frame equivalent. This ensures that the EXIF data will display the correct focal length. The only exceptions are cases when you are using a special optical adapter that changes the focal length of the adapted lens, such as a Metabones Speed Booster for the X-mount (focal length reduction).

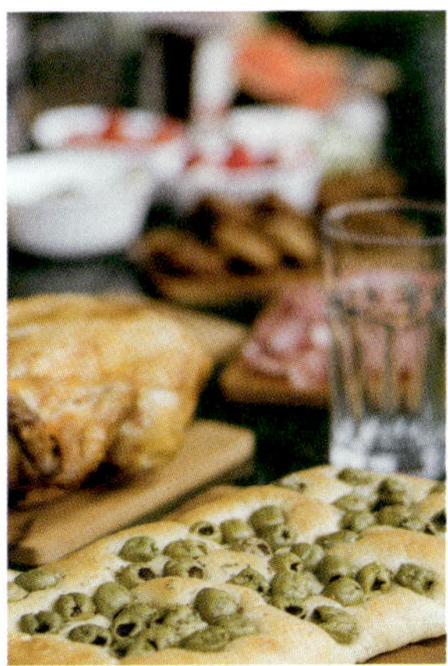
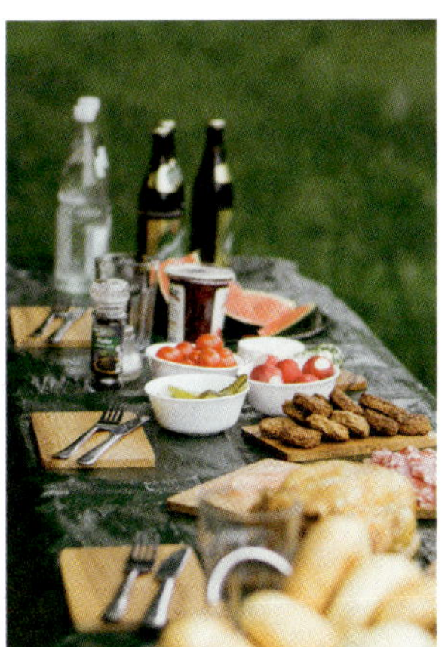
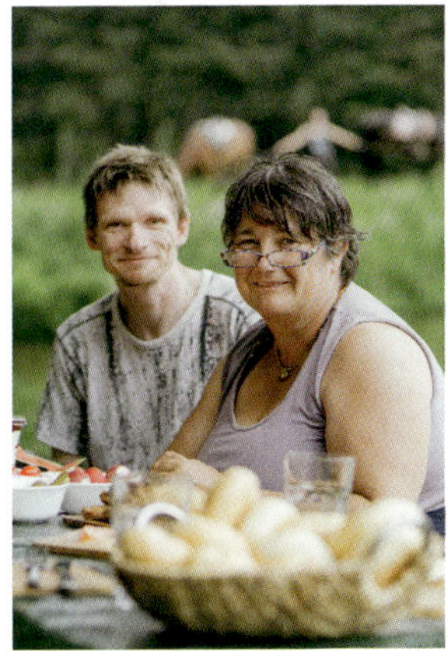

Fig. 186: **Third-party lenses with "character"** can help you achieve images with a distinctive look and bokeh. For this series, I attached a Voigtländer Heliar 75mmF1.8 M-mount and shot it wide-open at f/1.8.

**TIP 143    Exposing with mechanically adapted lenses**

Mechanically adapted lenses can be used in exposure modes **A** (aperture priority) and **M** (manual mode). There are also a few notable differences between exposing with native lenses and adapted lenses:

- Native lenses close down to the working aperture when the shutter is half-pressed or when the shot is taken. Mechanically adapted lenses always operate with the aperture set by the user. As soon as you stop down an adapted lens, less light reaches the sensor and the camera's exposure metering. Stopping down adapted lenses increases the depth of field in the viewfinder.

- Since less light reaches the sensor when the lens is stopped down, the camera must increase the live view image amplification to display an accurate WYSIWYG simulation of the scene. This decreases the quality of the live view image and can also negatively affect the live view's frame rate.

- Since the camera thinks there's no lens attached at all, the aperture is always displayed as F0 in the viewfinder (and f/1 in the EXIF data). There's no way for the camera to know which aperture has been set on a mechanically adapted lens.

- Shooting in poor light with mechanically adapted lenses can be tricky when you stop down the aperture. It's possible to reach the live view's amplification limit. Once this limit is reached, the live view and live histogram cannot display the actual brightness of the scene, so it appears darker than the image that will be exposed. However, exposure metering will still work correctly, and the camera will display the correct shutter speed.

- Since the electronic live view cannot control the aperture of a mechanically adapted lens, it takes longer for the camera to adjust to abrupt brightness changes. You can test this yourself by quickly panning the camera from a bright scene to a dark scene and vice versa. With adapted lenses, the camera may need a few seconds for the live view to adapt to the changing brightness levels.

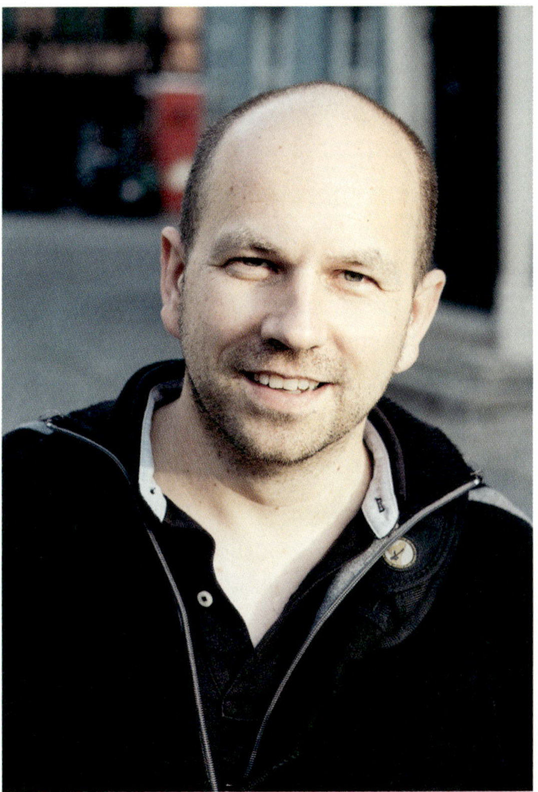

Fig. 187: With mechanical adapters, **exposing with adapted lenses** is limited to modes **A** and **M**, and metering always takes place at the set working aperture. No matter which aperture you set, EXIF data will always show f/1. For this street portrait, I attached a Helios 44M-4 lens to my camera using a Novoflex M42 adapter.

**TIP 144**    Focusing with mechanically adapted lenses

Mechanically adapted lenses can only be focused manually. Here are a few tips to make things easier for you:

- Set your camera to manual focus. This makes sure that MF assistants such as Focus Check, focus peaking, and digital split image are available.

- The electronic distance and depth-of-field (DOF) scale of your camera is useless in concert with mechanically adapted lenses. Instead, you must rely on analog scales and markers that may be engraved in the barrel of your adapted lens. Remember that the DOF scale on your lens is probably less conservative than what you're used to from the electronic scale in your camera. The analog scale doesn't guarantee pixel-sharp results at 100% image magnification. Instead, it will more likely resemble the FILM FORMAT BASIS option of the electronic DOF scale.

- The most important tool for focusing with adapted lenses is the magnifier tool. You can usually activate it by pressing the rear command dial (if you didn't change its default Fn button assignment). Turn the rear command dial to cycle between the available magnifications. Don't forget: instead of focusing and recomposing, it's better to select a focus frame position that covers the part of the image you want to be in focus.

- Use focus peaking or another MF assistant. You can cycle between these MF assistants and the standard view by pressing and holding the rear command dial. The magnifier tool can be combined with focus peaking, digital split image, and digital microprism. However, in concert with digital split image and digital microprism, only one magnification level is available.

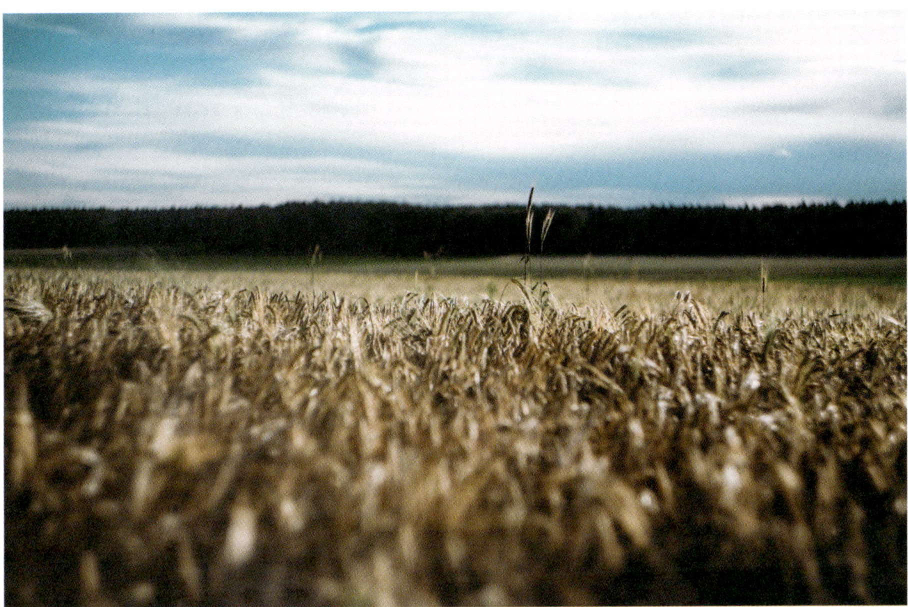

Fig. 188: **Focusing mechanically adapted lenses** can be tricky. My preferred method for obtaining manual pinpoint focus is to use focus peaking in concert with the magnifier tool. This example was shot with a Helios 44M-4 lens that was adapted using a Lens Turbo II focal reducer.

- The magnifier tool and MF assistants work best with the aperture wide open, when the DOF is as small as possible. However, some lenses exhibit focus shift, meaning the focus plane shifts when the lens is stopped down. The increased DOF from stopping down the lens may not be sufficient to compensate for the focus shift, so your carefully focused shot will end up out of focus when the aperture is closed. If you are using a lens with pronounced focus shift, it's better to focus with the actual working aperture instead of the wide-open aperture. Please note that focus shift isn't a matter of price—even a few high-end lenses from Leica and Zeiss exhibit it quite prominently.

| TIP 145 | Using the Fujifilm M-mount adapter |

Fuji's own Leica M-mount adapter is a little bit different from conventional adapters:

- The adapter features electronic XF lens contacts to identify itself to the camera. However, there's no transmission of lens data since the adapter doesn't know which M-type lens has been attached or what distance and aperture has been set. Sadly, the electronic contacts also make the inner adapter tube thinner than normal, so not all M-type lenses are physically compatible with it. To be certain, you can download a list of compatible and incompatible lenses [120]. Fuji also encloses a template with its M adapter that you can use to find out if your M lens measures up with the adapter.

- Pressing the function button on the adapter directly opens the camera's adapter menu.

- The camera's adapter menu offers a few additional functions when a Fuji M-mount adapter is attached. In addition to entering the focal length, you can also enter correction values for lens distortion, color shading, and vignetting. Those corrections affect the JPEGs during RAW conversion with the built-in or external RAW converters. As usual, the corrections are burned into the RAW file metadata where they can be interpreted by RAW conversion software. However, color-shade data is currently only processed by the camera's built-in converter. For each adapted lens, you must find out the right correction values for yourself before you can enter them. There aren't any reference lists you can use that I know of.

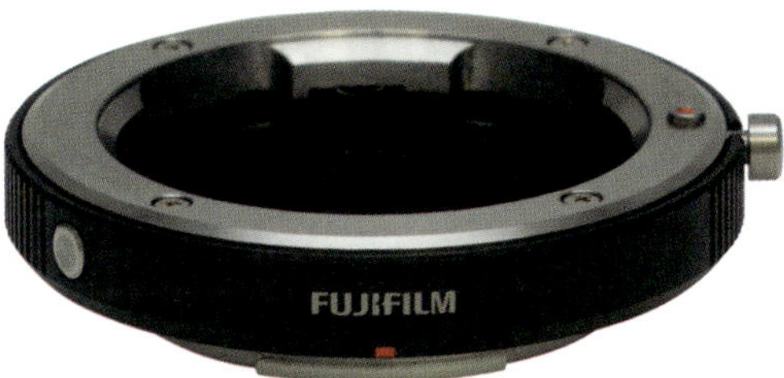

Fig. 189: Fujifilm's own **M-mount adapter** features electronic contacts and a function button that opens the camera's adapter menu.

| Electronic smart adapters | TIP 146 |
| --- | --- |

Electronic smart adapters have been designed for modern
third-party lenses like the Canon EF system. These lenses
have electronic contacts and they communicate with the
camera body to offer functions such as autofocus, electronic
aperture control, and optical image stabilization (OIS). They
also get their power from the camera body.

Connecting modern EF lenses on the X-T3 with a simple
mechanical adapter turns out to be a frustrating experience.
You cannot change the aperture while the lens is attached
to the Fuji camera, there's no autofocus, the OIS doesn't
work, and there is no EXIF data transmission to the camera.

The solution: use an electronic smart adapter. The major-
ity of smart adapters are designed to adapt Canon EF (and
other EF-compatible) lenses, but a smart adapter for current
Nikon DSLR lenses might also be on the horizon.

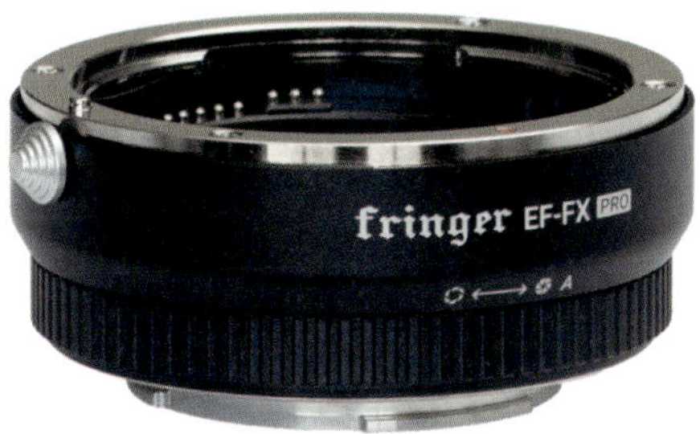

Fig. 190: The **Fringer EF-FX** was one of the first EF-to-XF smart
adapters. You can also get the EF-FX Pro version (pictured here) with
an integrated electronic aperture ring.

An ideal smart adapter should include the following features:

- Full electronic aperture control.

- Autofocus support (PDAF/CDAF, AF-S, AF-C, face detection, video, etc.).

- Support for built-in optical image stabilizers (OIS) in adapted lenses.

- Support for IBIS (X-H1) with adapted lenses that don't have built-in OIS.

- EXIF data transmission and recording (focal length, aperture, adapted lens model, serial number, etc.).

- Digital lens correction data transmission and conversion (chromatic aberrations, distortion, vignetting).

- Compatible with most or all lenses of the adapted system, including popular third-party offerings like Sigma or Tamron EF lenses.

- Frequent firmware updates to improve and maintain compatibility. New firmware updates should be easy to install from macOS and Windows computers. Alternatively, there should be support for adapter firmware upgrades via the lens firmware upgrade procedure of X-series cameras.

Smart adapters are available from several vendors. Some even offer built-in focal length reducers (like the Speed Booster) to project the full image circle of the adapted full-frame lens on the smaller APS-C sensor of the X-mount camera.

## 2.9 WIRELESS REMOTE CONTROL AND TETHERING

Fuji's own Camera Remote app works with wireless iOS and Android devices, and it allows you to remotely control your camera by providing a live view image and a touch-screen interface to set the focus point, change exposure parameters, and release the shutter.

| Using the Camera Remote App | TIP 147 |
| --- | --- |

Camera Remote allows you to control the X-T3 from an Android or iOS device running Fuji's Camera Remote app. To use Camera Remote, you must first download and install the free app on your smartphone or tablet. You can find download links, instructions, and additional information online [121].

Here's how Camera Remote works with iOS devices (it shouldn't be much different for Android users):

- Pair your camera to your smartphone or tablet via Bluetooth (SET UP > CONNECTION SEETING > Bluetooth SETTINGS > PAIRING REGISTRATION) and make sure that Bluetooth is switched on. This allows your smart device to automatically connect to your camera's Wi-Fi network.

- Open the Camera Remote app, make sure your X-T3 is selected, and choose Remote Control. The mobile device will now assume control over the camera and display a live view image along with options to adjust shutter speed, aperture, and exposure compensation. There's also a virtual shutter button and a basic shooting menu that allows you to adjust parameters like ISO, film simulation, white balance, macro, flash mode, or self-timer.

- To autofocus on a specific part of the live view image, double-tap on it with your finger. Focus will be confirmed with a green rectangle. If no focus lock can be established, the rectangle will appear in red.

- Adjust your exposure parameters as required. The brightness of the live view will change accordingly. Please note there's no live histogram.

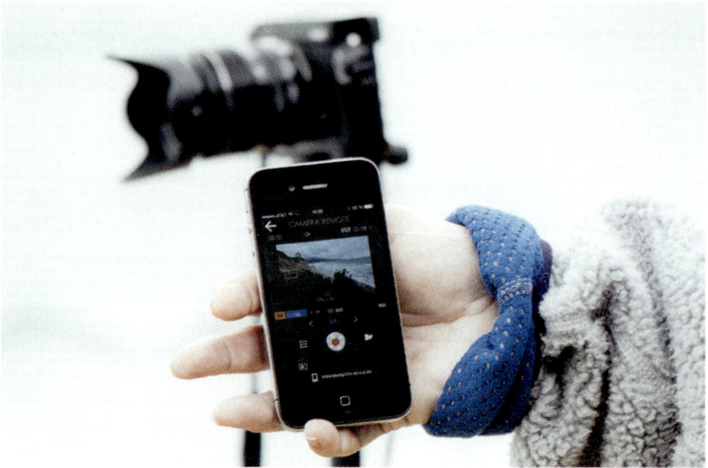

Fig. 191: **Camera Remote** offers a simple interface to control your camera with a smartphone or tablet. To autofocus, double-tap on a specific part of the WYSIWYG live view and wait for the green confirmation rectangle to appear. Sadly, there is no live histogram, and you can't magnify the live view. There is a rudimentary shooting menu and a virtual shutter button, and there is a playback button that allows you to review images and transfer JPEGs to your mobile device.

Here are a few things you might want to know about Camera Remote:

- Fuji's Camera Remote app allows you to adjust exposure parameters (aperture, shutter speed, ISO, exposure compensation), but you can't remotely change the camera's exposure mode. This means you must manually set the camera to either **P**, **A**, **S**, or **M** mode *before* you transfer control over the camera to the app. To change the exposure mode during remote shooting, you must first disconnect Camera Remote, make the desired changes in the camera, and then start over with a new connection.

- There's no electronic level indicator and no live histogram in the Camera Remote live view on your mobile device.

- You can change several shooting parameters from within the Camera Remote app (ISO, film simulation, white balance preset, macro, flash mode, self-timer), but other parameters (such as dynamic range or Auto-ISO minimum shutter speed) must be preset in the camera *before* entering wireless communication mode.

- There is no bulb functionality in Camera Remote, so your maximum exposure time is limited to the extent of the T setting. If you need more, it is better use a conventional (tethered or wireless) remote shutter release or the dedicated Bluetooth-based remote shutter release in the Camera Remote app.

- Changing exposure parameters affects the WYSIWYG live view. The live view in Camera Remote always reflects the currently selected film simulation and JPEG parameters. There is also a preview of manually selected DR settings (DR200%, DR400%).

A few more tips and hints:

- I use Camera Remote mostly in manual exposure mode **M**. I feel this is the most convenient and efficient way to adjust shooting parameters. Changing a parameter (shutter speed, aperture, ISO) immediately adjusts the live view brightness.

- Some users may suffer from connection losses caused by interfering networks that are transmitting on the same Wi-Fi channel as the camera. Sadly, there is currently no way to change the camera's transmission channel, and the X-T3 only supports slow 2.4 GHz connections.

- To transfer JPEGs from the camera to your mobile device with full resolution, make sure to select SET UP > CONNECTION SETTING > GENERAL SETTINGS > RESIZE IMAGE FOR SMARTPHONE > OFF. Otherwise, the transferred images will be downsized to 3 megapixels.

- Manual DR expansion settings (DR200%, DR400%) are reflected in the Camera Remote live view. The same applies to JPEG parameters such as contrast (HIGHLIGHT TONE, SHADOW TONE) or white balance settings. In manual mode **M**, the Camera Remote live view will also respect any settings made in SET UP > SCREEN SET-UP > PREVIEW EXP./WB IN MANUAL MODE.

Thanks to Bluetooth, location data and the current date and time can automatically be synchronized from your smartphone or tablet. There is also the benefit of a simple Bluetooth-based remote shutter release function, and there's the possibility to automatically obtain and install camera firmware updates. To use Bluetooth with Camera Remote, make sure to pair the camera with your smartphone or tablet. You can find more information on these and other function in the Camera Remote app online manual [122].

| **TIP 148** | Streaming the live view via HDMI |
| --- | --- |

The X-T3 offers HDMI live streaming, meaning that the contents of the live view (electronic viewfinder or LCD) can be transmitted to a monitor, TV, or projector via the camera's HDMI output. All you have to do is connect the camera's Micro-HDMI jack to a suitable monitor with a digital input (HDMI, DVI, etc.). Real-time streaming will start automatically once the connection is established.

This is a useful feature for workshops, product demonstrations, or professional productions, where customers can watch on a monitor what the photographer is seeing in the live view.

You can also use the HDMI live view output to connect the camera to an HD frame-grabber, which is then connected to your computer. With this setup, you can make video recordings and screenshots of the live view.

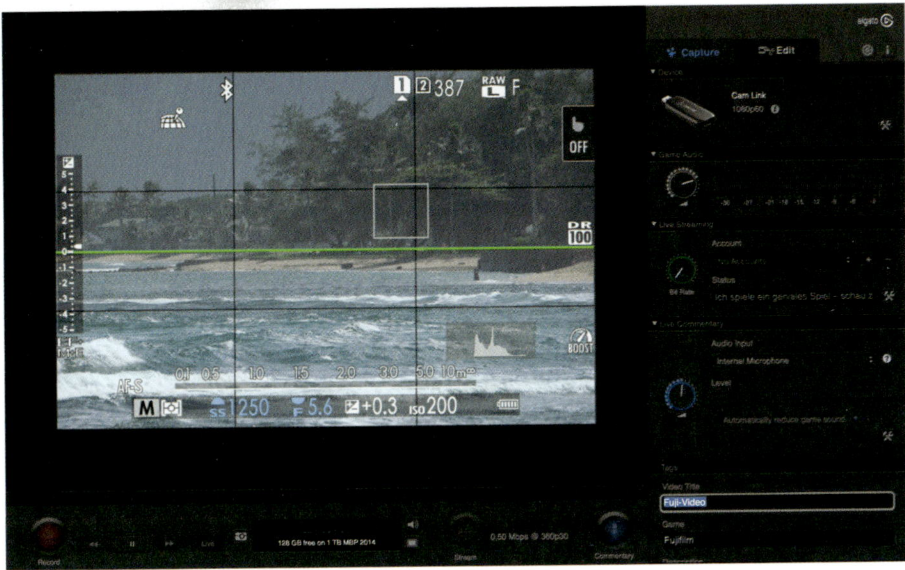

Fig. 192: The camera screenshots in this book were created by streaming the live view's HDMI output to my MacBook Pro, where I used **Elgato Cam Link** [123] with Game Capture HD software to capture screenshots. You can also use this hardware and software to create 60 fps HD video recordings of your camera's live view.

| Tethered shooting via USB or Wi-Fi | TIP 149 |
| --- | --- |

Tethered shooting involves controlling the camera via a computer that is connected (tethered) to the camera via a USB cable or a Wi-Fi connection.

In order to use USB tethering, you must select either USB TETHER SHOOTING AUTO or USB TETHER SHOOTING FIXED in the SET UP > CONNECTION SETTING > PC CONNECTION MODE menu. This way, the camera is either recognizing (AUTO) or even forcing (FIXED) a computer connection via

USB, yielding control to compatible tethering software on the computer. For Wi-Fi tethering [124], select WIRELESS TETHER SHOOTING FIXED.

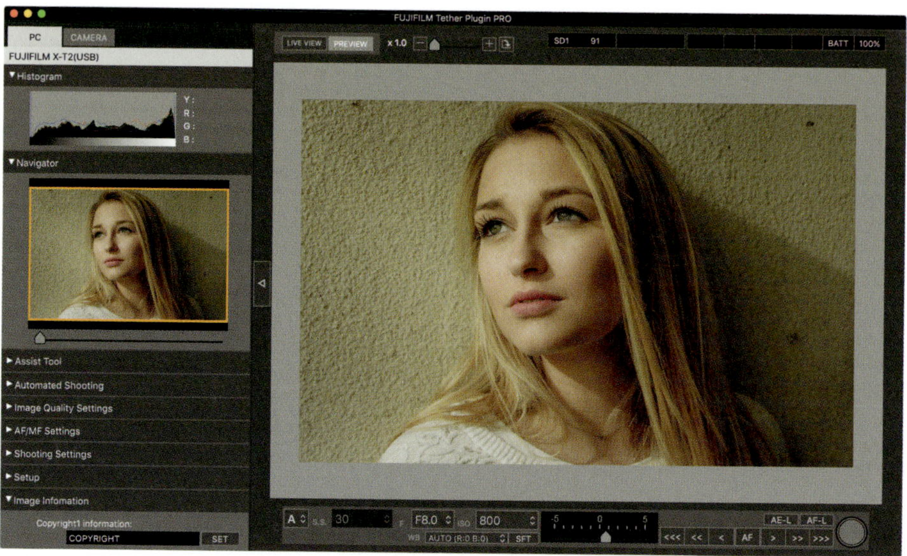

Fig. 193: The **Tether Shooting Plug-in Pro for Adobe Lightroom** includes a live-view image and comprehensive control over the camera. Features include color histograms, focus stacking, expanded bracketing, and the possibility to enter copyright information. You can also save and load full camera configurations.

**Fujifilm X Acquire** [125] is a simple freebie app for macOS and Windows that saves images to a hot folder from which other apps can obtain them. It also allows you to backup and restore full camera settings on your Mac or PC.

The **Fujifilm Tether Shooting Plug-in** [126] and **Tether Shooting Plug-in Pro** [127] are plug-ins for Lightroom/ACR. The Pro version offers shooting with a remote live view and remote control over most of the camera's settings.

In addition to that, **Capture One Pro** [128] also adds direct tethering support thanks to the 5-year partnership between Fujifilm and PhaseOne that was revealed at Photokina 2018.

## 2.10  ANYTHING ELSE?

Hopefully, this book has answered many of your questions that went beyond the user manual of your camera. However, this isn't the end: you can read my X-Pert Corner blog, participate in Fuji X forums, or join one of my Fuji X Secrets workshops.

| Forums, blogs, magazines, and workshops | TIP 150 |
|---|---|

- High-resolution versions of many images in this book are available on Flickr [129].

- At Fuji X Secrets [130], you will find articles and reviews covering specific features, new firmware, and new products for X-series cameras.

- My free X-Pert Corner blog [131] covers a variety of topics about the Fujifilm X series. You will find everything from service articles that go beyond this book to "First Look" previews of cameras and lenses.

- There are several online forums that focus on Fujifilm's X series: The Original Fuji X Forum [132]; The Ultimate Fuji X Forum [133]; and the Fuji X Series Forum [134].

- I am a regular contributor of gear-related articles in FUJILOVE [135], a dedicated monthly magazine for all things Fuji X.

- Books, blogs, and forums are great, but what about a more personal touch? My site, Fuji X Secrets [136], offers a series of advanced workshops for Fuji X series users. My workshops cover topics that are similar to those in this book, but on a more in-depth and comprehensive level, including practical demonstrations and plenty of sample images. We work in small groups, and our delegates set the agenda. It has everything you always wanted to know about X but were afraid to ask.

# ONLINE REFERENCES

Websites are not run by Rocky Nook, and are subject to change without our knowledge.

If necessary, we will update these references. For an updated version of this reference list, please download the available document at:

http://www.rockynook.com/fuji-x-t3-online-references/


[1]   http://www.fujifilm.com/support/digital_cameras/manuals/
[2]   https://charger.nitecore.com/product/fx1
[3]   http://digital-cameras.support.fujifilm.com/app/answers/detail/a_id/20151/p/8453
[4]   http://www.fujifilm.com/support/digital_cameras/software/
[5]   http://digital-cameras.support.fujifilm.com/app/answers/detail/a_id/19061/kw/firmware/p/43/c/1524
[6]   http://digital-cameras.support.fujifilm.com/app/answers/detail/a_id/18998/kw/firmware/p/43/c/1524
[7]   http://digital-cameras.support.fujifilm.com/app/answers/detail/a_id/18997/kw/firmware/p/43/c/1524
[8]   http://app.fujifilm-dsc.com/en/camera_remote/
[9]   http://app.fujifilm-dsc.com/en/camera_remote/fw_update.html
[10]  https://en.wikipedia.org/wiki/Live_preview
[11]  https://en.wikipedia.org/wiki/crop_factor
[12]  https://en.wikipedia.org/wiki/image_stabilization
[13]  https://en.wikipedia.org/wiki/motion_blur
[14]  https://en.wikipedia.org/wiki/panning_(camera)
[15]  https://en.wikipedia.org/wiki/depth_of_field
[16]  https://en.wikipedia.org/wiki/circle_of_confusion
[17]  http://www.cambridgeincolour.com/tutorials/diffraction-photography.htm
[18]  https://en.wikipedia.org/wiki/vignetting
[19]  https://en.wikipedia.org/wiki/distortion_(options)
[20]  https://en.wikipedia.org/wiki/chromatic_aberration
[21]  https://en.wikipedia.org/wiki/exif
[22]  http://app.fujifilm-dsc.com/en/camera_remote/index.html
[23]  http://app.fujifilm-dsc.com/en/manual/camera_remote/usage/remote_release/
[24]  http://app.fujifilm-dsc.com/en/manual/camera_remote/
[25]  http://app.fujifilm-dsc.com/en/manual/camera_remote/usage/live_view/
[26]  https://en.wikipedia.org/wiki/exif
[27]  https://en.wikipedia.org/wiki/dark-frame_subtraction
[28]  https://en.wikipedia.org/wiki/raw_image_format
[29]  https://en.wikipedia.org/wiki/jpeg

[30] http://www.fujifilm.com/support/digital_cameras/software/myfinepix_studio/rfc/
[31] https://en.wikipedia.org/wiki/wysiwyg
[32] https://en.wikipedia.org/wiki/live_preview
[33] https://en.wikipedia.org/wiki/zone_system
[34] http://www.cambridgeincolour.com/tutorials/histograms1.htm
[35] http://www.cambridgeincolour.com/tutorials/histograms2.htm
[36] https://en.wikipedia.org/wiki/depth_of_field
[37] https://en.wikipedia.org/wiki/motion_blur
[38] https://en.wikipedia.org/wiki/aperture_priority
[39] https://en.wikipedia.org/wiki/aperture
[40] https://en.wikipedia.org/wiki/depth_of_field
[41] http://www.cambridgeincolour.com/tutorials/diffraction-photography.htm
[42] https://en.wikipedia.org/wiki/shutter_priority
[43] https://en.wikipedia.org/wiki/shutter_speed
[44] https://en.wikipedia.org/wiki/motion_blur
[45] https://en.wikipedia.org/wiki/panning_(camera)
[46] https://en.wikipedia.org/wiki/long-exposure_photography
[47] http://www.cambridgeincolour.com/tutorials/camera-shake.htm
[48] https://en.wikipedia.org/wiki/image_stabilization
[49] https://en.wikipedia.org/wiki/crop_factor
[50] http://www.techradar.com/how-to/photography-video-capture/cameras/program-mode-explained-how-to-creatively-shift-aperture-and-shutter-speed-1321042
[51] https://en.wikipedia.org/wiki/bracketing
[52] https://en.wikipedia.org/wiki/dark-frame_subtraction
[53] https://en.wikipedia.org/wiki/neutral-density_filter
[54] https://en.wikipedia.org/wiki/Film_speed
[55] https://www.flickr.com/gp/ricopfirstinger/m8dvhf
[56] https://en.wikipedia.org/wiki/high-dynamic-range_imaging
[57] https://en.wikipedia.org/wiki/rolling_shutter
[58] http://www.fujifilm.com/products/digital_cameras/x/fujifilm_x_h1/features/page_05.html
[59] http://digital-photography-school.com/the-problem-with-the-focus-recompose-method/
[60] https://fujifilm-x.com/af/en/
[61] https://en.wikipedia.org/wiki/hyperfocal_distance
[62] https://en.wikipedia.org/wiki/circle_of_confusion
[63] https://www.youtube.com/watch?v=7FR3l6S12JA
[64] https://www.youtube.com/watch?v=rnkib7FZ8S8
[65] http://www.cambridgeincolour.com/tutorials/hyperfocal-distance.htm
[66] http://www.fujifilm.com/products/digital_cameras/accessories/pdf/mcex_01.pdf
[67] https://en.wikipedia.org/wiki/depth_of_field
[68] http://www.cambridgeincolour.com/tutorials/diffraction-photography.htm
[69] https://photography.tutsplus.com/tutorials/how-to-calculate-the-sharpest-aperture-for-any-lens--cms-25153

[70]   https://en.wikipedia.org/wiki/focus_stacking
[71]   https://www.heliconsoft.com/heliconsoft-products/helicon-focus/
[72]   https://en.wikipedia.org/wiki/panning_(camera)
[73]   http://www.cambridgeincolour.com/tutorials/white-balance.htm
[74]   https://en.wikipedia.org/wiki/exif
[75]   https://en.wikipedia.org/wiki/gray_card
[76]   http://www.fujifilm.com/support/digital_cameras/software/application/
[77]   https://en.wikipedia.org/wiki/contrast_(vision)
[78]   https://en.wikipedia.org/wiki/colorfulness
[79]   https://en.wikipedia.org/wiki/color_space
[80]   https://en.wikipedia.org/wiki/srgb
[81]   https://en.wikipedia.org/wiki/adobe_rgb_color_space
[82]   https://en.wikipedia.org/wiki/gamut
[83]   http://www.fujifilm.com/support/digital_cameras/software/application/
[84]   https://fujifilm-x.com/en-us/stories/fujifilm-x-raw-studio-features-users-guide/
[85]   https://www.howtogeek.com/342416/what-is-hevc-h.265-video-and-why-is-it-so-important-for-4k-movies/
[86]   http://www.deltadigitalvideo.com/wp-content/uploads/H.264-vs-H.265.pdf
[87]   http://www.premiumbeat.com/blog/differences-all-i-ipb-compression/
[88]   https://en.wikipedia.org/wiki/PAL
[89]   https://en.wikipedia.org/wiki/NTSC
[90]   https://theappliancesreviews.com/why-frame-rate-is-25-30-or-29-97-fps/
[91]   https://www.premiumbeat.com/blog/advanced-look-into-frame-rates/
[92]   https://nofilmschool.com/Aspect-Ratio-Examples-For-Filmmakers
[93]   https://en.wikipedia.org/wiki/IRE_(unit)
[94]   http://www.fujifilm.com/support/digital_cameras/software/lut/
[95]   https://www.filmconvert.com/download/camera-profile
[96]   https://www.premiumbeat.com/blog/the-video-editors-guide-to-color-grading/
[97]   http://www.fujifilm.com/support/digital_cameras/software/lut/pdf/F-Log_DataSheet_E_Ver.1.0.pdf
[98]   https://www.itu.int/dms_pubrec/itu-r/rec/bt/R-REC-BT.2100-2-201807-I!!PDF-E.pdf
[99]   https://en.wikipedia.org/wiki/gamut
[100]  https://en.wikipedia.org/wiki/non-linear_editing_system
[101]  https://cameramanben.github.io/LUTCalc/LUTCalc/index.html
[102]  https://images.apple.com/final-cut-pro/docs/Working_with_Wide_Color_Gamut_and_High_Dynamic_Range_in_Final_Cut_Pro_X.pdf
[103]  https://www.premiumbeat.com/blog/filmmaking-techniques-mastering-rack-focus/

[104] https://www.lensrentals.com/blog/2016/03/mythbusting-parfocal-photo-zooms/
[105] https://www.youtube.com/watch?v=alyzgdR8ET0
[106] https://en.wikipedia.org/wiki/neutral-density_filter
[107] https://nofilmschool.com/2017/07/new-gimbals-here-are-few-basic-camera-movements-you-should-know
[108] https://photography.tutsplus.com/tutorials/how-to-use-a-gimbal-minimizing-up-and-down-motion--cms-27764
[109] https://fstoppers.com/education/balancing-any-gimbal-stabilizer-smooth-cinematic-video-280764
[110] https://nofilmschool.com/2016/11/learn-how-read-6-different-scopes-ensure-proper-exposure-and-color-balance
[111] https://en.wikipedia.org/wiki/chroma_subsampling
[112] http://en.wikipedia.org/wiki/through-the-lens_meter-ing#Through_the_lens_flash_metering
[113] https://en.wikipedia.org/wiki/neutral-density_filter
[114] https://en.wikipedia.org/wiki/flash_synchronization
[115] https://en.wikipedia.org/wiki/neutral-density_filter
[116] https://en.wikipedia.org/wiki/red-eye_effect
[117] https://en.wikipedia.org/wiki/catch_light
[118] http://www.metz-mecatech.de/en/lighting/flash-units/system-flash-units/mecablitz-m400/data-sheet/mecablitz-m400-fujifilm.html
[119] https://en.wikipedia.org/wiki/teleconverter
[120] http://www.fujifilm.com/products/digital_cameras/accessories/lens/mount/fujifilm_m_mount_adapter/compatibility_chart/index.html
[121] http://app.fujifilm-dsc.com/en/camera_remote/
[122] http://app.fujifilm-dsc.com/en/camera_remote/
[123] https://www.elgato.com/en/gaming/cam-link
[124] http://app.fujifilm-dsc.com/en/tether/tether_wireless.html
[125] https://fujifilm-x.com/en-gb/stories/fujifilm-x-acquire-features-users-guide/
[126] http://www.fujifilm.com/products/digital_cameras/accessories/others/
[127] https://fujifilm-x.com/global/stories/fujifilm-tether-plug-in-pro-features/
[128] https://www.phaseone.com/fujifilm
[129] https://www.flickr.com/gp/ricopfirstinger/717gpx
[130] https://fuji-x-secrets.net/
[131] http://www.fujirumors.com/category/x-pert/
[132] http://www.fujix-forum.com/
[133] http://www.fuji-x-forum.com/
[134] http://www.fujixseries.com/
[135] https://fujilove.com/
[136] https://fuji-x-secrets.net/

# INDEX